LECTURES

ON THE

MORAL GOVERNMENT OF GOD.

BY

NATHANIEL W. TAYLOR, D. D.,

LATE DWIGHT PROFESSOR OF DIDACTIC THEOLOGY
IN YALE COLLEGE.

"Of Law there can be no less acknowledged than that her seat is the bosom of God — her voice the harmony of the world."

VOL. II.

NEW YORK:
PUBLISHED BY CLARK, AUSTIN & SMITH,
3 PARK ROW & 3 ANN STREET.
1859.

RENNIE, SHEA & LINDSAY,
Stereotypers and Electrotypers,
81, 83, and 85 Centre-street,
New York.

Printed by
C. A. ALVORD,
15 Vandewater-st.
New York.

CONTENTS.

SECTION III.

THE MORAL GOVERNMENT OF GOD AS REVEALED IN THE SCRIPTURES.

LECTURE I.

LECTURE II.

LECTURE III.

LECTURE IV.

LECTURE V.

THE MOSAIC LAW A THEOCRACY.

LECTURE VI.

THE MOSAIC LAW A THEOCRACY.

LECTURE VII.

THE *NATURE* OF GOD'S MORAL GOVERNMENT AS REVEALED

LECTURE VIII.

THE *NATURE* OF GOD'S MORAL GOVERNMENT AS REVEALED.

LECTURE IX.

THE *NATURE* OF GOD'S MORAL GOVERNMENT AS REVEALED.

LECTURE X.

PAGE

THE *NATURE* OF GOD'S MORAL GOVERNMENT AS REVEALED.

LECTURE XI.

THE *NATURE* OF GOD'S MORAL GOVERNMENT AS REVEALED.

LECTURE XII.

THE *NATURE* OF GOD'S MORAL GOVERNMENT AS REVEALED.

LECTURE XIII.

THE *NATURE* OF GOD'S MORAL GOVERNMENT AS REVEALED.

APPENDIX—No. I.

ESSAY ON JUSTICE AS THE ATTRIBUTE OF A PERFECT MORAL GOVERNOR.

PAGE

PART I.—CONCEPTION OF JUSTICE ANALYZED AND EXPLAINED.

PART II.—DIFFERENT SPECIES OF JUSTICE WITH APPLICATION TO THEOLOGICAL ERRORS.

APPENDIX—No. II.

ESSAY ON THE PROVIDENTIAL GOVERNMENT OF GOD.

PART I.—RELATION OF PROVIDENTIAL TO MORAL GOVERNMENT.

PART II.—THE PROVIDENTIAL PURPOSES OF GOD.

APPENDIX—No. III.

ESSAY ON THE QUESTION—IN WHAT DIFFERENT RESPECTS MAY GOD BE SUPPOSED TO PURPOSE DIFFERENT AND EVEN OPPOSITE EVENTS?

APPENDIX—No. IV.

ARE ANY OF THE PUNISHMENTS OF CIVIL LAW LEGAL SANCTIONS EXCEPT THE PUNISHMENT OF DEATH?

(VIDE LECTURE VII., SECT. I., VOL. I.)

APPENDIX—No. V.

THOUGHTS ON THE EVIDENCE FOR DIVINE REVELATION, AND ESPECIALLY THE ARGUMENT FROM MIRACLES.

THE MORAL GOVERNMENT OF GOD.

SECTION III.

THE MORAL GOVERNMENT OF GOD AS REVEALED IN THE SCRIPTURES.

LECTURE I.—THE FACT AND THE PROOF.

The nature of Man.—Man, from the first, placed under Moral Government.—This relation of God formally claimed throughout the Scriptures.—The history of God's Providence.—The Theocracy of Israel.—The leading Doctrines of the Scriptures.

To present God to men as their perfect Moral Governor, and to unfold the nature, the mode, and the issues of his moral administration under its different forms, is obviously the great design of Revelation, and that to which every other is subordinate and subservient. The manifestation of God in this august relation to man, carrying with it the relation of man to God as the subject of his moral government, and implying its foundation and its origin in the character of God, and in the nature and condition of man—man's duty, character, and destiny, the influences under which he must act, the progress and results of the system—may be justly said to be the comprehensive theme of Revealed Theology.

In attempting to unfold a subject so comprehensive, it is often necessary to discuss singly some of its prominent and essential parts. Especially must this be true when every such part of the whole subject has been one of long, extensive, and continued controversy. The part which has called forth the discussion and the controversy may be more or less comprehensive; it has usually been so in theology, as different circumstances and occasions have given rise to these partial and insulated discussions. Witness for example, without going further back in dogmatic history—the Augustinian and Pelagian, the Calvinistic and Arminian controversies, and also those far more restricted and limited themes and topics which have employed the labors of such men as Butler, Howe, Edwards, and many others. Such have been the forms in which the ablest and most distinguished theologians have professedly given to the world the theology of the Scriptures, the substantial truths of God's Revelation. In this way we have had, with more or less of Natural Theology, Institutes of the Christian Religion, Bodies of Divinity, Systems of Theology, Confessions of Faith, Creeds, and Catechisms. It is not my design to raise the question concerning the utility of what may be called Systematic Theology, but to say that all the attempts made by theologians to systematize the great and substantial truths of both Natural and Revealed Theology, have hitherto proved utter and complete failures, by a necessity arising from the manner in which they have been made. For, in all these attempts, there never has been any full and thorough exhibition, nor even a professed attempt at an exhibition, of that great and comprehensive relation of God to men, to which all things besides in creation and providence are subordinate and subservient;—*his relation to men as administering a perfect moral government over them as moral and immortal beings created in his own image*,—I do not say, that on some *parts* of this commanding relation of God to men, nothing has been said nor even much which is true, with however, much more that is false, or if true, not decisively proved. But I say, in all the theology of uninspired men, there has been to this hour not even an attempt formally and fully to unfold the comprehensive relation of God to men as their perfect moral governor, in the nature, the essential principles, and actual administration of this government.

But if God actually sustains this comprehensive relation to men; if he is actually administering a system of perfect moral government over men; if all his works of creation and providence are subordinate and subservient to this high and comprehensive relation, then all theological truth must be comprised either in the truths which are essentially involved in this system of moral government, or must be in entire and perfect harmony with them.

It is not then my *immediate* design to call your attention to a full view of God's moral government as exhibited in the Scriptures. My present design in this series of lectures is,—

I. To establish from the Scriptures the general FACT of God's moral government over men; and,—

II. To unfold the nature of this government as presented in the Scriptures. I proceed then on the authority of the Scriptures,—

I. To establish *the general fact* of God's moral government over men.

Of this fact, the Scriptures furnish such manifold and abundant proofs, that it is quite impossible to present them in all their fullness and force. What I propose is, to present some of them with as little amplification as may be, though at the sacrifice of their fullness and weight. These proofs will, of course, necessarily relate to the general fact of a moral government, as distinguished from any particular mode of its administration. A moral government, whether it consist of a merely legal system, or of law and grace combined, is still a moral government, and may be proved to exist by arguments which prove either particular form of it, or which prove neither in distinction from the other. I argue the fact of God's moral government over man, then,—

1. From the account given of man's nature as a creature of God.

The first description of man is one which imparts the highest significance and grandeur to the work of creation as at first recorded. "God created man in his own image." What were this world in all its beauty and sublimity, without this creature man in the likeness of the Being that made him! No other being so exalted in the essential elements of his nature, could have been created; for he was essentially God-like. He was therefore immortal; and as endued with intellect, affections, and elective power, *a free agent*, and from the necessity of his condition, as created male and female, as well as in his relations to his Maker, *a moral agent;* capable of moral character and of moral action—fitted to do the will, to accomplish the designs of God,—thus to live and act in eternal fellowship with God, in doing good. The great end of his being was thus to bless God, to bless a sentient universe, and to bless himself in the highest degree; and yet he was not less capable of defeating this end, and promoting its fearful opposite in the highest misery. He was destined to be the progenitor of other myriads like himself. Would the benignant Father of existence forsake this work of his own hands, and leave these children of his power to the darkness and dreariness, to the self-disposal and ruin of an unguided and unprotected orphanage? or, would he assume that relation, and adopt that system of control which should combine every influence of wise and benignant authority, of discipline, of guidance and of guardianship, which is adapted in the highest degree to secure the end of their creation in perfection of character and of happiness,—the system of a perfect moral government? Can we, in any case of moral reasoning, infer with greater assurance any truth from any reason? The first and most momentous fact then of divine revelation concerning man, decides that he was created, so that from the beginning he might live and act forever under the perfect moral government of God.

2. Man at the first was actually placed under the perfect moral government of God, when created and put into the garden of Eden to dress and keep it,—"the Lord God commanded the man, saying: Of every tree of the garden thou mayest freely eat; but of the tree of the knowledge of good and evil, thou shalt not eat of it; for in the day that thou eatest thereof, thou shalt surely die."

Man indeed, by the institution of the Sabbath and the creation of Eve, may perhaps have already come under the full measure of moral obligation to obey, what are commonly called the first and second commandments of the law. Be this as it may, God first and formally instituted his moral government over man when he gave the law in Eden, which has now been cited. In giving this law, he in the first instance formally assumed his rightful authority as a moral ruler, claimed in his true character as "the Lord God" the right to govern, which imposes an obligation to obey, gave a perfect rule of action, which demands the spirit of unqualified loyalty, and sustained his absolute dominion by the requisite legal sanction. Without here attempting to interpret, in its more particular meaning, the language of the requirement and of the penalty of this law, it is sufficient for my present purpose, that it requires that spirit of loyalty, or that unqualified submission in all things which is due to an infinitely perfect Being in the relation of a moral governor, and fully sustains his authority by the legal sanction which is annexed to the requirement. God then, from the beginning, assumed the high relation of perfect moral governor over men, as moral and immortal beings.

3. This relation of God to men, is set before us, in different instances throughout the Scriptures, with similar formality and explicitness.

The moral government, as given in its first form to our first parents in Eden, was a merely legal dispensation. Immediately after their apostasy however, is revealed a promised Redeemer; and now this simply legal system, though it ceases not to be a perfect moral government, is greatly *modified*, by a divine and wonderful combination of law and grace in one system; in which, while there is an ample provision for the pardon and acceptance of penitent transgressors, neither the obligation of the law as a perfect rule of action, nor the authority of God as a perfect moral governor, is impaired. The reason is, that in pardoning the penitent or believing transgressor under the provision of an atonement, the authority of the lawgiver or moral governor is as fully sustained—every iota of the influence of law to secure perfect obedience is as fully established, as it would be by the infliction of the legal penalty on the transgressor. And thus it is, as we shall see, that God throughout his entire Revelation ever presents himself before his moral kingdom in his untarnished glories as a just God and yet a Saviour; with his authority undiminished and unobscured, and with his claim to perfect obedience unconcealed and unrelaxed. And this he does, whether he claims obedience to the perfect rule of moral action, or compliance with the condition of his pardoning mercy. He ever appears enthroned in the high and absolute authority of a rightful moral governor. In proof of this assertion, the appeal is sufficient to the three more formal and signal dispensations, in which after man's apostasy, God is presented in the Scriptures in this exalted character. As the first then, I refer to the covenant made with Abraham (Gen. xvii.). As in the law given to our first parents, the authoritative preface is, "THE LORD GOD commanded," &c.; so in the covenant made with Abraham,—the Gospel thus preached to Abraham (Gal. iii. 8), we find substantially the same authoritative preface, "I am the Almighty God; walk before me and be thou perfect." Here, the obligation to obedience to this great and comprehensive command is rested on God's authority or right to command, which imposes an obligation to obey; and his authority is rested on his perfect character, as "the Almighty God." I next refer to the Mosaic law—the Jewish theocracy. I assume this to have been a *representative* system, exhibiting God's system of moral government over all men, as I shall hereafter attempt to prove that it was. Viewing it then as identical with God's moral government in its great requirements at least, God gave this law, saying: "I AM THE LORD THY GOD, &c., thou shalt have no other gods before me" (Ex. xx. 2). And again, Deut. v. 6, 10, and 12. But it is unnecessary to quote instances to our purpose. For we may say, the obligation of every command and every prohibition of the law as given by Moses, is made to depend on God's simple, naked authority, as this depends on his perfect character. Nor can it well be imagined that more abundant proof should be furnished, that God ever and constantly presented himself in the Old Testament in the one relation of a perfect moral governor, directly to Israel, and indirectly through the Mosaic dispensation to the rest of the world. If now we refer to the New Testament, what do we find there presented, but God in the same grand relation to men? What too is the comprehensive theme of the revelation which, by its light, is to eclipse in comparative darkness all prior revelations? what, but the kingdom of God—the reign of God—the perfect moral government of God through grace! What was the message of the forerunner, but a summons to prepare to receive this in its complete and final development? "Repent, for the kingdom," —the reign,—"of heaven is at hand;" and how was a nation moved by this announcement? What employed the ministry and life of the Messiah himself, but to affirm and establish the fact, that this kingdom of God had come as the consummation of all God's prior dispensations? When by the wonders of his divine power, he arrested the human mind to universal, thoughtful consideration, and excited it to every form of emotion,—to admiration, surprise, anxiety, reverence, submission, sympathy, gratitude, joy, love, enmity, hate, and malice, as he unfolded the nature, object, end of this kingdom, with the duties and the character of its subjects; when the people followed him from place to place, and multitudes into the city, as with the heart of one man, what was the subject, whether rightly apprehended or not by others, which he presented to consideration, and which produced this commotion among the people,—what but the moral government of God? When he aimed to kindle and fill the hearts of his disciples with intense desires like his own, for the success and triumphs of this kingdom, by teaching them to pray, "Thy kingdom come, thy will be done on earth as it is in heaven;" when to arouse thoughtless men to become his servants, by strenuous effort, and by action that should never falter, he told them that the kingdom of God suffereth violence, and the violent take it by force; when every command, invitation, exhortation, promise, threatening, was only a summons to duty; what was his design, but that God should be obeyed by men?

When, after entering on his ministry, in all his intercourse with men, in villages and cities, at the house of the Pharisee, with the woman of Samaria, by the wayside, in the synagogue, in the market, before the high priest and Sanhedrim, and at the bar of Pilate, he recognized men as it were only as *moral* beings, and under God's authority; taught them their duty, and summoned them to perform it; called men to act, and by acting to obey God; when by his instructions, by his example, by his whole life, and even by his death, he taught not the philosophy of the Porch or the Academy, not physical nor political science, not the arts of intellectual culture, not even the relative and social duties by insulating men from God, but chiefly, subjection to God and God's authority in all human doings; when he required men to forsake all, to let the dead bury their dead, to take up the cross and follow him, to hate father and mother and wife and children, and even life itself, and go and proclaim the kingdom of God;—what else was to be thought of, what else to be done, till the souls of men were brought under the moral dominion of God? And further, how absolutely did he ratify the standard of all moral perfection—the perfect rule of action for all moral beings, first in relation to God, when in answer to the lawyer's question, he said, measuring man's duty by man's ability, "The first and great commandment of the law is, thou shalt love the Lord thy God with all thy heart, and with all thy soul, and with all thy strength, and with all thy mind." And then assuming that he who should obey this *first* and great commandment, would love *himself* only as he ought,—i. e., in that degree only which would be consistent with the glory of God, or with the highest good of all,—he adds, in relation to man, "And the second is like unto it, thou shalt love thy neighbor as thyself;" in that degree, which is consistent with the glory of God, or the highest general good. And with this absolute moral perfection required of man by God's authority, is there no moral government on the part of God? In respect also to the condition of pardon or justification,—the great and only rule of final judgment,—how constantly and peremptorily did our Lord enforce compliance with this rule on the part of sinful men and on God's authority! "This," said he, "is the work of God, that ye believe on him, whom he hath sent." "If ye believe not that I am he, ye shall die in your sins." "Whosoever forsaketh not all that he hath, he cannot be my disciple." In order to demolish the self-righteousness of the young ruler, and to convict him of the want of even the least moral rectitude, he says, "Sell that thou hast, and give to the poor, and then thou shalt have treasure in heaven, and come and follow me." When he fixed the terms of eternal life and death, he declares, "He that believeth and is baptized, shall be saved, and he that believeth not, shall be damned." What then, I may now ask, was the ministry of Christ while on earth, what in its aim and in its result, but a vindication and explanation of God's perfect moral government through grace over this sinful world? If now we refer to the apostles of our Lord, what engrossed the heart and soul, the labors, the toils, the life of these men, even unto death, especially of the great apostle, except the fuller exhibition of this moral system, in its nature, its principles, its comprehensiveness, its results, its glory,—the whole foundation and superstructure of this kingdom,—the moral government of God through grace? What, in a word, is the Gospel, but an exhibition of God's moral government, developed and established in all the strength of its authority, and in all the riches of its mercy, for the present obedience of a sinful world, for its speedy adjudication at the last tribunal, and the unchangeable retributions of eternity? And what will be when the end cometh? He to whom, for its administration in this world, is given all power in heaven and on earth, will deliver up the kingdom to God, even the Father, that God may be all in all. With what emphasis and fullness of import then, may it be said, that the one single comprehensive relation, to which every other is subordinate and subservient, in which God is presented to men throughout his entire revelation, is the high and august relation of their perfect rightful moral governor. I remark—

4. That the history of God's providential government, exhibits its administration as subservient to his moral government.

I can only advert to some of the more striking events of his Providence as recorded in revelation, the design, tendencies, and effects of which are so obvious to a reflective mind, that they scarcely need be stated. Consider then, the condition of our first parents in Eden. This garden, as we may suppose, more beautiful and lovely than any elysium which the human imagination ever pictured, at once bespeaks its design and its fitness to become what it actually became, the happy residence of purity, love, and joy. If angels and archangels were not there, our first parents were there, adorned with absolute moral perfection; and God was there, a frequent, welcome visitant, with whom they walked in that filial affection and confidence which the presence and love of such a Creator must inspire. Could sin ever enter such bosoms as these and in such a place; or, if it did, could it find the slightest palliation in the circumstances or character of its inmates? Must not temptation, however powerful, still be weak amid such heavenly influences? Could it invade a place so much the emblem of the paradise above? It did; but when and only when, with astonishment it must be said, in the true meaning of the language, God had done what he could do to prevent the direful catastrophe of a necessary probation to these immortals. For what in any case, is any thing, which can be called the *power or the strength* of inducements to disobey the living God, greater than the power of motive to obey him? All that can be supposed of fitness or tendency to disobedience, is a comparative trifle. It is not, then, for man to surmise a condition of moral beings, whatever temptation to sin be supposed, more auspicious to their endless moral perfection than was that of our first parents in Eden.

I next advert to the providential condition of our race, as the consequence of the entrance of sin into the world, and of its foreseen universal prevalence. The moral government of God over man in Eden being a merely legal system, was now greatly modified by an economy of grace. The moral character of our first parents was changed, and with it, consequentially and prospectively, as the result of this trial of human nature, their descendants like themselves, on becoming moral agents, were from the first to become sinners. Man is no longer sinlessly obedient to the divine law under a merely legal dispensation, according to the principles of which, by *one sin* all must be lost, the world is to be no longer a paradise. The race, mankind, now consequentially and prospectively sinners, are at once placed under an economy of grace, with a divine provision for justification from many offenses. This change in character from sin to holiness in man, carried with it a corresponding change in the condition of human existence. A new system, not of retribution, but of trial and of moral discipline, was now imperiously demanded, and at once adopted. The world became one of thorns and thistles, and man was doomed to toil, to suffering, to sorrow, and to temporal death; not as the legal penalty of sin, but rather as such an expression of God's displeasure for his sin, that with other tendencies it might subserve the purpose of a reclaiming influence under the new economy of mercy, where one act of sincere though imperfect obedience would insure God's everlasting acceptance and favor. And now, who shall say that this condition of human existence, compared with that of Eden itself, in adaptation to promote and to secure man's moral well-being, is on the whole, and as a system of influence for this end, aside from its known effects, not for the better instead of for the worse?* Be this as it may, who can fail to discern the subservience of these permanent providential arrangements of God, under a system of mercy, to the great design and end of his moral government? Who does not see in the fixed providential condition of every moral being in the world, a system or part of a system of moral discipline involving both goodness and severity eminently, even divinely adapted to the great ends of a moral probation for the allotments of eternity? Who, in view of the goodness of God, does not think of repentance for his sins against such a Benefactor, and even wish for and intend to secure, on this condition, his pardoning love and eternal friendship? Who, were there no disappointment, nor

* What is the leading object of the Apostle in Romans v. but to enforce this truth?

sickness, nor sorrow, nor suffering in the world, and especially no prospect of death, would be reclaimed to virtue, or be confirmed in her paths of pleasantness and peace? or rather, without these evils felt or feared, how hopeless in sin, how desperate in crime, would the world become! And yet, who that should pervert no gift of divine bounty, nor chastening of divine love in its kind and gracious design, would not be reclaimed to holiness, to happiness, and to God? Nor would it be difficult to trace the benign influence of the present system of moral discipline on this world, in the confirmation of the saved in eternal holiness in another, nor to unfold the divine wisdom as well as love, which dictated the intercession, 'I pray not that thou shouldst take them out of the world, but that thou shouldst keep them from the evil.' But not to dwell longer on this topic—who does not perceive in the permanent arrangements of God's providence over sinful men, a most necessary and useful subservience to the great practical design of God's moral government,—a constant tendency, an ever-urgent influence in human experience, and resulting from the ceaseless operation and effects of physical laws, directed to this one great end? What but the most unreflecting presumption can deny their fitness to this end, or venture to propose a change for the better? What are they but so many proofs of God's moral government over men; and so many signal illustrations, that where sin abounds, grace doth much more abound?

The next event in the providence of God, which I notice, is *the destruction of the world by the deluge.* This is an instance, not of chastening love, but of vindictive wrath; of the infliction of the full penalty of sin;* of the full and just retribution of impenitent, unbelieving sinners. Fifteen centuries had elapsed since man was created; his wickedness had now become great in the earth; the warnings of Noah had been dis-

---

* Temporal death, as common to both the righteous and the wicked, is a *proof* of sin, and the certainty of it, this death to all, a part of the moral discipline under which all men live. But temporal death *in sin*, i. e., *to die in sin*, to *die in impenitence and unbelief*, is more; it is *a part* of the evil included in the whole legal penalty, or at least *proof* of the infliction of this penalty in every such case. Hence, in Jewish usage, *to die in iniquity, to die in sin*, &c., describes such a case; and all *known* cases of this class are spoken of as such. (Ezek. xviii. 18, 30; xxxiii. 8, 9; John viii. 21, 24; Luke xiii. 1–5; 1 Cor. x. 11; 2 Pet. ii. 6; Heb. iv. 11; Jude 7.)

regarded for one hundred and twenty years; wickedness was triumphant; it repented God that he had made man on the earth, and now the hour of retributive judgment has arrived. Nothing stays the execution of the threatening. The heavens are clothed in blackness; the light of day is extinguished by clouds thickening, darkening, and foreboding the hastening tempest; the awful artillery of the skies shakes the earth; the guilty millions are appalled with consternation and dismay; agonies are depicted on every countenance; the child clings to its mother, the wife to her husband in unutterable terrors—but does God desist? The waters rise rapidly; earth, air, and sea tremble; the fountains of the great deep break up—and where now are the myriads of these creatures of God? Save one family, the wrath of God has swept the world of every inhabitant. Never since the earth stood, have men witnessed such a terrific, and, as it were, sensible demonstration in the execution of the legal penalty of sin—such a manifestation of the wrath of God in upholding his authority as the just and rightful moral governor of men. Nor is there any thing, in this fearful retribution, to surprise us. It was for the wickedness of a world, which had proved itself incorrigible under the government of the God who made it, and who, though punishment is his strange work, must either inflict it, or abandon that rightful dominion over his moral universe, which has all the worth of his own infinite Being.

Here I might dwell on another event, though less extensive in its effects, scarcely less impressive than the former—the destruction of Sodom and Gomorrah. Sodom and Gomorrah, and the cities about them, saith an apostle, are set forth as an example, suffering the vengeance of eternal fire.

I might here appeal to another providential event, as not less explicit in giving the same instruction. The confusion of tongues, and the dispersion at Babel, are prominent among the events of patriarchal history, which were brought to pass only in subservience to the designs of God as the moral ruler of the world.

And next, that event which, in its relations and results, pervades the entire history of God's providence over this world to the present hour, the calling of Abraham, with its typical covenant and promises of earthly blessings, here demands a particular consideration, of which subject however, I shall speak only in general terms. I ask then, what was the calling of Abraham, with that covenant of earthly promises, which was made with him and his posterity? It was plainly, and as it were exclusively, a typical dispensation, comprising in all its prominent details, probably the fullest, richest, most impressive instruction concerning God's moral government which, in that age of the world, could be given, with the faintest prospect of its utility. If we interpret it and understand it, as the apostle has taught us to do, in its higher spiritual import, what is it in its precept, "walk before me, and be thou perfect," but an authoritative rule of action, as the condition of God's acceptance and favor; in its promise of an earthly country, but the promise also of a heavenly country, wherefore God is not ashamed to be called their God; in its promise to the patriarch of an only son, and from him the innumerable multitude of children of the promise counted as his seed; in its commanded sacrifice of this only son on Mount Moriah, received again by Abraham as from the dead, in *a figure;* in the promise, not to seeds as of many, but to thy seed as of one, which is Christ; and I may add, in the indirect but distinct recognition by the act of Abraham, of Melchisedec *as a priest of the Most High God*, authorized, by divine designation, to officiate for all the true worshipers of God, as the medium of acceptable worship, being also king of righteousness and king of peace, and typifying another priest according to the same order; even in its prescribed right of circumcision, as the seal of the righteousness of faith—the token of the covenant—sealing the validity of its every higher, as well as of its every lower promise,—I say, if interpreting this covenant with Abraham, as that which, in its representative character, was designed to instruct men in these higher truths, what is it but such a representation of God's moral government through grace, over this sinful world, that the Apostle justly calls it, "the Gospel which before was preached unto Abraham?" In its primary import, how was it fulfilled in its every promise! In its spiritual, or secondary import, how were its practical effects secured in that cloud of witnesses who embraced it, who confessed that they were strangers and pilgrims on earth, who died in faith, looking for a city which hath foundations, whose builder and maker is God! Thus God, as it appears from his own history of his providence, had, for so many long centuries, been, as it were, compelled by the degradation and incorrigible wickedness of men, to adopt the severer modes of his moral administration to sustain his authority. These, from the apostasy in Eden to the calling of Abraham, though blended with many decisive forms and proofs of his mercy, were yet so ineffective that now, as if it were all that divine wisdom and mercy could do, he seems to abandon,—with the exception of one family—the rest of the world, and to leave them without the reclaiming influence of any further revelation of his truth. In respect to this one family however, by a fuller and brighter revelation of divine truth than any he had before made, he adopts a new expedient for the accomplishment of his great design as a moral ruler. He does not, in apparent discouragement, as by the wickedness of man before the deluge, now, as then, destroy him in his wrath, but resorts rather to a new and more perfect system of influences to reclaim and to save; confining it however, in its first form, to a representative mode of revelation, and this to a single family, as they may be able to bear it—and designing, as the subsequent history shows, further additions, through successive generations, and even through protracted ages. What significance and moment does such a course of providence impart to God's determination to maintain a perfect moral government over this world, unto its full and final consummation! His providential purposes will not fail through want of providential expedients. Delay in the execution of these purposes is not abandonment; counteraction is not defeat, nor hindrance discomfiture. What are the rage and the wrath, the vain imaginings, the contempt and the scoffs of a world, as ignorant and weak as it is wicked? "He that sitteth in the heavens shall laugh!" What too, are the sins, and sorrows, and sufferings, and death of this temporary scene; what the rise and fall of empires; the desolations and carnage of war; the ravages of famine and pestilence; the prolonged reign, crimes, cruelties, of despots and tyrants—what are all those evils of earth, which seem to human hope perpetual; what though that adversary of God, so successful in Paradise, seems ever since to be achieving new and more permanent conquests; what if, from the beginning, the many be lost and the few saved; and all things continue as they were; what of all this;—what is *time* to Him who inhabiteth eternity; what is earth even, with all its moral beings, in all their generations, in all their interests, in all their immortality;—what is all this but an infinitesimal, when the question is—whether God shall be God, and reign in the glories of a perfect moral governor, in the eternity which is yet to come?

5. I now refer to the Theocracy of Israel—the national government, which God himself administered over that people by Moses.

In this event, or temporary dispensation of his providence, especially as an appendage to the Abrahamic covenant, it is claimed, that God is revealed in a still more decisive, full, and impressive aspect of a rightful moral governor, than under any prior dispensation. Unfortunately however, for our own present purpose, there is in respect to the character and nature of the Jewish theocracy, so much that is unsettled among theologians and commentators; there is so much, in my view, that is imperfect and erroneous in the views and opinions commonly entertained respecting it, that it can scarcely be made use of in our present argument; at least, that it cannot be so used as to give its full force to this argument. On this account I shall defer any attempt to present it in this manner, until I have more fully investigated its character and its relations in several subsequent lectures. In the mean time, I will only say here, that in my view, the law which God gave to Israel by Moses, was, in its primary and proper character, simply a national government; and one which, while resembling in its essential characteristics the civil government of Egypt, and the civil governments of contemporary nations, yet, compared with modern systems of civil governments, was peculiar in many prominent respects. It was thus peculiar, inasmuch as God assumed toward this people the twofold relation of National King and Tutelary Deity; established this government as a representative system, i. e., to represent his higher system of moral government over men as moral and immortal beings, and administered it through grace, and by a supernatural providence. That such were the essential features of this system in its primary and proper character, so prominently presented and decisively proved, as to be eminently fitted to arrest the attention and control the practical convictions of this nation, I hope fully to show hereafter. Proceeding on this assumption respecting the nature of this system of civil government, I need only to ask any one at all acquainted with the Scriptural narrative, to reflect on the extreme degradation, ignorance, and stupidity of this idolatrous people, now just delivered from their Egyptian bondage, and then say whether the human mind can devise a system, especially as an appendage to the Abrahamic covenant, so perfectly fitted to reclaim them from their idolatry, to the worship and service of the only living and true God? To be convinced on this subject one needs but to know that this people, from their prior education, habits, and usages, in Egypt, knew, and could know nothing of a civil government, except in the form of a theocracy, and of course, as representing another and higher system of government over men as moral and immortal beings; and then to reflect on what, in the providence of God, preceded, attended, and followed the giving of their national law on Mount Sinai, even from their deliverance from Egypt to the coming of their Messiah. It may be surely said, if it be possible to show one thing by another, clearly, unambiguously, impressively, then the theocracy of Israel, as a symbol or type, representing God's higher system of moral government, is without a conceivable parallel. What a striking proof of this relation of one system to the other must thus have been furnished to this people, and thus what a constant memorial in their engrossing ritual and other services, in their ceaseless assemblages, in their signal prosperity when obedient and loyal to their national king and their national God, and in their signal calamities when disobedient and rebellious, must have been presented before them every day and every hour of God's perfect moral government through grace over them as moral and immortal beings.

6. I now refer to what are commonly called the great or leading *doctrines* of the Scriptures.

Concerning the reason or the propriety of this somewhat limited application of the term, I shall not now inquire. Under this name are included certain great and prominent facts or truths of the Scriptures, which have a most important relation to, and connection with, the moral and immortal interests of men. Among these I shall notice as briefly as may be, the doctrines of the depravity or sinfulness of all men; of the atonement of Christ; of justification by faith through grace; of decrees and election; of regeneration by the influence of the Holy Spirit; and of the final, general judgment. Assuming the truth of each of these doctrines, in its just, Scriptural form of statement, I claim, that it incontrovertibly and necessarily implies and proves, that God administers a perfect moral government over this world of human beings.

We refer in the first place to the doctrine of the depravity or sinfulness of all men in their first moral character. What then is sin, as presented in God's revelation, but the transgression of law? Not only is the transgression of God's law, sin; it is the only thing which in the Scriptures is called sin. All other theories, conceptions, notions of sin, formed by theologians, orthodox or heterodox, or to be found in confessions, creeds, and catechisms, are brought to naught by the light of God's word, and that of human consciousness. Miracles, if the solecism of supposing them for the purpose may be allowed, could not, without disproving the intuitions of the human mind, prove the contrary. But if sin on the part of men is the transgression of the law of God, then there is a law of God to be transgressed—a perfect rule of action sustained by the requisite legal sanctions, and having the full authority of the Lawgiver: in other words, God administers a perfect moral government over men in this world.

I next advert to the atonement of Christ. This is a measure of God's providing, that he might sustain his authority as a moral governor; or that he might be just in the justification of the believing sinner. The Logos of God, by the most intimate union, by the closest possible approximation to identity of being with the man Christ Jesus, became, with him, what is, and what must be conceived and spoken of, according to all analogous modes of conceiving and speaking, as one person, one at least for the great purpose of the intimate union. He was the Messiah of the Jews, the Redeemer of the world, the Lord of glory, who was crucified, the man that is God's fellow. He who thought it not robbery to be equal with God, in the form of a servant and fashion of a man, became obedient unto death. It is Divinity humanized to suffer; it is humanity deified to atone. His atonement for sin is an event without a parallel—the mightiest miracle of earth—the wonder and joy of heaven—revealing the manifold wisdom of God to principalities and powers in heavenly places, and showing God in all the majesty of his justice, and in all the riches of his mercy, toward this sinful world. No similar transaction, can we suppose, has ever taken place on the theater of the universe, nor will ever take place again in the annals of eternity. "It stands amid the lapse of ages and the waste of worlds, a single, solitary monument" of that august relation of God to which itself and all things else are subservient; and when these heavens and this earth shall be no more—when, at the final consummation, God shall be all in all, there will still be the Lamb in the midst of the throne—eternity's memorial of God's perfect moral dominion, through grace, over this sinful world.

I next refer to the doctrine of justification by faith. Without here noticing the variety of opinions on this subject, I shall only state my own. Justification before God, according to the Scriptures, is that act of God whereby, as the righteous Lawgiver and final Judge of men, he authoritatively determines or causes believing sinners to stand right in respect to the sanctions of his law. The doctrine of justification, as it asserts or teaches this act of God, unfolding it in its dependencies and relations, its processes, its conditions, its attendants, its issues, and these in all their own intrinsic harmonies and perfect adaptation to the grand ultimate result, may, not inappropriately, be viewed as entire Christianity—the whole of God's revelation, as it is related in every part and every element, to the manifestation and glory of God in his moral dominion. If we go back to the counsels of God before the foundation of the world, and trace them as developed in all his works of creation and providence, and in all his acts and doings of grace and of mercy toward men as moral beings, terminating with his one great and last act of earth and of time—*the justification* of the righteous at his final tribunal—what else do we see but God in the administration of his perfect moral government through grace?

The doctrine of God's decrees claims our notice, as one, according to the Scriptures, simply teaching one great fact or truth of purely practical relations—the fact or truth that God wills or purposes the existence of all actual events. Without it, without the great fact which constitutes the doctrine, the sole basis of many of the most momentous duties which God requires of men would be wholly subverted. Without it, what ground were there for gratitude under blessings, for submission under trials, for trust in the present, for hope in the future? On the throne of Providence we could see only some blind, fortuitous energy, with utter indifference to the wants and the woes of dependent creatures, disposing of their allotments without a thought of good or of evil to them. We should indeed be the children of an infinite Being ; but exiled from his paternal love and care, we should have no Father! Thus forsaken of its Maker, what a dark and somber world were this! But how is the scene changed and brightened with a designing God on the throne—an all-perfect Being, whose wisdom and whose will direct every event! Under a Providence which executes such counsels of the Most High, how obvious and imperious are the claims of his authority for that class of ennobling virtues, which arise from the diverse and almost ever-varying conditions of our earthly existence, whether prosperous or adverse—virtues which have eminently adorned the character of righteous men among saints and martyrs, and pre-eminently of Apostles, imparting patience and perseverance in their labors and toils, to the end—constant rejoicing in life and signal triumph in death! Under the accomplishment of such "decrees," whose gratitude shall not express its praise; whose song shall be silenced, even by afflictions and trials; whose heart shall be made faint with the trembling of fear, or caused to sink by the chill of despair; whose submission, trust, confidence, hope, peace, joy, shall not cheer and bless his existence on earth, come what may; in a word, whose will shall not be one with and lost in God's will? If this be duty—if any other thought be impiety, rebellion—then how does the doctrine—the fact that God, for reasons worthy of himself, purposes every actual event in this world and in all worlds—show his rightful and authoritative claim to all those virtues and graces of human character which he demands under all the various changes and dispensations of his providence? If God has no will that what takes place shall take place, how can his will be recognized in respect to any event? And then, what can exempt from hardened ingratitude, or save from distrust and fear, from murmuring, repining, and despair? But in view of such a will of God—a will of which every event, as providential, is the expression—how are enforced the requirements of his authority, that in the reception of blessings "we render to the Lord according to his benefits;" that in the perplexity and severity of our trials we say, "Though he slay me, yet will I trust in him;" and when in the deepest midnight of mystery, his mighty hand seems to be crushing us, how welcome and sustaining his own voice—"Be STILL, and know that I am God!" How God's providential dominion thus reveals and enthrones him in his moral dominion! What assurance for the righteous, that from behind the darkest clouds and tempests the Eternal Sun of light, and life, and joy will soon break forth to cheer every scene of earth, or, as in a moment, in the far more exceeding and eternal weight of glory! With what an emphasis of authority then, does God ever summon us to those moral duties which alone and so eminently fit us for our earthly condition, be it what it may.

The next doctrine which I have specified as worthy of notice in this connection, is the doctrine of Election. As I propose largely to consider this doctrine hereafter, and particularly to exhibit its practical relations and tendencies, I shall here only say concerning it, that, in my view, it has an eminently salutary *practical* tendency in respect to both the saint and the sinner; that in these relations it is revealed and employed in the Scriptures, as subservient to the great design of God's moral government, and thus becomes one of the most decisive illustrations and proofs of such a government on the part of God over this sinful world.

I now refer to what by theologians is commonly called the doctrine of Regeneration through the influence of the Holy Spirit. The term *regeneration* in the New Testament occurs in only two instances, and in both in a highly figurative meaning, as is also all other correlate phraseology in these writings. I shall now assume, what I hope satisfactorily to prove hereafter, that this change in man is a *moral change*—a change of his moral character, consisting in an intelligent elective preference of God to the world; that change which is required in such divine commands as, "make ye a new heart and a new spirit;" or as, "repent ye, and be converted;" and in description, as, "for it is God who worketh in you to *will*," &c.; or, "the love of God is shed abroad in your hearts by the Holy Ghost;" or, "ye have purified your souls in *obeying the truth* through the Spirit." This change then, in sinful man, thus presented in literal language, should not be mistaken and misrepresented in its true nature, as it has so commonly been by theologians and in confessions of faith, merely because to describe the greatness of the change, it is spoken of as a *new birth*, or as *a resurrection from the dead*, or as *a new creation*. It plainly cannot be *literally* all these, nor yet any one of them. It is true, that the change is never brought to pass in the human mind without the supernatural influence of the Spirit of God. Is it not therefore man's own act as truly as any other? Did not apostles *remember* through a supernatural influence of the Holy Spirit, and yet was not the act of *remembering* their own act—the act of their own mental power called *memory?* If God works in men *to will*, is not the act of willing *exclusively* their act, and done *proximately* in the exercise of their own power to will? If the love of God is shed abroad in our hearts by the Holy Ghost, is not the act of *loving exclusively* our own, and *proximately* the act of our own power to love God? If we obey the truth through the Spirit, is not the act of *obeying* our own act, and as such, an act of our power to obey? If it be said that God in regeneration gives man *the power* to will morally right, or to obey, or produces some other constitutional change in the mind, called a *new taste* or *relish*, diverse from right moral action; I answer, that to create any new mental power or property, is not to produce a new moral character, nor that which necessarily insures such a character; that such a change in man is never taught in the Scriptures; and further, that the Scriptures have not only never taught that man is unable to do his duty perfectly, i. e., to act morally right, but the contrary, in the express terms of the divine law, the only standard or rule of absolute moral perfection. In this perfect rule, man's duty to love God is made to consist simply in the use of his power to love him, and limited by his power to love. And has man then no heart, no mind, no soul, no strength, i. e., no power to love God, until he does love him? Is it said that he has power to love God if he will, i. e., *can will morally right, if he will?* This is plain nonsense in every possible meaning of the language. Is it then said, that he has power to love God, or to act morally right, when he does, or when he certainly will, love God, or act morally right? This is plainly impossible and absurd, unless he has the power prior to the act, and of course power used or exerted in the act. Should man then do what he can do, in respect to loving God, as God's law requires, he would become absolutely morally perfect.

In this view then, of *the nature* of the change in regeneration; in view of God's authoritative requirement of the change on the part of man, and especially in view of the work of the

Spirit of God in the production of the change; a more decisive manifestation of God, as the perfect moral governor of men cannot well be imagined, than that furnished by the Scriptural doctrine of regeneration. The change in the mind is no other than the change, by a sinful moral being, of his own moral character. It is, thus viewed, the change which takes place, by changing as his own act that *governing principle*—that controlling disposition*—which is no other than an elective preference of God to Mammon, and which alone constitutes a good or holy heart,—the good treasure of the heart, —the good tree which bringeth forth good fruit,—the pure fountain which sends forth the sweet waters. Hence the authoritative requirement, "Make the tree good;" and again, "Purify your hearts." It is that change in which man, in the use of his own moral powers ACTS ALL; and God, by his Spirit, causes him thus to ACT ALL;—a change in which man, through the supernatural influence of the Spirit of God, uses his own complete powers of a moral agent in acting morally right, when he had before used them only in acting morally wrong. Now, when this is the only conceivable morally right change in man; when God, by the whole weight of his authority as an all-perfect Being, requires and justly requires, and can justly require no other change in man; when this change, as an act of obedience to God, cannot be demanded, or even conceived to exist, except as an act of submission to God's authority as the rightful moral governor of man;—what can be said or thought, but that God according to the Scriptures, sustains this high relation to man? But this is not all. When man, thus a complete moral agent, and as much so as were he to become perfectly obedient to God; when thus able to obey God perfectly, without the least influence of the Holy Spirit; and when therefore, he ought thus to obey him without such influence, he yet willfully, i. e., with *willfulness*, disobeys him,† and will in fact thus continue, without the interposing influ-

* The ambiguity of these important terms renders it necessary to say, that there can be no *morally right principle*, or *holy disposition*, or *godly disposition*, which does not involve *the supreme* love of God, or which is not an act of the will and heart, *electively* preferring God to every other object as an object of choice.

† I do not say, as some do, *refuses to obey him;* for this, in my view, would be saying *he chooses to disobey*, which, in this connection, would be choosing *a wrong moral choice;* i. e., choosing a choice, which is absurd.

ence of the Holy Spirit, to disobey forever—God, in his compassion to man in this self-ruined condition, is moved to send his Holy Spirit into the world. And now, what is, what can be the design, the END aimed at by the mission of this divine Agent into this world of redeemed sinners? Is it to transform the trees of the forest, or "the stones of the street," into moral agents; or to change the physical properties or physical laws of things created—things, including man himself, pronounced by their Creator to be "very good?" The thought were irreverent, for it were contemptuous of the work of God. Is it to impart to sinners, in any sense or degree, the powers of complete moral agents? This thought were still more irreverent—not to say, were blasphemous. For shall a perfect God count, or consider, or treat any of his creatures as sinners, who have not sinned in the use, and therefore in the full possession, of the powers of moral agents? Who has heard of this sort or species of sinners, except under the orthodox patent of Saint Augustine? Who has ever supposed, except some early converted heathen philosophers (converted long after the death of the apostles), and their more modern disciples, that the grand errand on which the Holy Spirit is sent into this world, is either to create powers in the soul of man, which, if men are sinners, are already created in it; or, so to finish God's work in the creation of the soul, that what at first is a moral automaton shall become a moral agent, and so capable of moral action? Surely, the mission of the Holy Ghost into this world of redeemed sinners, planned and purposed in the eternal councils of the Godhead, must have an object worthy of such an embassy. Was it then, under the moral exigencies of a lost race, to make other beings either animate or inanimate than *moral* beings, partakers of God's holiness? Or was it, by a mysterious influence, which he knew how to employ for the godlike purpose—a purpose not less godlike because so obvious—that of leading moral and immortal beings to use their high powers morally right, which hitherto they had used morally wrong? The true answer to this question shows at once how intent God is to accomplish, so far as may be, his great design as the moral governor of men. It must thus appear, that when God saw that law and authority, all the love and mercy of redemption, all the awards of eternal retribution; all argument, persuasion, entreaty, motive; even all that truth could utter,—would be in vain to save;—then, rather than abandon to hopeless sin, and so lose these alienated, sinful men forever from his friendship and favor, he determined to send his Holy Spirit to reform, and thus to save some of an otherwise hopeless race. By what higher proof, can we well imagine, could God evince the august and eternal reality of his moral dominion over men? I add but one more of these proofs—

Lastly, The doctrine of final judgment.

This is not the place to unfold the Scriptural account of this transaction, nor is it my present purpose to attempt it. The principal *fact* with which I am now concerned, is, that God will then "RENDER TO EVERY MAN ACCORDING TO HIS DEEDS;" that "we must all appear before the judgment-seat of Christ, that every one may receive the things, done in his body, *according to that he hath done, whether it be good or bad.*" Such is the object, and such will be the issues, of the last day of man's history in this world—that day, for which all other days are made. The scenes, the events, all the transactions of this day—according to the Scriptural representation—in their grandeur and glory, their terrors and their triumphs, befit the catastrophe of earth and of time, and not less, the Being who sitteth on the throne, for the consummation of his moral dominion over a world of moral and immortal beings. How the results of this day will dissipate all human doubt, respecting the most prominent truth—the greatest FACT, concerning God made known by God's revelation—God on the throne; God, in his own right, by virtue of his eternal power and Godhead; God, in his intrinsic majesty and glory; God, with that investiture of authority which his infinite perfection gives; God, on the throne of perfect moral dominion!

REMARKS.

1. In this view of the moral government of God, I am constrained to ask, Have the orthodox part of the Christian ministry, in one important respect, rightly divided the word of truth?

I do not ask whether they have denied, nor whether they have not recognized by distinct implication in many forms, nor whether they have not assumed in some general form, God's moral government over men. But I ask, whether, according to the Scriptural standard of exhibition, they have not given an inferior prominence to God's moral government compared with that which they have given to his providential government? Have they not, in their sermons and other writings, placed God's moral government in the background, and his providential government, as including what have been esteemed and called the great doctrines of the Scriptures, in the foreground? Have they even attempted to unfold the former in its nature, in its elementary and fundamental principles, and its momentous relations,as fully and thoroughly as they have the latter? Have they not dwelt upon, and given an almost exclusive prominence to the so-called *doctrines*,—e. g., the Five Points of Calvinism, such as the doctrines of decrees, election, depravity, justification by faith only,—regeneration, the perseverance of the saints; or, what is worse, such dogmas as imputation, imputed sin and imputed righteousness, original sin, limited atonement, man's inability to perform his duty or act morally right? Even without supposing error in what they have taught, have not their teachings respected man's dependence on God, rather than man's moral obligation to obey God? Have they ever and always held man, as the Bible does, up to his high and ceaseless relation to God, as subject to his authority in all his doings and bound to act in all, under the influence of this authority, so that without acting under it, he cannot act morally right in obedience to God in a single instance; as that influence, under which he is able to act and bound to act without any other; as that influence under which, whatever other influence may coincide with and be concomitant with this, he must act, or he violates his ceaseless moral obligation and sins against God? He must work out his own salvation, under God's authority requiring him so to act and to do, though God works in him to will and to do; and is as truly bound to perform the work under God's authority without the co-operation of God as with it. Have the orthodox ministry then, thus pressed men to act morally right under God's authority, grace or no grace? Have they not taught them to depend on the Holy Spirit to give them power to act morally right, rather than with some hope, more or less, for God's undeserved, unpromised, sovereign influence, to put themselves at once to the use of their own perfect moral powers to act morally right in so acting? Have they not, to a great extent, taught *a mode of dependence* on the Holy Spirit, which, instead of enhancing, as it does, man's obligation to act morally right in immediate obedience to God's authority, absolutely subverts man's obligation so to act, and God's authority to require him so to act? How momentous the difference between teaching the one, instead of the other of these *modes of dependence* on the Spirit of God! If the latter is error, how great is that error! And yet how common! On this question of fact, I appeal to the ablest theologians, from Augustine to President Edwards, and to the more eminent of those who have followed of the same general class of divines; and I ask, who has placed the human conscience under the weight and pressure of God's authority to immediate duty as the Bible does? Who has presented man's dependence on the Holy Spirit, and man's obligations as a moral agent, *in such a manner* as to make the precise impression in respect to right moral action, which the authoritative commands of God are designed to make and should make,—that such action is man's duty, and only duty; the act which under every summons of God to duty, even in the thought of it, is to be done, or God will be disobeyed? And more than this,—where in the whole range of theological literature can be found any thing, which even in pretense can be esteemed a thorough treatise, on the high relation of God, to which his every other relation is subservient,—that of the supreme and rightful moral governor of his moral creation? I deny not that this subject has been taken up and considered in parts, and in parts applied as the exigency may have required, to some particular questions in theological controversy, though with very defective and false views of the very parts of the subject thus considered. And how should it be otherwise, than that erroneous and false views should result from the partial mode of treating a subject so comprehensive? But when or by whom, either in Natural or Revealed Theology, has any satisfactory or even plausible attempt been made to unfold the moral government of God, in its comprehensiveness, in its fundamental principles, its essential and immutable relations, and its diverse forms of administration? No such attempt is known, or suspected by the writer. If this be so, is it as it should be? If this be so, to what purpose is what is called systematic or scientific theology, except to incur, as it has often incurred, the censures of many eminent men, both theologians and others? If this be so, to what purpose can it be claimed, that hitherto there has been any consistent, truthful interpretation of the sacred oracles, any which exempts them in some most important respects,—I do not say from groundless, but from unanswerable objections? And if this be so, how can the honest mind believe without doubts, and difficulties, and perplexities, the teachings of Revelation, beyond certain general forms of truth, or truth combined with diluting error, which may suffice for moral responsibility and the conversion of a few sinners,—oh! how few!—but scarcely for the perfecting of the saints, or the edifying of the body of Christ? And if these things be so,—and the greater part of Christendom, even the greater part of the visible Church of God, are not the better but rather the worse for divine revelation, having only that knowledge of God, which will not save, but rather destroy,—then to what purpose does the meridian sun of Christianity shine on the world? Comparatively, how ineffectual are its beams on the hardened soil! God intended that its light should be—and so it would have been but for the sloth and perverseness of men—as the light of seven days, with its benign and rejoicing efficacy. But in this respect, how impaired and lost are its splendors! how dark and dreary the moral desolation of the earth! God intrusted his revelation to his Church,—to men no longer taught by his inspiration, to be defended and explained, to be unfolded to the intellect, and impressed on the conscience of a world, in all its riches of truth and grace, as the power of God to salvation. But how soon, and for long ages, did its combination with error, and its consequent obscurity and weakness, betray the human instrumentality which so imperfectly, and even faithlessly discharged the sacred trust! Sad waste of the treasure committed to earthen vessels! Fearful catastrophe of this gift of a benignant God,—not yet alleviated, still less retrieved! It is the fault of man—it is the fault of the Christian Church: it is more—it is the fault of the Christian ministry.

2. How obvious and imperious is the demand on the Christian ministry for the thorough investigation of the nature and principles of God's moral government over men!

There was a time when what was called *doctrinal* preaching usurped a pre-eminence in our pulpits over what was called *practical* preaching. The occasion of this prevalence of doctrinal preaching was the doctrinal errors or false doctrines, which it was designed and required to expose and overthrow. The calamity was, that it combined the severity of gospel truth with much error respecting man's inability and dependence, opposed to common sense and the Scriptures,—a combination peculiarly fitted to render it offensive to a large portion of the people. And yet the truth which it so prominently inculcated, being often blended with exhortations to immediate repentance, and softened by the appeals of divine mercy,and pressed on the conscience, had more real gospel in them—more of the worth, and light, and power, and efficacy of truth—than any and all other cotemporary preaching; the latter being little more than the denial of all wholesome truth, and the inculcation of a soulless morality. But not to go further in historic details, useful as they might be, I wish to say, that according to the Scriptural standard, all doctrinal preaching should be practical, and all practical preaching should be doctrinal. The truth of the Gospel—God's truth—is both. Distinguish its elements as you will by words, every divine precept involves doctrine, and every divine doctrine involves precept. Doctrine has a causative relation to precept, and precept a dependent relation to doctrine. Take away these relations between them, and you destroy both, by depriving each of one essential element of its relative nature. The doctrine *furnishes* the obligation, the reason, the motive, the nature and direction of the precept, and the precept, of course, derives all these reciprocal relations from the doctrine. Doctrine is the teaching which instructs the mind of the people in that truth which is authoritative and designed to influence and control the whole man as a moral being; which enlightens, guides, determines, consecrates the whole moral activity of a self-active nature to its true end, and so fashions immortal energies into perpetual and perfect moral character. It is truth then, as practical or productive of *action;* truth as binding, fixing the whole inner and outer man to action and doing; truth, controlling, reigning, authoritative; truth, manifested by revealing God's moral government in its nature, its principles, relations, power, results, which is the Gospel of God. And who, if not they whose high calling is emphatically to be workers together with God in the harvest of God's husbandry; who, if not they who are to be honored as wise master-builders of God's spiritual temple; who, if not they who are called to promote, and, as far as may be accomplished, secure the end for which God created and governs this world; who, if not the ministers of Christ, ought to arouse this dead world to life and action? What mighty energies are here perverted *in* sin, and devoted to its work! How ought they to be summoned by the cry of the watchman, as in thunder tones, to that new, and highest, and holiest productive exercise and activity which shall constitute co-operation and companionship with God! I speak not merely of overt external acts or doings. I speak of the energies of the moral man,—the energies of the intellect, of the heart, of the will, of affections, emotions, as these are the life and soul of all overt doings. Who, in preaching the Gospel, shall not aim at the same end at which God aims in revealing the Gospel; that end to which creation, providence, laws, precepts, ordinances, grace, reason, conscience, revelation, every thing else, is subservient,—*right moral action* in principle and practice? Who shall not use the same means for this end which God uses,—that truth or system of truth which is embodied in his perfect moral government; which ever places man in the attitude of an agent, teaching his dependence on God only as a reason for acting and doing? Who shall not aim to make the same impression on the human mind which God aims to make by his commands to act, his exhortations to act, his invitations, his entreaties to act, thus throwing every iota of responsibility for the issues of eternity on man, as an agent,—*for what he does;* for the deeds done in the body? What shall hinder? Not one doctrine or truth, except perverted and distorted into falsehood—and then hated and fit to be hated; not one, in its just, real nature and aspect as truth, or as the truth which it is, does not carry with it all its light and beauty and loveliness to the human mind; not one which is not the voice of mercy to those who need mercy, which is not attractive and winning like the music of heaven. Oh! how little do they who hate, oppose, and reject the great and peculiar truths of Christianity, know of these truths! Even cold indifference cannot be maintained and cherished in any mind, without a cherished, willful ignorance of their nature—their divine fitness to bless man. But how shall the people understand without hearing? And how shall they hear without the Christian ministry? Ay, and how with a Christian ministry, who do not understand that system of divine truth, which is nothing more and nothing less than a revelation of God's perfect moral government;—and how shall they understand it so as to give, I do not say, a tolerable degree of perfection to their teaching, but so as to give it that increased power on the human mind, which may be given it, and which one day awaits it; how, without a more, a far more laborious investigation of its nature, its relations, its harmonies, and its divine adaptations, than has yet been furnished by the incoherent and clashing systems of even Protestant Theology;—how, at least in such degree, that if they assert some of its momentous truths, they shall not as often contradict them;—how, so as to show that God's revealed moral government, the glorious Gospel of the blessed God, is by him designed and fitted, not to hold a world of moral beings like this in the slumbers of spiritual death, but to rouse and move and stir them to the instant, the ceaseless, the joyous activities of that spiritual life which is the only and absolute perfection of a spiritual being

LECTURE II.

PRELIMINARY.

Introduction.—Discussion involves the consideration of the Mosaic Economy.—Mistaken or defective views.—As preliminary, we ask, What is a Theocracy ?

I PROPOSE to unfold my views of the nature of God's moral government, as presented in the Scriptures, by considering the law by which this government is administered.

In the proposed discussion of this subject, I shall confine my inquiries to three forms in which God has given law to man, viz., the law which he gave to our first parents in Eden; that which he gave to Israel by Moses; and that which he gave to the world by Christ and his apostles.

In pursuing the investigation of this comprehensive subject, it would seem to be the most natural method, to direct our attention in the first place to the law of Eden. This has been the common method with theological writers; and has, if I mistake not, occasioned serious difficulties and many errors in the interpretation of important parts of the sacred writings.

There have been, I think, two common assumptions in respect to the law of Eden which are groundless. The one is, that this law, which, in the sum of its requirement, was both a rule of action and of judgment, as first given to our first parents in Eden, has continued to be such to their descendants, without modification or change. It is indeed, quite undeniable that this law of God, requiring absolute moral perfection of man, is, ever has been, and ever will be, obligatory on all men as a rule of action. But it is obviously impossible, that under that economy of mercy which was instituted and revealed on the first apostasy, it should also be a rule of judgment. This would secure the final condemnation of all, and render redemption nugatory. God will judge the world according to the Gospel. I say no more on this topic at present, as I shall have occasion to resume it in another connection.

The other assumption to which I refer is, that the law of

Eden is given to us by Moses in the very words in which it was given to our first parents by their Creator; and that hence the real question concerning its import is simply how *they* understood the language of this law.

Without however, provoking a controversy respecting the origin of language, and without attempting to show how Adam did or could understand the law from the words of the law, I advert to a fact which wholly supersedes the necessity of such inquiries, viz., that the language of the law given in Eden is the language of Moses, the Jewish historian; and this, whether he compiled the narrative from prior records or not. As the narrator of this transaction, Moses must have used the language of his own age and country. Of course his language must have conveyed those ideas, or that meaning, to his countrymen, which their usage gave it, and this meaning must have been the same which was originally conveyed by the Creator to our first parents. Whether, therefore, the terms of this law, as it is recorded by Moses, be the *ipsissima verba* which God addressed to them or not; or whether any language, properly so called, was the medium of communicating to them what these words now express, as employed by Moses according to Jewish usage; this is wholly immaterial to our purpose. If we can determine the import of this language, in the time of Moses, we can determine the true import of what we call the law given to Adam.

These remarks, with a little acquaintance with the controversies respecting the import of the law of Eden, will be sufficient to show, that if we would obtain just views of this law, our inquiries must be directed first to the import of the Mosaic law. At the same time, many other of the great questions in Scriptural theology, and among them that of our justification before God, depend on correct and adequate views of the law given to Israel. Before then, proceeding to the topics proposed respecting the law of God's moral government, I shall attempt, as preparatory to the discussion of them, to present to some extent, what I consider just views of the Mosaic law.

Here a wide field of inquiry opens before us. I propose only to give you some general views which may serve to guide your own future investigations.

It has been extensively maintained that the government which God administered over Israel was a *theocracy;* in other words, that God, as the governor of this people, simply assumed toward them the two great relations of national king and tutelary deity; and that accordingly, the laws which he gave them by Moses were simply national laws, and were enforced simply by temporal sanctions, involving to a great extent, supernatural interpositions in their execution. On this ground the learned Warburton has founded an argument for the divine legation of Moses, of this nature, viz., that Moses is the only human legislator who ever attempted to enforce his laws by temporal sanctions involving supernatural interpositions; and for this reason, that none but the true God could control the laws of nature, and execute such promises and threatenings as those by which the Mosaic code was enforced. In this argument Warburton rested much on the premise, that no future state of reward and punishment was taught in what he calls "the Mosaic religion," or "Mosaic dispensation," by which he must be understood to mean at least, that the Mosaic code was in no respect enforced by such sanctions. He denies that Moses, or the people of Israel, disbelieved a future state. He admits that the Mosaic dispensation, as a typical system, taught the doctrine of a future state, and that many passages in the Old Testament, in their typical sense, teach the same doctrine. What he seems to mean and maintain is simply, that the Mosaic dispensation, as such, does not, in *literal language*, or in the primary meaning of its language, teach the doctrine of future rewards and punishments; nor of course, make any use of this doctrine in enforcing obedience to its laws. What is true in this respect we may see hereafter. I only remark now, that the argument of Warburton for the divine legation of Moses must be admitted to be conclusive, whether we suppose the doctrine of a future state to be revealed and known or not; for if the laws given to Israel were enforced by constant supernatural interposition of God, the divine mission of their lawgiver was established.

Various opinions have been entertained in respect to the nature and design of the Mosaic dispensation. Some have maintained, that the laws of Moses respected only the external conduct or overt doings of men, because, like civil laws in modern times, they were enforced only by temporal sanctions, and in their administration made external conduct the *criterion* of obedience or disobedience, as if because such conduct under civil law is the proof, it is therefore the whole constituting element of loyalty or disloyalty.* Others seem to deny or overlook the peculiar character or nature of this government as a theocracy, and to contemplate it only as a religious system which exhibits God solely as the moral governor of men. Others speak of it as requiring obedience, in the most unqualified manner, to all its precepts, under the penalty of death, and allowing no mercy to any sinner, however penitent.† Others still have considered the Mosaic law as a system by which Church and State were united—a union of which I am not so fortunate as to have seen any satisfactory explanation by those who maintain it.

Indeed, I must confess myself by no means satisfied with any view or explanation of the Mosaic law which I have seen. Even Jahn, one of the latest and best writers on the subject, appears to me to have overlooked entirely that material characteristic of the system, to which the writer of the Epistle to the Hebrews has given the most prominence—its characteristic *as a representative system*. The grand error of commentators—of all who have attempted to unfold the nature of the system—has been, as it seems to me, one of the following: either that they have regarded it as so exclusively a religious or moral polity—what I have termed God's moral government over men as moral beings, as to overlook, and virtually deny, its primary, essential, and in one sense, its *only* character, that of a merely *national institution;* or, that they have regarded it—I do not say as exclusively a civil institution, for such I think, in one use of language, it is and is properly said to be, but that as such, it neither furnished nor was designed to furnish, any important instruction respecting God's higher system of moral government over men as moral and immortal beings; or, that they have regarded it as so combining the two systems—so uniting Church and State—under one system, that it is impossible, even for practical purposes, to trace a clear distinction between them. On this subject there is an ambiguity of language which also deserves notice. In speaking as modern writers do of this system, as a *national or civil institution* of government, their language naturally leads the reader to

* Vide Erskine's Dissertations, p. 3, et seq.; also p. 37.
† Vide McKnight's Trans., note, vol. v. p. 188.

understand that it does not in its nature include a representative system. But to speak of a national system of government, in that age of the world, when every such system was a theocracy, was to speak of a national system which, in its essential nature, was a representative system. To omit therefore, this idea or conception of a theocracy, by using the language described, is to give an essentially imperfect and false view of the thing in one of its most important relations.

Jahn, in his able treatise on this subject, appears to me to have misled himself by this unauthorized use of language; and in some instances to have fallen into the second, and in others into the third, of the errors above specified.* Certainly, I cannot discover that he ever exhibits a theocracy, or the Jewish theocracy, as a *representative* system. Without this view of this theocracy, or with either of the views of it above specified, it is not strange, I think, that very imperfect and erroneous views should be formed of the reasons, the nature, the design of this amazing economy.

The proposition on this important part of the subject, which, with requisite explanations, I shall attempt to establish, is, that the Mosaic law or system of government was a theocracy, and as such, designed to exhibit God's moral government over men as moral beings under an economy of grace.

I propose to show—

I. What a theocracy is;

II. That the Mosaic law was a theocracy; and,

III. That it was designed to exhibit God's moral government over men as moral beings under an economy of grace. I inquire, then—

I. What is a theocracy?

That we may the better understand the nature of this kind of government, it is necessary to recur to the actual state of the world, and to the prevailing views of civil government, especially in Egypt, when Israel was called out of that country, to be organized as a distinct and peculiar nation under the superintendence and government of the true God.

The following facts demand particular consideration:

1. The notion of tutelary deities—which has been supposed to be originally Egyptian—was universal throughout the Gentile world.

---

* Hist. Heb. Commonwealth.

This notion was, that the earth was divided by its Creator among a number of subordinate deities, each of which was employed in the protection and care of his own country and people, and wholly unconcerned for every other.

2. On this universal belief of an idolatrous world, in Egypt and all other nations, was founded all civil government.

These ancient legislators adopted into their civil code, not only laws which were strictly municipal, or designed to regulate civil conduct, but laws requiring and regulating, so far as such laws can control, the worship and service of their national gods, always claiming that they imposed their laws by the authority and sanctions of some divinity. And so, it may be said, the people believed.

3. All these were civil laws, or laws of the civil magistrate, having divine authority, whether they respected the worship of their national divinity or other conduct.

They were enforced by temporal sanctions, and the belief was as absolute as it was universal among the nations, that as they obeyed or disobeyed these laws of kings and rulers, they should receive both as individuals, good or evil from the hands of the civil magistrate, and also as nations, blessing or cursing from their tutelary deities, in the present world. Thus temporal good and evil, as dispensed in these modes, became exclusively and directly the sanctions of civil government in Egypt and in other nations—sanctions of sure execution, in the popular belief, except arrested, in case of disobedience, by such rites of sacrifice and lustration as were ordained for propitiating their offended deities.

4. Every such national institution involved another characteristic or relation: it was regarded as a *representative* system.

By this I mean that the theocracy, or national system which, as such, respected the conduct and condition of men, as beings of earth and time, implied another and a higher system of government over them as moral and immortal beings, so that the latter was represented by and inferred from the former. The theocracy, as I understand it, was in every respect a *merely national system*, though of that peculiar kind in which God, or the divinity of the nation, was both national king and tutelary deity, and which also implied and represented a higher system of government in relation to a future state of existence.

The popular belief in this other and higher system, and its

intimate connection with the theocratic government, seems to me, as a general fact or truth, to be placed beyond all reasonable doubt by Bishop Warburton in his Divine Legation of Moses, and also by other writers. I say as a general fact or truth, for I by no means commit myself to the defense of all the details of Warburton on the subject. Assuming then, as I think I may now safely assume, that the national government of Egypt, during the bondage of Israel in that country, was a theocracy and, as such, a merely civil or national institution as we have described it, we may now see that it would naturally, and did in fact in the view of the nation, become a representative system, implying another and a higher system of government over men, as moral and immortal beings; so that the latter was inferred from, and represented by the former. Let us look at the nature and circumstances of the case.

This form of civil government—for as a theocracy it was simply such—though wholly of human origin in fact, was founded, in its earlier forms at least, wholly in the pretense of divine revelation and divine authority. The ancient kings and legislators pretended, and secured the admission of the pretense, that they were commissioned by some god, by whose authority and direction they imposed their laws on the nations.* The design of this claim to a divine mission and to divine authority, was of course, to establish their control, and to perpetuate their power and their institutions. The more effectually to accomplish this, they availed themselves of the false religious systems of their people, especially the doctrine of tutelary deities, who, it was believed, exercised a particular providence over the affairs of men, and would bless with prosperity or curse with calamity, the nation over which they presided, as they should obey or disobey the laws of the civil ruler. Hence these rulers artfully employed these *quasi* religious opinions of the people, and especially encouraged their mysteries or rites of worship, that they might increase their veneration for these tutelary gods. This was done that so they might establish and render effective, the popular belief of the superintendence of these gods over the affairs of men in this world, by giving full force to the divine but temporal sanctions of civil government and its laws. Accordingly, the belief, as we have before said,

* Vide Jahn.

was as absolute as it was universal among the nations, that as they obeyed or disobeyed the laws of kings and rulers, they obeyed or disobeyed their gods, and should receive at their hands as tutelary deities, both as nations and individuals, good or evil, blessing or cursing, in the present world. Thus temporal good and evil, as dispensed by the providence of the national gods, and by their authority through the hands of the civil magistrate, were the sanctions, the only proper *legal* sanctions, of a theocracy or national government in Egypt and in other nations.

But this is not all. Equally universal was the belief of a future state of rewards and punishments. Nor did the ingenuity prompted by the love of power fail to employ this belief for the purpose of enforcing submission to the authority, and obedience to the laws of civil government. This belief, however, was not inculcated or adopted, under the assumption that eternal sanctions were a part of the theocracy or national government; for this was not a government directly instituted and administered by the gods, without the intervention of men as civil rulers. It was administered in its ordinary course by men, who, according to the popular belief, were directed by divine inspiration; and so far as sanctioned by the providence of the gods, it was sanctioned only by means of temporal good and evil.

But then this belief of a future state of rewards and punishments involved the belief of a great and momentous fact inseparable from it—the belief of another and higher system of government than a national theocracy—a government which, in its origin, authority and administration, would be regarded as directly and exclusively in the hands of the national divinity, whether of one supreme god or of many gods. This would be naturally regarded as a *moral*, as distinguished from a *civil*, government, and as determining the allotments of men in a future state of existence, when they had passed beyond the reach and control of earthly rulers, and all that could be called civil government. It would necessarily be regarded as a government, with its law as a rule of action and of judgment, and with its final issues in happiness and misery, as suited to an untried state of existence, and as exclusively in the hands of the national divinity. It would also involve other and higher relations on the part of men while living and acting in this world, than those of the subjects of a merely civil and temporal institution, for it would hold them responsible in respect to the higher rewards and punishments of an eternal retribution. As instituted and administered by the national divinity, it would naturally and surely be regarded as having a strong resemblance, in certain great principles and modes of administration, to that which the same being had established and administered over them as their tutelary deity. The administration of some of the laws of a theocracy would necessarily be confined to the civil magistracy. This part of the theocracy, consisting of these laws, some of them perhaps, admitting of satisfaction for their violation by offerings and sacrifices, and others not, would not naturally, being thus exclusively in the hands of men with the errors and imperfections of its administration, be supposed to bear an exact or even a striking resemblance to the higher system. It would be far more natural and reasonable to infer a resemblance between that part of the theocracy whose administration, in respect to sanctions, was reserved in the hands of the tutelary god or gods, according to the promises and the threatenings which were to be executed by an extraordinary providence. This, I cannot but think, would be the most natural view of the subject, though we may not be warranted by the records of antiquity to say that it was actually taken. But that the theocracy, or lower system—so far as its administration was viewed as *in the hands of the tutelary divinity*, and *as involving an extraordinary providence*, whether it respected individuals or the nation generally—would be considered as resembling, and so representing, the higher system in its general nature and great principles, cannot, I think, be reasonably doubted. It is true indeed, that from the essential differences in the nature of the two systems as pertaining to different states of existence, would obviously, in the view of all, naturally arise differences in their administration. But how could it be supposed, that the same Divine Being who reigned supreme in both systems, should prescribe a rule of action requiring less or more in either, than the spirit of loyalty due to a divine being? The natural conclusion would be, that this rule of action, though sustained in the one system by temporal, and in the other by eternal sanctions, would be the same in both, and especially if it were absolutely perfect in the lower, would not be less than absolutely perfect in the higher system. Further, if the lower system assumed, and proceeded on the assumption, that this perfect rule of action was universally transgressed, this would be unavoidably implied in respect to the rule of the higher system. If this perfect rule of *action* was modified as a rule of *judgment* under the theocracy, by an economy of grace and forgiveness in respect to penitent transgressors, through propitiatory sacrifices, how could it be supposed that less benignity would characterize the government of the same being, under the higher system, in forgiving transgression through some adequate propitiation. Under both systems, the perfection of the law as a rule of action could scarcely fail so far to convict the human conscience of sin, as to render welcome the doctrine of forgiveness by sacrifice, and to secure the belief of it, especially as sedulously inculcated by kings, hierophants, &c., in the mysteries and rites of national worship. It is true, that the mode of determining who is obedient and who disobedient to the rule of judgment, would widely differ under the two systems. In one it would be only through the medium of external action; in the other, by the direct inspection of the heart by an omniscient judge. In neither would the claim for the true principle and spirit of loyalty to the reigning divinity be dispensed with as a matter of obligation. In each system, as a system of law and grace, the rule of *duty*, as prescribing the whole duty of the subject, would differ from the rule of *judgment* as prescribing the condition of acceptance and favor. While the rule of duty in each system must be the same, and the rule of judgment in each the same, yet, in the lower or national system, external action, though not full compliance with the rule of judgment as being merely external action, must be the evidence or proof, and therefore the criterion of such compliance. But in the higher system, not external action but the direct inspection of the heart, would determine the question of compliance with the rule of judgment. Hence they who were judged obedient to the national system according to the rule of judgment under it as a system of grace, would, if *actually* obedient to *this* rule, be rewarded under the higher system; or if judged disobedient to the national system, according to the rule and mode of judgment under it, would, if *actually* disobedient to this rule, be punished under the higher system. Thus, a higher influence than any furnished by the theocracy, or merely national government, with its temporal sanctions, and its mode of adjudication, was employed, not as a part of the national government as such, but still as tending to secure obedience to the national government. It was the influence of the authority of Him who was their national god, but not as their national king, reigning over them as beings of earth and time, but as their moral governor, reigning over them as moral and immortal beings. The two relations of national king and moral governor were combined in one being. The authority was one and the same in both. It was divine. It was as if God should become the national king of this State, and thus impart his authority to our particular form of government and each particular law of this government. This would not confound, but present in perfect distinctness, the two great relations of national ruler and moral governor. His assumption of the former would not in the slightest degree obscure the latter, especially if we suppose him to give us a national system of government, resembling in its more prominent and substantial characteristics his moral system. We should still distinguish the one from the other as clearly as the Saviour did, when he said, "Fear not them which kill the body," &c.; or, again, "Render to Cæsar the things," &c.; or as the apostle, "Submit yourselves to every ordinance of *man*," &c. In like manner, if we suppose ourselves in the condition of the heathen nations, without the knowledge of God by revelation, and yet believing in a supreme divinity as a national god and tutelary deity, and at the same time believing in a future state in which this being would dispense future rewards and punishments, it would be natural—it would be reasonable to believe—it would be nearly incredible that we should *not* believe, in a higher system of government than the theocracy, while the latter should *represent*, and satisfactorily illustrate, the nature and great principles of the former. So in the case of a heathen theocracy, the resemblance being rationally assumed, so far as the nature of the two systems would admit, the lower system, in its essential nature and substantial principles, being constantly acted upon and familiarly known—being regarded as a revelation from the supreme divinity and having his high sanction; how can it be doubted that a theocracy, though as such a mere national system would be, and was regarded by its subjects, in all supposable and substantial respects, as implying, proving, and representing a higher system of moral government, whose judgments and retributions were to follow when the soul left the body; in a word, that a theocracy, though simply a national system administered over men as beings of earth and time, was a *representative* system also, exhibiting a moral system as administered over men as moral and immortal beings?

A theocracy then, may be said to be *the civil government of a nation or people in which the supreme divinity, whether one god or many gods, assumes the two relations of national king and national god or tutelary deity, and administers by his extraordinary providence, their entire civil polity under a system of grace; thus exhibiting, by inference and representation, his higher system of moral government over them as moral and immortal beings.*

LECTURE III.

THE MOSAIC LAW A THEOCRACY.

Plan of argument.—Certain characteristics of the system are undeniable, viz., the Mosaic system reveals God as national king and tutelary deity.—All its laws are from God.—It was administered to some extent by a human magistracy, as well as by an extraordinary providence.—It involved political propitiatory rites, &c.—It was sustained *expressly* only by temporal sanctions.—External action is the criterion but not the rule of judgment.—That it was a theocracy evident from its religious services; also from its direct or primary design.—It was a *positive*, as distinguished from a *moral* institution.—It was *a civil government, administered by God*, as distinguished *from a civil government, administered by man*.—Its late beginning and transient continuance.

HAVING attempted to show *what a theocracy is*, I now proceed to show—

II. That the Mosaic law was a theocracy, i. e., *that the government of Israel by Moses was one in which God assumed the two relations of national king and tutelary deity toward that nation, and by the civil magistrate, and also by an extraordinary providence, administered their entire civil polity, through propitiatory rites, under an economy of grace; thus exhibiting, in a natural and representative method, his higher system of moral government over them, and over all men, as moral and immortal beings.*

Before I proceed directly to offer the proof of this proposition, I remark, that there is one great and prominent *fact*, and a principle resulting from it, which are ever to be remembered in all our reasonings on this subject. The fact is, that the Israelites when delivered from Egypt, and when receiving the law from Moses, were thoroughly Egyptian in their character, education, language, modes of thought, opinions, habits, and usages. The principle resulting from this fact is, that the true God, in revealing himself to this people in the two great relations of their king and their God, would and ought to be understood, and would intend to be understood, in the true Egyptian meaning of the language employed in this revelation of himself. Especially are these things so, provided that there is no evidence to the contrary, and that every consideration supposable in the case to confirm this meaning of the language, actually exists. Assuming then, what I claim to have decisively proved, that the government of Egypt was a theocracy, and that the Israelites when brought out of Egypt could have had no idea or conception of any other government than that of a theocracy, it follows, according to *the principle* above stated, that the government which God by Moses instituted over Israel, in the only authorized and just view of it, must have been regarded by that people as a theocracy, and therefore was a theocracy.

I shall now attempt to establish the truth of my leading proposition, by considerations which not only prove its truth, but which will more fully unfold the nature of the Mosaic system, than could well be done in a somewhat general definition. These considerations will be derived—

In the first place, from some prominent and undeniable characteristics of the Mosaic law as given to Israel.

In the second place, from the character, views, opinions, &c., of the Israelites, as wholly Egyptian, when they received the law.

In the third place, from a common use of language in the early ages of the world, in which one thing is spoken of chiefly to denote another.

In the fourth place, from the New Testament.

That the Mosaic law was a theocracy is evident—

I. *From some obvious and undeniable characteristics of the law as given to Israel.*

That the government of this people was, in some general and essential respects, a theocracy, according to the view now taken of such a government, I suppose will, to a great extent, be admitted. I suppose that it will be admitted—

First, that God assumed toward this people the two great relations of national king and tutelary deity.

Secondly, that the whole Mosaic system—all its laws—emanated from God, and were clothed with his authority.

Thirdly, that this government, while administered to some extent by a human magistracy of divine institution, was also administered by an extraordinary providence.

Fourthly, that it involved through propitiatory rites and sacrifices suited to its nature, a system of grace in the forgiveness of *civil or political* transgression.

These essential characteristics of a theocracy in the government of Israel, I suppose to be too obvious to require proof.

There are yet others which may be more questionable. I remark therefore—

Fifthly, that this government over Israel was directly sustained and enforced by no other than temporal sanctions.

Here the question is not, whether a future state of rewards and punishments is revealed in the Old Testament. What is now maintained is, that the Mosaic law or Jewish theocracy, was enforced only by temporal sanctions. For proof of this, I deem it sufficient to refer only to the 27th, 28th, and 29th chapters of Deuteronomy. In the 27th, the Jewish lawgiver directs the manner in which the curses of the law shall be published to all the people and assented to by them. In the 28th, we have a full and unambiguous description of these curses, and of the opposite blessings. Both are exclusively of a temporal nature. Nor could the language have been more explicit to this purpose, according to ordinary usage, had there been no future state. In the 29th chapter, it appears that the threatened evils were not exclusively *national*, or such as could be inflicted on the whole nation, but that the individual who violated the law became liable to similar punishments. Vide verses 19, 20, and Heb. ii. 2.*

Sixthly. I allege that external or overt action, though not the rule, is the only *criterion* of judgment in the administration of the law of the theocracy. God, in assuming the relation of national king toward Israel, and giving them law, never lowered or obscured the standard of right moral action, but required them to love him with all the heart, mind, soul, and strength,—the only spirit of loyalty due to a Being of infinite perfection. As tried by this perfect rule of action, he ever assumed, and proceeded on the assumption, that all were sin-

---

* I cannot here dwell on this topic without transgressing my prescribed limits. Warburton has largely dwelt on it. Vide Div. Leg., vol. iv. B. 5, Sec. 4, 5, 6; B. 6, Sec. 1. After considering the Book of Job in Sec. 2d of his 6th Book, he examines in Sec. 3d, 299, all the passages in the Old Testament which have been supposed to teach a future state of rewards and punishments. His view is not, that this doctrine is not taught in the Old Testament, nor yet that Moses and even the people did not believe it; nor that it was not taught by the later prophets; nor yet that it was not taught by the Mosaic law, or Jewish theocracy, *as a representative system;* but that it was not taught by this system, in the primary import of the language, and as an essential or constituent part of the system. Of several passages, in my view, especially in the later prophets, his interpretation is not just.

ners or transgressors, and as such must be condemned or cursed. Deut. xxvii. 26, and Gal. iii. 10. The light of truth shone so strongly on this fact, that the people, at least the candid and enlightened, fully conceded it by their frequent and formal confessions. Their offerings and sacrifices, voluntary and commanded, proved the same thing. And especially did the great sacrifice, made once a year for the sins of all the people, show that all were transgressors of *that perfect rule of action* which was common to both the national and the moral government of God, and that God never relinquished the prerogative of searching the heart and trying the reins. And yet the omniscience of God, as the national sovereign, never interposed in the administration of the national law, or theocracy. The laws of this system, as such, like other national laws, were designed to secure that spirit of loyalty due to the national king, and thus to secure such overt action as would promote, and to prevent such as would hinder, the well-being of the State, as a temporal or earthly community. It was also designed to secure those outward forms of worship, which were appointed to produce an almost constant recognition of the only living and true God as the tutelary deity of the nation, and thus strongly to impress on them their dependence on him for their national prosperity. This was the direct design of those civil laws in which their burdensome ritual was enacted and enforced.

And here, that we may not confound, as is too often done, the two co-existing kinds of government—the national government of God over this people, as citizens of the State, and his moral government over them and all other men, as moral beings—it becomes important to show wherein these two kinds of government, in the present case, agree, and wherein they differ.

The law of requirement then, that is, the substantial rule of action, is necessarily the same in both the moral and the national system. This results from the fact, that the same perfect Being is the supreme sovereign and lawgiver in both, and therefore, in the form of a rule of action, could require in both nothing less than that spirit of loyalty which is due to his perfect character, with all its specific expressions in subordinate action demanded by circumstances. Thus God, in this law or rule of action, required every Israelite as a subject of his national government, in every act whether of worship, or other overt service or conduct, to love him with all his heart, and with all his soul, not less than as a subject of his moral government. Every Israelite, viewed in relation to either government, was under this perfect rule of action for all moral beings, and if tried and judged by this perfect rule of action, must be convicted of not having observed all the words of this law to do them, and by it must therefore be condemned. But none but the Omniscient King could justly judge the people according to this perfect rule of action; nor he, without making the law of his moral government both a rule of action and a rule of judgment. Had he done this, the national government would have terminated at once, as it were, in the eternal retribution of its subjects as moral beings. Besides, that this perfect rule of action is not the rule of judgment in either system is evident, since each system, instead of being administered on strictly *legal* principles, is combined with and modified by an economy of grace, providing mercy and forgiveness on condition of repentance. Hence, legal sanctions are not adjudged or executed under either system according to the perfect rule of action under each, but under each according to a rule of judgment instituted and modified by grace. This rule of judgment also is and must be the same under both systems. From the character of the lawgiver, this must *require* some degree of personal holiness as the condition of acceptance; nothing being more incongruous and unsupposable, than that such a lawgiver and judge should, even under a gracious economy, lower the condition of the slightest favor to entire impenitence and unbelief, i. e., to the utter want of personal holiness. This would be a formal exemption of the impenitent from punishment, and an avowed relinquishment of all claim to the lowest degree of that spirit of loyalty which is due to such a lawgiver. The rule of judgment then, so far as made known by the language of the lawgiver—so far as clear promulgation, or precise specification in terms can determine it, is the same under both systems. It requires, in formal and explicit specification, REPENTANCE, i. e., some degree of personal holiness. No subject, as related to either system, however *according to some other principles he may be treated*, has any warrant to conclude or suppose that he is *truly* accepted, or regarded with *actual favor*, by the lawgiver, any further than he is *truly penitent* in his sight. The lawgiver has said nothing, done nothing, to authorize on this point any other conclusion.

But we now come to a difficulty, or at least, what is very commonly supposed to be a difficulty—one which, if I mistake not, has occasioned very unsatisfactory exhibitions of the Jewish theocracy. This difficulty arises from overlooking the necessary principle in the administration of a national government, though it be a theocracy—that of making overt or external action the *criterion*, but not *the rule* of judgment. This distinction between the *rule* and the *criterion* of judgment, though it seems not to be at once obvious to every mind, is of vital importance. The necessity of adhering to this principle in the administration of all civil law, does in no respect change the *rule* of judgment, which requires in all cases, a true spirit of loyalty to the ruler,—in the present case, to God, the national king of Israel. Adherence to this principle is only the necessary mode of determining the question of the spirit of loyalty —compliance or non-compliance with the actual rule of judgment. Instead of determining it by the direct inspection of Omniscience, the Omniscient National King himself conforms to this universal and necessary mode of determining conformity to the rule of judgment. Nor does he in this way in any degree obscure, or render doubtful to reason or common sense, the actual rule of judgment as requiring the loyalty of the heart. The subject tried and judged, even when accepted and rewarded on account of merely external action as the only criterion of his loyalty, still knows that he has not secured the favor of his Omniscient Sovereign, but only the external expression of his favor. Such hypocrisy is the subject's own fault, not that of the sovereign or the law. The *rule* of judgment is plain, and if the necessary criterion of judgment is, through the perversion of the subject, made the occasion of hypocrisy, still this criterion is the best which the nature of the case admits of, and the evils resulting from it are far less than would result from adopting any other. For, while a spirit of loyalty furnishes the best security that the ends of civil government, in overt action and its results will be obtained, and ought therefore to be required, still the well-being of the State is secured by that overt action which is the *expression* of this spirit. I add, that the administration of this system in adjudging and executing sanctions, was to a great extent, committed to rulers and judges with whom external action could, of course, be the only criterion of judgment. Accordingly, as in other cases of civil government, a rule of evidence was prescribed, and external action only made the proof of loyalty or disloyalty to the national king.

The same thing is substantially true in respect to that part of it which God reserved to himself, and administered by an extraordinary providence. God here proceeded as rigidly on the principle of making overt action on the part of the nation and of individuals, the criterion of obedience and disobedience, and of conferring good and inflicting evil, as ever did any human magistrate. So far as subjects were externally obedient, they were, according to the only possible mode of administering a civil government, adjudged and treated as *in principle* obedient to the rule of judgment; and so far as they were externally disobedient, they were adjudged and treated as *in principle* disobedient to the rule of judgment.

Thus God was pleased to give to his chosen people a political or civil government, and to proceed *more humano* in every part of its administration. Every step of his providence, in awarding temporal sanctions, and the mode of it, show that he disposed of their civil affairs only in accordance with the principles of civil government; and though he interfered by a supernatural providence, he did so only in conformity with these principles.

Seventhly. That the Mosaic system was a theocracy, is evident from those laws of the system which respected what are commonly called "the religious services" of the people. Most writers on this subject speak of the laws of this system as "political laws, requiring *religious* duties, rites, sacrifices, offerings and worship." Now I cannot but regard this not only as a false, but as a peculiarly unfortunate use of the word *religious*, as fitted to conceal the distinction between what was strictly and simply "*political*," and what was, in the lowest authorized sense, "*religious*." The error in my view, consists in overlooking the fact, that the twofold relation of national king and tutelary deity is merely a *political* relation—the latter as truly as the former. It is true, as I have already said, that in every law of the theocracy, the *requirement* reached the heart. This is true in every instance of rightful civil or national government—the specific nature of this spirit of loyalty being determined in each case by *the character* of the national king or ruler. Still, in each case it is a merely *political* requirement, as enacted by political authority and for political purposes. Obedience and disobedience to such a requirement are merely political obedience or political disobedience; and this, whether God or man be the national ruler, and whether the spirit of loyalty be due to the one or the other. The former indeed, contemplated under certain relations, would be a morally right or religious principle or state of mind. But it has also other relations which are by no means essential to it as a *religious* principle, and which result from it solely as commanded by, or as obedience to, civil law. As such obedience, it secured by promise the favor of the tutelary deity, in long life and great temporal prosperity; while contemplated simply as *religious principle*, it had no such connection. To call any of the services, even the morally right principle, as claimed by the law of the theocracy or civil law, *religious* service or religious worship, or by any name when contemplated as obedience to civil law, which shall imply that it sustains any other or higher relations than those of mere civil obedience, is a false and unfortunate use of language. Even the word *holy*, when applied to this people, denoted nothing beyond obedience to civil law, and as such simply described it as related to the promises of the national system. From *the mere word*, no inference could be made of any higher relation of those to whom it was applied, than that of subjects of civil government, who evinced by external conduct a spirit of loyalty to their national king, and were thus entitled to the temporal blessings which he, as national God, had promised to such obedience. Thus it appears that God, as the national king and tutelary deity of Israel, in the administration of a theocracy over this people, and in its true and proper effects and consequences, no more held them responsible for religious service properly so called, or personal piety, or true spiritual religion *in its higher relations to the allotments of men in a future state*, than does any wise and good human ruler. It is true, that God, as a national ruler, in claiming of his subjects a spirit of loyalty, claimed more as his due, than any human ruler can properly claim as his due. Still, this spirit of loyalty to him as national ruler, no more sustained, as such, those relations which pertain to what is properly called religion, piety, spiritual holiness, than does the spirit of loyalty to a human magistrate sustain these relations. I am not saying that those services required by the theocracy, which are often called "religious," were not peculiar, and did not sustain a peculiar relation. They were peculiar, and yet common to every theocracy. Their relation was peculiar on account of the peculiar arbitrary relation of God, as the tutelary deity of the nation, dispensing by a supernatural providence, national blessings and national calamities. They were services rendered to him in view of his relation to them, and their consequent relation to him, in respect to these temporal blessings and evils, and not to him as their moral or spiritual ruler, nor as arising from their relation to him as moral or spiritual beings.

It will greatly confirm the views now given of the Mosaic law, to show in this place, how decisively they refute a common objection to it. It has often been said, that as a civil or national law, it punished its subjects for matters of opinion, and the instance especially appealed to, is that of the sincere idolater. This dishonorable imputation has been commonly countenanced by the advocates of its divine authority. It is now denied as entirely groundless. God as we have seen, could not, consistently with his own character, claim in the form of requirement any thing less of men than that truly spiritual state of the heart which is his due, and which of course implies a just conception of his character. But then we have seen, that this same state of mind as required by God as the moral governor of men, and as required by God as national king of citizens in their relation to the State, must sustain very different relations. Viewed as required by the moral governor, it is piety, spiritual religion, with its eternal relations. Viewed as required by the national king, it is simply political loyalty in temporal relations. The same things, *mutatis mutandis*, are true of the opposite act or state of mind. In its relation to God as national king, *idolatry* is not to be viewed as spiritual impiety, but only as *a civil offense* with its essential relations. As such, it was simply *treason—crimen læsæ majestatis.* This relation was not destroyed or changed by any other relation to God's moral government, no more than the same political crime is with us. As a civil offense, it was therefore justly punishable by civil law. This is decisively confirmed by the fact, that God, as a civil though an omniscient lawgiver, never judged and determined any subject of this law, by the omniscient inspection of his heart, to be an idolater. The law was never applied to the internal belief, which was manifested by no overt act, and which of course, could not be tried before a civil tribunal. The secret idolater, believing and trusting in false gods, was indeed guilty of spiritual impiety; but no law of the theocracy could punish him for this. And further, in this same state of mind, he was in principle guilty of rebellion against the national king. But for this, so long as it was not manifested in overt action, no process of civil law could reach him. On the contrary, the civil law gave him full protection, until, by overt action, he showed his practical denial of the authority of the national king. It was then, *in such a case*, and *for such a reason*, and not for a matter of mere opinion, that he was to be punished as a political offender. A *conscientious* idolater—if we suppose such an one—could no more be punished for a mere matter of opinion under the Mosaic law, than could be a conscientious murderer or blasphemer, &c., and neither could be punished for a matter of opinion, but only for action, which simply as a civil offense, showed him to be an enemy of the State.

Eighthly. I infer the same thing from the *direct* design of the Mosaic institution. By this institution God designed, primarily and directly, to reveal himself as the only living and true God, in the single relation of the national king and tutelary deity of Israel; though, as we may see hereafter, indirectly by this means, in the higher relation of moral governor. That such was the primary design of the theocracy is as obvious,as that the Mosaic system was a political or national system in every essential respect, or even in any respect at all. God's spiritual or moral government over men as spiritual, moral, and immortal beings, and a civil government even in his hands, are in their very nature, ends and modes of administration so essentially diverse, that they can not be identified, or made to coalesce in one system of government. How for example, could a civil government as such, require personal religion, spiritual religion, piety, holiness, of its subjects in its true and essential nature and relations; or how be administered according to the direct inspection of the heart by omniscience; and how could the moral government of God require spiritual religion, except in its spiritual relations, or be administered in any other way than by the direct inspection of the heart? If these two kinds of government, though in the hands of the same Being, are, as we have seen they are, entirely distinct, then God, when revealing himself as the only living and true God, in the single relation of national ruler, does not, as *identical* with this relation, nor as any essential part of it, reveal his higher relation of the moral governor of men as moral and immortal beings. I am not saying that the latter relation may not be in some way *inferred* from or represented by the former. But I maintain that each is distinct from the other; that each is complete in itself; that each might exist by itself without the other; and that therefore two things, so different and distinct, cannot be so combined as to lose their distinct and separate nature and identity. God then, in revealing himself to Israel as the only living and true God in the comprehensive relation of national king and tutelary deity, did not in so doing *directly* reveal himself in the higher relation of the moral governor of men, but only as the one true God in the former relation. The Mosaic institution therefore, was simply a national or civil institution. All its relations were civil, temporal relations. Even the requirements, which were the same as those of God's moral government, and when viewed as elements or parts of it, were spiritual and holy, in the highest sense, yet as elements or parts of the Mosaic system, sustained only civil and temporal relations. The Mosaic institution therefore, was primarily and *directly* designed to reveal God to Israel in the single relation of national God and tutelary deity; and was of course in its only true and essential nature, a national or civil institution of that peculiar kind called a theocracy.

It may serve to illustrate and confirm the foregoing view of the subject to remark, that, when in common language, we speak of *what a thing is*, we speak, at least for the most part, not of its *absolute*, but of its *relative* nature. Thus we say of a stone, it is *heavy;* meaning its *relative* nature, or its absolute nature *as related* to the earth, and within the sphere of its attraction. But the same stone with its *absolute* nature unchanged, were it to be removed at a certain distance from the earth, and placed within the sun's attraction, would cease to be *heavy*, in this new condition of existence. All such terms as right, good, bad, holy, righteous, &c., and such also as hard, soft, heavy, &c., are *relative* terms. Thus, when we speak of action as *holy* in its highest or spiritual sense, we mean its *relative* nature; i. e., its nature *as related* to the highest interests of moral beings. Viewed however, in its nature *in relation* to the State, or to the well-being of the body politic, especially in its *relative nature* in the Hebrew commonwealth under its theocracy, it has another *relative nature* than its *relative nature* in the highest sense. This *relative nature* of such action, so peculiar, and arising exclusively from the relation of this people to God as their national king and tutelary deity, in Hebrew usage was called *holy*. Thus the same action is properly conceived and spoken of as *holy*, in the highest sense, without including in it the conception of its political relation under the Hebrew theocracy; and also as *holy* denoting its political relations, without including the conception of its holy nature in the highest sense. This shows how entirely distinct, in the true conception of things, was the civil government which God administered over Israel as a State, from the moral government which he administered over them as moral and immortal beings; and how it is that the former could wholly cease, and the latter remain immutable and eternal.

Ninthly. I infer the same thing, from the nature of the Mosaic system, as a *circumstantial* or *positive*, in distinction from a *moral* institution. In the use of these terms however, I must briefly explain my meaning. By a *moral* institution or government of God over men, I mean that which necessarily results from the essential nature and essential condition or circumstances of men as moral beings. This essential nature and these essential circumstances are absolutely unchangeable so long as men are moral beings; nor can the moral government of God over such beings cease for a moment, let circumstances change as they may. By a circumstantial or *positive* institution of God over men, I mean one which arises from and depends on other things or circumstances than those which are essential to their high relation as moral beings; that is, on circumstances which are changeable and often change. It is appointed by a perfect God in one set of variable circumstances, and not in another, because the circumstances in which it is ordained furnish the reason for its appointment or ordination. It is indeed, authoritative and binding in all circumstances in which it is ordained, for it is ordained only in those variable circumstances, which are the reasons for investing it with the authority and obligation of a divine command; all which is proved to its subjects by the character and promulgated will of its author. It is therefore changeable and changes, as certain variable circumstances of moral beings change, while moral government over moral beings is unchangeable, so long as they are moral beings. A theocracy therefore is not immutable as is *moral* government, but is in an important respect circumstantial, arbitrary, or positive. It is *circumstantial*, as its establishment depends on the variable circumstances of moral beings; and it is arbitrary or positive, as its universal obligation and authority are wholly determined by a formal positive enactment of unexplained sovereignty. Its whole nature as a *civil* law or institution, is an *arbitrary nature*—a nature which so entirely depends on the will of God, that he can create or annul it and its obligation, by imparting to it, or withholding from it, civil relations at his pleasure, without changing its nature, relations, or obligation, as a *moral* law or institution. It is thus, I may say, that the apostle has described the whole Mosaic institution in Eph. ii. 15, and in Col. ii. 14. This will appear hereafter, from his use of the word δόγμα, of which the plural form used by him cannot, I think, be better rendered than by *positive institutions* as now explained.

Such, beyond all denial, was the Mosaic law—the theocracy of Israel. It resulted wholly from the peculiar circumstances of this people. It was a law or system to them which in some sense it was not to any other. Without specifying these circumstances in detail, it is sufficient to say, that God had made peculiar promises to their fathers concerning these their descendants—the promise of great temporal prosperity—the promise that the knowledge of himself should not be utterly lost in the world by the encroachments of idolatry; that through them it should be imparted to other nations, and that from them the seed of Abraham, should the Redeemer come, to the end that these promises so peculiar might be fulfilled, and this peculiar and high destination of this people accomplished; a theocracy—a civil government, clothed with God's authority—became, from the condition of circumstances of this people in Egypt, so far as man can see, the fittest means, that by connecting the knowledge of the true God thus intimately, even essentially with their civil government and their existence as a nation, the former could not be annihilated without the annihilation of the latter. Such a government, in its general nature and form, was in accordance with the civil government of other nations, and peculiarly adapted to the peculiar circumstances and usages of those over whom it was established. How plainly then, was it what I have called it, a circumstantial, or better, a *positive* institution? How plainly incredible that God, in becoming a civil ruler—a political king of one nation, or of all nations—should so lower the two great spiritual requirements of his moral government—the one the perfect rule of action, and the other the actual rule of judgment to men (as moral and immortal beings), that these rules or laws should sustain simply the relation of civil laws, awarding only temporal rewards and punishments through external action as the sole criterion of adjudication, except this government was merely a *circumstantial* institution.

Tenthly. The same view of the Mosaic law will be corroborated, if we consider the difference between a civil government administered by God, and civil government administered by man. Of all civil government, the true object or end is to secure by the influence of its authority, the highest well-being of the State as a community of earth and time. This authority of the civil governor, or the civil authority which is to be employed for the temporal well-being of the State, though always absolute while acknowledged by its subject, is to be estimated and measured in its degree by the degree of the governor's qualification to rule, i. e., by his competence and disposition to govern in the best manner. At the same time, the spirit of loyalty on the part of subjects, founded in a due regard for the well-being of the State, as a temporal community, is to be graduated by the known qualifications of the governor for his office, supposing him always to possess the degree of qualification which justly entitles him to reign. Thus his authority and their loyalty would properly vary in degree, as the governor might be a superior man or a higher being, as an angel. Still, his authority would be merely civil authority, i. e., merely a right to govern according to the principles of such a jurisdiction; or, in general, to enact and enforce law for the temporal well-being of the State. He has and can have no right to enact laws designed to control or to secure the spiritual well-being as such of his subjects, or to regulate or determine the religious faith or opinions as such of his subjects, either Pagan or Mohammedan, Infidel, Jewish or

Christian, Protestant or Catholic. Such prerogative pertains to no civil ruler, whether man or angel; nor so far as we can say, to God himself under this relation. If God, as the national king of Israel, may be said in claiming the spirit of loyalty due to himself, so far virtually to claim a right religious belief, still he never assumed the prerogative of enforcing either claim by *temporal rewards and penalties*. It was not disobedience to either claim as such, or as seen and known by his omniscient eye; but it was such disobedience, *only as evinced by overt action*, for which he inflicted or ever threatened to inflict, the pains and penalties of the national law. If then, we suppose God himself to assume the relation of a civil governor of a State, taking the whole civil authority which had before existed in the hands of men into his own, he would indeed possess a higher *degree* of civil authority than his predecessor; and the spirit of loyalty due on the part of subjects to their king or civil governor, ought to be that which is fitted to his infinitely perfect character, and perfect qualification to govern the State in the best manner. Still, the civil authority which he has assumed, and had a right to assume, though taken from the hands of another, is in its essential nature and relations *civil authority*, and it is nothing more. He was the perfect moral governor of men before assuming the relation and prerogatives of a civil ruler over the State.

Civil government then, as *a kind* of government, is one and the same thing (though differing circumstantially in *the degree* of its authority in different cases), whether in the hands of man, or of an angel, or of an archangel, or of God. It is, at the same time, so diverse as a *kind* of government from that higher kind of government which God administers over men, as moral beings, in their high relation to eternity, that, while they are easily confounded, they should be accurately distinguished according to their essential difference. Thus distinguished, what can be more rationally believed, than that God, the rightful moral sovereign of all men as moral beings, should, in view of the condition of this lost world—in view of his relation to Abraham, and of the condition of his descendants in Egypt, and especially for the great purpose of accomplishing his highest design and richest promise of mercy to our sinful race—assume the relation of a national king and tutelary deity over the people of Israel—hold and perpetuate, for long centuries, the administration of this national or civil system of government over that people in his own hands—keep the entire administrations of the two systems wholly distinct—render the inferior system ever prominent and subservient as a temporary *representation* of the higher, until its object and end should be fully accomplished in the advent of the Great Redeemer of all—then entirely abolish the inferior system, so leaving all civil authority and power to revert to human hands, —and all this as an overwhelming and everlasting confirmation of the higher system, so worthy of himself, as one to be consummated in the issues of eternity?

To a clear apprehension of the subject before us, there is yet in some minds perhaps, a difficulty which it is desirable to remove. Thus it may be inquired—since the authority of God as the moral governor of men as moral beings, remains unimpaired over them, and especially since the apostles Paul and Peter (Rom. xiii. 1, &c., and 1 Pet. ii. 13) so expressly and earnestly enjoin submission to existing civil government as the ordinance of God and for conscience' sake—how is it, that every civil government is not clothed with divine authority; or, that the authority of God as a moral governor does not, in its own proper influence, directly reach the duties and conduct of men, as citizens or members of the State, and bind them to obey the enactments of civil government? I answer, that a true rendering of the passages referred to, instead of one dictated by the assumed doctrine of the divine right of kings, will correct some common mistakes of commentators, and show what is the meaning of these apostles. I remark then, that nothing is plainer in these passages, than their distinct recognition of *the difference* between God's authority as a moral governor over men as moral beings, and the authority of civil government over men as its subjects; for both apostles simply employ one kind of authority, viz., God's authority as a moral governor to enforce submission to another kind of authority, viz., man's authority as a civil ruler. When or where had these governments of the nations derived their authority from God, as had the national government of Israel? Or how, in any way, came they to possess this divine authority? We know the method and the means by which the civil government of Israel was clothed with God's authority. He assumed every prerogative of an absolute national king over this people. He became their legislator, enacting with his own authority their every law. Nor was there the shadow of any other civil authority than his own, or that which was directly and expressly derived from it, in the entire administration of their national system. When has he done this for any other nation? Now the apostle Paul speaks of "the powers (*ἐξουσιάι*, authorities) that be; which of course, are not mere *abstractions*. He speaks not of civil government in the abstract, but of civil authorities or governments *actually existing*, which they to whom he wrote knew, and which we know, were as exclusively of human origin as is the authority of a city or of a school. This is placed beyond all denial by the passage in 1 Pet. ii. 13, where the apostle says, "Submit yourselves to *πάσῃ ἀνθρωπίνῃ κτίσει*, *every human creation*, for the Lord's sake, whether it be to the king as supreme, or unto governors as unto them as sent by him," &c. What can be more plainly taught, than that the authority of civil government is simply *human* authority, and has solely a human origin? Thus while both these apostles represent every civil government in its essential, inherent authority, as a merely human institution, and do not weaken this authority, or the obligation of the subjects arising from it, they lay upon them in addition to this, another and higher authority, *even God's authority over them as moral beings*, to submit to this civil human authority, whenever or wherever it exists.

To confirm this view of the subject and to remove any doubts arising from the common translation, and the more common interpretation of the passages referred to, I shall, as briefly as may be, further present my own views of the meaning of these apostles, in the context. Paul then, plainly asserts, that there is no instance of the existing power or authority, of which he speaks, which is not generally speaking from God; and then, to show his more particular meaning, adds: These *existing* powers (*οὖσαι ἐξουσίαι*), authorities of human origin, are *ordered* (*τεταγμέναι*) not by revelation, but *ordered*, appointed, in his *providential purposes*—arranged in his providence, and designed to be in each case the existing thing which it is, neither more nor less—a human institution with its own peculiar human authority, obviously fitted while existing as such, and shown to human reason, by the nature and condition of human society, to be fitted to promote the well-being of the State, and indirectly the highest good of the universe, and thus to swell the sum total of good. They are like many other human institutions, originated, devised, and adopted by men, as obviously dictated by human reason, as parts of *the providential arrangement* (διαταγῇ, v. 2.) of God, for the well-being of men on earth: for example, as parental government in the family, that of tutors and governors in colleges, schools, &c. The parent and the schoolmaster are each bound, or under obligation to God to assume authority, to devise and administer government in their respective relations in view of its necessary utility to the family and the school. But they are under this obligation to God not as a national king or ruler, but as the moral governor of men as moral beings. The Jews entertained the false and almost invincible prejudice, that human authority was no authority, and that no national government had the least authority whatever, except God's express and direct authority as given to it, and assumed on his part by formal revelation enacting its laws, &c. Accordingly, the apostles are at great pains to show the contrary. They not only distinctly and expressly recognize the authority of every existing civil government, as originated by man (ἀνθρωπίνῃ κτίσει), but inculcate submission to this simply human authority by a still higher authority. Thus Paul: Whosoever resisteth (ἀντιτασσόμενος, *arrays himself against*) this human authority of an existing civil government a providential arrangement of God, or an establishment of God brought into existence by his providence—resisteth in so doing, what? Not an ordinance of God clothed with his authority as a national ruler, by express revelation as in the case of the Jews; nor yet even as that which *in this manner* he had required men themselves to establish, or, in respect to the form of it, given the least direction or instruction; but a merely human institution brought, under God's providential ordering of human agencies and instrumentalities, into existence by men for the temporal well-being of States or nations. By resisting any such human institution, man could not resist what is properly called *a divine ordinance*, involving the universal divine right of kings, the most foreign and even contemptible idea to a Jewish mind as applied to the kings of the Gentiles, but a merely human institution (ἀνθρωπίνῃ κτίσεί), purposed, and brought to pass, in the providence of God, for the temporal well-being of the State. He therefore, who should resist, overthrow or destroy in any case, such a means of good, or any other means of good so important, so useful and even necessary to men as social beings here on earth, acts wickedly as a *moral* being: instead of doing good from right moral principle, he does evil from wrong moral principle. To show this, if possible still more plainly, the apostle says (v. 5): "There is a necessity that you should be subject, not only to avoid the penalty of the civil institution, by which only its authority can be supported when resisted, but also for another and far higher reason—*on account of conscience*, which will condemn you for acting morally wrong, as moral beings, in contravening the will of God as the moral governor of men, though this will is shown, not by revelation but by the utility of civil government." He then proceeds to inculcate, FOR THE SAME REASON; their duties as citizens of the State to pay tribute, and then their duties in social life, from the great moral principle of love to their neighbor. The apostle Peter also inculcates submission to civil authority, as exclusively from men (*ἀνθρωπίνῃ κτίσει*) from respect to the will of Christ, whether it be to the king, &c. (v. 13)—"as the servants of God" (v. 16)—enjoining upon them, in two distinct precepts, *to fear God, and to honor the king* (v. 17). He then recognizes the same *moral* obligation to another merely human institution, saying, "Servants, be subject to your masters (*δεσπόταις*), with all fear, &c., and this for conscience toward God" (verses 18, 19). But not to dwell longer on this part of the subject, I only ask, When, since God abolished the Jewish theocracy, has he assumed the relation of national king or tutelary deity over any other nation, or promised national temporal blessings, or threatened national temporal calamities to nations, as they should obey or disobey his laws as the moral governor of men as moral beings?

These considerations are deemed quite sufficient to show how entirely distinct the moral government of God over men is from a national or civil government, whether the latter be a theocracy like the Mosaic law, or a merely human institution; and that while the former or Mosaic law, was merely a civil government in the form of theocracy. What under the national government were primarily and properly civil enactments, as the ten commandments were, would indeed lose this character after the abrogation of the Mosaic or national law;

but so far as they were *moral* precepts, or could with the shadow of propriety or truth be called such, they were binding on all men before the Mosaic law was given, and equally so as moral precepts while that law existed, and after its abrogation. *Lex stat, dum ratio manet.* Should any of these be enacted by the civil law of a State as involving overt action useful to the State, they would as such be merely civil laws, to be enforced only by civil authority with only temporal sanctions, and not by such authority as being in their nature moral precepts. Under this aspect or character, they are not civil laws but divine, and can be enforced by no authority, even that of a whole senate of kings, but only by the authority of God as the moral governor of men.

Finally. That the Mosaic law was simply a national institution appears from its late beginning and transient continuance. What the apostle has said on this subject, in Gal. iii., we shall presently see. I advert to it in the present connection to show, that had the Jews reasoned from the known facts in the case, as they ought to have reasoned, they would have adopted the same argument, and come to the same conclusion with the apostle. From the creation of man in paradise, God assumed toward him the high and immutable relation of a perfect moral governor—a relation to which every other was forever to be subservient. The first form of this government was that of a strictly legal system, consisting of a perfect rule of action to men as moral beings, which was also a perfect rule of judgment, and designed as such to secure their absolute moral perfection. From the hour of man's apostasy however, this particular form of this system was greatly modified. Without impairing in the slighest degree its adaptation to secure the absolute perfection of men *as moral beings*, a method of grace was combined with it, by which its rule of judgment was changed. It was as thus modified, not only divinely fitted as before to restore to obedience to its perfect rule of action a race of *sinful* moral beings, but also by its rule of judgment, to restore them as fully to the favor and friendship of their offended sovereign as had they never sinned. Such became now the form of God's perfect moral government over men, permanent and eternal, with a perfection excluding, in every essential respect, all further modification or change. His system of moral government for a sinful world, in its substantial fullness and glory, though not in its minuteness of detail, was revealed to the first parents of our race immediately on their apostasy, and with its heavenly light shone on the world from the beginning of the patriarchal dispensation. Its reclaiming power and saving influence were effectually disclosed in Abel, in Enoch, in Noah (Heb. xi. 4, 5, 7), and doubtless in multitudes besides. There were it is true, sad and awful counteractions of its benign tendency which only proved its reality, while God by his vindictive judgments in this world for two thousand years, more impressively upheld and enforced his authority as the moral governor of men, than he ever has since in this world's history. Thus, for this long period, God presented himself to men, in one, it may almost be said in *only* one—every other being subservient to this—high and august relation, that of their perfect moral governor, "merciful and gracious," which his absolute right to reign over them fully sustained. Nor can it be said with the least plausibility of truth, that he did not impart by revelation all that religious and moral truth to men, and in every essential form of doctrine and of precept, which was sufficient to reclaim every individual to whom the revelation came. From the calling of Abraham and during the Abrahamic dispensation, God greatly in some respects, augmented both to this patriarch and to his descendants, the light of that truth which he had before revealed in the promise of Eden. This advance in revelation however, consisted in greater particularity of detail, and greater clearness and fullness of exhibition, rather than in any essential addition to its comprehensive import. Indeed it would be difficult to find, either in the decalogue or in any subsequent part of the Old Testament, one moral precept viewed in its moral aspect, and as universally binding on men, which cannot also be found clearly revealed, or at least well understood, under the Abrahamic dispensation. So greatly was the light of religious and moral truth increased by this covenant—this *διαθήκη*—so rich, abundant, and superabundant were its promises to the righteous, not merely in temporal, but in eternal blessings (Gen. xvii),—so clearly and fully did this covenant unfold the only way of acceptance with God—the nature of religion and of moral duties—all truth which was necessary, if unperverted, to form the character of the perfect man (Gen. xvii. 1), that the apostle (Gal. iii. 8) calls it the Gospel preached before unto Abraham. With this revelation of God's moral government to Abraham and his descendants, and through them designed for all nations, comprising every thing of moment to men as moral and immortal beings, and being as constituting the Gospel itself, incapable of higher perfection—being the Gospel itself—we come, in the history of this people, within less than five centuries, to another peculiar, widely, even essentially different dispensation from any which had preceded it. Twenty-five centuries since the creation of the world had passed away, and neither the Mosaic law, nor any thing essentially like it from God, had been heard of by men. This dispensation could add nothing to, and take nothing from that which already existed, and was already perfect and unchangeable. It has been distinguished as the Mosaic dispensation. It was that in which God, after delivering the descendants of Abraham from a long and cruel bondage of four hundred years in Egypt, placed and continued them under a system of government, which he established and administered over them by Moses. But was it that perfect moral government and only moral government, which God had administered over men as moral and immortal beings since the first apostasy—the only one which he will administer in common to all men to the end of time, and according to which he will judge the world in righteousness and fix the allotments of all in eternity? Was the Mosaic law in its true and essential character, the covenant made with Abraham—was it the Gospel? Plainly whatever else it was, it had not one essential characteristic of God's moral government over men; not one, in respect to its authority, its requirements, its administration, its sanctions, or its retributions. For these as we have seen, were each and all political or civil in their nature and relations. In all these respects, it was a separate distinct institution, and as such might have subsisted in its peculiar individuality, though God's moral government had never been revealed, or even had had no existence. What then, I ask again, was the Mosaic law given to Israel at so late a period of this world's history? Did it add any thing to, or take any thing from that moral government of God, which was already absolutely perfect and unchangeable? What addition to or subtraction from such a government of God—a government which, from its very nature and the nature of its promises, could be justly viewed in its high and essential characteristic only as *moral*, and therefore in duration, eternal—what addition to, or subtraction from such a government of God, either in its authority, its theology, or its ethics, could any unperverted rational mind conceive to be made, by an institution which had not a single characteristic except that of a national or civil government? Could it be supposed that the latter should annul the former?

And now I further ask, what could these descendants of Abraham, with unperverted minds, with their Egyptian education and notions of government, and especially with their knowledge of the recent origin of this Mosaic law as a new system of government, now just instituted for them by the God of their fathers, judge this law to be? If they knew any thing of the covenant with Abraham, the *moral* government of God, they knew in one respect, what the Mosaic law was not. They knew well what a theocracy was. They well understood, that in and of itself it was simply a peculiar—compared with what we call such—national institution, deriving its whole authority, in every instant of its existence, directly and solely from a National Divinity, who assumed and acted in the relation of the national king and tutelary deity of the nation over whom he thus reigned; and who administered such a government over his subjects as *a representative* system—thus representing another and higher system of moral government over them as moral and immortal beings. What else then, could these descendants of Abraham rationally and honestly believe the Mosaic law—a law before unheard of since the creation of the world as coming from the one only living and true God, now given by Abraham's God exclusively to them as his descendants—what else could they conclude this new law from the God of the fathers to be, but a theocracy with its unquestioned and unquestionable characteristic of *a representative* system?

If now we appeal to facts, we cannot doubt after what the apostle has told us (Heb. xi. 29), that among those who came out of Egypt, and among those of subsequent generations, there were some, more or less, at different periods of their history, who were the sincere worshipers and true servants of God; who like Abraham and other patriarchs died in faith, and who not having received the promises, i. e., the things promised, embraced them. This in its true import, can involve nothing less than embracing the comprehensive promise of justification by faith, unto eternal life. This was universally the method of justification relied on by pious Israelites, from the giving of the law at Sinai to the coming of the Messiah. Now whence had these men the knowledge of this method of justification before God, as the moral governor of moral and immortal beings? Not directly from the Mosaic law; for this, though a revelation from God to this people, revealed nothing *directly* or *expressly* of this method of justification for men as moral beings. Were this people then, living under this grand and only system of revelation given to any portion of the human race, left by it for fifteen centuries as destitute of all instruction concerning the true method of justification to eternal life, as had this revelation not been given? Was God's revelation during this long period, stationary, or retrograde? Was the light of salvation by the Abrahamic covenant, left to go out in darkness? or was it, as commonly supposed, progressive? But how progressive, or rather how did the Mosaic law shed one solitary ray of the light of truth on the most momentous of all subjects to sinful men, their justification to eternal life; how, unless as *a lower system* of national government it did *represent*, and *was proved* to right reason to represent God's *higher system* of moral government through grace—the covenant made with Abraham—the substantial Gospel itself; and then how, by any conceivable *mode of representation*, could this higher system of truth have been so clearly, so fully, so impressively unfolded to the minds of men, as by that supernatural system of national law and national providence which God administered over Israel? If we imagine ourselves to have lived thus, as it were with God in sight every day and hour—with such sensible manifestations of his presence and majesty as a jealous God, yet showing mercy to thousands, it would seem that the impression of his method of salvation might have been stronger than that from the transcendent intellectual and moral grandeur of the glorious Gospel, as now given by the Great Teacher and his apostles. That such was the tendency of the former mode of revelation compared with the latter, and considered in relation to the degradation, and prejudices, and perverseness of the minds of those to whom it was given, there can I think be no doubt. Indeed, if we would form some just estimate of the fitness of the Mosaic economy to its high and ulterior design, we must consider the almost noon-tide light and splendors of the Gospel, which broke through the clouds of that economy when approaching its end and consummation. How sweet, and rapturous, and heaven-anticipating were some of the songs of David! How grand, how sublimely entrancing, some of the themes and visions of Isaiah, as of one standing before the throne of God! How did some of the later fervid prophets of Israel already begin to summon a sinful nation to repentance and faith, as with the last trump, announcing eternal retribution as at hand! And how in so doing was the Mosaic economy, so to speak, used and appealed to, as a system of illustration and representation! And what was all this, but the progress of God's revelation, begun in the promised redemption in paradise, enlarged by the divine comprehensiveness and rich and wonderful details of the Abrahamic covenant, and still brightening onward, in the most impressive illustrations conceivable of the Mosaic economy, till the meridian sun of Christianity is ready to break in full effulgence on a benighted world!

LECTURE IV.

THE MOSAIC LAW A THEOCRACY.

The Mosaic law shown to be a theocracy by its adaptation to a people trained in Egypt, particularly as designed to exhibit, by *representation*, God's moral government.—The Israelites accustomed in Egypt to such a system.—They would naturally infer the new government to be similar.—Given from God, it could not but *suggest* some higher truths.—Reflection would confirm the suggestion.—The Hebrew ritual similar to the Egyptian in many particulars.—A representative system adapted to the great ends which God must have proposed.

Having attempted to show that the Mosaic law was a theocracy, from some of the prominent characteristics of the law itself, I now proceed, as I proposed, to show the same thing—

II. From the fact that the character, views, modes of thought, of the Israelites were wholly Egyptian, when they received the law.

It seems to be quite undeniable, that the earlier revelations of God were comparatively obscure, and that the light of divine truth, which was by this means to be shed on the world, was, in the wisdom of God, to be progressive. Many of the most important truths were delivered in such a manner as to convey only very general conceptions of their nature, and scarcely to disclose at all the great principles on which they were founded. Witness the law given to our first parents as compared with its subsequent fuller form, the first promise of redemption, the covenant with Abraham, and as illustrating the same thing, the disclosures of our Lord respecting the event of his death and the nature of his kingdom. If such concealment was maintained in these cases; if principles, relations, designs, of highest moment as we might account them, were left to mere inference, why should more be expected on the subject under consideration? In accordance with this fact, the whole system of God's administration by Moses, as presented in the Old Testament, is, we claim to have shown, presented in language and which, in its primary literal meaning, can be applied to nothing but a national or political system of government—the Jewish theocracy.

It becomes then an inquiry of deep interest to the interpreter of the Scriptures, of what importance to us is a very considerable part at least of those ancient Hebrew writings called the Old Testament, especially as teaching religious truth? Or thus; we may inquire, what truths if any, are taught by this national institution respecting that higher and more perfect system of moral government which God administers over the world of moral beings; and *how*, or in what way or mode, are these truths respecting the latter to be learned from the former? What has been already said is sufficient to show that these truths are not to be ascertained from a large part of the language of the Old Testament, interpreted in its primary and literal import. The few passages in the later prophets, which as revelation progressed are exceptions to our general remark, need not be noticed as qualifying the proposition that the Old Testament interpreted as above stated, to a great extent simply unfolds the facts and principles of *the national* institution as such. The question then, still recurs, how can we learn, or rather how could the nation of Israel for long centuries learn any thing concerning God's higher system of moral government from the civil government which he administered over that people? I answer in two ways, which in some respects differ, but which it is not perhaps easy, and certainly not necessary in all cases to distinguish; viz., by *inference*, and by *representation.*

I shall now proceed to a course of remark which will serve to explain and confirm the proposition—*that the Jewish theocracy was designed to exhibit by inference and representation, God's higher system of moral government over men as moral beings, under an economy of grace.*

God then originally revealed himself to the first parents of our race, in the high and immutable relation which necessarily results from his own character, and from the nature and condition of his moral creatures—that of their perfect moral governor. The moral government thus instituted was one, *as we speak*, of mere law, of which the rule of action was also a rule of judgment. Its great design was defeated by the apostasy; and immediately after this event, God combined with this institution an economy of grace: in other words, he revealed himself as henceforth administering his moral government over men under an economy of grace. This institution in its present form was afterward more fully revealed to Abraham, being in the language of the apostle, "the Gospel before preached unto Abraham" (Gal. iii. 8). Here then, we have that form of moral government which God has administered since the apostasy, and still administers over this sinful world. This is perpetual, universal, unchangeable. This institution—*διαθήκην*—the Mosaic law, which was four hundred and thirty years after, could not disannul (Gal. iii. 15–17). It remained unchanged and in full force over Israel and over all men, as the one and only form of God's moral government over them as moral beings. The Mosaic law or theocracy was added, not to set it aside, to alter, to ratify or perfect it, in any respect whatever; but "because of transgressions"—because of its actual failure through the idolatry and wickedness of men, to accomplish the end for which it was designed. To this universal, unchangeable system of moral government over men, "the law," the Jewish theocracy, was wholly subservient, being designed and fitted as a means of preventing its perversion and securing its end. This Mosaic law was, as the apostle describes it, "our schoolmaster to bring us to Christ, that we might be justified by faith."

What then, was this Mosaic law—the Jewish theocracy? It was as we have said, a national or civil government, in which God in addition to that higher relation of a perfect moral governor, which he sustained toward Israel and toward all men as moral beings, assumed the new and comprehensive relation peculiar to that people, of their national king and national God or tutelary deity.

The Israelites, by their residence in Egypt through successive generations, had become thoroughly Egyptian in their views, opinions, and modes of reasoning, respecting civil government and religion. Though they had not wholly lost all knowledge of the God of their fathers, they had evidently lost it for all practical purposes. They had no confidence in the success of the mission of Moses to deliver them (Ex. xiv. 12), nor were all the miracles which they witnessed in Egypt, at the Red Sea and Mount Sinai, sufficient to cure them of their idolatry, or to break up their purpose to return to Egypt. That such was their character, such their extreme degradation and perverseness as idolaters, when they left Egypt, with all those practical views in respect to government and religion which were universal under the idolatrous theocracy of that country and other nations, so clearly appears from their history by Moses, that to prove it would be superfluous to any one who reads and believes that history.

With these facts before us, the principle of our argument as hereafter to be presented, may be thus stated: that as the Israelites when in Egypt, had in their views, opinions, and modes of reasoning in respect to government and religion, become thoroughly Egyptian, and that as the Egyptian theocracy or national government implied in their view, another and higher system of government administered by their national Divinity, so the theocracy or national government, instituted by God over this people would naturally, and should according to the prevailing modes of thinking, be in like manner understood to imply another and higher system of government.

It would be so understood by *a natural conclusion*. By this I mean, by one of those conclusions which is given not by formal reflection—not by a well-considered reasoning process—but by that ready and almost unavoidable *suggestion*, which arises from familiarity with the subject in similar cases.

That we may the better estimate the force of this argument, let us advert briefly to the more prominent and familiar facts of the case. God then had formed the design of introducing and preserving the knowledge of himself as the only true God in an idolatrous world. This design was to be accomplished by separating the descendants of Abraham who were now in Egypt, from all other nations, and by establishing over these descendants the same kind of government as that to which they had been accustomed—a theocracy. They were now groaning under the yoke of oppression, and wholly given to idolatry with the people among whom they dwelt. One of their own brethren was sent to them with a message from God, who was to become under God, their divinely authorized leader and lawgiver. This was no mere pretense of Moses, as was that of other political rulers. He proved his mission to be divine, by such miraculous works and such superior wisdom as no other lawgiver could pretend to. This message, accompanied with signs and wonders and proved to be from the God of their fathers, whose virtues he had promised to reward with distinguished blessings on their posterity, announced their speedy deliverance from Egyptian bondage, and the sure possession of the land of Canaan as the scene of the promised inheritance. The people hearken to the voice of their leader, and are delivered. On the third month after their departure from Egypt, they come to Mount Sinai. Here God first informs them of his great design toward them—and it is worth while to inquire how his language would be understood by this idolatrous people—saying, "If ye will obey my voice indeed, and keep my covenant, ye shall be a peculiar treasure to me above all people, for all the earth is mine; and ye shall be unto me a kingdom of priests and a holy nation" (Ex. xix. 5, 6). The people at once consent, saying, "All that the Lord hath said, will we do." And now God amid thunderings and lightnings, and under the name of the Lord their God, that brought them out of the land of Egypt, delivers the covenant or code of laws by which they were to be governed. This as we have seen, was on the face of it a system of laws given to this people by Jehovah, as their national king and national God.

It is to be remembered also, that the notion of tutelary deities, which we find then in Egypt, was universal throughout the Gentile world. This notion was, that the earth was divided by its Creator among a number of subordinate divinities, each of which was employed in the protection and care of his own people, and was the *local* deity of the country—its exclusive and rightful possessor. Thus, after God selected Judea for his peculiar residence and dominion, it was called "his land" (Jer. x. 16; li. 10). In confirmation of this view, we refer to Deut. xxxii. 8, 9; 1 Kings, xx. 23; 2 Kings, xvii. 23; 2 Chron. xxxii. 19. There was also a sort of intercommunity of the gods of one nation with the gods of another; so that when the people of one country removed to another, they were expected to recognize the gods of the country to which they removed, though they did not abandon the worship of their own. Those also who conquered and possessed another country were obliged to maintain in all their accustomed honors, the gods of the conquered country. Whatever gods of their own they might bring with them, they were to render all due service to the *local* god of the acquired country. Even mere sojourners from a foreign country refusing to sacrifice to the god of the place where they sojourned, were esteemed guilty of impiety. Great benefits were supposed to result from this; so much so, that it became in part the cause of the idolatry of the Israelites who visited foreign countries. (Vide 2 Kings, xvii. 24, *sqq.*) It was this superstitious reverence for the tutelary gods of Canaan which was one cause of the defections of this people, when Canaan became their own possession.

With these things in view, let us now suppose that this people had left Egypt for some other country than Canaan, and under the patronage and direction of some other God than Jehovah—would they not have transferred those views and opinions in which they had been educated concerning their relations to the king and tutelary gods of Egypt, to the king and tutelary deity of the country to which they should go? Especially if he whom they should now acknowledge as their king and their god, should institute a similar form of government with similar rites of worship, would they not regard them as instituted for similar purposes? If they had believed in a future state of rewards and punishments, would they not still believe in it? If they had performed the services, rites, and ceremonies of the Egyptian theocracy, and submitted habitually to the authority of its laws, with the full conviction that it implied or was connected with a higher system of government founded on a future, immortal existence—would they not still retain these views of the subject, and be led to regard their present relations to the system of government as substantially the same? And when the true character of their national king and national God should be, as it was in respect to Israel, more fully unfolded with its new relations, and with the most distinct correction of former false opinions—would not their views of the higher system be changed and modified accordingly? Would not the *natural conclusion* still be, that the lower system of a theocracy now was designed to exhibit, even with increased advantages, the higher system of moral government, as well as formerly in Egypt? I mean, would not all this be natural and highly probable?

I now remark again, that—

1. The same conclusion would result from more formal *inference.* By this I mean, *reflection in formal reasoning.*

Here it is to be remembered, that the question is not what inferences or conclusions were actually derived by this people from the premises—but the question is, at what conclusions had they the means of arriving by due reflection, and without mental perversion on their part? It is also to be specially considered, that we have already shown that man under the mere light of nature, *could* come to the knowledge of God as administering a perfect moral government over this world under a gracious economy. And still more especially, that God had revealed this system of government from the fall of Adam to the patriarchs, and pre-eminently to Abraham, Isaac and Jacob, the ancestors of this people, and this in the form of a covenant which it would seem could never be forgotten—of a covenant from which Paul, as the chief source of his argument with Jews proves the reality and unfolds the nature of God's system of moral government through grace, over both Jews and Gentiles. The question now is, what further means of knowledge and faith on this great subject, was furnished by the Jewish theocracy?

Here the first thing to be noticed is the full and formal promulgation of the perfect law of his moral government—the perfect rule of action—revealing the sum of all duty on the part of moral beings. Less than this, according to the principles before stated, he could not require *as a rule of action*, in the relation of a national ruler. This was also a thing too momentous to be left to be decided in any other way than by the most clear and explicit disclosure in such a revelation. In assuming therefore, the relation of a national king, God did not jeopardize the great interests of holiness, or of perfect moral excellence by lowering or obscuring the perfect rule of action or duty. He did not endanger or sacrifice the moral perfection of man by presenting a false standard of moral character. He made a full and formal promulgation of the perfect law of his perfect moral government.

I now ask, what was the rational inference from this fact? Was it that God did not administer a perfect moral government over them? Plainly such a fact considered in itself and without opposing evidence, would as we have seen, require according to every principle of just reasoning, the opposite conclusion—that God is administering a perfect moral government over men.

Further, God as national king revealed another rule of action *as the rule of judgment*, which as we have seen was not, and could not be, any thing less than the same requirement under a perfect moral government through grace—the requirement of some degree of personal holiness. But was there any thing in this fact to impart doubt or uncertainty to our main *inference?* Not surely the fact that God did not proceed on the strict principles of a merely legal system, for the very system itself as a system of grace, necessarily excluded a merely legal system. God was ever showing himself under the theocracy or lower system, as a national ruler, forgiving iniquity, transgression, and sin against the civil government, on condition of repentance and making external conduct, *more humano*, the *criterion* of judgment. God as an infinitely perfect Being, could require nothing less than some degree of personal holiness—true spiritual piety—as the rule of judgment; and as national ruler administering a civil government, he could make nothing the *criterion* of judgment but external conduct. Who could suppose that God, who always revealed himself as the omniscient searcher of the heart—who had so clearly revealed his perfect law as the rule of action, and the law of personal holiness in some degree, of spiritual repentance, as the rule of judgment, could ever be satisfied with or *receive to actual favor*, a subject even under the national system, on the ground of external conduct, merely because, *more humano*, he on this ground *treated* him with favor? Could any civil ruler *regard* with affection a known traitor, merely because through overt action he could not be convicted of treason? Plainly here again, God left no possible ground of mistake even under the national requirement, in respect to *the rule of judgment*, except by the most palpable and inexcusable perversion. No principle of a perfect moral government is abandoned in the lower system of civil government; but rather every essential principle of the former is preserved and clearly inculcated in the latter, so far as it is possible from the nature of the case; while none is adopted in the latter, which is not manifestly inseparable from its nature. Indeed, the very principle so palpably adopted in the lower or civil system, not merely of requiring perfect holiness as a rule of action, but of requiring imperfect personal holiness as the rule of judgment, though external conduct is the criterion of judgment, sheds a constant and strong light on the fact that personal holiness would, and that nothing else would, render any one even as *a mere citizen or subject of civil government*, an object of the *actual* friendship and favor of the moral lawgiver. But if God as national king and tutelary deity, actually promised even by an extraordinary and miraculous providence, and subverted the laws of nature in execution of the promise to confer earthly happiness in effect for merely external conduct, with what higher approbation must he regard, and with what richer gifts would he bless, not merely the sinless obedience of a perfect heart, but the full, actual compliance with the known rule of judgment in a penitent and contrite heart? Be it here remembered, that this people fully believed in a future state of rewards and punishments. Through their Egyptian education, if in no other way, they also believed in a lower system of divine government with pardon; and a higher system of divine government through grace. And with these premises admitted, how could they believe that God should as he did *in effect*, confer the richest earthly rewards for merely hypocritical service under the one system, and leave sincere, true-hearted compliance with the only revealed or even possible rule of judgment unrewarded under the other? Could any honest, reflective reasoning on the subject, have resulted in a doubt? Difficult as at first sight it would seem to be, I know that the error, the grand error, of the Jew, was that he legalized mere external conformity to the Mosaic law as a rule of action and of judgment, into full compliance with the claims of God upon him, and thus, on principles of law and equity, expected acceptance and favor with God. From what could such an error—an error under the light of so much truth—a practical error of such serious, everlasting moment—result, except from a most palpable and fearful perversion of the mind? Which was the most rational *inference* from the premises,—that because God as a national king, like other national rulers awarded earthly good, in effect, for mere external compliance with the rule of judgment, for the mere show of actual obedience, this was the full claim of God as a moral ruler, or—in view of the express and unqualified language of requirement as reaching the heart—that a spiritual obedience would, and such obedience only would secure the higher reward of a future world? No degree of intellect which pertains to a rational being, if unperverted, it would seem, could in such a case fail to adopt the latter conclusion. How too, do the reproofs and denunciations of God for the want of spiritual service—the homage of the heart—on the part of this people, show the manner in which he expected them to reason on this subject, and with what unqualified wrath he regarded them, in every relation, for this failure?

I remark again, that—

2. What was thus clearly exhibited to the rational and unperverted mind on this subject, in the mode of obvious and palpable *inference*, was decisively shown in another mode, viz., by *representation.*

Our first argument on this topic may be thus comprehensively presented—The theocracy or national government of Egypt, was a representative system. Under this government, the Israelites who were delivered from Egypt by Moses, had been born and educated. They had imbibed the strongest attachment to this kind of national government—not to say, they had no conception of any other. It was difficult to bring them to leave Egypt, and to receive a theocracy from the true God. It is incredible that they ever should be brought to receive and submit to any other than one that, in their view, was a theocracy. When God therefore, had actually established such a government over this people, and when they had consented to receive it, it is reasonable to conclude that they understood and regarded it and that God designed that they should understand and regard it, as a theocracy—the same kind of government as that to which they had been accustomed in Egypt—and therefore a *representative* system, exhibiting in its great and general principles his moral government over them as moral and immortal beings. The very establishment of such a system of government, in view of its known nature and design, involved the proof of its *representative* character.

This argument is much confirmed by considering the particulars included in it.

This people as already intimated, were so thoroughly Egyptian in their notions, opinions, and usages—they were so profoundly degraded by their idolatry, and as a consequence so violently attached to a theocracy, to its shows, its rites, its pompous services, as their subsequent history from its very beginning through long ages proves—that nothing is more incredible than that they should ever have been brought to acknowledge Jehovah as the only true God, by any other means than by his administration of such a government.

Again: a prominent and principal difficulty in restraining them from idolatry shows the same thing. When they came into the possession of the promised land, they expected great blessings from the tutelary gods of the nations which they conquered, as truly as from their own national Deity; and it was this expectation which made it so difficult to secure, not indeed the acknowledgment of Jehovah as their God, but the renunciation of other gods. Thus they persisted in all their accustomed views of a theocracy, and must have regarded it as a representative system. God therefore, in establishing such a government over them, must have intended that they should so regard it. What should lead them, according to the laws of rational belief, to separate from their conception of a theocracy in the hands of God, their conception of every other theocracy—its relation as a representative system? While these laws of belief—their assumed premises instead of being contradicted, being fully confirmed—show that they ought not, and their inveterate attachments, that they would not separate these conceptions; the facts of their history down to the abolition of the national system, show that they did not.

This leads to another remark—that the truly righteous among this people must have practically relied on and used this characteristic of the national system, while the wicked grossly perverted and abused it. The truly righteous must have had a sufficient, even a divine warrant for their faith in God as their rewarder in a future state of existence. That a theocracy was a representative system, had become throughout the earth a settled, undoubted truth—a plain principle as it were of common sense, or rather of divine authority. Now how could any of those idolatrous Israelites who left Egypt, or any of their descendants, placed under a mere theocracy, find in such a system a divine warrant for that faith which looks to another world for its reward? If this system required this principle, did it promise aught but temporal good? If the covenant with Abraham was still not disannulled and in full force, how could they learn its nature or its import from a system of mere national law, which in its primary and obvious character and import, contained not a word either in the explanation or inculcation of that covenant? How then, under this protracted Mosaic dispensation, and by means of it, was the least divine warrant furnished for the prospects or the hopes of a truly religious faith, unless it was divinely constituted and regarded by every true believer as A REPRESENTATIVE system? Otherwise it is plain that the theocracy or national system could afford no authorized instruction respecting God's higher system of law and grace, as the moral governor of moral beings; his revelation so far as what was taught or revealed by Moses, instead of being as commonly supposed, progressive, was retrogressive; and instead of attesting the righteousness of God without law, it held forth a mere *political* justification and temporal happiness and not eternal life as its only promised reward. All that is said in the New Testament, of its relation to Christ and salvation through him—of which we shall speak more fully hereafter—would be groundless and unwarranted.

Here too, I may appeal also to that "cloud of witnesses," who, under the Mosaic dispensation, "obtained a good report through faith," and ask, what could warrant the faith of these holy men in this dispensation, unless it were justly viewed as representing the Gospel itself, shadowing faintly but still more brightly than before under the patriarchal dispensation, the covenant made with Abraham—the grand charter of the Christian church and of human hope? And then again how could God through the whole history of this people, with their established views of a theocracy, be constantly presenting himself to them by the wonders of his power, as the Creator of the heaven and the earth—as the only living and true God—ever both by his goodness and severity, causing all his glory to pass before them in the administration of a national system of law and grace, and yet they fail to see, in a temporal system so glorious, a higher system which "doth exceed in glory." If Abraham, when "receiving Isaac *in a figure*," saw the day of Christ and was glad, did not "many righteous" also see it with like emotion, through that august economy for Israel, so plainly designed and adapted as a representative system, to reveal that day in still brighter splendors? But on the other hand,not all; for of still greater multitudes, it must be said in the language of the apostle, "their minds were blinded;" for "until this day, when Moses is read, the vail is on their hearts." Here we have the cause of the grand error of this nation finally rejected of God for their unbelief. This error to the last was, that by a gross and palpable perversion of the representative character of their theocracy, instead of distinguishing as they ought, the national from the moral government of God, they so identified the two systems, as to reduce the whole government of God practically to a merely national or political system for both this and a future world. In this view, what the RULE of judgment under both systems required—personal religion, true holiness—was lost sight of, and the CRITERION of judgment under the national system, or mere overt action, was substituted in its place. Hence according to the apostle, they attained not to a law of righteousness—because they sought it not by faith but, *as it were*, by works of law—not even by conforming to the requirement—the true rule of judgment—of their national law, but as if *it were so;* by substituting external obedience the *criterion* of righteousness before a civil tribunal, for that spirit of loyalty, personal holiness, which the national as well as the moral system required, and which would have justified them under the latter. But failing in this, they attained to nothing beyond the mere *criterion* of righteousness under the national system. They thus sought a mere *quasi* righteousness as citizens, or as subjects of civil government. Of course they attained to nothing more, and utterly failed of attaining to righteousness under the moral government of God. What then pertained to the theocracy, or national government, except its *representative* character, which could be thus perverted into this grand error of an unbelieving nation? God clearly presented himself to this people as their national king or ruler, making the rule of action and the rule of judgment as plain as language could make them, requiring in his rule of judgment that state of heart—that spirit of loyalty, with its prescribed expressions in overt action, which was due to him as a being of infinite perfection, even under a gracious economy. This national government as a representative system also, would clearly show, that God as a moral governor reigning through grace, required the same state of mind as a rule of judgment. But now, in the actual administration of his national government, mere overt action necessarily became not *the rule* but *the criterion* of judgment, and actually secured the justification of the externally obedient subject. Hence as subjects of civil government, and so it commonly is in like cases, the criterion of judgment was substituted for the rule of judgment, and all their solicitude and aim directed to the *criterion* of judgment, i. e., to mere external obedience. This, with that want of thorough reflection so common and natural to man, would be regarded as the fulfillment of every claim of God, and so be relied on as a legal righteousness. Such was undeniably the grand error of this people, and such plainly the process by which they fell into it. At least, what else in the theocrăcy of this people, except its representative character, could be made by their depraved heart and perverted intellect (2 Cor. iii. 14, 15), the occasion of believing that righteousness by works of law was to be attained before God as a moral governor, it seems difficult to imagine. Is it credible that a Jew, or any other man, with a just and full apprehension of the broad and spiritual import of God's perfect law, should persuade himself that he fulfilled its claim, and by so doing had or could have a righteousness *in law?* Is it any more credible that he should persuade himself, that any merely external morality or ritual service was all that the law required, in view of its abundant claims on the heart? Is any thing credible in the case, except that he was willfully ignorant of the true spiritual import of the law—that assuming that the rule of action and of judgment were the same under the national and moral system, he further vainly and falsely assumed, that his exact and scrupulous external conformity to the national law was decisive *proof* of entire conformity with its demand on the heart; and thus arrived at the conclusion, that he met and satisfied every claim of God as a lawgiver and was therefore righteous *in law?* Was not this the error of the young ruler, who so vainly supposed that he had kept the whole law—an error so plainly exposed by the Saviour, when applying the test of true moral principle to the heart? Was it not the error of Paul before the commandment came, and which he so frankly confesses when he says, "as touching the righteousness of the law, blameless"—an error exposed only by the saying of the law, "thou shalt not covet?" Was it not the error of supposing that the rule of action and of judgment under the national law, with its whole demand sunk to the mere criterion of judgment under this law, was the rule of action and of judgment under God's moral system—an error which has ever been, and is now, the grand and fatal obstacle on the part of this people to their reception of the Gospel? Now it would seem, that there must be some characteristic of the national system—some existing relation of it to the moral system, as the original occasion of this grand Jewish error. Otherwise, an error so flagrant could not possess the semblance of plausibility, even in the most perverted mind. The representative character of the national system affords in the manner described, an obvious and natural account of the origin of this error, when it cannot I think be accounted for in any other way. If this be the true account of it, then was the theocracy of Israel a representative system.

Another consideration, which shows that God designed the theocracy of Israel should be, and that therefore it was, a representative system, is that it so far, or in such degree, resembled the Egyptian theocracy. By this I do not mean that there was a resemblance in all the minute details or peculiarities of the two theocracies. Nothing is more remote from the truth. In the Jewish system, every thing was changed and made different from the Egyptian, which was required by the great object or end of the former, viz., to bring the people to renounce idolatry, and to understand and receive the higher or *represented* system of God's moral government. But I mean such a resemblance in certain general and essential elements as determine each system to be a theocracy. In proof of this I remark, that—

3. Both systems, in their primary character, were simply systems of national or political government. In this character, as we have shown, the laws of each respected only the political conduct of their subjects—inculcated that spirit of loyalty which was due to the exalted character of the supreme national ruler, but only in this relation—were enforced only by temporal sanctions, and administered only according to the principles of a civil government.

Both systems distinctly and prominently recognized the divinity as the national king and tutelary deity, a determining element which greatly modified the political government or theocracy of all nations. Hence,

Both systems included the general, comprehensive requirement of obedience to the national king, as sustaining also the relation of tutelary deity in the administration of a particular and an extraordinary providence. From this latter relation, as combined with the former, resulted the laws requiring what may be called *political* rather than *religious* worship, since obedience to these was as truly obedience to the national ruler as any other. As such obedience, it was required and rendered only as the appointed means of securing temporal blessings, and averting temporal calamities. Thus, a spirit of loyalty with its overt doings, in what was called in heathen language a life of *piety and virtue*, or in Jewish language *holiness*, as obedience to the divinity in the twofold relation of national king and national God, was inculcated and enforced in both systems. It is not of course, to be pretended that the things meant by this language in the two cases were the same things, especially in view of the difference between the character of a pagan divinity and that of the true God. The terms were used to denote the conceptions, which were formed under widely different standards of piety and virtue. Under one system it may be difficult to say what they did denote, beyond a vague and general notion of obedience as satisfying the divinity. Under the other, they denoted in one relation true spiritual religion, or what was *visibly* such and properly spoken of as such.

Each of the two systems was a system of law and grace combined. That each was a system of law, as including authoritative rules of action, will not be denied; while, as we have seen in the pagan rites, the performance of lustrations which cleansed from guilt, and the offering of sacrifices and incense, to win the favor and avert the wrath of the gods, are not less obvious than the atonements and consequent forgiveness under the Mosaic institution.

Further, both systems included *a rule of action* and *a rule of judgment*, differing from each other and plainly distinguished. I do not say that the nature and import of these rules were unfolded with equal plainness and precision under the two systems. But that the difference between these rules—the rule by the transgression of which sin and condemnation begin, and the rule of repentance by which pardon and acceptance are obtained—was not less real, or less actually distinguished in the Egyptian than in the Hebrew theocracy, is as truly evinced in the lustrations and offerings of the former as in the sin-offerings and especially in the great annual atonement of the latter.*

* Without going into the question, whether the sin-offerings of individuals for individual transgressions were *atonements* in any higher sense than mulcts or fines, on account of which, in cases of smaller offenses against civil law, the

Once more: The most surprising resemblance between the Egyptian and Hebrew theocracies, is in the ritual parts of the two systems. On this part of the subject, I shall only refer again to the learned work of Spencer, *De legibus Hebræorum ritualibus et earum rationibus*,* remarking, with Warburton, "that the RITUAL LAW when thus explained, is seen to be an institution of the most beautiful and sublime contrivance, which, without its *causes* (nowhere to be found but in the road of this hypothesis), must lie open to the scorn and contempt of libertines and unbelievers." Like this author, "I mean to charge myself with no more of Spencer's opinions than what directly tend to the proof of this part of my proposition, viz., that there is a great and surprising relation and resemblance between the Jewish and Egyptian rites, in circumstances both *opposite* and *similar*."† Spencer has not only assigned an adequate reason for the resemblance of the Hebrew rites to the Egyptian, in the design of God by their splendor to attract the people and to prevent their return to Egyptian superstition, but has given, as has Warburton also, decisive proofs that the Egyptians did not borrow from the Hebrews, but the Hebrews from the Egyptians.

To form the present argument, we have now to put two things together. The Egyptian theocracy was, and as we claim to have shown, ought to have been considered by the Israelites who were brought out of Egypt, *a representative system*, exhibiting a higher system of moral government. Be-

---

offender is passed over, they must be admitted at least to be *atonements* in the general sense of *a ground of forgiveness*. The word *atonement*, at least according to English usage and as a general term, is *a ground of forgiving a fault*, and is applicable of course to a variety of cases. An atonement in the above *specific sense*, differs widely from atonement in that specific sense in which it is necessary to sustain *the authority of a ruler or lawgiver*. And here, is it not a question whether the only atonement under the Hebrew theocracy, which accomplished this end, was not the great annual atonement. (Vide Lev. xvi. and Heb. ix.) Between this *atonement* and the sin-offerings of individuals, the difference in many respects, is obvious. These were required as acts of *individuals*, and were plainly acts of individual obedience, the want of which incurred an individual penalty, as did individual disobedience to any other command. But the great annual atonement was the act of the high priest only, made by him for the sins of the people, and characterized and distinguished by peculiarities which show its universal efficacy for the sins, i. e., the civil offenses of all the people, and that it must sustain some peculiar relation. Hence as we should expect, the apostle compares this great annual atonement, and no other, with the atonement of Christ.

* Vide lib. iii. p. 16. † Div. Leg., vol. iii. p. 338.

tween this Egyptian theocracy and the theocracy which God established over the same people, there was, so far as the form or kind of government is concerned, in every substantial respect a resemblance—a resemblance so complete as to show that the latter system was substantially copied from the former. I now ask, why this resemblance between the theocracy which God established over this people, and that under which they had been educated in Egypt, and for which they had such strong and almost invincible predilections, unless like the latter, God designed that they should regard it as being, and thus that it should be a *representative* system?

This view is further confirmed by the consideration, that no other satisfactory account can be given of his adopting such a system of government, for the great purpose or end proposed. The more direct object of this institution may be said to be, *to reclaim them from idolatry to the knowledge of himself as the only living and true God, and thus to true religion.* But why should God adopt a mere national or civil polity for such a purpose, which, neither in the language in which it is revealed, nor yet in any authorized way or method could afford increased instruction, or even the least instruction concerning that moral government of God over men, without the knowledge of which true religion on the part of man is utterly hopeless (Heb. xi. 6)? To have left the acquisition of this knowledge to mere *inference*, sufficient as this would be to the unperverted mind, would have been in vain, as is fully proved by the entire failure of even the higher instruction and stronger light furnished by the covenant with Abraham. Will it then be said, that the design of God in this political government, was according to literal promise simply to make the nation politically great? But such plainly, was not his great and ulterior end, nor an end which, as his great end, was in the lowest degree worthy of himself. This is to suppose that the God of the patriarchs, by this new institution, should throw all his prior revelations into obscurity and darkness in respect to this paganized nation; that he should only confirm them if not in their idolatry, in the utter irreligion and impiety involved in it; that he had forgotten his covenant with the father of the faithful; that the God of eternity, in revealing himself to successive generations of creatures made in his own image, sunk his relation as reigning over them in the glories of a perfect moral dominion, to that of a mere civil ruler of men as the insects of a day (Heb. xi. 16). If these things are incredible, what can we conclude, but that God by the theocracy of Israel designed, in the way of *representation*, to exhibit in clearer light than he had done before, his perfect moral government over men?

Another consideration worthy of notice is, that this system of government was pre-eminently fitted to the great end proposed, and thus renders the wisdom and goodness of God conspicuous in its adoption. That he *could* have adopted any other means so well fitted to its end as this, is beyond the power of human reason to show. It is God himself who asks, "What more could have been done in my vineyard, that I have not done in it?" In our ignorance on this question, and therefore without affirmation or denial, and also without aiming to unfold all the particular adaptations of the system to its end, I proceed to say—

4. That this system of government with their very existence as a nation, connected the manifestation of the only living and true God, and in the manner already shown, his almost constant worship and service as their tutelary God. How obvious then in this respect, and especially in view of the idolatry and extreme moral degradation of this people, is the fitness of the system to its high and ulterior design? The great, comprehensive requirement of the system, including the perfect rule of action and the rule of judgment considered in their relations as political rules, were presented in terms as plain as language could furnish, so that of these nothing but perverseness could be ignorant. At the same time we may safely say, in view of their subsequent conduct, that nothing but a theocracy would be regarded by them with respect; nothing but the strong *sensible* impressions of such a system would furnish the slightest hope of their moral elevation. On the other hand accustomed as they were to such a government, they were prepared to understand the character of that under which they were placed—the latter scarcely differing from the former except in one great fact, and what it necessarily involved—a fact which it would seem could not be misunderstood or misapprehended—that, instead of an Egyptian idol or dead men deified, the God of the nation is Jehovah. Moses also, who under God was their lawgiver—"king in Jeshurun"—as "learned in all the wisdom of the Egyptians," and under constant divine direction, was signally

qualified to give, and especially to administer a theocracy—conformed, except in that respect just specified, to that with which this people were familiar. By such conformity, it was in no degree consistent with its high design, fitted to offend their previously cherished attachments and prejudices. It rather coincided with them, and was in many respects, especially by its splendid ritual, fitted to attract their regard and to secure an entire and welcome reception. No innovations are introduced, no new burdens imposed, no prior usages changed, except what every rational mind must approve, when he who alone is God, whose are the heavens and the earth and all that in them is, is their national God instead of heathen idols. Nor was this system of government given and perpetuated without its high authority being established and kept constantly in view, as a system coming from him who is God over all. The whole nation saw the mighty hand and outstretched arm of the Almighty in their miraculous deliverance from Egypt, and at the giving of the law heard his voice amid the awful grandeurs of Sinai, while in blessings and calamities, and by an extraordinary providence, he shook the heavens and the earth throughout their subsequent history. If aught that can allure or terrify—if aught of kindness and severity—if aught could avail of sublimity, grandeur, glory, addressed to the sensible apprehension of a people hopeless in respect to all other impressions; when were the majesty and awful love of God in his rightful dominion, in this manner so presented to any people? If now we add to these things, that this national system was fully proved by its own nature, and according to all the laws of reasoning applicable to the case, to be a REPRESENTATIVE system, thus showing God in brighter manifestation than any prior revelation, in his higher relations—how signal its adaptation to its end—how conspicuous the condescension of God to this idolatrous and rebellious people! Human ingenuity may be defied to suggest a system of government and a course of providence, so perfectly adapted to the end designed, so illustrative of the wisdom and goodness of its author, in view of the character, the condition, and the necessities of this people.

And further, it will be generally admitted that the Mosaic system or law was designed to furnish a most convincing *proof* of the substantial nature and divine origin of Christianity. In what manner was this design accomplished? Not a word nor sentence, as we have before intimated, can be found in the Mosaic law—the theocracy, as such—which in its *primary, literal import*, teaches or implies the moral government of God. Indeed, the express and full revelation of this system, as one afterward to be introduced in its fullness and perfection, and to supersede the national system, would doubtless have defeated another design of God, of indispensable accomplishment to his ulterior end—the design of training them by a long course of discipline under this preparatory dispensation. For had this people—this whole nation—degraded and corrupt as they were, been fully convinced that their law was temporary and to have an end, they would have despised it, and, as they were wont to do with far less inducement, have rejected the authority of Moses, before "*the fullness of time*" had brought into the world "the Desire of all nations." They would not have so prized it, under their burdensome ritual, as to wait for their spiritual deliverer. Hence divine wisdom and goodness conveyed this information with comparative obscurity—an obscurity not so great but that sincere and honest inquiry would know and understand the higher system, and yet so great that perverseness and willful ignorance could not augment guilt by rejecting a clearer revelation. How was this accomplished by the Mosaic system of national government, unless it was *a representative* system exhibiting substantially the nature of God's higher system? How can any such correspondence be otherwise traced between the two systems, or any such dependence of one on the other, as shall prove that if one had a divine origin, the other had also—a correspondence and dependence which show that not man, but God only, could be the author of either, and is therefore the author of both?

LECTURE V.

THE MOSAIC LAW A THEOCRACY.

The Mosaic law shown to be a theocracy from the prevalence in early ages of *representative* language and symbolic actions—as also from the nature of the case.—From examples in the Scriptures: Gen. iii. 15; xxii. 2; xii. and xvii.; Psalms 2, 22, 47, 67, 72.—From the prophets.—From Christ's manner of teaching, confirmed by his striking declarations in Matt. v. 17; John, xviii. 33; Luke, xxiv. 44, 45.

THAT the Mosaic law was a theocracy, I shall now further attempt to show—

III. In the third place, from a common use of language in the early ages of the world, in which one thing is spoken of chiefly to denote another.

This use of language, which is frequent in both the Old Testament and the New, is of various species or kinds; and is distinguished in these respects by the various epithets of figurative, parabolic, allegorical, typical, &c. It consists, generally speaking, in *so using* language as to direct thought first to one thing either real or imaginary, for the purpose of representing another thing, and turning the thoughts to it as the main or principal thing intended to be thought of in the case.

I am not now approaching the question whether the language referred to, or any other language, has a *double sense;* nor shall I attempt formally to discuss this question, until at least *the sense* of the phrase *double sense* itself is accurately determined, and so distinguished from the variety of other *senses* in which the language has been used by the parties in controversy. Nor shall I now enter particularly into an inquiry concerning types, allegories, fables, parables, &c. I only take the more general ground, that truths of the highest moment were revealed to men under the Old Testament dispensation, in what I shall call *the representative mode.*

Nor can I, within my prescribed limits, pretend to do any thing like justice to this subject. I shall rather state my own views of some parts of it, and refer you to authors who have treated it more largely than is possible in the present discussion.

And here, *the propriety* and *reasonableness* of this mode of revelation demand consideration, as well as *the fact*.

The object of all that can be called language, whether significant things or arbitrary sounds, is to convey some ideas or conceptions from one mind to another. This is its principal object or end. These ideas or conceptions constitute at least its principal meaning—a meaning always designed, and without which the language would not be used. There is only one kind of language, since language has been so greatly improved and perfected by culture, which is fitted to express this one meaning and nothing more. This is true not only of scientific language, but of all ordinary literal language when *properly* used and interpreted in its logical connection. That such language, in the present improved state of it—by which I mean literal language, language which expresses one meaning and nothing more—should, to a vast extent, even for the ordinary purposes of life, be used, is of the highest importance not to say of absolute necessity. It is so, because it is the best language for its purposes, and because, since the degree of culture which language has received, any other kind substituted for this would occasion in many cases great perplexity, if not absolute uncertainty, in respect to its principal meaning, or what is to be understood.*

But while all this is readily admitted, it does not follow either that this kind of language was, in any high degree of perfection, the language of the earliest ages of this world. Nor can it be shown that the very earliest language did not consist of significant things—either actions, sounds, or other things—nor that the earliest records were not made in the language of *picture;* nor that this was not followed by or connected with the language of *representation;* nor that whatever progress or improvement had been given to language by the introduction of *arbitrary* signs, in the time of Moses or earlier, the language of *representation* had not then more or less prevalence in the Hebrew nation. Nothing is more obvious in respect to language, than that it was at first formed not for scientific purposes, but with almost no true or exact knowledge of things;

* Vide this objection stated by Warburton, from Sykes. Div. Leg., vol. iv. p. 477.

—formed with almost no reflection, and for the more direct and limited purposes of practical life;—formed from mere *sensible appearances*, and that therefore it expressed, to a vast extent, only hasty, and hence false conceptions of things. This *language of appearance*, we know on reflection, is *false* in its actual meaning. For example, it is *false* in the actual meaning of the common language of life, that the sun rises and sets, that the sugar is sweet, that the ice is cold, that the kite flies, that the body moves, &c., &c. This language has become *proper* by usage, and answering the common purposes of practical life, the only thing which gives to such language its value or importance, it is of no consequence whether it be true or false. If the sun will be at a given time in a given point of space in relation to the earth, and this is all that we have occasion for common purposes to express, it is wholly immaterial whether we predicate self-motion of the body or not. Accordingly, *the language of appearance* ever has been used, and ever will be to the end of time.

And now why should there not be from the beginning, a language of representation, common and sanctioned by usage, as well as a language of appearance? Moreover if there are—and we expect to show that there are—important ends, even those of divine wisdom and mercy, to be answered by its use; and if in many instances all uncertainty in its use may be avoided as effectually as in the use of any other language; or if in others it involves a peculiar but useful degree of obscurity, then instead of any valid objections against its use there are decisive reasons for it. In short, if in all cases of its use there was no other kind of language which would as well answer the same useful purpose, then its use has an ample vindication.* This is what is now to be maintained, and particularly on the subject under consideration. If, for example, of the two great dispensations of God by Moses and by Christ, the former was *representative* of the latter, it is easy to see what an overwhelming proof is furnished of God's revelation to the world; the two dispensations in this way affording the most decisive confirmation of the divine origin of both.† Nor

* Warburton has dwelt on the propriety and reasonableness of this use of language, Leg., vol. iv. pp. 454, 464, 511. Vide also vol. iii. and B. 4, Sec. 5, p. 413.

† Warburton, vol. iv. p. 411.

is this all. In view of the supposed fact that the theocracy or God's national government over Israel, represented, and was known to represent, in all substantial respects, his moral government over men, language as applied to the former, must, to every unperverted mind, convey corresponding conceptions of the latter. Thus all perplexity and uncertainty in respect to the great object or end of the writer or speaker would be prevented, and his language might be interpreted with as much precision and accuracy, according to the laws of usage in the case, as in any other case; and on the same general principle, viz., the object of the writer or speaker manifested in his language and manner of using it. When the use of the language of representation is common, has become conventional, and is familiarly employed in the communication of thought, it may be as easily distinguished from other language, by the nature of the subject and the logical connection, as language which has a metaphorical and a literal meaning.

I now come to the FACT that such a mode of imparting knowledge was adopted as I have described. And here I may say, that it was not only adopted extensively by the writers of the Old Testament, but was the principal mode of conveying that knowledge of the great truths of God's moral government under the patriarchal and Mosaic dispensations, which in more direct language is conveyed under the Christian dispensation.

Of the FACT now specified, the *proof* seems to me to be so obvious and abundant, that it can scarcely be necessary to attempt any full exhibition of it to the readers of the sacred writings. I propose therefore, only to give some illustrations of it, and to make some references which I think will be satisfactory.

The first instance is—

1. (Gen. iii. 15.) "And I will put enmity between thee and the woman, and between thy seed and her seed; it [He] shall bruise thy head, and thou shalt bruise his heel."

I do not here propose to enter into any consideration of the many questions which have been raised respecting this text. I only say, on the authority of Jewish usage, it contains the great promise of a Redeemer. The proof, to say nothing of the allegorical structure of the language, is decisive, in the distinct allusions to it as such by Paul and John. (Vide Rom.

xvi. 20; Col. ii. 15; Heb. ii. 14–15; 1 John, iii. 8.) This passage should also be viewed in its accordance with Gen. xxii. 18; xxvi. 4; xxviii. 14; Gal. iii. 8; and with Isa. vii. 14; Jer. xxxi. 22; Mic. v. 3; Matt. i. 23; Rev. xx. 1–3, and xii. 9. Now, whether the language of this passage be interpreted in one specific meaning or another given by different commentators, it says nothing in its *primary literal import* respecting the Redeemer of the world. How then, according to Jewish usage, should it be understood as a promise of this Redeemer in its *principal*, and according to subsequent allusions to it, in its *only* meaning, unless it were regarded as the language of *representation*—language used at least chiefly to describe one thing by describing in its primary import another?

3. (Gen. xxii. 2.) "Take now thy son, thine only son Isaac," &c.

In the purport and object of this command, I agree with Warburton so nearly, that I shall state my own view of the passage nearly in his words. The language of this command, in my view, directs to an *action* which *represents* the great sacrifice of Christ for the redemption of mankind. This view of the passage is shown from the words of Christ (John viii. 56); nor less clearly in Heb. xi. 19, where the apostle tells us that Abraham offered up Isaac, accounting that God was able to raise him from the dead, whence also he received him *in a figure* (ἐν παραβολῇ). The question put by the Jews to Christ, "Hast thou seen Abraham?" shows that they inferred this from what Christ had said of Abraham's seeing his day. But Warburton has, with so much ingenuity and truth, shown that the offering up of Isaac was an action which represented the sacrifice of Christ, that I shall refer you to what he has said on the subject, with the single remark, that if this was so, then the language used to describe the sacrifice of Isaac is the language of *representation*—language which, while it primarily describes one thing, is employed chiefly for the purpose of denoting another.

4. (Gen. xii. and xvii.) The covenant made with Abraham. Compare Gal. iii.; Heb. xi. 16; also verses 8, 9, 10.

In respect to this covenant it may be said, that the apostle evidently considered some part of the language, viz., "I will be a God to thee," &c., as *literal*, and thus including the promise of the heavenly country. But I ask, in reply, is there any thing in the language of this covenant in its primary import, beyond the promise of great temporal blessings from God as a tutelary deity? Would Abraham, Isaac, and Jacob, or even Paul, aside from the language of *representation*, and adhering strictly to the *usus loquendi*, have justly understood the language, "I will be a God to thee," as promising the heavenly inheritance? Why must the mere promise, so far as words are concerned, of an earthly country, and limited, as in Gen. xii. 1, and xvii. 7, to great earthly blessings, be understood to mean even by implication, more than the terms of the covenant express, even of an inheritance in heaven? And further, if this were so in the literal import of the language, how was it that the Sadducees denied a future state with such decisive proof, as they argued; and especially, that the Pharisees, so anxious to find the proof of a future state, in their controversy with the Sadducees, entirely overlooked one so obvious and so prominent? Is not the evidence decisive, that both these Jewish sects, through their false views of justification before God on the ground of political obedience, and through their national pride, had been led to consider the promise as simply one of national greatness; and thus perversely blind to that higher spiritual system of grace clearly but *representatively* revealed in the Abrahamic covenant, were entirely ignorant of what both Christ and the apostle, with just views of its representative character, understood this covenant to teach?

A similar objection to the view now taken of this covenant may be supposed to arise from the language of this apostle in Gal. iii. 16: "Now to Abraham and his seed were the promises made. He saith not, and to seeds as of many," &c. My view of this passage, without here giving a critical exposition of it, is, that the apostle means to say—not that the covenant with Abraham included no promise to numerous natural descendants of Abraham, which cannot indeed be supposed—but that THE promise of which he is speaking, the promise of justification before God by faith, was not made to his natural descendants as such; for though the word *seed* in the covenant is broad enough to *admit*, and did even require a promise, or some promise, viz., that of an earthly country, to Abraham's *natural* descendants, yet, according to the well-known principle of representing one thing by another, the higher promise was made only *to* Christ, as the following context clearly shows, viz., to Christ, including as one in him the *believing* seed of

Abraham. And to prevent all evasion of this conclusion, the apostle, proceeding on the true mode of interpreting the covenant, is careful to say, there is nothing in the *wording* of the covenant that confines this higher promise of justification, taught only by representation or inference, to any other import.

5. (Psalms 2d, 22d, 47th, 67th, 72d.) The predictions in these psalms evidently respect chiefly the coming and reign of the Messiah, and the admission of the Gentiles into the church of God. And yet the language is wholly theocratic, without a word, which in its primary and literal meaning, carries the thoughts beyond the temporal prosperity and extension of the national kingdom.

To instances of the use of this kind of language already mentioned, I might add many others in which it is employed by the prophets. I refer only to Ezekiel's vision of the valley of dry bones (chap. xxxvii.), and to one in Isa. xix. 18, *sqq.*, remarking, that the predictions of the prophets, in which they foretell the future greatness and glory of the kingdom of Christ in language merely *theocratic* (Isa. lvi. 7), thus describing one thing by another, are so numerous, that to transcribe them would be tedious and unnecessary. (Isa. xx.; Jer. xiii.; Ezek. iv. v. vii. xii. and xxiv. are instances to our purpose). I only add, that of the *three* great festivals—the Passover, the feast of Pentecost, and the feast of Tabernacles—while the two first commemorated Israel's deliverance from Egypt and the promulgation of the law, so were they clearly *representative* of the sacrifice of Christ, and that miraculous effusion of the Holy Spirit by which the Gospel was disseminated over the world; while the feast of Tabernacles, as commemorative of their dwelling in booths, and on the eighth day returning to their houses (Lev. xxiii. 34–36, and 42, 43), seems not less clearly to *represent* the future conversion of the Jews, if not their return to their own land.

From these examples, the reader of the Old Testament must see, I think, that the revelation of the Redeemer and his work, or of God's moral government over this sinful world through grace, has, since the first apostasy, to a great extent been made in the language of *representation*. How undeniably true this is in respect to the language of the Abrahamic covenant—that revelation of God's system of moral government so full and so complete that the apostle calls it "the Gospel, before preached unto Abraham!" If such symbolic language was employed to unfold the import of this covenant promulgated before Abraham's descendants entered the promised land, why should not similar language be employed in exhibiting God's national government over them when about to take, and after they had actually taken possession of this promised inheritance? Why are we not constrained to admit the fact, especially when we reflect that it would greatly increase the fullness of the revelation of the higher system; while, if such were not the fact, God, in a series of revelations through many centuries, did not in any other mode reveal himself in that highest and most august relation to men, in subservience to which he made and governs the world?

I might dwell on the present topic at much greater length were it necessary. Antiquity is full of examples, which show, as Livy tells us, that "this was the ancient mode of teaching." It prevailed among all the eastern and western nations long before the time of Christ. Especially was it used by the Jews. Some examples among the Jews are Judg. ix. 7; 2 Sam. xii. 1; 2 Kings, xiv. 9; 2 Chron. xxv. 18; Jer. v. 6; Ezek. xvii. 3. Others still might be cited.

I now propose to show the same thing from the New Testament, and particularly to show to what an extent the language of the Mosaic law, as well as other language of the Old Testament, is recognized and reasoned from by Paul, as being the language of representation. So far as the teachings of Christ are concerned, it cannot be necessary to say that he spoke many things in parables, and in other forms of figurative language. One obvious reason for adopting this use of language, at least in many cases, was, that his hearers could not so readily apprehend his instructions, nor so easily retain them when in the form of simple didactic discourse, as by means of similitude and examples derived from other things, whether real or imaginary. In what other manner than the story of the prodigal son, is it conceivable that our Lord could have so clearly and impressively imparted the instruction which is contained in this justly admired parable? How could that great problem with philosophers—that *crux theologorum—the existence of moral evil in the world*, have been so clearly explained, not merely to the philosopher according to true philosophical principles, but to every husbandmen, to all the people, even those of the most humble life, as by the parable of the householder and that of the fisherman? (Vide Matt. xiii. 24, *sqq.*; xiii. 47.) And now could no light concerning God's moral government over men as moral beings, be added to his prior revelation on the subject, by the Mosaic law or Jewish theocracy as a system of *national* government *representing* or symbolizing his system of *moral* government? Let the former be supposed to be, what I claim it to be,—a *representative* system; and can the ingenuity of man devise another method so adapted to impart and to impress instruction respecting God's moral government on the idolatrous and besotted mind of the people of Israel? Say not that it was for a long time and to a fearful degree, ineffective in respect to its supposed design. This proves nothing but a palpable counteraction of what must be admitted to be the means to an end, and divinely fitted to accomplish that end. Say not that far more salutary effects would have been produced on the minds of this people by the earlier introduction of Christianity into the world. How they treated Christianity when it was introduced into the world is told by the crucifixion of its author, and also in the destruction of their temple and their city and their dispersion over the earth for their unbelief. Far be it then from the pride and presumption of human judgment, to pronounce that God could have done more for the eternal salvation of this people at any period of their history, than he actually did by that national law and national providence which he administered over them. Let critics wrangle as they may about double sense, the theocracy of Israel as a *representative* system stands forth through many centuries a memorial dispensation of God, eminently designed and fitted to save a nation and a world lost in sin. And if the teaching of the Great Teacher—the Light of the world—was to such an extent, by parable, and similitudes derived chiefly from things imaginary, why is it incredible that substantially the same mode of instruction, derived from a reality of knowledge constantly experienced, should have been adopted and relied on in the previous history of the same people?

But my object is not merely to vindicate the use of this kind of language, but to show from the New Testament, that it was in fact used in giving the Mosaic law to Israel. For any direct and full statement of this fact however as involving the temporary character and approaching termination of the Jewish theocracy, we are not to look in the early teachings of Christ. The Mosaic law was not as yet abolished; nor did Christ unnecessarily awaken Jewish prejudice and hostility against himself and his instructions, by asserting its speedy destruction. The time had not come for revealing to the Jews a fact so unwelcome and so incredible to them; nor did it come except in some intimation or obscure prediction, made necessary by circumstances, until after his crucifixion—that great fact which was to furnish the decisive evidence of the abolition of the Mosaic law, and to render it even plausible or in the lowest degree credible to Jewish pride and prejudice. I shall only refer to some two or three declarations of Christ, in which, by intimations more or less distinct, he recognized the Mosaic law as a representative system, whose design or end was to be fully accomplished by his mission, and which, as a national system, was to be done away when its design should be thus accomplished. (Matt. v. 17, 18.) "Think not that I am come to destroy the law or the prophets; I am not come to destroy, but to fulfill. For verily I say unto you, till heaven and earth pass, one jot or one tittle shall in no wise pass from the law till all be fulfilled" (*ἕως ἂν πάντα γένηται*). By "the law," must here be meant the Pentateuch, in which are included the covenant with Abraham and the Mosaic law. The meaning of the whole passage must be that which is applicable to the *law* of which he speaks, as well as to the prophets. So far as "the law" is concerned, his meaning, in my view, is, that he came not to loosen, slacken, impair (*καταλῦσαι*), the law spoken of, i. e., the Pentateuch in relation to its object or end either as a preceptive or sacrificial system; but (*πληρῶσαι*), *to fill it out* or to complete it in this respect, and that not one iota shall pass from the law till all is done which is necessary for this purpose, i. e., to accomplish the end of his mission. This last clause faintly implies that when all these things are done (*πάντα γένηται*), something may, if not shall, pass from the law, i. e., when the ulterior end of the law shall be fully accomplished or the law in this respect be filled out—some change may or will take place in it. Now in respect to the Abrahamic covenant, all that remained to be done by Christ to give it completeness was, that He, the promised seed in whom all nations shall be blessed, should come, and teach, and do, and suffer, and die, as he did. What then did he do in respect to the complex system now called "*the law?*" He fully unfolded the nature of its two great requirements,—the one as a rule of action, the other as a rule of judgment, and both in their high *spiritual* import: thus showing that as such requirements, whether viewed as pertaining to God's *moral* government over men as moral beings, or to his *national* government over Israel as citizens of the State, they were so far the same, that there was no true obedience to either short of spiritual obedience; and that no Pharisaic righteousness, no external conduct, being at best the mere *criterion of political obedience and favor*, could without the obedience of the heart, secure God's acceptance and favor as a moral governor. By thus fully unfolding the spiritual nature of the requirement of "the law" of which he speaks, he so far *filled it out*—gave it its completeness—while by correcting the grand Jewish error in respect to external doings, he gave still further completeness to the law in respect to its great object and end. But this is by no means all the things which should be accomplished—πάντα γένηται—by the mission and work of Christ, in order *to fill out*, or give completeness to "the law." Christ by his great sacrifice for the sin of the world, was yet to supersede and cause to pass from the law spoken of—the revelation of God as contained in the Pentateuch—the Levitical offerings and sacrifices 'for the weaknesses and unprofitableness thereof.' 'For the law in these things made nothing perfect, but the bringing in of a better hope did, by the which we draw nigh to God.' With the Levitical atonements must of course pass away the temporal sanctions of the national law, and with its sanctions also the national law itself, i. e., all the peculiar *political* or *civil* relations of God's revelation contained in the Pentateuch. Not one of these comparatively unimportant things—nor even "one jot or tittle," was to pass from this part of revelation till this part itself was *filled out*, or completed, by the work of Christ. But when all that was essential to "the law" spoken of in respect to its great object and end, should be thus fully accomplished, then the theocracy, i. e., the national law, meaning only *the national or civil institution* of the Pentateuch—a mere appendage introduced four hundred and thirty years after the only true substantial reality, to represent this reality as the shadow does the substance, would pass away leaving the substance unobscured, complete, perfect, even effulgent in its own light. Thus Christ does not *deny*, but rather by his guarded and qualified language intimates, that such *will be* the issue of the work which he came to do.

7. (John, xviii. 33.) "Art thou the King of the Jews," &c. From this record of the interview between our Lord and Pilate (v. 28, *sqq.*), it appears that Jesus was accused by the Jews, and understood by Pilate to be accused as a malefactor against the *civil law* (v. 30, 31). When charged by Pilate on the ground of the representations made to him by the Jews, with claiming to be the King of the Jews, the important question I now raise is, what was our Lord's answer? He did not say in unqualified terms, 'I am the King of the Jews;' for this, according to the import of the question, would have been saying that he was the *national* King of the Jews, which was not true. Nor yet does he deny but rather implies, that in some sense or respect he was the King of the Jews. "Jesus answered, My kingdom is not of this world; if my kingdom were of this world," &c.; thus clearly implying that he had a kingdom and was in some respect a king. This implication led Pilate to ask again, "Art thou a king, then?"—if thou art not as thou sayest a *temporal* prince or king, in what sense art thou a king? Jesus now answers explicitly and positively, that he was born and came into the world that he should bear witness to the truth, and all who are of the truth are his obedient subjects. He does not in express terms assert the abrogation of the Mosaic law as the design and effect of his mission. But he denies that he is the national King of the Jews, or of any other people (v. 36). And yet he most explicitly asserts his *moral dominion* over all men, Jews and Gentiles; and that in this respect therefore, he is the King of the Jews. Can it be supposable that Christ should thus declare, that for this end he was born, and for this cause he came into the world, to assume this absolute moral dominion over the Jewish nation as also over every other nation, without the fullest conviction and most distinct recognition in his own mind that the Jewish theocracy—the Mosaic law—was soon to pass away? Did not Christ know that when his work as a teacher of truth, or rather the whole work of his mission should be

finished, as it was in his sacrifice on the cross, that the national government given to Israel by Moses would come to its end—its consummation—and he himself should reign king in Zion, the sole King of Israel? And further still, did not the instructions which he gave to the Jews concerning himself as their Messiah, so disclose the design of his mission and the nature of his work as the sum and consummation of all God's previous revelations, and especially as superseding the Mosaic law, that denial or doubt was possible only to willful ignorance and perverseness?

8. (Luke, xxiv. 44, 45.) "And he said unto them, These are the words which I spake unto you, while I was yet with you, that all things must be fulfilled which were written in the law of Moses, and in the prophets, and in the psalms, concerning me. Then opened he their understandings, that they might understand the Scriptures." In verse 27, we read,—"And beginning at Moses," &c., "he explained unto them in all the Scriptures the things concerning himself." We learn from Acts, i. 3, that in this conversation our Lord spoke to his apostles "of the things concerning the kingdom of God." In the passage now cited we learn that he told them as he had done before, that all things written in the Pentateuch or law of Moses, as well as in the other Scriptures, concerning him, must be fulfilled; and that he explained what was written to their just apprehension. Of course, he must have taught them substantially, all which was written concerning him in the Pentateuch or law of Moses. He must have explained the first great promise of redemption (Gen. iii. 15), the nature and design of Abel's acceptable sacrifice, and of the sacrifices offered by Noah, and especially that of Abraham in offering Isaac; he must have unfolded the Abrahamic covenant with its promise to Abraham, 'in thy seed shall all nations be blessed,' together with that prediction concerning Shiloh (Gen. xlix. 10), so exactly and wonderfully accomplished in the final issue of intervening centuries with all their revolutions and changes. (Compare Deut. xviii. 8, and John, v. 46.) What is more directly to our present purpose, he must have developed with equal fullness the Jewish theocracy or national government of Israel—the law given by Moses, in its nature, design, and end—in all its prominent relations and characteristics, and of course, in accordance with the more explicit and full de-

velopments made by his apostles in their subsequent writings. The resurrection of Christ seems to have removed all their lingering doubts of his Messiahship, and to have resulted in that docility of spirit, which with all the means that we have seen, they possessed as Jews, of understanding the grand, ulterior, though indirect design of their national government, would render them apt scholars under his present instructions. Nor can it be reasonably doubted, that in the conversations which he had with them during the forty days between his resurrection and ascension, in which he so instructed them from their own Scriptures, he gave to them some just and adequate comprehension of the import of these writings. It was evidently from this source that he drew his instructions as we may say, exclusively, "speaking of the things pertaining to the kingdom of God" (Acts, i. 3), and saying when opening their understandings, that they might understand the Scriptures, "Thus it is written, and thus it behooved Christ to suffer" (Luke, xxiv. 45, 46). They seem indeed, probably from his direction to them not to depart from Jerusalem but to wait for the promise (in John, xvi. 8), to have inferred that the entire Jewish nation would receive him as their Messiah, shake off the Roman yoke, and perhaps suddenly rise to universal dominion. To their inquiry on this subject, our Lord's answer (v. 7) clearly intimates that substantially but not circumstantially, what they spoke of should come to pass—even a kingdom for Israel. It was not indeed, to come to pass immediately, nor for them to know the times and seasons which the Father had reserved to himself for the accomplishment of his great design, to give them as he had said, the kingdom. But this was to be accomplished in a way suited to its own nature, not as a *temporal* but as a moral or spiritual kingdom; for he assured them that they were to receive power in respect to the setting up and establishment of this kingdom, after the Holy Ghost should qualify them for their work, *as witnesses for him*, both in Jerusalem, and in all Judea, and in Samaria, and unto the uttermost parts of the earth. How strikingly adapted was this answer to correct their circumstantial and imaginary mistakes, and to exhibit to their minds just views of the symbolical and evanescent characteristic of their national law, and of the spiritual nature as well as of the permanent and universal extension of the kingdom of their Messiah! Compare Luke, ii. 30, *sqq.;* Luke, xxiii. 43; John, iv. 25, as showing that, to a limited extent, just views on this subject actually existed; and also Luke, xvii. 20, 21, and John, xviii. 36–38, showing that Christ actually approved and justified these views.

I only add on this particular part of the subject, that Christ in his personal instructions, not only never taught that the national law of the Jews was in any respect *a moral* institution or sustained any moral relation to that people whatsoever; but, on the contrary, always implied, in what he said of it, that it was not *a moral*, but a merely *positive* institution. Proceeding on this assumption, he ever distinguished it from, and contrasted it with God's moral system; and thus as a teacher of true religious ethics, he ever presented himself as inculcating spiritual morality—the religion of the heart. In proof of this, it is quite sufficient to read the severe and even terrible rebukes which he administered to the scribes and Pharisees: while conceding without qualification, that they outwardly appeared righteous to men, he at the same time charged them with being full of hypocrisy and iniquity. If he spoke of the obligation to tithe mint, anise, and cummin, or of the external acts of judgment, mercy, and faith, it was not of the *moral obligation*, as implying their *moral* quality, but merely their *fitness or rightness to the particular ends* of such action. Or if he reproved for the omission or commission of external doings, it was not for their *moral quality*, but simply as *proofs* of the morally wrong or the want of the morally right state of the heart. (Vide Matt. xxiii. 1–33.) He never approved or commended *in a moral regard*, any subordinate action as such, nor only as a complex act involving morally right principle; nor disapproved or condemned subordinate action as such nor only as a complex act involving morally wrong principle. He always, and in all things, inculcated morally right principle, and condemned the want of it as involving the morally wrong principle. How remote was such a standard of morals from that of the scribes and Pharisees, and of the people generally, whom he instructed! How fitted to show them that unless their righteousness consisted of something more than the mere criterion of obedience to their national law, they could in no case meet with God's acceptance as a moral governor; that through the perversion of their national law, they defeated its ulterior and grand design in their moral reformation, and hence it was important and probable that the national system thus perverted and abused, was to be displaced by that spiritual kingdom or reign of God, which he as their Messiah so plainly taught, that he came into the world to establish!

LECTURE VI.

THE MOSAIC LAW A THEOCRACY.

The views of Paul in respect to this system.—The premises from which he argued familiar to him and to the Jews: Rom. i. 17, 18; ii. 1, 2; ii. 20; iii. 21; vii. 3–6; Gal. iii. 16, *sqq.*; Eph. ii. 15; Col. ii. 14.—The Epistle to the Hebrews.

HAVING attempted to show by various considerations, that the Mosaic law was a theocracy, I propose also to unfold the views of the apostle Paul on the subject.

We shall see if I mistake not, that the apostle, as a Jew reasoning with Jews, derived his great, not to say all his arguments, in support of the doctrine of one common method or way of justification before God for all men—in support of the Gospel in its great and essential truths, or God's moral government through grace over this sinful world—from the great facts of the Jewish theocracy or the law given by Moses, in connection with other known and familiar facts of the Jewish revelation. We shall further see that he derived them from the same great facts from which, as I claim to have shown in the preceding discussion, the Jews, from the beginning to the end of their theocracy, ought to have derived the same, and would, aside from their almost incredible perverseness, their idolatrous degradation and stolidity, have actually derived them, and so have come to the same momentous conclusions with the apostle.

If these things shall appear from the epistles of Paul, then it will also be seen, not only what abundant instruction God furnished to men in the earliest ages of the world, especially by the Abrahamic covenant, but how this instruction, without withdrawing one ray of the light of revealed truth already given, was signally and impressively augmented by that theocracy in which God became the national king and tutelary deity of Israel. We shall further see how the great apostle of the Gentiles, in fully unfolding by revelation God's system for the salvation of a lost world, relied not on any merely legal system and its principles, but on a system modified by grace. Since man's apostasy in Eden there had been no such law, either moral or political, not even in any heathen nation. Nor of course did the apostle reason as theologians have commonly done, on the assumption that any of our race, much less that all of them are finally condemned for sin as the transgression of law as distinguished from unbelief. Nor yet, for the accomplishment of his purpose, did he rely simply nor even chiefly, on his authority as an inspired teacher, but on the Jewish theocracy and the known facts of the Jewish revelation. As Luke tells us (Acts, xvii. 2, 3), "Paul, as *his manner* was, went in unto them (the Jews), and three Sabbath-days reasoned with them out of the Scriptures, opening and alleging (*παρατιθέμενος*, fully evincing) that Christ must needs have suffered," &c. This mode of reasoning was, on this occasion, in a degree successful, as it was, after the close of the apostle's labors, eminently triumphant. Judaism and Christianity, in the time of this apostle, were in active conflict. A crisis had come in which one or the other must triumph. And now in the Jewish theocracy itself (with an occasional, and for some subsidiary purposes, a necessary reliance on the light of nature), our apostle finds his chief citadel of defense against every assault on the truth by Jewish ingenuity. From this also he takes his brightest armor and most effective weapons of onset on Jewish error and perverseness, even almost his whole equipment for victory in that conflict, which was to overthrow Judaism and to subdue all nations to the obedience of faith.

I cannot here pretend to refer to all the proofs and illustrations of the view now given which are contained in the writings of this apostle, but only to some of them, which must, I think, be satisfactory to any one who will even slightly examine the subject. Indeed, I shall confine myself chiefly to those facts respecting the Mosaic law to which I have before referred, as these are employed by the apostle in his reasonings with Jews, especially as these will show that the Jews had the same means of coming, and were therefore bound to have come, to the same great conclusion respecting justification with the apostle. And here it may be well briefly to advert to some instances in which the apostle makes a simple appeal to the authority of the Old Testament in support of his doctrine. In some of these, it is true, he appeals to the later prophets;

but then not on the hypothesis that a later and new revelation of the doctrine was made to them, as many are apt to suppose. For there is not only no intimation of such a fact, but as we shall see, he appeals to the Pentateuch and even to the decalogue, which shows that he did not consider the later prophets as acquiring new knowledge on the subject by any *new and special* revelation made to them, but only by more justly interpreting and more fully understanding the revelation by Moses.

(Rom. i. 17.) "For I am not ashamed of the Gospel of Christ," &c. Here he affirms that "the Gospel is the power of God to salvation, &c.—*to the Jew first.*" How to the Jew first? Plainly as first revealed to Jews not by the preaching of Christ, but in their own Scriptures; for he adds that therein, i. e., in the Gospel, "the righteousness of God by faith—the ground of justification by faith (ἐκ πίστεως), which is of God's providing, is revealed (εἰς πίστιν) to faith, as it is written, The righteous by faith (ἐκ πίστεως) shall live."* Here then, in the beginning of this epistle, he affirms the fact by no means unimportant to his purpose, that the Gospel was first revealed to the Jews in their own Scriptures.

(Verse 18.) "For the wrath of God is revealed from heaven against all ungodliness and unrighteousness of men, who hold the truth in unrighteousness." Here the kind of revelation spoken of is evidently the same as that in v. 17. The revelation of the one fact (v. 17) is based on the revelation of the other (v. 18). The *revelation* of the truth spoken of in the New Testament is, for the most part, supernatural revelation. Thus, the apostle not only asserts that the doctrine of justification by faith, now fully revealed in the Gospel, was first taught the Jew in his revelation, but also that the wrath of God was revealed in the same as the original basis for the doctrine of gratuitous justification.

By "the wrath of God revealed from heaven," we are not to understand *temporal* death, for to this, simply as such, the righteous by faith were hopelessly doomed (Gen. iii. 19). Indeed, to them it is "gain" (Phil. i. 21). But the wrath spoken of is the penalty of sin—the full expression of God's anger against sin—that *eternal death* which is the wages of sin (chap. vi. 23). This is the wrath of God, revealed in the Jewish

* The ἐκ πίστεως in the last clause so plainly denotes *by faith*, that I wonder, with Doddridge, that it should have been translated differently in the former.

Scriptures and in the Gospel, "against all ungodliness and unrighteousness of men," of all men "who (as a universal characteristic of determined sin, John, iii. 20) hold the truth in unrighteousness." The meaning plainly is, that they know the truth sufficiently as the basis of *moral* responsibility, but *practically* disregard it. Refusing reflection, they practically place the truth known in utter abeyance. Shutting away from the mind the full discernment of the practical relations of truth because they dislike them, they thus yield themselves to the control of their selfish and sordid inclinations with as little disturbance as may be, fostering their mental quiet by such false speculations, groundless convictions, and vain hopes, as only evince their willful ignorance as opposed to thorough *reflective* knowledge, and their mad desperation in sin.* I need not say how explicitly this meaning of *τῶν τὴν αλήθειαν ἐν αδικίᾳ κατεχόντων* is shown in the following context. Thus the apostle, that he may convince the Jews of the clear manifestation in their own revelation of God's wrath toward the wickedness of all mankind (vide his proofs derived from the Scriptures, chap. iii. 10, *sqq.*), proceeds to confirm the fact in that respect in which Jews might question or deny it (viz., in respect to Gentiles), by appealing to such flagrant and notorious wickedness on their part as no Jew could deny, and which rendered them worthy of the wrath which the Scriptures revealed in common against all, both Jews and Gentiles. With this digression, it is still apparent that he makes the Scriptures, God's revelation, the ulterior ground of his argument in placing Jews and Gentiles on a common level, as sinners justly exposed to the wrath of God.

(Rom. ii. 1, 2.) "Therefore thou art inexcusable, O man, whosoever thou art, that judgest; for wherein thou judgest another, thou condemnest thyself, for thou that judgest doest the same things. But we are sure," &c.

We shall now see how the apostle in this verse, and in the following context to v. 17, continues his appeal to the Jewish revelation, in support of his views and principles concerning the final judgment.

In the passage now under consideration, his reliance on this revelation for his argument is obvious. As if he said, If the

* Since writing the above, I am gratified to find, from Tholuck, that Chrysostom gives the same interpretation as I do to the clause (v. 18) under consideration.

Gentiles under the light of nature are as you judge them to be in view of their flagrant wickedness wholly inexcusable and worthy of death the penalty of sin, you cannot be less so under your own revelation from God. In judging them therefore, you condemn yourselves; for you do the same things. You must therefore, in your view, be under the curse of your own law. To enforce the argument he adds, 'And we know that the sentence of God, in accordance with this law, is according to truth upon them which commit such things.'* Thus the apostle, in this argument with Jews respecting the final judgment, appeals to and relies on their own revelation. And to place this view of his argument beyond all doubt, he distinguishes (v. 3) their common judgment of the Gentiles and of themselves from the sentence of God. As if he had said, If you cannot escape your own judgment of self-condemnation, how can you escape "the sentence of God?" He then proceeds (v. 4, *sqq.*) to expostulate with them for the vain and presumptuous thought, that those thus exposed to this sentence of God at the final judgment, should escape it, while despising the only hope of so doing, furnished by the riches of his goodness and forbearance and long-suffering, "not knowing," &c. —should thus go on 'treasuring up wrath against the day of wrath, and revelation of the righteous judgment of God who will render to every man according to his deeds'—good, in perfect and eternal blessedness to them that do good, and evil, as the full expression of his wrath for sin, to them that do evil. Thus then the apostle unfolds and affirms in this argument with the Jews, on the authority of their own revelation, the fact of the last judgment with its great and eternal issues.

On the same authority he still proceeds in his reasoning, still showing that his argument is a Jewish argument. In v. 11 he asserts the absolute impartiality and perfect justice of God in his treatment of sinners whether Jews or Gentiles, according to the great principle of judgment already specified (v. 6). In verses 12, 13, he still recognizes the same rule of judgment, affirming that as many as have sinned (i. e., shall be found on the day of account to be *sinners* as distinguished from *saints*) without a revelation, shall perish without a revelation; and as

* No Jew would ever, as some suppose the apostle does in this case, call any decision of reason or conscience, "*the sentence of God,*" except a sentence of *revealed* law.

many as shall be found on that day to be sinners in the same sense (for such only can be the true meaning of his language), under revelation, shall be judged (condemned) by revelation. He then adds, in obvious rebuke of the Jews, and giving greater precision and particularity to his meaning, to convince them of their entire practical deficiency, that "not the hearers of the law (τοῦ νόμου) are just before God, but the doers of the law (τοῦ νόμου) shall be justified." By "the doers of the law" he must mean those described in verses 7 and 10 (vide James, i. 21, 22), i. e., he must mean those who obey the revealed rule of judgment. He can mean no other, especially in view of the absolute form of his language, "shall be justified." By thus using *the article* in this verse, he shuts the word *law* down to a particularity of meaning which it had not in v. 12, and thus administers a most pointed rebuke to the Jews for their entire disobedience to their own law. And now as he proceeds, he still presents the same authority of *revelation* as the only rule of judgment for all men. Thus in verses 14, 15, by asserting that when the Gentiles do by nature substantially the same things to obtain acceptance with God which are required by revelation, they show that substantially the same rule of judgment is written on their hearts—he says in other words, that they know substantially the same "work" to be necessary to justification before God, which is required for this purpose by the Jewish law. Thus the apostle again shows his Jewish readers contrary to their preconceived opinion respecting Gentiles, that there is but one and the same rule of judgment for all men, viz., that which is prescribed on the authority of their own revelation.

But I now come to the main question: *What warrant had the apostle thus to derive his argument from the Jewish revelation, and what reason had the Jews to admit its conclusiveness?* The manner of the apostle shows that he had no suspicion that the validity of his reasoning would be questioned, nor indeed was it—at least there was no question raised respecting its validity. But had the Jewish revelation—either the Abrahamic covenant or the national law given by Moses—in plain and express terms presented or authorized this view of the final judgment? This will not be pretended. What warrant then had the apostle for this argument from the Jewish revelation, for requiring or even expecting the Jews to receive it? Is it said that this knowledge of that revelation was now for the first time imparted to Paul by a new and special revelation to *him?* Be it so. Then the force of his argument depended wholly on the fact that such new revelation was made *to him*, and on his own authority as an inspired teacher, and not at all, even in the slightest degree, on the Jewish revelation as made to the Jews. How preposterous! He reasons *ex concessis*, from what had not been conceded. He reasons from a fact as made known to those with whom he reasons, when it had only now been made known for the first time to himself! His argument therefore for aught that appears, was entirely groundless and illusory—one which he had no warrant to make, and the Jews no warrant to receive. And yet he makes it, as if, when plainly presented to popular conviction and consideration, it would not and could not be questioned. What then shall we say—what can be said—to vindicate the apostle in this mode of reasoning? What, except that the revelation made to the Jews, especially that part of it which consisted of their national law—their law given by Moses—was A REPRESENTATIVE SYSTEM of government, as already explained, a fact which, though speculatively and practically overlooked and disregarded by the Jewish nation, was still so well known to any one who would honestly reflect on their own history, that it need but to be stated to shut off denial, and actually to convince and silence every adversary. Who in view of the apostle's reasoning, can, notwithstanding all the perverseness, and error, and suppression of the truth on the part of the Jews, entertain a doubt that the Jewish theocracy was a symbolical system of government, divinely designed and adapted to unfold God's moral government over men through grace, in its nature, mode, progress of administration, its principles of adjudication, and also in its final issues on the judgment-day?

(Rom. ii. 20.) "An instructor of the foolish, a teacher of babes, having the form of knowledge and of the truth in the law" (ἐν τῷ νόμῳ). In this verse the apostle, in my view, expressly asserts that characteristic of the law which I maintain. In v. 17 he says, "Behold thou art called *a Jew*"—one having that revelation from God which we call the national law, given to Israel by Moses. I claim the word νόμος is used by the apostle in verses 17, 18, 20, to denote this national law. The question now is, what is the meaning of the apostle's assertion that the proud and boasting Jew has τὴν μόρφωσιν τῆς γνώσεω; καὶ τῆς ἀληθείας ἐν τῷ νόμῳ? The word μόρφωσιν denotes an *image—a representation;* in one connection it denotes *semblance* without that which is real (2 Tim. iii. 5), and in another a correct representation of what is real, as the verb in Gal. iv. 19. Now it cannot be supposed, that the pride and boasting of the Jew respected what he *himself regarded* as the mere semblance of knowledge and of the truth, and still less that the apostle meant to say that the Jew *in the law* which God had given him, possessed nothing but a mere semblance of what was not real. What then can be the meaning of the apostle, except that the Jew, in the national law which God had given him, possessed the correct representation of knowledge and of the truth on the great subject of God's moral government, of which the apostle was treating. This meaning not only accords with what, as we have seen, the apostle had before assumed as the characteristic of this law, but gives great point and force to his rebuke of the Jew for his vain boasting and formality in respect to true religion and morality. As if he said, You claim to be superior to all others because you are a Jew; to be their guide, instructor, teacher, because God has given you your national law, regarding this *merely representative system* as imparting all truth which need be known, demanding a mere ritual service as constituting on your own part and on the part of others, the substance of all virtue and true religion—even that righteousness of law which commends you to God's everlasting favor and friendship. And what is the practical effect of all this pretension and pride? Just what is to be expected. You who teach another, teach not yourself. You who preach that a man should not steal, steal yourself. You who say a man should not commit adultery, yourself commit adultery. Thus by perversely overlooking the representative character of your national law and the moral system represented by it, you rest on what you consider a complete legal righteousness while breaking your own law, dishonoring God, and even causing his name to be blasphemed among the Gentiles (verses 23, 24). Thus the apostle, in this part of his argument, is led expressly to assert *the representative* character of the national law given by Moses, that he may the more fully expose Jewish error by showing its origin in mistaken and false views of this law. In confirmation of this view of his course of thought, he pursues the same in the following part of the chapter, passing from the decalogue to circumcision—telling the Jews, for the correction of their error, what circumcision is in its essential nature; what it is in substance instead of the shadow, i. e., *what it represents*, this being *all that it is* of any real moment, viz., the circumcision of the heart, in the spirit and *not* in the letter, whose praise is not *from men* but from God. The represented reality of which it is the sign or seal is "the righteousness of faith" (Rom. iv. 11). Thus the apostle as it were, constantly establishes the truth of his great doctrine of justification by faith in the sight of God on the final day, by appealing to acknowledged *Jewish authority*—to the law given by Moses.

I might greatly multiply these general forms of proof, that the apostle rested his great argument for the leading doctrine of this epistle on what he calls ὁ νόμος—the national law of the Jews, or rather its requirement for justification, as *representing* God's rule of judgment under his higher system of moral government. (Vide Rom. iii. 2 and 7; iii. 21; iv. 6; vii. 1, *sqq.;* ix. 33; x. 11; xi. 25.) I deem it necessary here only to ask what force or even plausibility, can pertain to this argument, unless this national law was in truth designed by God, its author, to be a *representative* system, and ought therefore ever to have been regarded by the Jews as such; and therefore, when justly interpreted in connection with the great and familiar facts of their own history, as being in its pre-eminent characteristic an exhibition of God's higher system of moral government through grace—the Gospel—the covenant made with Abraham. Thus, while there is no pretense that the Mosaic law, directly or expressly, taught any thing on the subject of man's justification before God, the apostle in this epistle to the Romans, compelled the Jews to see and know (what some of the later prophets substantially saw and knew from the same source) that their own national law, the theocracy of Israel, indirectly, but *very clearly and impressively*, taught the same great doctrine of justification before God—the same Gospel which he preached.

I shall now, in accordance with what I have said in introducing the present argument, proceed to show in what manner Paul used the national law or theocracy of Israel, and particularly its recent origin, its temporary duration, its representative character, its design, and other striking peculiarities of it as a national system, to establish the truth and unfold the import of the Gospel which he so triumphantly defended and maintained.

The first of a particular class of passages to which I refer, is Rom. iii. 21: 'But now the righteousness of God without law is manifested, being witnessed by the law and the prophets.' This is one of the most striking and decisive passages in which the apostle places in the strongest light, the ground of justification of God's providing—without law (χωρὶς νόμου), without legal righteousness, in opposition to the ground of a legal justification. (Compare v. 20 and context.) But he expressly asserts generally, that this righteousness of God without law, which is wholly of God's providing, is witnessed by *the* law (ὑπὸ τοῦ νόμου) and the prophets; but the logical connection in v. 25, *sqq.*—his language being taken from the Jewish ritual and applied to Christ—shows that he considered, and meant his readers should believe, that that part of the Jewish revelation, or of the Mosaic law, which ordained liberty by a ransom, and by a mercy-seat or propitiatory sacrifice, revealed or taught *in some mode*—witnessed—the righteousness of God by faith as the ground of man's justification before God. But how could the apostle say, or Jews be authorized to believe, that this particular part of the Mosaic or national law revealed this doctrine of the righteousness of God by faith, unless they viewed, and were authorized to view, this national law as a *representative* system? Every one must see how exclusively the apostle derives his doctrine of justification by faith, without deeds of law, from the Mosaic law; not indeed a *national* justification which is all that as a national law it could give or *directly* teach, but a justification before God for men as moral beings; for it is by proving the latter, and surely not by proving the former, that he infers (v. 29) that he is not the "God of the Jews only, but of the Gentiles also." The apostle has derived the doctrine not merely from the law and the prophets, but from that part of revelation called the Mosaic law—the *civil* or *national* law of Israel, even from the *ritual* or *ceremonial* part of it—by which God instituted *propitiatory offerings or sacrifices* for national sin. In no other meaning could an honest Jew understand the passage, Rom. vii. 3, 4, 5, 6. It is undeniable that what he calls *the law* (ὁ νόμος), in vs. 4,

5, 6, is the Mosaic law, or national law, which God gave to Israel, for there was no other law which the apostle could have called *the law* (ὁ νόμος), and have said that the Jews were freed from it, as the woman is freed from the law of her husband when he is dead, or that they had become dead to it by the body of Christ, or that the motions of sins by it did work in our members to bring forth sin unto death, or that the Jews were delivered from it as a dead law. What can be made of this language of the apostle, if he did not mean that the Mosaic law was a temporary institution which had now come to its end? How did he know this in respect to this law? In *words*, its author had not given it this character in the Old Testament. How then could the apostle know what he affirms of it to be true, unless he knew it to be a national law—a theocracy—and as such, *a representative* system now dead, or done away by the accomplishment of what it represented?

I might advert, in confirmation of the present view of the Mosaic law, to other passages in this epistle. I propose, however, to consider some of the prominent, and to me peculiarly forcible passages on the subject in some other epistles of the same apostle.

(Gal. iii. 16, to the end of the chapter.)—"Now to Abraham and his seed were the promises made," &c. Without fully commenting on this passage, I deem it sufficient to say, that the apostle clearly teaches the following important truths: that the covenant made with Abraham was the Gospel (v. 8); that it contained the promises of all the real good which God, since the apostasy, has ever made or could make to man (Rom. viii. 28, 31, 32; 1 Cor. iii. 21, 23); that these promises (what the apostle so often and emphatically calls "the promise" and "the promises") were not made directly, but only *indirectly* or *representatively*, by the Mosaic law, and were made to none as binding to their actual fulfillment or the conferring of one real blessing, except to Christ and to those who as being Christ's by faith, were Abraham's seed (vs. 28, 29), so that God never promised, either in the Abrahamic covenant or in the Mosaic law, that he would not cast out of his favor, at any moment, the *natural* as distinguished from the *spiritual* seed of Abraham; and further, that the covenant made with Abraham was no other than the perfect moral government of God, established and administered over all men in every essential respect,

—being substantially what the apostle calls it, the Gospel; that this perfect moral government, this institution (δίαθήκη), which was before confirmed of God in Christ, the Mosaic law, which was four hundred and thirty years after, must have left unchanged in its full force and absolute perfection, and that this law was not added as a part of the Abrahamic covenant, but was introduced because of transgressions, as a temporary appendage, till the seed should come to whom the promise was made. Can it then be supposed that what the apostle calls "the law" was an essential part, or even any part, of God's moral government over men as moral beings? Did this law in any respect change this unchangeable and perfect system, either by taking any thing from it, or adding any thing to it? Did God, after having given Israel a perfect moral government through grace, change this government, by giving them, several hundred years afterwards a *civil* government? The chief, not to say the only *direct* reason for giving them this national government, was according to the apostle, because of transgression; that is, the object was to restrain idolatry as an overt crime with other overt crimes and abominations resulting from it, which in their prevalence and influence had become fatal to the *moral* reformation of this people. By this method idolatry was made a *civil offense*, even *treason*, against the *national* king of Israel. It thus became punishable, and was actually punished, as some other overt crimes were, simply as *a civil* offense, with temporal death as a civil penalty. Such a law, or any number of such laws, could no more add aught to, or take aught from, God's perfect moral government over men as moral beings, than could a similar law with a civil penalty enacted by this State against intemperance or theft, change God's moral government over us as moral beings. Whatever *direct*, useful effects to the State might then be aimed at or accomplished by the Mosaic law, or whatever *indirect* useful effects preparatory to bringing the idolatrous people to submit with the heart to the moral government of God, still God's perfect system of moral government through grace, confirmed before of God in Christ, in its perfect rule of action, in its rule of judgment, in all its particular moral precepts, in all its exceeding great and precious promises, and in its fearful penalty, remained unchangeable and unchanged in its glory.

In the 23d verse and onward, the apostle unfolds a further but an indirect design of the Mosaic law, with the reason of its continuance until the way of justification by faith should be more fully revealed. This design was, that as a schoolmaster, a conductor of children, it might bring the Jewish nation to Christ, to be justified not by the law but by faith. He then asserts that after faith is come, after this full revelation is made, the Jews are no longer under a schoolmaster. Thus the Mosaic law—the law which was four hundred and thirty years after the covenant made with Abraham—wholly ceased on the full introduction of the Gospel. Nor was this law, as many have supposed, the ceremonial or ritual part of the law. It was the whole law given by Moses, after the lapse of the four hundred and thirty years specified by the apostle. It was the Mosaic law, the entire national law of the Jews, or the Jewish theocracy. It was this as distinguished from that everlasting covenant which God made with Abraham, or from that system of moral government which God administers through Christ, under an economy of grace over all men. It was that covenant which God made with the fathers, when he took them by the hand to lead them out of the land of Egypt, because they kept not *the better* covenant which was established on better promises. It was that covenant which, instead of being faultless and so superseding the better covenant, was in no substantial respect according to, but essentially diverse from that better covenant, and which God by his prophet promised not to *make*, but to *finish* or *complete* with the house of Israel and the house of Judah, in writing his laws in their hearts, and remembering their sins and iniquities no more. But the Mosaic law contained no promise, and revealed no purpose of renewing or sanctifying grace, nor contained the least provision or ground for the forgiveness of the sin of the heart. In respect to sin in this high sense, whatever provisions it made for the sanctifying of the flesh or the pardon of civil offenses, it left the perfect law of God's moral government over men as the true and only criterion of such sin, and as both a rule of action and also of judgment in its full force and application, without one ray of hope of deliverance for the transgressor from its fearful and endless penalty. It had revealed God's abundant mercy for the penitent transgressor of its rule of action as a national or civil system, while it revealed nothing of God in his high relation of the moral governor of men, except as a *representative* system. However momentous, clear, abundant, convincing, were its instructions to every unperverted mind in its representative character, it was as a national system, utterly barren of all instruction in respect to the higher relations between man and his Maker. It could not give eternal life—in this respect it was weak and profitless; it could not make him who performed its services perfect, as pertaining to the conscience; it was pre-eminently, not to say *only*, a system of *positive* institutions (δόγματα);* it was imposed only *until* the time of reformation, it therefore waxed old, decayed, and vanished away.

Eph. ii. 15, next claims consideration. "Having abolished in his flesh the enmity, even the law of commandments in ordinances." Here the question to be answered is, *what is the law of commandments in ordinances* (τὸν νόμον τῶν ἐντολῶν ἐν δόγμασι)? As a somewhat general answer to this inquiry, I should say that the apostle means "the revealed law of requirements in positive precepts." I have already said enough to show what I mean by *positive* precepts, especially as they are in a peculiar respect arbitrary, circumstantial, and changeable. Nor do I suppose there is any room for the question according to New Testament usage, whether such is the meaning of the word δόγμασι in the present case. To this so far as I know, respectable commentators assent. But another question arises on which they are not so well agreed, viz., what are the requirements or commandments of the Mosaic law, or of the Jewish theocracy or national government of Israel, which are *positive* in distinction from *moral*? I answer, each and all so far forth as they were national or civil requirements, or sustained this relation. Even what our Saviour calls the first and great commandment of the law, and the second which he says is like unto it, and also that requirement of repentance or faith which was the rule of judgment, were as truly *civil* or *national* requirements as any other. I do not say that they were nothing more. I simply affirm that they were requirements of the national law of Israel—principles sustaining *civil relations*, de-

* Even the requirement of a spirit of loyalty to God, as *national king* of Israel, was a circumstantial temporary requirement, arising from circumstances and ceasing with a change of circumstances. It was, therefore, a *positive* precept or requirement—a *dogma*.

pending solely as such on the relation of God as their national king. If it here be said that these rules of action and many others, e. g., those of the decalogue, were *in their very nature* moral requirements—I admit and maintain most strenuously that they were *moral* requirements *in their very nature*, as their nature was *related to men as moral beings*. At the same time I also maintain that they were civil or national requirements, given by God as the national king of Israel, and this *in their very nature* as they *related to that people* as subjects of his civil government. They were civil requirements *in their very nature* in respect to that people, when given by God as their national king, though they are not and never have been such in respect to any other people—as much civil requirements in one relation of their nature, as they were moral requirements in another relation of their nature. But as civil or national requirements, given by God to the people of Israel, they were *positive* requirements, arbitrary, circumstantial, changeable, as changeable circumstances may change. Thus the whole Mosaic law or Jewish theocracy or national law of Israel, was, as such, a revealed system of requirements, consisting of *δόγματα*. It was *τὸν νόμον τῶν ἐντολῶν ἐν δόγμασι*, a revealed system, which in its requirements consisted wholly of *positive* precepts. This view of the apostle's meaning appears to be decisively established by the logical connection. In the preceding verses (13, 14), the apostle tells the Gentile converts at Ephesus, that "now in Christ Jesus ye who were once far off are made nigh by the blood of Christ; for he is our peace who hath made both one, and hath broken down the middle wall of partition between us;" and proceeds thus (v. 15), 'having abolished in (by means of) his flesh the law of commandments, *consisting of positive requirements*.' Now can there be a doubt that the Mosaic law, as the national law of the Jews, was that which separated them from all other nations? What else made the people of Israel so peculiarly and exclusively as they were, the people of God? Were not the moral law of God as a perfect rule of action, and the covenant with Abraham, the Gospel as the rule of final judgment, common alike to both Jews and Gentiles? Was there nothing in the Mosaic law but its ordinances respecting *rites and ceremonies*, by which it distinguished and separated Jews and Gentiles? What then were the municipal requirements of this system, every one of which, as resting on every Israelite, required of him what it did not require of any other human being—a spirit of loyalty to the true God as a national ruler—and was enforced on him as it was not on any other human being and never has been, through a civil process by sanctions of *temporal* good and evil? Plainly it was the Mosaic law—this law of the Jewish theocracy as a national or civil law which was the middle wall of partition between Jews and Gentiles, which absolutely shut off the latter from all its immunities, its peculiar obligations, its worship of God as the tutelary deity of Israel in the temple at Jerusalem, its promises of national prosperity by his miraculous providence, its reflected light as revealing God's higher system of law and grace for men, as moral and immortal beings—this law, this national law given to Israel as a single nation, so necessary to introduce into even one small spot of earth the knowledge of the true God, and gradually to unvail his glories as the God of grace and salvation to a lost world, was that wall of partition rising as it were to heaven between Jews and Gentiles—this national law of commandments, consisting as such simply of *positive*, i. e., of arbitrary and circumstantial, requirements, Christ by his atoning sacrifice has abolished, that he might make in himself of twain one new man, and reconcile both unto God in one body by the cross.

(Col. ii. 14.) "Blotting out the hand-writing of ordinances (*χειρόγραφον τοῖς δόγμασιν*) that was against us, which was contrary to us, and taken it out of the way, nailing it to his cross." So far as the mere words of this passage are concerned, I deem it quite unnecessary, after what I have said on Eph. ii. 15, to show that the apostle here asserts that the Mosaic law—the hand-writing graven on the tables of stone included—is blotted out, taken away (*ἐκ τοῦ μέσου*), from between Jews and Gentiles.* The interpretation of this text now given is confirmed especially by the following context. To spoil (*απεκδύειν*), is to take spoil as from a conquered enemy, or *divest thoroughly*. To make a show openly (*δειγματίζειν*), is to expose to just reproach. The question now is, who are the *τας ἀρχὰς, καὶ τὰς ἐξουσίας*, the rulers and authorities? Plainly those who, by defending the Jewish institutions—the Mosaic law—of which

* I think it may be easily shown that the word *δόγμα*, in such a connection as the present, always denotes *a royal mandate*, or a *positive*, arbitrary enactment, or decree, of civil authority.

the apostle is speaking, had chiefly hindered the progress of Christianity. Christ, by his death, resurrection, and ascension, effectually baffled the designs and overthrew the power of the Jewish rulers and priests, and publicly exposed these enemies of true religion to the reproach they merited, in the triumphs of the Gospel. In view of these facts—the blotting out of the hand-writing in ordinances, and the full and complete victory of Christ over its powerful and malignant defenders—the apostle derives his practical inference (v. 16), "Let no man therefore judge you in meat, or in drink, or in respect to a festival, or of a new moon, or of Sabbaths." Can we then suppose the apostle to exclude from what he calls the *χειρόγραφον τοῖς δόγμασιν*, the hand-writing on the two tables of stone—i. e., the decalogue or ten commandments—the hand-writing so emphatically called, being written by the very finger of God? Especially, can we suppose this when he has so explicitly asserted that these commandments are done away (2 Cor. iii. 11, 13)—a fact which had been wholly impossible had they not been *positive* requirements—and when also he calls the whole Mosaic law (Eph. ii. 15) the law of commandments (*ἐν δόγμασι*), in *positive* requirements? What can be more obvious than that the apostle thought of the same *subject* in these three cases—the Mosaic law, conceived of it as a national system of *positive* requirements, and as such done away in the coming and work of Christ? But it may be asked why, in this 16th verse, did he not say, Let no man judge you in respect to any part of this abolished law, instead of forbidding such judgments in respect to mere ritual service, as meats, drinks, &c.? I answer, because in respect to keeping the ten commandments there were none among the Judaizers to cast the first stone, or to complain of such delinquencies on the part of those to whom the apostle wrote. These Judaizers counted nothing delinquency in respect to the Mosaic law, except failure in ritual services. No other proscription of uncharitable judgment by the apostle, therefore, was called for, or could be even pertinent to the case. But it may be further said, that the apostle extends his prohibition beyond mere ritual services, as meats, drinks, festivals, and new moons, by the specification of *Sabbaths*, which shows that he had respect to the fourth commandment of the decalogue. But to this it may be replied, that there were other Sabbaths besides that of the fourth commandment, which were as truly merely ritual, festival days, as were the new moons and the others specified by the apostle; and we may suppose that these were the only Sabbaths in respect to which the Colossians were, for their non-observance, liable to censure from the Judaizers—so the apostle neither spoke of nor meant any other. The connection shows a much higher probability of this than that the apostle here includes under this term, *that Sabbath* which was not Jewish in its origin, but instituted when the work of creation was finished. Indeed, when the fact of such an institution is once admitted in respect to a Sabbath, it is incredible that Paul should refer to it in this passage, and place it on the same level with these merely Jewish ritual observances which were to perish with the using. Besides, let it be supposed that the apostle did refer to the Sabbath of the fourth commandment, so as actually to include, under the word *sabbaths*, the particular Sabbath in some respect, and that he says in respect to this precept what implies its abolition, and that Christians are not therefore to be judged or censured in respect to the non-observance of this Sabbath. What did, or could he mean? This is shown at once by the preceding context. For he was speaking *only*, as we have seen, of the dogmas—the *δόγματα*—the *positive precepts* of the Mosaic law, or of the law of the Jews. In saying then what he is now supposed to say, he must be understood to mean, *at most*, that the Sabbath of the fourth commandment considered as *a positive* precept of the *civil law* of the Jews, was abolished with its other *δόγματα*, and that therefore no man was to be censured or judged for not considering it as still in force in this character. He might have said the same thing of every other particular command of the decalogue (a fact involved in what he said generally concerning this civil law in v. 14, as also in 2 Cor. iii. 11, and Eph. ii. 15), had the same occasion occurred, or the same reason existed, in respect to any other particular command, which led him to say it in respect to this particular command. The time had come, when what was peculiarly Jewish in this command, e. g., the observance of *the seventh day* of the week, was no longer binding. This, at least in respect to the seventh day, was shown by the practice of the apostles and other Christians. The Judaizers at Colosse, therefore, would of course falsely insist that this was a plain and inexcusable violation of the Mosaic law, and Paul would of course be led to expose the error on the ground he had taken in v. 14, viz., that this law "was blotted out and taken away." This would be merely putting an end to *the civil obligation* to observe the Sabbath—a day of holy rest—which could no more lessen *the moral obligation* to observe it, than the same thing could lessen the moral obligation to obey the fifth or any other command of the decalogue, *the moral obligation* of no one of which can depend,nor ever did depend in the slightest degree on the Jewish civil law. On the question whether the fourth commandment is what is properly and truly called *a moral* precept, I shall only say, that in my view it can be shown as decisively to be such, by showing what is properly called its universal tendency, utility, and necessity to man's highest well-being, or to be the dictate of true virtuous benevolence, in the *universal* circumstances and condition of men, as can be any other moral precept by the only mode of showing it to be such.

I shall here briefly notice some remarks of McKnight in his notes on v. 14. He says, "that though these precepts (the decalogue) are all founded in the nature and reason of things, they are with sufficient propriety called δόγματα, an appellation which *denotes* precepts founded in the mere will of the lawgiver, because the penalty of death, with which they were sanctioned, depended on the will of God." It is plain that McKnight did not distinctly *apprehend* the very distinction, which he so justly states, between what have been called *moral* and *positive* precepts. For if these precepts of the decalogue "are founded in the nature and reason of things," and if this is the only nature or character of these precepts, then they are not "founded in the mere will of the lawgiver;" for such precepts, as we have seen, are circumstantial and changeable as circumstances change, while the former are immutable in all circumstances. Now, are these precepts *moral* only, or *positive* only, or are they in different relations? Both—plainly both. They are in their nature *moral*, contemplated in their relation to men as *moral beings*, and they are *positive* in their nature, contemplated in their relation to the people of Israel as subjects of God's civil government, or as citizens under a theocracy. In their former *relative* nature (for we have nothing to do with *absolute* nature, as strictly distinguished from *relative*) they are *moral;* in their latter *relative* nature they are *positive.* As such, they derive all their authority from the will of the law-giver in the peculiar circumstances in which they were given, and when these circumstances changed, they have been blotted out taken out of the way, so removing an otherwise insurmountable obstacle to the union of Jews and Gentiles in one body in Christ. Notwithstanding the error of McKnight in respect to the true distinction between the two characteristics of the precepts of the decalogue, a distinction in respect to which the minds of many other interpreters and theologians have been as confused as his, he was still compelled to adopt the true meaning of the apostle's language. He says: "It is evident that the law of Moses, in all its parts, is abolished and taken away. Consequently, that Christians are under no obligation to obey even the *moral* precepts of that law, *on account of their having been delivered to the Jews by Moses.*" Is it not strange that others should not see this as well as Dr. McKnight? For what is more undeniable than that these *moral* precepts were binding on all men as moral beings, with the full authority of God as their moral governor before the giving of the Mosaic law—an authority which could not be increased by a merely *civil* law given to Israel, nor diminished by the abolition of that law. We come next to—

THE EPISTLE TO THE HEBREWS.

After all that the apostle had written on the subject in his epistles, especially in those to the Romans and Galatians, most of the Jews still adhered to the Mosaic law with perverse obstinacy, while such were the plausible reasonings of the Judaizing teachers, as not only to prevent many of their countrymen from receiving Christianity, but to weaken the faith of those who had received it, and even to bring them near to apostasy. The apostle therefore found it necessary to write this epistle to the Hebrews, for the purpose of showing that the Gospel in all its substantial elements, was founded on God's former revelations to the fathers of the Jewish nation, and especially on the Mosaic law. To this law the Jews of his time cherished an unalterable attachment, and a consequent inveterate hostility to the Gospel. In the first sentence he unfolds comprehensively his design in writing the epistle. The only possible mode of reasoning, from which there was any hope of convincing these gainsaying Jews, was by an argument *ex concessis*—by proofs derived from their own Scriptures, especially from the Mosaic law. This mode of reasoning the apostle adopted, insomuch that this epistle may be emphatically esteemed an argument *ex concessis* to the Hebrews, founded in the acknowledged testimonies of God's revelations to their fathers, and, more than all in the Mosaic law, as an evanescent *representative* system of civil government.

Fully to support this view of the epistle, a full exposition of the whole of it would be necessary, while to justify in the strongest manner the remark concerning the Mosaic law, would require a similar exposition of the 7th, 8th, 9th, and 10th chapters. Such an exposition of these chapters, which is what my present object more directly requires, would be quite superfluous. Nothing can be plainer, from the perusal of these chapters, than that they were written as an argument *ex concessis* with the Jews; in other words, to show them that according to the facts and principles which they believed and admitted respecting the Mosaic law, *this law was a system of national government, a theocracy, and, as such, a system representing God's higher system of moral government.*

(Chap. vii. 11, 12.) Is not the necessity of a priest, of an order so entirely different from that of Aaron, a declaration of the utter inefficacy of the priesthood of the latter, and of the design of God to change it? And if the very priesthood under which or on account of which the law was given (v. 11), is changed, is there not also a necessity of a change in the law?

(Chap. vii. 18, 19.) The priesthood then being wholly changed, there is of course an entire abolition of the prior commandment, i. e., of the Mosaic law, by which it was instituted, because of its utter insufficiency and failure to procure acceptance with God; for the ὁ νόμος, the Mosaic law, made no man by its priesthood, acceptable to God, but, &c.

(Chap. vii. 28.) Hence it is plain that Christ, as a priest made by the word of the oath, supersedes the high priests which the law maketh, and of course the law that maketh them.

(Chaps. viii. ix. x.) I need not say how utterly insignificant and useless, according to the apostle, were the atonements and sacrifices under the law, nor how effectual and glorious was the great sacrifice for sin, even the sacrifice of the Son of

God himself, now set down at the right hand of the Majesty in the heavens, as the abiding High Priest in "the holy places"—"the Lamb in the midst of the throne;" nor the difference, or rather the contrast, which the apostle draws between the sacrifices under the Mosaic dispensation and the sacrifice of Christ, and how manifestly these things are alleged by the apostle to show that the Mosaic law, its priesthood, its offerings and sacrifices for sin, had come to an end. I shall only call attention to some declarations of the apostle which are explicit to my purpose.

(Chap. viii. 5.) The priests under the law, in their services, furnish a *representation* and *shadow* of heavenly things.

(Chap. viii. 6, to the end.) The superiority of Christ's ministry is here estimated by his being the mediator of a covenant established on promises of eternal blessings, compared with a covenant which promised only temporal blessings. We have next the fatal weakness and deficiency of the Mosaic law, and the fact of its being entirely superseded by completing, *perfecting*, a new covenant in respect to the house of Israel, &c. (v. 8). This new covenant is entirely different from the Mosaic law, even as different as are temporal and earthly things from spiritual and heavenly things (vs. 9–12). And from calling the latter *new*, the apostle infers that he hath made the first *old*, and infers that "that which decayeth and waxeth old is ready to vanish away."

But without dwelling thus on what can need no explanation, except what a correct translation of some passages would furnish, I will only refer to the ninth chapter, from the seventh verse to the end, and the tenth, from the first to the thirtieth verse, requesting attention to the apostle's assertions of the utter inefficacy of the provisions of the Mosaic law, except to procure forgiveness of national sins—of its *representative* character, not to say its double sense (ix. 8, 9, 23, 24; x. 1), and of the entire abrogation of the Mosaic system of law when the Messiah should come (ix. 10).

Thus it appears that Paul, in this epistle to the Hebrews, by an argument *ex concessis*, and, as I may say, by this only, professes at least to establish Christianity on the basis of God's former revelations—especially on that revelation called the Mosaic law. In the exhibition of this argument he neither assumes the authority of an apostle, nor rests his interpretation and explanation of the Mosaic law on his inspiration or any revelation of its import peculiar to himself; nor resorts to any novel interpretations, either figurative, typical, or literal. What have these things to do with an argument *ex concessis?* Had the apostle relied at all on either of these things, his argument would not have been what he pretended it to be, nor have proved what he pretended to prove by it. It would have had no weight, nor be fitted to have any, with either the believing or unbelieving Jews to whom he wrote. The reply would have been as unanswerable as it would have been obvious: We have never understood nor known any among us, learned or unlearned in the law, who have interpreted and understood it as you do. This great argument in this great epistle of the great apostle, unless the commonly received and universally admitted interpretation of the Mosaic law by the Jewish people was that now assumed and reasoned upon by the apostle, would have been an argument founded on facts and principles assumed by him to be conceded, which were not conceded. But what right or warrant has any man, especially an apostle, thus to reason on fictitious or false premises? And now if the facts and principles of the apostle's argument were conceded universally by the Jews, then they knew or believed that the Mosaic law was what Paul assumed it to be. This view of this law must have been not only that of the learned of that age, and the popular view as derived from the expounders and teachers of the law but with the highest probability that of the ancient prophets, which was perpetuated through successive generations to the time of the apostle. Nor is the least evidence to the contrary furnished by the interpretation of this law on the part of modern Jews, with their hostility to the divine origin of Christianity. What then is this view of the Mosaic law so well established by Jewish usage, and assumed by the apostle in the argument of his Epistle to the Hebrews? It is, that the Mosaic law was a national system of government, which, whatever other peculiarity it involved, was *a representative* system exhibiting God's higher system of moral government over men under a gracious economy. In the language of the apostle, it was *a representation and shadow of the heavenly things* (ὑπόδείγμα καὶ σκιᾶ); it *had a shadow of good things to come* (σκιὰν τῶν μελλόντων ἀγαθῶν); in one essential respect it was *a parable* (which signifies an information either by speech or action), in which one thing is put for another (ix. 8, 9), of the time then present, &c. Nor is this all. It was a representation—a shadow (not the very image or substance) of the good things to come—a parable for the time which interposed between the tabernacle service (v. 8) and the time of reformation (v. 10), during which the gifts and sacrifices could in no degree expiate moral offenses, or relieve a guilty conscience, or deliver from final condemnation; but being at most *δικαιώματα σαρκὸς* (ix. 10), *ordinances*, or *institutions for the righteousness* of the flesh—grounds of acceptance before *a civil* tribunal (ix. 9–13), imposed UNTIL the time of reformation. It was an institution, a *διαθήκη*, so incomplete, so inadequate, in respect to God's great ulterior design, that on this account he said by his prophet, "I will complete *a new* covenant," &c., thus making the first old; and that which decayeth and waxeth old is ready to vanish away. On the whole then, whoever was the author of this Epistle to the Hebrews, he has, on the acknowledged divine authority of the Jewish revelation, and especially of the Mosaic law itself, silenced every Jewish objection to the divine origin of Christianity; and thus compelled every Jew either to abandon the divine authority of Moses in the law, or to admit the divine authority of Christ in the Gospel. In addition to this, if Paul or any other inspired writer was the author of this epistle, then is it clothed alike in its argument and its conclusion with the authority of God; and the theocracy of Israel was a system of national government, late in its origin and temporary in duration, and as such designed to *represent* God's higher system of moral government over all men as moral and immortal beings. *The Mosaic law was a theocracy.*

LECTURE VII.

THE *NATURE* OF GOD'S MORAL GOVERNMENT AS REVEALED.

Introduction.—Plan unfolded.—The subjects of six sections announced.—Section first: *Law immutable in its authority.*—Dogma of man's inability discussed.—Three theories in support of it: The Augustinian, the Arminian, the Edwardian.—These theories discussed.—Section second: *The law immutable in its claim.*—Claim defined.—Can never be satisfied in case of disobedience.—Neither by the infliction of penalty, nor by repentance, nor by an atonement.

I HAVE attempted to establish from the Scriptures, the general FACT of God's moral government over men, and given what I consider the true view of the Mosaic law or Jewish theocracy. By this discussion the way is prepared, as otherwise it could not be, to show

THE NATURE of God's moral government over men, as exhibited by Revelation.

What I maintain and hope fully to evince is, generally speaking, that the Scriptures exhibit God as administering over men a perfect moral government under an economy of grace.

A perfect moral government, as before defined, *is the influence of the rightful authority of a moral governor on moral beings, designed so to control their action as to secure the great end of action on their part through the medium of law.*

Law, in this general forensic import, is *an authoritative, perfect rule of moral action, fully sustained in its authority by the requisite sanctions.* In this general forensic import of the word, law is essential and common to every form of a perfect moral government.

There are two kinds of a perfect moral government. Law as above defined, is common and essential to both. In the one, this law is also the rule of judgment, according to which the transgressor must be condemned to bear its penalty. In the other, another rule of action under an economy of grace, is the rule of judgment. The one may be called a system of mere law; the other, a system of law and grace combined. The former was adopted in Eden in respect to our first parents, before their apostasy; the latter, after their apostasy, was adopted in respect to them and all their descendants. It is this particular form of a perfect moral government which, as I maintain, God is shown by revelation to be administering over men, namely, *a perfect moral government under an economy of grace.*

This system of God's moral government may be justly viewed as consisting of two great and essential parts, which, while sustaining to each other the most important relations as parts of one system, may with advantage be separately considered. The nature of the system can be unfolded only by the exhibition of *the law* which is included in the system, and also of *the economy of grace* which is included in it. The latter, with the many great and prominent facts and truths with which it is connected, on which it depends, and which it implies—facts and truths which are commonly called *the doctrines of grace*—I design to make the subject of future investigation. The former, *the law* of God's moral government—law as essential and common to every system of perfect moral government—is the subject of our present inquiry.

So different are the two particular forms of God's moral government to which I have referred, that to form just views of either, they need to be clearly and accurately distinguished, especially by precise conceptions of *law* as a general forensic term, or in that import of the word in which the thing is common to both forms of a perfect moral government. Indeed, on this subject I am constrained to say that to my own mind the views of theologians are in a high degree unsatisfactory, and wholly inadequate to a consistent system of Biblical theology. So little attention has been given to the essential nature and principles of a perfect moral government, both by theologians and interpreters, that while they have seen that an economy of grace must greatly *modify* the law of *a merely legal system* of moral government, they have *not* seen that an economy of grace can in no respect modify *law* as an essential, eternal, immutable element of such a government.

The inquiry now before us is, What, according to *scriptural usage*, is the divine law in *the general forensic import of the term*, and when employed to denote the perfect law of God's perfect moral government over men? Law, under a merely legal system, specifically differs in some respects from *law* under an economy of grace, while yet it has a meaning which is common to both cases. What then is *law* as common to both a merely legal system and a system of grace? I propose to answer this inquiry, in the following sections, by considering *law* in this import:

1. As immutable in its authority, its claim, and its sanctions.
2. As a rule of action, and not a rule of judgment.
3. In its requirement as a prohibition of its opposite, and *vice versa.*
4. In the sum of its requirements.
5. In the import of its sanctions.
6. As an expression of the lawgiver's preference of obedience to disobedience.

Sect. 1.—Law as immutable in its authority, its claim, and in its sanctions.

I proceed to show that in the sense in which the language is now used, the law of God is immutable in the three respects now specified.

(1.) In its authority.

The authority of the divine law, or the authority of God as a lawgiver, is his right to command which imposes an obligation to obey, and results from his infinitely perfect character. That God possesses this character, is here to be assumed. That on the ground of this character, he claims authority over men, as their moral governor or lawgiver, we have attempted to prove in a former lecture (Lect. I.) from the Scriptures. When, in the account of his giving law to man in Eden, we read that "The Lord God COMMANDED the man;" when we read that he said to Abraham, "I am the ALMIGHTY GOD, walk before me, and be thou perfect;" and again, when giving his law to Israel, "I am the LORD THY GOD, &c., thou shalt have no other gods before me;" and when in the New Testament we find the first and great commandment to be, "Thou shalt love the LORD THY GOD;" and again, "GOD now COMMANDETH all men to repent;" we cannot fail to see God presenting himself throughout his entire revelation, in the character of infinite perfection, and on this ground resting his rightful authority over men as their lawgiver. Nor can we, admitting the reality of such a Being and of his revelation, question his authority.

Nor is it supposable that any Christian theologian should *directly* deny or imagine himself to deny, that God reigns in this unabated, rightful authority over men. But there are strange things in the theology of man's devising. And here I am constrained to ask, Whether in all this theology both Catholic and Protestant, theologians, in maintaining the doctrines of grace, have not extensively maintained opinions—philosophical dogmas, unscriptural principles—and held them as essential doctrines of the word of God, which are palpably inconsistent with and utterly subversive of God's authority as a lawgiver? Without referring to more remote incongruities on this subject, may it not be said to be a prevalent doctrine of the Christian Church from the time of Augustine, and emphatically in the two great divisions of the Reformed Church known as the Calvinistic and Arminian, that "God commands what man *cannot* perform;" "that man by the fall lost all ability of will to any thing spiritually good;" "that God did not lose his right to command, though man lost the power to obey?"*

Nor have any attempts of theologians to justify, to palliate, or to conceal this doctrine of man's inability, been even plausibly successful. There are but three theories on the subject which I deem worthy of notice—the Augustinian or Calvinistic, the Arminian, and the Edwardian. According to the first, we are told, and this on the pretended authority of the word of God, but without a text to prove it, that all mankind, as they were *created* one moral person in Adam, had this power to obey God, but that they utterly lost it by sinning in him, and that all his descendants thus *created and existent* in Adam, are *born* without this power as truly as the beasts of the field, and yet are responsible for the use of it. This dogma involves the absurdity of saying, that power which is necessary to the beginning and essential to the very existence of moral obliga-

* Vide Calvin's Inst., B. i. 6, 7. The error of Pelagius is, not that he maintained man's ability to obey God without grace, but that man does *actually* obey God without grace. Some, who would seem to think themselves to be well-read theologians, appear not to know the difference between affirming that man *can* obey without grace, and affirming that he *does* or ever will obey without grace. I affirm the former, and deny the latter. I suppose a *necessity* of grace, not to constitute men moral agents, or able to obey God, but to influence those to obey God who can, but from willfulness in sin never will obey him without grace.

tion, is not necessary to its continued existence, and that it is fit and what ought to be, that power which has no existence, should be used; and that when all the responsibility in such a case pertains to the single act of destroying the power, men are responsible for not using it after it is destroyed. The Arminian theory of man's *inability* or *want of power* is the same, excepting a vain attempt to conceal its revolting aspect by the still greater absurdity of what is called *a gracious ability*. The advocates of this theory plainly subvert and virtually deny the grace of God, in their very attempt to magnify it; for if man has not ability or power to obey God *without grace*, then he does not sin in not obeying, since a being who cannot act morally right cannot act morally wrong. Such a being cannot be truly said to receive or be capable of receiving grace, for grace is favor to sinners. Besides, what does the supposed grace of God do? Does it give man *power* to obey, then man has power to obey as he must have before he obeys. But even this is no security that he will obey. Adam sinned with this power. The grace then does not meet the exigency of the case. Is it said he has power to use the grace furnished? But what power is this? Until man has *power to obey*, it is absolutely inconceivable that he should obey, for the act of obedience is *his own* act, done in the use or exercise of *his own power* to obey. Thus the grace of God according to this scheme, must by a direct act of creation impart some new essential mental faculty or power to the soul of man, to qualify man to act morally right or wrong. Without the grace of God man has not a human soul, for he has not the true and essential nature of such a soul—the *power* requisite to moral action. He cannot be a sinner, and of course grace to him cannot be favor to a sinner. Grace is no more grace.

The Edwardian theory of *inability*, what is it? The *inability* to love God, which it maintains, is the inability to love and hate the same object at the same time, or *the inability to will opposites at the same time*.* The *ability* which this scheme affirms, to soften it may be, the revolting aspect of the *inability* which it maintains, is the wonderful power of man *not to will*, or to avoid willing opposites at the same time, or *power to will without willing against his will*. Now as to this

---

* Vide Edwards' Inquiry, &c., P. iii. Sec. 4.

inability, it is an absolutely fatal possession, for God can never remove it, i. e., he can never impart power to man to will opposites at the same time, any more than he can impart power to a body to move in opposite directions at the same time. And then again, as to *the ability* or *natural ability* of this scheme, there is the same difficulty; for the mind neither has nor can have in the nature of things, the *power* or *ability* specified. It has doubtless power to will, but has not *power* in willing to avoid willing against its will, any more than a part has power to be less than the whole, or than two and two not to be four. There is a *possibility*, *in the nature of things*, in each of the three cases, that the thing affirmed should be; but this *possibility* does not result *from power* to make it so. A part is less than the whole, *in the nature of things*, and not as the result of *power*. So man in willing, wills without willing against his will *in the nature of things*; but not as the result of power, either natural power or any other power. That he wills is owing to his power to will; but that he wills without willing opposites at the same time, is not owing to his power. Such power or ability is inconceivable. Power to cause that to be which is necessary in the nature of things, as power to make two and two to be four, can have no existence, nor pertain to God or man. God can give no such ability to man. The *natural ability of man* to obey God, as defined by Edwards and others, has no existence and can have none. It is an essential nothing. Thus according to this Edwardian theory, while there is not the shadow of *ability* or of power on the part of man to obey God, the *moral inability* of the theory, the inability to love and hate the same object at the same time, though undeniable, is unchangeable either by man or his Maker. Nor is this all. Such *an inability* furnishes not the slightest evidence, that when one wills morally wrong, he has not in the proper and true use of language, power or ability to will morally right; nor that when he has willed morally wrong, he has not power or ability to will morally right the next moment.

It is worthy of remark, that the theologians who have denied man's ability as a moral being and a sinner, have felt themselves obliged to base his moral responsibility in something which they call *ability to obey*. The Augustinian rests it on ability *created* in man when Adam and all his posterity in him were *created*, but lost or destroyed by their sinning in Eden; the Arminian devises the solecism of *a gracious ability;* and the Edwardian a *natural ability*, which is utterly inconceivable *in rerum naturâ.* All this clearly shows how impossible it is for the mind to assent to the absolute, unqualified proposition that man's obligation to obey is not founded in his ability to obey. These assertions of *ability* indeed, amount to nothing which can be real or true as the basis of moral responsibility; while the doctrine of an inability which is subversive of all moral responsibility, is constantly inculcated.

I shall hereafter attempt to show, that the Scriptures always proceed on the assumption of man's *ability or power* to obey God; that there is not a passage in the sacred volume which teaches or implies any inability of man to act morally right; that the passages commonly relied on to prove man's inability to act morally right assert no such inability, but an inability in respect to something widely different; and particularly an inability or impossibility with a morally wrong heart to act *right* in subordinate or executive action, which is not *moral* action. This inability is inculcated to show how vain the hope is of pleasing God with a wrong heart, and as *a reason* for changing the heart; thus clearly implying, not that the sinner *cannot* change his heart, but that he *can.* (Rom. viii. 7, 8; Matt. vii. 18; xii. 33, 34; John, xv. 4, 5.)

What philosophy has taught on this subject we have to some extent seen already. What the Scriptures teach respecting it, I propose to inquire more fully hereafter. I will only call attention to some general features of their testimony. We find, that in all cases the Scriptures exhibit the *moral change* in man, either as that which man is bound to accomplish in the use of his own power, as in the command, "Make you a new heart and a new spirit;" or as that which he has accomplished in the use of his own power, as in the assertion, "Ye have put off the old man with his deeds, and have put on the new man;" or as that which through a divine influence they are required to perform in the use of their own power, as in the requirement, "Work out your own salvation," &c., "for it is God which worketh in you *to will and to do* of his good pleasure;" or as that which they through a divine influence, have accomplished in the use of their own power, as in the assertion, "Ye have purified your souls in obeying the truth through the

Spirit." Thus, in all these prominent forms, and I might say in other forms, this great moral change in man is presented in the most guarded manner as his own *act*—done of course from its very nature *proximately* and necessarily in the use or exercise of *his own power*. It is *his heart* with which he is required to exercise new and holy affection; it is himself who has changed his own character as his own doing; it is his *will* which is "to will," and *his power* to work or do, which is to work and do; it is his power to abandon sin and to obey God, with which he purifies his soul and actually obeys the truth. What if the change is "through the Spirit"—this fact no more interferes with the fact that it is accomplished in the use of the sinner's own power, than were it done without the Spirit in view of truth and motives. On the contrary, the very work of the Spirit in this change consists in bringing the sinner to use his power in morally right action. Even could we suppose new *mental power* to be given to the sinner, something more—certain mental states, antecedent thoughts, desires, &c. —would be necessary to give *certainty to the right use* of the power. The mere *power*, whether given in the creation of the soul or afterward, cannot supersede the necessity of that peculiar interposition of the Spirit, by which alone the right use of the *power* is made certain. Thus in what the Scriptures teach respecting the work of the Spirit, *the power* of man to act morally right is presupposed. If it were not so, what would there be for the Spirit to do? Do you say to create *new powers* in man? But if this were all, it might only make the matter worse. I only add—

That the law of God, in the very terms of it, settles the question. How does it read? "Thou shalt love the Lord thy God with all thy heart, and with all thy soul, and with all thy mind, and with all thy strength." And is this God's right to command, without man's power to obey? Is this the doctrine of man's inability to obey God,—an inability to be removed by an ability through grace; an inability because ability was lost in Adam; an inability to effect the metaphysical impossibility of loving and hating at the same time;—ay, inability in man to do what he can do? Or is it the fullest and most unqualified recognition of man's power to obey his God which language can furnish? Is not this law of God the standard of absolute moral excellence in man? Is not the man who should obey it absolutely, morally perfect? And is not its entire claim on man limited to a specified use of his power—his power of heart, soul, mind, and strength? If this use of his own power is not claimed in the law, what is claimed? Is it possible in the nature of things, that man should comply with the claim of this law except in the use of his own powers? or as some imagine, in the use of any other power than *his own*—*his own* as existent under the claim and its obligation? And has man *not* power or no power, to obey a law which claims nothing but the use of his *own power*—can he not love God as much as he can love him? Is man, by this law, required to love God in the use of the high powers which exalt him into a resemblance of God himself—are these the powers which the divine Lawgiver specifies in the very words of his law as man's powers, and yet does the same Lawgiver affirm nothing so often as that man has not power to obey his law? Have men made after the similitude of God, no power to love God? Any conscience, from above or beneath, can answer this question. Shall all theology then, venture to teach and inculcate the doctrine that man cannot love the all-perfect God?

After all the attempts that have been made to vindicate this doctrine—whether on the theory of our identity in Adam, or on that of a gracious ability, or on that of a *natural* ability and a moral *inability*—is it not true that that ability on the part of men which is necessary to moral responsibility, has been and is still denied by the evangelical and orthodox ministry and Church? Are they not in fact and justly, understood by the people to teach and maintain an inability on the part of men to obey God without grace, which exempts them from all moral obligation to obey God, without grace to furnish ability? If their language on the subject is such that, *de usu loquendi*, or when justly and properly interpreted, even with all their vain attempts at explanation, it means and is understood by the people to mean, an inability without grace on the part of men to obey God, as real as that of an inanimate substance, or as that to make a part equal to the whole, then are they not justly charged with teaching this doctrine? It is on this ground—that of the proper meaning of the language—that I claim that they maintain and teach that man, without the grace of God, has not that ability or power to obey God which is requisite to moral responsibility.

It is this doctrine which I claim to have shown extensively prevails, and which carries with it the subversion of God's authority as a lawgiver. Shall the Christian ministry then, continue to assert man's inability to obey God, and in words only assert, or rather faintly assume God's authority without assertion and without proof? Is this to make the just, the true, the useful impression of God's authority on the human mind? Is this after the manner of God? When "the Lord God" gave law to man in Eden, was there a doubt or a question concerning his right to reign—I do not say warranted but possible—in the mind of a creature formed in the image of himself? Was there any thing in the promise of a Redeemer; any thing in the expulsion of our first parents from the garden; any thing in the sentence pronounced on the race; any thing in the history of Cain and Abel; any thing in the whole patriarchal dispensation, in the destruction of the world by the deluge, in the destruction of Sodom and Gomorrah by fire and brimstone, in the calling of Abraham, and the covenant with him;—any thing so fitted to arrest and absorb human thought, as God in his supreme and rightful authority as a lawgiver? When God delivered Israel from their Egyptian bondage, when he led them through the wilderness, when he lifted his voice of authority amid the thunderings and lightnings of Sinai, spreading terror and dismay among the assembled hosts and constraining their vows of allegiance, was his right to reign obscured or relinquished? Did even his attendant proclamation of "keeping mercy for thousands of them that love me," produce this effect? In their subsequent history, under the administration of the Mosaic theocracy as *a representative system*, amid altars smoking with expiatory victims, and shaking heaven and earth in execution of his law as the tutelary deity and national king of this people, and thus shadowing forth his higher relation of the moral governor of men, who or what was to be thought of, but God in his supreme and rightful authority?

If we appeal to the New Testament, what meets us in this meridian light of revelation but the long-promised Messiah, the incarnate Logos, God manifest in the flesh, King of kings and Lord of lords—who came, not to destroy *the law* or the prophets, but to fulfill, i. e., to accomplish the whole design or end of God's revelation—to consummate all God's prior dispensations (Heb. ix. 26)? I need only refer to what every reader of the Gospels must know, to show how He to whom was given all power in heaven and on earth, always and in all things exalted God's authority as a lawgiver (Luke, xxii. 36). And what appears in equal fullness in the rest of the New Testament, in the life and labors, in the preaching and the writings of apostles, especially in those of the apostle Paul, is the same God in the same supremacy and splendors of his moral dominion. To deny this manifestation of God throughout the New Testament, is scarcely less than to deny that God is therein revealed at all.

In accordance with what has been said, I now ask, Is there any way to magnify the grace of God in this world's redemption from the power and the doom of sin, except by unfolding his rightful authority as a lawgiver? Can any adequate manifestation of the riches of his grace and mercy—an object so dear to the heart of all who love him—be made, while the Church and its ministry deny to men that essential characteristic of every subject of law—the ability to obey it? Can this be done, and God's authority as a lawgiver be apprehended and felt? Shall the friends of God and of his truth forever reiterate man's *inability without grace* to obey the living God, and not so much as tell us what they mean by *grace* to a being so utterly devoid of all moral responsibility without the grace? Or shall they maintain and teach that men are made after the image of God, and with that power either to obey or disobey their Maker which qualifies them to be subjects of his perfect moral government? Shall they or shall they not honor and magnify the grace of God *as favor to sinners*—to moral beings who can and who ought, and yet who in fact never will obey God without the supernatural grace of his Holy Spirit? Shall they or shall they not enthrone God in his supreme and rightful authority as the moral governor of men, without a shadow to obscure its cloudless majesty?

On this subject I cannot but suggest the most cautious reflection and thorough reconsideration of the views and opinions of the most distinguished theologians who have gone before us. Grateful to God for their labors, I do not forget that the greatest and best of men are "but darkly wise," and that in the word of God there are rich treasures of knowledge yet to be revealed. How desirable that the whole Church should, in faith, apprehend God in the unimpaired glories of his justice and his grace! How much is lost, if one truth concerning God in these high relations is lost to a sinful world!

I proceed, as proposed, to show that the law of God's moral government is *immutable*—

(2.) In its claim.

By the claim of law, I intend its claim on the subject for that action which is to be performed by the subject. God as a lawgiver has specified such action, and *claims* its performance by every subject on the ground of his rightful authority. It is this claim in his law which I now say is *immutable.* This is at once obvious from the essential nature of all that was ever called law in the forensic use of the word. Law in this use of the word, which should express no claim on subjects for action or conduct with the design of the lawgiver thereby to regulate such action, would be an anomaly. More need not be said to convince any reader of the Scriptures, who believes that God is what he is and that man is what he is, that the claim of God's law as exhibited in the Scriptures, is and must be, like its author, absolutely immutable. Nor is there any occasion for saying any thing on this important part of our subject, in addition to what has been already said in preceding lectures, except what arises from what a large class of Christian theologians maintain. I allude to their favorite and frequently repeated theological dogma, that the law and justice of God are satisfied by the atonement of Christ, in respect to all those for whom it is made. I shall not stop to inquire whether this or equivalent language can be true, in some arbitrary and unauthorized meaning which may be given it. The meaning of those who employ it is, for the most part, too obvious to be mistaken. They mean, that every claim of the law and justice of God in respect to the elect, is as fully satisfied by the atonement of Christ, as had they sinlessly and perfectly obeyed the law, so that the penalty of the law cannot be inflicted on them, nor its reward withheld from them, according to any principle of justice.

It is not my present design to examine fully what the advocates of this view of the atonement allege in its support. This belongs to another part of our course of lectures. I can only say here, that in my view, when the subject is thoroughly examined, it will be found that the doctrine of *Christ's satisfac-*

tion has resulted solely from a false philosophy respecting the principles of law and moral government, which has not the least plausibility or support from the Scriptures. I know of no passage in the word of God which expresses even a semblance of the idea of an atonement, as a satisfaction of the claim of law and justice on the transgressor of law. The Hebrew word כפר, copher, I am aware is rendered in Numb. xxxv. 31, 32, by the word *satisfaction*, which ought to be rendered by the word *atonement.* To render it *satisfaction*, however, is even worse than a mere begging of the question, for the connection shows decisively that there may be a *copher* which shall not be taken or accepted, and which of course could not be a *satisfaction.* But my present object is not to examine the pretended scriptural arguments for this view of the atonement, but rather to show its inconsistency with the known nature and principles of law. I proceed then on this ground, to show that—

The claim and only claim of the divine law on its subject, can, in case of disobedience, never be satisfied.

Law has but one claim on its subject. It claims his obedience to law, and it claims of him nothing else. The lawgiver does not *claim* punishment of the subject in case of transgression, as *the act* of the subject nor indeed in any sense whatever. The lawgiver *threatens* punishment for transgression, and executes the threatening if it be executed at all, as his own *act*, and not as the act of the disobedient subject fulfilling a claim on him. The same is true of law and of justice, for though they may be said to require or to claim the punishment of the transgressor as the necessary means, under a system of mere law, of sustaining the authority of law or of the lawgiver, this claim for punishment is not a claim on the subject for an act on his part, but solely a claim on the lawgiver as his act—his act of justice to vindicate his own rights and the rights of his kingdom. Under any other aspect or relation, punishment could make no expression of supreme disapprobation of sin, and of course could not sustain his authority nor be a legal penalty. Besides, it is inconceivable and impossible that a perfectly benevolent lawgiver should be *satisfied* with sin, and with the infliction of the legal penalty on transgressors, as a substitute for their perfect obedience and consequent perfect blessedness. In the one case, with all the miseries involved, he would simply sustain his authority or vindicate his justice as a lawgiver; while in the other, not only the same result would be secured, but his own perfect blessedness would also be secured by the perfect holiness and perfect blessedness of his kingdom. And could perfect benevolence be satisfied with the former result instead of the latter? And if benevolence could not be satisfied with the former result, then neither the claim of law nor the claim of justice for obedience could be satisfied with it. Neither justice nor law ever claimed the perfect obedience of every subject of law, except as such obedience was necessary to secure the rights of God and of his kingdom in their perfect blessedness. In case of transgression, neither law nor justice can execute the legal penalty as the means of the perfect blessedness of all. It is too late for this. And can the claim of law and justice be satisfied by an act of the lawgiver sustaining his authority, and showing him to be just when every claim of law and justice on his subjects in respect to its object and end is utterly frustrated by so much sin and misery, instead of satisfied by the perfect holiness and happiness of all? Can a benevolent lawgiver, a perfect law, inflexible justice, be *satisfied* with such results of a moral government? It is impossible. The lawgiver, his character, his law, his authority, his justice, are maintained in their unobscured perfection—shining in cloudless glory; but their every claim on the subjects of law is by sin utterly and forever unsatisfied in its object and end.

And further, while law and justice do not claim the punishment of the transgressor of law as an equivalent for his not satisfying the claim by obedience, neither do they claim repentance after sin as a satisfactory substitute for perfect obedience. Nor do they claim the obedience or the imputed righteousness or any sacrifice by an atonement, or any thing else on the part of another, as a satisfactory substitute for the obedience of the subject. Law and justice are enthroned in a perfect moral government to define, protect, and enforce rights. This is an absolutely universal principle, which must be carried out unless the possessor of a right consents, or chooses for good and sufficient reasons to waive or abandon his right. The moral governor has rights. His kingdom has rights. Every subject has rights as an individual. It is important here to contemplate some of them. The moral governor then, in addition to such rights as the right to reign, the right to give and uphold law, has the right to claim of each and every subject of law his perfect and perpetual obedience to law. To deny this, is to say that the rights of God and of his kingdom—the rendering to all their due from every subject—can in case of transgression, or without universal perfect obedience to God's perfect law, be secured by some other means or method than by such obedience. But if this be too absurd to be said, then how shall the claim of law and justice without the perfect obedience of every subject of law, ever be met and *satisfied?* Will it be said that such is not the necessary and only means of the end specified, and that the existence and miseries of sin with the atonement of the Son of God, were as good a means of this end as the supposed obedience? I answer, that this is utterly impossible and inconceivable; for how can a system of means, involving sin and its miseries with the sufferings and sacrifices involved in atonement for sin, produce as good a result as the highest conceivable happiness—the necessary result of universal and perfect obedience? Besides, to suppose otherwise is to suppose that the Lawgiver had no right to claim such obedience. This claim on his part, if it is any thing, is a declaration that such obedience is the necessary and only means of the end specified, and that nothing else can be substituted for it as such a means. If therefore, it is not such a means, the claim of law is not true nor just—is not dictated or demanded but is forbidden by justice. Law could not be law, unless obedience to it were the necessary means of the highest conceivable good. If it is such a means, then its claim for universal perfect obedience is dictated and demanded by justice; and without such obedience, this claim can never be satisfied. It must remain, if once violated, and to any extent in which it is violated, remedilessly and forever unsatisfied. The Lawgiver indeed, in his claim for universal perfect obedience, plainly declares that he will be satisfied with such obedience. But in the sanctions of his law, he says as plainly that he cannot be satisfied with any thing but such obedience. How can he be? What else will secure the rights of all; not only the rights of the Lawgiver himself, and of his subjects, but the voluntarily surrendered but otherwise the inviolable rights of the eternal Logos? What else will secure to the Lawgiver himself, and to his kingdom, the highest possible blessedness, but the universal perfect obedience of his kingdom and its result in this blessedness? Not sin followed by repentance; for then the law would not claim obedience or forbid sin, but only claim repentance after sin: not sin and the execution of its fearful penalty; for how could the infliction of such miseries be, to the infinite benevolence of the Lawgiver, a satisfactory substitute for the perfect obedience and blessedness of his kingdom: not sin and an atonement made by the agonies of the Son of God on the cross, and the sacrifice of the Father in delivering the Son to these agonies, or rather in inflicting them; for what satisfaction from all this, compared with that of the fulfillment of the claim of law, in the perfect holiness and blessedness of its subjects: not sin, and the so called imputed righteousness of Christ to the elect or to believing sinners; for how can the mystical absurdity of imputing and thereby making the righteousness or obedience of one subject of law, which could only answer the claim of law on himself, the righteousness or obedience of others, satisfy a violated claim for their own personal absolute moral perfection? It is true, that if sin occurs, God can, and God only can sustain his authority or right to reign, and this either by the execution of the penalty or by an atonement, and that can be done by either. But what has this to do with satisfying the claim of law for obedience under this sustained authority and its influence? Obedience which alone satisfies the claim, presupposes the validity of the claim; the validity of the claim presupposes the authority of the Lawgiver; and the authority of the Lawgiver presupposes the manifestation by himself of his perfect character, or perfect qualification to govern. What the Lawgiver is, and what he does, is the sole basis and source of his authority, and it is his exclusive prerogative to sustain it. He neither derives it from the acts or the doings of his subjects, nor intrusts its support or continuance to them. The obedience of the subject though it satisfies the claim of law, is not that on which the authority of the Lawgiver in the least degree depends. The want of obedience, that is, the act of transgression, unpunished or unatoned by the Lawgiver himself, would result in the subversion of his authority. This result would follow the want of obedience, not because obedience is the *source* of the Lawgiver's authority, but solely because the Lawgiver would neglect by his own act either to execute the penalty, or as an equivalent to provide an atonement. But neither of these acts of the Lawgiver, in case of transgression, *satisfies* the claim of law on the subject of law. They are the acts of the Lawgiver himself, and not the sinless perfect obedience of the subject. Such obedience, had it been rendered, could neither originate nor sustain the Lawgiver's authority, by *satisfying the claim of law;* for his authority, as we have said, must exist and be fully sustained prior to being satisfied by obedience, or there could be no authoritative claim, that is, *no* claim of law to be satisfied. In the administration of his government by authority therefore, it is alike his prerogative and his function as a moral ruler, to perpetuate the authority which has its origin in his own character, exclusively by his own acts and doings. Thus he shows his supreme approbation of obedience, by conferring the requisite reward on the obedient subject, as the necessary and only means in this case of sustaining his authority. Thus he shows his supreme disapprobation of disobedience, by inflicting the requisite penalty on the disobedient, or by providing an atonement, as the necessary and only means in this case, of sustaining his authority. His authority is thus sustained by his own acts, and not by the acts of the subject. His own perfect obedience, though it *satisfies* the claim of the law, does not, *as such a satisfaction*, sustain its authority, but the Lawgiver's act in conferring the reward. But neither an atonement nor imputed righteousness, can do or effect any thing more than the perfect obedience of the subject of law, in satisfying its claim or sustaining its authority. Of course nothing, *as such a satisfaction*, can sustain this authority. In case of transgression, neither subsequent perfect obedience, nor the execution of the penalty, nor the atonement, nor the so called imputed righteousness of Christ, nor his active or passive obedience, nor any of these things, nor all of them together, can *satisfy* the claim of law on the subject. Nor if they could, could they thereby sustain the authority of the law. Nor is there the least necessity of satisfying this claim of law or of justice, that its authority may be perfectly sustained.

Nothing can be plainer than that the authority of law may be sustained by the acts of the lawgiver, though its claim on the subjects be wholly unsatisfied and violated by the acts of the subjects. The law may be transgressed by every subject, and yet authority sustained by the execution of its penalty or by the provision of an atonement. By either, the lawgiver would fully express his supreme disapprobation of transgression, reveal his perfect character, and establish his authority. He would thus establish his right to reign as a moral ruler, and also, in the plenitude of his power, secure the object of this right, by still holding his throne in unobscured, unimpaired, rightful dominion. But in case of transgression he cannot secure the objects of other rights, the securing of which depend on the perfect obedience of all his subjects, viz., of his right to the highest conceivable blessedness, and of his right to the highest conceivable blessedness of his kingdom. One sin impairs this blessedness—much more the sins of a world. Some of the most momentous rights in the universe, rights of God, and I may add, rights of his moral kingdom involving reciprocal obligation on the part of every subject, must be waived in respect to their objects, if his authority be sustained, whether by the execution of the penalty or by the provision of an atonement; for these rights are irretrievably violated by sin, and their objects hopelessly and forever sacrificed and lost. Such is a part of the work of sin. God is not as blessed—his kingdom is not as blessed, as law and justice claimed of every subject, that they should be as the effect of obedience; not as blessed as they might and would have been, had there been no sin violating every principle of law and justice, and thus impairing the amount of blessedness. This deficiency, greater or less, is to be traced only to the offense and fault of each transgressor of law—each violator of the immutable claim which law and justice held in respect to *him*. And now, how can eternal justice—the watchful, inflexible, benevolent guardian of the rights of God and of his moral universe—ever be *satisfied* with the irretrievable violation of such rights, with its irretrievable results, or with these guilty authors? God indeed, as we have said, can sustain his authority or his right to reign, and secure the only object of this particular right in the glories of a perfect dominion, either by the execution of penalty or by an equivalent sacrifice in an atonement. But how much better had it been—how much more grateful to infinite benevolence and perfect justice—had this authority been upheld without sin, with the rewards of the perfect and universal obedience of his moral kingdom! Such a result would have *satisfied* every claim of eternal law and eternal justice, which nothing else could *satisfy*. God has done, in this view of the subject, as I have before shown, what he could as a perfect moral governor, to secure all the objects and ends of the best conceivable system of means, and of course of perfect benevolence and perfect justice. But he has been crossed and thwarted in this highest, greatest design, by sin. He is indeed truly said to be perfectly blessed, because he secures to himself the highest blessedness, which, in the nature of things, he can secure; because in a moral system the best conceivable, Omnipotence, by the mere dint of power could not avail to prevent an infringement of his rights, and the marring of his own highest blessedness, as well as that of his kingdom by sin; because when sin took the responsibility of this fearful achievement, he did what he could to counteract and redress the remediless calamity by an atonement. By this measure however, he has not *satisfied* his justice as a lawgiver, so that justice cannot punish the sinner. The perfect obedience of the sinner would have *so satisfied* law and justice, that justice could not punish. This effect could not be produced by an atonement, nor by any thing else, except by perfect obedience to the claims of law and justice. But while justice as the attribute of the lawgiver, is not under an atonement compelled to pardon or justify any sinner, neither is it compelled to condemn and punish. It can do either the one or the other, as the highest general good shall dictate or demand. What the atonement does, and all that it does as an atonement, is to render it *consistent* with justice to pardon the sinner, by fully sustaining even in such a case, the authority and the justice of the lawgiver in the best manner possible to him. Still this is not done *in absolutely the best manner possible;* nor could it be, without the perfect obedience of his whole moral kingdom. This, with its results—his supreme approbation of it expressed in its rewards—would have not only vindicated his right to reign, sustained his authority and justice as a lawgiver, but have vindicated all other rights—the right of his kingdom to the highest conceivable blessedness, and especially his own right to his own highest conceivable blessedness—for it would have fully secured the objects of these rights;—rights which in respect to their objects, he has consented, in compassion to a sinful race, to waive, that he might accomplish the highest good possible to him in view of existing sin. It is by such a sacrifice, with all it involves, that God sustains his authority and his justice as a lawgiver, through an atonement in the pardon or justification of the sinner. How then can it be pretended that his claim of law and of justice for the perfect obedience of his subjects, is or can be *satisfied* in view of universal sin, and that on the ground of such a satisfaction, sin is or can be pardoned or the transgressor justified? Plainly the claim of his law for the perfect and uninterrupted obedience of his disobedient subjects never has been and never can be satisfied. It is immutable like its author, and so long as he is what he is, and his subjects what they are, there can be no satisfaction for one violation of this high and holy claim of this eternal and immutable and perfect rule.

LECTURE VIII.

THE *NATURE* OF GOD'S MORAL GOVERNMENT AS REVEALED.

Section third: Law immutable in its sanctions.—Law used in a generic sense.—Theologians too often confine it to a legal system.—Consequent errors.—Error of Dr. John Taylor in asserting that the transgressor can be pardoned by and only by the *prerogative of the sovereign*.—Similar error of those who hold that the legal penalty can be executed (by *imputation* or mystical union) on another than the transgressor.—Contrary to known principles of law and justice.—The authority only of the lawgiver sustained by penalty and an atonement.—Pardon not a matter of right, nor merit, nor claim.—General view of sanctions from the Scripture history.

I SHALL now attempt to show that the law of God's moral government, now under consideration, is immutable,

(3.) In its sanctions.

To prevent misapprehension I here remark again, that I use the word *law* in that somewhat general forensic meaning in which the word is employed in the Scriptures, to denote that which exists alike under a merely legal system and also under an economy of grace, or in that meaning which is common to the word under both these systems of moral government.

The importance of precise views on the present topic, in my estimation, results chiefly from the errors of theologians respecting it, especially when considered in connection with the doctrine of forgiveness or justification. I do not indeed suppose that theologians have to any extent formally and explicitly denied the immutability of the sanctions of the divine law. They may in words affirm this immutability. But of law in what sense—of what law do we so often hear the predicates, *eternal* and immutable? Of law I apprehend, in that sense in which it pertains exclusively to a merely legal system; of law, as both a rule of action and of judgment; of law in that meaning in which it can have no existence under an economy of grace; of law which, instead of being absolutely immutable, admits of a most important modification through grace. If law, in the specific sense in which it pertains to a merely legal system—law as both a rule of action and of judgment—admits of no change or modification, who of this sinful world can be saved? Some theologians of distinction trace, as we shall see, all that can be esteemed grace and mercy in behalf of transgressors directly to the sovereignty of the lawgiver. Others however, and a very large class of theologians, have rigidly maintained the absolute immutability of law as pertaining to a merely legal system, and hence have attempted to vindicate and uphold the essential principles of such a law, in the pardon and justification of sinful men, by the *quid pro quo* conception of an atonement, and of an atonement provided only for the elect, by the doctrine of a mystical union between Christ and believers, of the imputation of their sins to him and of Christ's righteousness to them and the satisfaction thereby of all the claims of law and justice in their behalf, &c., &c.

My object now is not fully to examine these palpable errors, for so I esteem them, but to show how entirely subversive they are of the known nature and principles of law. If, as theologians have commonly assumed, law, in the specific form in which it pertains to a merely legal system, be incapable of change or modification, then the utter, hopeless inconsistency between the nature and principles of law and the sinner's justification would be palpable. The attempt to reconcile them on this assumption of theologians, would be an attempt to reconcile an eternal and immutable contradiction with itself—to show how a sinner's justification, which cannot be according to the principles of law, can be according to these principles. But theologians, shut up by their false assumption concerning the nature of law, have felt themselves under a necessity of reconciling this palpable contradiction, and for this purpose have plainly racked their ingenuity to the utmost, and propounded as the exigency required, yet other contradictions in the form of dogmas no less palpably absurd.

What I now maintain is, that law—the law of God's moral government as common to a merely legal system and to a system of law and grace combined and yet peculiar to neither—*is immutable in its sanctions.*

This proposition I shall endeavor to establish, chiefly from the known nature and principles of law and the necessary scriptural import of the *word.*

It may seem quite unnecessary, especially after what has been before said, to show that *law* essentially involves sanctions. And perhaps it would be were it not for the almost constant *virtual* denials of this truth, in the speculations of theologians, in their views of the great doctrine of justification. So unreflective and careless on this subject have been the prominent theological writers—Catholic and Protestant, Orthodox and Latitudinarian—that from the times of Origen, not to say of Irenæus, they have scarcely to any extent worthy of notice, given any form to the great scriptural doctrine of justification, which has not in my view involved downright Antinomianism—the subversion of the law of God in one of its essential elements.

What I have now said, I expect sufficiently to justify in the following remarks.

Law without sanctions can possess no authority. A perfect rule of action may indeed commend itself to the conscience of a moral being with more or less power or influence. But this influence is not that of *authority.*

If we suppose the lawgiver to give the most perfect rule of action without sanctions, or if we suppose him to give it with them and then so to separate them from the rule, or so to annul them in any way or by any measure or expedient that they cannot, according to strict legal principles or according to the principles of law and justice, or according to the merit or demerit of any and every subject of law be executed—then in neither case can the moral governor, nor his moral government, nor his law, be conceived to possess the least authority. Nor is this all. Sanctions are not only the necessary proof of the authority of the lawgiver, but the want of them is decisive proof against his authority. For if he actually felt the highest approbation of the best kind of action, and the highest disapprobation of the worst kind of action on the part of his subjects, as he must if he has the right to reign, he would actually express these feelings in the requisite legal sanctions, and thus enthrone his authority as the best means of securing the highest happiness and preventing the highest misery of his kingdom.

What follows? Where there is no law there is no transgression. Transgression being an impossibility, an atonement for sin, forgiveness of sin, a Saviour from sin—all that we call the gospel, are also impossible absurdities. It is only when *law* stands forth to the apprehension of its subjects as a full manifestation of the lawgiver's estimate of obedience and its opposite, in the light of the requisite sanctions, that it can with the least truth or propriety be called *law* either by man or his Maker. If we suppose these sanctions not to pertain to law in their full character, force, and influence; if we suppose them to be separated from law, weakened, mitigated, nullified, then law is divested of its authority, and can with no more propriety be called *law* than an utterance from the lips of infancy.

Such then, undeniably, is the universal conception which the human mind forms of the *thing* called *law*, when the word is employed as a general forensic term, as before defined and explained. This conception of the thing therefore, *de usu loquendi*, constitutes the meaning of the word—the meaning in which the sacred writers often use it, and intend that it should be understood. If this be not so, then God in his revelation employs human language to no purpose for the instruction of mankind.

I shall now attempt, as proposed, by some further explanation, to vindicate this view of the import of the word *law* as used in the Scriptures, by exposing what I regard as certain theological errors opposed to it, which result from confounding one of its *specific* meanings with its general forensic meaning.

The first of these errors which I shall notice, and which has had no inconsiderable prevalence with the opposers of orthodox theology, is that which is plausibly set forth by Dr. John Taylor of Norwich, a celebrated scholar and critic. He says, that "trangress and die is the language of law. And therefore every transgressor, the moment he is such, is dead in law, and for any thing in law, he must continue so as long as it is true that he has violated law, that is, for evermore. The law which condemns him can give him no relief; for law would not be law if its sense and language were this—*the transgressor who doth not repent and obtain pardon shall die;* seeing this would be to allow transgression by law upon the uncertain conditions of repentance and the sovereign's mercy."

The truth and justice of these remarks respecting *law*, in *one specific sense* of the word—*law* as pertaining to a merely legal system—law as a rule of action and a rule of judgment—*law* in the form in which it was first given in Eden—are beyond all denial. In this sense of the word *law*, "the transgressor is dead for evermore, and the law which condemns him can give him no relief." But with this view of the law as an absolute declaration that sin *shall be* punished, comes the apparently insurmountable difficulty—*how can sin be pardoned?* How shall this great problem be solved? The ingenuity of our theologian readily devises a theory, in his view, fully adequate for its solution. He says, "It is the prerogative of the sovereign or lawgiver to remit penalty altogether on the repentance of the transgressor." This assertion is not only wholly gratuitous, but it plainly involves the Lawgiver in palpable self-contradiction. For it is claimed that in his law, he affirms in the most absolute manner and meaning that the transgressor shall die—shall not be pardoned—and yet that the same Lawgiver, by virtue of his prerogative as a sovereign, can, and in effect that he will pardon the penitent transgressor. Thus, the language of the Lawgiver in his law, and his language in the promise, justly interpreted, are self-contradictory. His language in both cases cannot be true. And thus this theory of our author by convicting the Lawgiver of self-contradiction, denies his veracity and subverts his authority.

Nor is this all. This theory involves two errors, the one being the consequence of the other, while the two propositions which constitute the theory are both false. One of these errors is, that the *execution* of the penalty of law in case of transgression is absolutely unavoidable from the very nature of law. The other is, that it is the prerogative of the sovereign to pardon on the repentance of the transgressor. It is true, that in case of transgression, the penalty of one *particular kind* of law—of law as pertaining to a merely legal system—is absolutely unavoidable. But then this *kind* of law admits of one great and material modification or change through an atonement, so that it shall cease to be a *rule of judgment*, and its penalty be averted. It may still be *law* in every essential element—law in absolute perfection—law unchanged and unchangeable in its high authority, its holy claim, and its righteous sanctions—all that constitutes it law—and yet through an atonement it may cease to be a rule of judgment, and its actually existing penal sanction may be, not separated from the law, but left unexecuted.

Here obviously, is the source of our author's error. He assumed that *law*, as a rule of action and *a rule of judgment*, is the only thing which can be perfect law, in the forensic use of the word. Hence his unqualified assertion, that "Transgress and die" is the language of law; meaning not merely that the penal sanction of death is inseparable from law, but that, if law be transgressed, the penalty *must be executed.* This is plainly an error, if the provision of an atonement intervene, as it may. For an atonement, as the means of pardon, would accomplish nothing, or rather its effect in pardon would be worse than nothing, if it did not change law as a rule of action and of judgment into simply a rule of action, leaving law in its authority, its claim, its sanctions, unimpaired and unchanged. An atonement which did not sustain this authority, would involve the destruction of all law.

Not less plainly would this effect follow from the pardon of transgression, in the exercise of "the prerogative of the sovereign." This is undeniable, on the authority of Dr. Taylor himself. He says: "Law would not be law, if its sense and language were this—the transgressor who doth not repent and obtain pardon, shall die; seeing this would be to allow transgression by law." But what difference can it make in respect to allowing transgression, whether the Lawgiver proffers pardon to the transgressor on repentance in the words of his law, or reveals the fact in some other mode, that he will pardon sin on repentance, in the exercise of his "prerogative as the sovereign and lawgiver?" It is the fact revealed by the Lawgiver, and not the mode in which he reveals it, which would destroy law. If it be said, that the fact is not revealed by the Lawgiver, then I ask, why is it asserted? If it be said that it is a fact or truth known by reason, then law is known to be a very different thing from what our author says it is. Besides, it is wholly a gratuitous assertion, and who but a madman would risk his salvation on such a basis? If it be said, that there is no other way of reconciling grace in the pardon of the transgressor with the import of the word law, or with the essential nature of law, this not only shows how entirely gratuitous the theory is, but it also betrays the source of the error, in the false assumption respecting the general forensic meaning of the word *law.* He assumes that in this meaning, law in its essential nature *as law*, not only involves a penal sanction, or threatens transgression with punishment, but absolutely and inseparably connects *the execution* of the threatening with transgression. In other words, he assumes that law *as law* in its very nature is both a rule of action and judgment,—mistaking *a species or kind* of law, the law of a merely legal system, for the genus law; and assuming that this *kind* of law is incapable of any modification or change by grace through an atonement, whereby, retaining its absolute perfection as *law*, it shall cease to be a rule of judgment.

This fundamental error respecting the essential and immutable nature of law is not peculiar to this celebrated divine, and to those who with him have maintained "the prerogative of the sovereign and lawgiver to remit penalty altogether on the repentance of the transgressor." The same assumption, that the immutable law of God is both a rule of action and of judgment, has long been and is still common on the part of most orthodox theologians, and though it has not always occasioned precisely the same form of error in respect to pardon and justification, yet it may appear that it has occasioned *substantially* the same error, with many others not less inconsistent with the nature of law, not less opposed to the Scriptures, and not less revolting to common sense.

Of this assumption concerning the nature of law, the natural consequence on the part of theologians, are theories devised for the purpose *of reconciling law and grace*. Nor has theological ingenuity faltered even at so formidable an attempt at explanation ; but according to its wont, regardless alike of the decisions of the oracles of God and of common sense, and welcoming mysteries to be believed as especially honoring *revelation*, has fearlessly shot the gulf of theological absurdity and self-contradiction.

To remove or explain away the inconsistency now referred to, orthodox theologians have devised and adopted some theory of *equivalency*, which, at least since the time of Anselm, has extensively prevailed. The object of this scheme is to show how every essential principle of law and justice, in the pardon and justification of the transgressor, is sustained and carried out by the work of Christ. This is obvious at once, from its prominent features. Thus it maintains that God, in his sovereign supremacy and right, constitutes a mystical union between Christ and the elect whereby they become *one moral person ;* that in consequence of this constituted union, God imputes the sins of the elect to Christ, and in his sufferings and death inflicts the legal penalty of their sins on Him ; that he also imputes the righteousness of Christ to them ; that by these acts of imputation and this mystical union, the sins of the elect become the sins of Christ as really as had He committed them, and the righteousness or obedience of Christ becomes as really the righteousness or obedience of the elect, as had they rendered it; that thus every justified sinner is *regarded* and *considered* and treated, not merely *as if he had*, but as having really and truly—*in re ipsa*—in his own person, never sinned, but perfectly obeyed the divine law; and thus every justified transgressor, having in actual verity fully met and satisfied and sustained every claim of law and justice, can *meritoriously* claim, before God, justification and eternal life.

It is apparent on the face of this theory of justification, that its design is to show that the justification of the transgressor rests strictly and literally on the veritable ground, that every claim of immutable law and justice are as fully sustained and secured in their objects or ends as they would be by the perfect sinless obedience to law, rendered by the transgressor himself.

I do not here propose a minute examination of this theory of justification, but to inquire how far it accomplishes the object it professes to accomplish—that of showing the act of justifying the transgressor of law to be, so far as the principles of law and justice are concerned, a strictly legal and juridical act —an act not only done in accordance with these principles, but literally and wholly based on these principles.

This theory, in two respects, proceeds on the same assumptions as that which has just been considered. And first, it assumes that the immutable law of God not only legally sanctions, but also that both law and justice necessarily involve in case of transgression, *the inevitable execution of the legal penalty*. This is obvious at once from the mere statement of the scheme already given, and also from the familiar asseveration that the legal penalty must be executed either on the transgressor or on his substitute. And further, like the theory referred to, it so assumes "the prerogative of the sovereign and lawgiver" as to show in two respects the act of justification to be wholly arbitrary—an act in direct violation of every known principle of law and of justice. For whence come the constituted mystical union of Christ and the elect, and the making, by imputation, *their* sins *his* sins, *their* ill-desert *his* ill-desert, and *his* righteousness *their* righteousness, except from "the prerogative of the sovereign?" The acts of pardon and justification in both cases are acts of mere arbitrary prerogative, for they depend ultimately in both on the simple exercise of such prerogative. Were it not for the supposed *mystical union*, the supposed *imputation* of sins and of righteousness could have no basis; and were it not for this supposed imputation of sins and righteousness, the acts of pardon and justification could have no basis. Both acts therefore are without a pretense, wholly arbitrary, without a reason or shadow of a reason. Both would contravene the essential nature and principles of a perfect moral government, imply the right and the prerogative of a lawgiver to annihilate his law by an act of absolute sovereignty, and to rule for the weal or woe of his kingdom, according to his own caprice.

Thus on this scheme, the acts of pardon and justification rest precisely on the same ulterior ground on which that of Dr. John Taylor, and of a large class of latitudinarian divines places them—" the prerogative of the sovereign"—a ground which our opponents will admit to be no ground at all. But if the acts of pardon and justification depending *directly* on " the prerogative of the sovereign" depend on nothing, the same must be true if they depend *indirectly* or *ultimately* on this prerogative. Whence then arise the acts of constituting this mystical union, and of imputing sins and righteousness? Not from law or from justice, nor yet from the sufferings and death of Christ, for these according to the scheme under consideration are the effects of the mystical union and of imputation. The mystical union and imputation result simply and solely from " the prerogative of the sovereign," which is *indirectly* the basis of justification. But if this prerogative as a *direct* ground of justification amounts to nothing in one scheme, it can amount to no more as the *indirect* ground of it in the other.

I ask then, what possible influence or effect on the great principles of immutable law and justice can be ascribed to the phantasms of a mystical union and an imputed righteousness? What warrant or authority, either in law or justice, has the lawgiver to pardon the transgressor on the ground of *considering* by prerogative, things to be realities which he knows are not realities, rather than to pardon him *arbitrarily* and *directly*, in the exercise of this prerogative without the intervention of a mystical union and an imputed righteousness? Will these vain and imaginary appendages to his moral administration change the principles of eternal and immutable righteousness? If not, then how by the gratuitous (theological) asseveration of them, can the pardon of the transgressor be more consistent with law and justice than it is in the scheme of the theologian of Norwich? Both schemes are substantially the same. Both rest on one and the same basis—that of the prerogative of the sovereign. There can be (words only excepted) no reality in one scheme which is not in the other. If one scheme falls, the other falls. If both stand, then law and justice furnish not the slightest obstacle to the pardon of the trans gressor, which "the prerogative of the sovereign" on condition of repentance cannot wholly remove, and we have only to proclaim the latitudinarian dogma, that God pardons the transgressor of his law solely on the ground of his repentance. Nay, worse than this if possible. For the scheme now opposed denies that repentance, or reformation, or any thing else can be the ground or condition of the exercise of the sovereign's prerogative in the act of pardon, without the antecedents of mystical union and imputation.

But the theory of justification now under consideration is not only substantially the same as another which its defenders would earnestly reprobate, but is flagrantly opposite to every principle of law and justice. If we know any thing of these principles, we know that no perfectly obedient subject of law *can deserve* its penalty. Suffering may indeed, in some supposable case, be inflicted on such a subject *with his consent.* But it cannot be inflicted even with his consent as a *legal penalty* or sanction—in other words, it cannot be inflicted on such a subject on the principle, or under the assumption of *his ill-desert* as the ground of the infliction. No mystical union, nor imputation, nor any thing else on the part of a sovereign God, can impart *ill-desert* to a perfectly obedient subject of a perfect law. We know this with a higher degree of mental assurance than that with which we do or can believe that there is a perfect God, and to suppose any degree of evidence which should disprove or contravene this knowledge of this principle, is to suppose the moral perfection of God to be disproved. Miracles are only a species of *moral* evidence, and this always admits of the *possibility* of the truth opposite to that which it proves. But that a morally perfect being, even Christ Jesus cannot be ill-deserving, is an intuition. For an omniscient God to regard or consider such a being to be ill-deserving, is as impossible as it is that he should know that to be true which he knows to be false; and to treat him as such would be, and be known to be as gross a violation of law, and as high-handed injustice on the part of an infinite as on the part of a finite being. Unless man then can unknow his necessary cognitions; unless he can know that to be false which he knows to be true; unless he can know that to be true which he knows to be false; unless he can know that to be just which he knows to be unjust, he cannot but know that ill-desert cannot be truly affirmed of a perfectly obedient subject of a perfect law, and of course that such a being cannot be capable of bearing, *de merito*, the *legal penalty* of such law. He who asserts the contrary, only proves that through the want of reflection he overlooks his own knowledge. This is indeed no uncommon error on the part of good men, especially of theologians in this imperfect state. He who falls into this error in respect to the all-perfect God in his high relation as the moral governor of men—who imputes to him in this relation what the human mind as a knower necessarily knows to be falsehood and injustice—ought to remember that to call evil good and good evil, to put darkness for light and light for darkness, is to encounter a fearful exposure.

A more minute examination of this scheme would show that every material part of it is entirely unknown to law or justice—that it involves principles entirely foreign and directly repugnant to every principle of both, as well as utterly subversive of the Gospel plan of redemption—principles which, instead of pertaining to the high relation of a perfect lawgiver, render the conception of such a relation impossible to the human mind. Indeed, if we are to rely on the necessary decisions and judgments of the human intellect—without which we can rely on nothing as true—then in this scheme these necessary decisions concerning law, justice, truth, equity, veracity, moral government, every thing which lies at the basis of faith, of confidence, and repose in God, are changed into their opposites. Law ceases to be even respectable advice; for the lawgiver abandons its claims by sovereign prerogative. Justice is converted into injustice; for the lawgiver makes our sins the sins of another, and inflicts the legal penalty which is due only to us, on him who is perfectly holy and perfectly obedient to law as an act of justice to him! This, according to the scheme under consideration, *satisfies* the perfect justice of the lawgiver. And thus, in his sovereignty, by imputing our ill-desert to our substitute, and inflicting on him the penalty which we only deserve, but which he is said to deserve, he exempts us from all ill-desert and from the entire legal penalty. But this, according to the scheme, does not meet all the exigencies of the case. The lawgiver therefore, in a mode equally unauthorized, is supposed to make in the same arbitrary manner the obedience of the substitute our obedience, or perfect righteousness; and on the ground of this perfect righteousness, thus made really ours by sovereign prerogative, we are justified according to the principles of law and justice and the exactest truth of things. Sinners as we are, and deserving the whole penalty of a perfect law, we do yet, by the metamorphoses of *mystical union and imputation*, come to *merit* eternal life—acquire a *right* to it as our legal reward!

Without pursuing for the present these details of absurdity and self-contradiction, I ask if this whole theory of justification is not the merest phantasm of the imagination instead of the reality of truth? I ask if it is not most flagrantly to transmute the essential nature and relations of things into their opposites, and thus to lead the mind to conceive what it necessarily conceives to be true, to be false, and what it necessarily conceives to be false, to be true? I ask if a theology thus produced is entitled to a moment's consideration as even in the slightest degree plausible, unless the mind disciplines itself into the belief that known phantasms are realities, and known realities phantasms; that known justice and known injustice, known transgression of law and known obedience to law, known merit and demerit in law, the known moral perfection of God, his benevolence, goodness, justice, veracity, grace, and mercy, when compared with their opposites, have changed places; in short, that every necessary conception which the human mind forms of what is true and what is false on the most momentous of all subjects, changes place with the necessary conception of its opposite? Can an all-perfect lawgiver by sovereign prerogative make eternal truth falsehood, and eternal falsehood truth? Can he by sheer despotic authority set at defiance, transmute, abolish, every principle of eternal, immutable rectitude, and substitute its opposite in the actual administration of his government; can he by his mere *sic volo* make myriads of beings one being, and yet each to retain his personal individuality—make one perfectly holy being to *deserve* the legal penalty due only to these sinful myriads, and these sinful myriads perfectly righteous by the perfect righteousness of one, regard such an exploit and its effects as a reality, proceed to adjudicate the retributions of eternity on the basis of such transmutations, and yet reign in the glory of his justice and in the majesty of his authority?

Some may think that to ascribe such views and opinions to wise and good men, demands an apology. This however, will be thought only by those who know too little of the history of theological opinions to believe such errors credible, not to say probable. I have no apology to make for these representations except my own full conviction of their truth; I do not question what some may be disposed to call the *sincerity*, in their opinions, of this class of theologians; in other words, that they actually believe without due reflection what they so often and zealously affirm, and that they will in most cases continue thus to believe, because this will supersede the labor of further reflection.

The great desideratum is to show *how* law and grace can be reconciled—*how* law in every essential element can be perfectly sustained and the transgressor be pardoned.

I remark then, that the law of God's moral government, immutable in its high authority, its holy claim, and its righteous sanctions, may exist in its absolute essential perfection as law, and through an atonement cease to be a rule of judgment to the transgressor, and its penalty for transgression be unexecuted, and the transgressor be justified. This must be admitted to be possible, or the pardon and justification of the transgressor under a perfect law would be an utter impossibility in the nature of things.

Again: law, as appears from what has been already said, must be perfect in all its essential elements before it can be obeyed or disobeyed.

From the mere giving or existence of a perfect law, with its authority and claim fully sustained by the requisite sanctions, cannot be determined that any subject or subjects will be punished, for all may obey the law; nor that any will be rewarded, for all may disobey the law. Perfect law does not reward or punish its subjects as subjects, but only as obedient or disobedient. If the subject is obedient, the reward follows as a matter of justice; for the lawgiver, his kingdom, and the individual subject have *a right* that the obedient subject be rewarded. If the subject be disobedient under a merely legal system, then punishment follows as a matter of justice, not because the disobedient subject has *a right to be punished*, and thus a personal claim to be punished, but because the lawgiver has a right, and his kingdom has a right that the disobedient subject be punished. The lawgiver is pledged from the essential nature of his perfect law to protect all these rights, and to secure the objects of these rights to their possessors *so far as it is possible to him.* This is the essential and the entire function of his relation as a perfect lawgiver. Now these rights may be comprised in the right of the lawgiver to the obedience of every subject; in the right of the obedient subject to the legal reward; the right of the lawgiver to reign by sustaining the influence of his authority as a perfect ruler; his right to his own highest blessedness as this depends on the perfect and universal obedience and blessedness of his kingdom, and the right of his kingdom to its perfect blessedness. Of all these rights, with their objects, there is one, and only one, of which it can be said it is possible to him, from the nature of the best system, that of a perfect moral government, perfectly to secure, viz., *his own right to reign as a perfect ruler.* Free moral agents, as the subjects of a perfect moral government must be, must have power to disobey law, notwithstanding any power of the lawgiver to prevent their disobedience. If they disobey law, then the right of the lawgiver to their perfect and universal obedience, his right to his own perfect blessedness and that of his kingdom, and the right of his kingdom to the perfect obedience and blessedness of all, are hopelessly and forever violated. The objects of these rights can never be perfectly accomplished. Nothing can be substituted for the violation as an *adequate* redress of the evil done. I do not say that the evil cannot be redressed in some imperfect measure and degree. It is manifest however, that no complete or adequate redress for the evil can be conceived possible. To suppose it, is to suppose that the highest blessedness of God and of his kingdom should be secured by something besides the only thing which can secure it—the perfect and universal obedience of all his subjects. The perfect protection and security of these rights in their objects and ends must be waived, abandoned, whatever partial redress of the evil be supposed. But, as I have said, there is another of the violated rights, which, notwithstanding disobedience, can be perfectly protected and secured;—THE RIGHT OF THE LAWGIVER TO REIGN, OR HIS AUTHORITY AS A PERFECT RULER. This right can be upheld by the lawgiver himself, not by his subjects. This can be done by him, not as some suppose, by a sovereign act of absurdity and self-contradiction, but either by the execution of the penalty or by an atonement which shall sustain his authority as truly.

That the moral governor's authority would, in case of transgression, be fully sustained by the execution of the legal penalty, will not be denied or doubted. In like manner if a provision of grace, whether called an atonement, propitiation, or ransom, which nothing in the essential nature of *law* forbids, can be made, and which shall as perfectly sustain the authority of the lawgiver as the execution of the penalty, then can the pardon of transgression be made consistent with the perfect authority of the lawgiver. This provision made, the lawgiver evinces his right to reign, though every subject of his kingdom be in revolt. This provision made, all is done which it is requisite should be done, or which in the circumstances can be done, to sustain every right which the justice of the lawgiver requires him to sustain. In the atonement an equivalent for the execution of the penalty is provided, which fully sustains his right to reign, and secures the unimpaired *influence* of his authority. In sustaining this right and fully securing its object—the influence of his authority—he sustains so far as it is possible in the nature of things, every other right in the moral universe, and also the object of every such right. Transgression having occurred, and the lawgiver fully manifesting his perfect character and thus sustaining his authority, he sustains his own right to the obedience of every subject, though through the fault of disobedient subjects, he does not, as he cannot perfectly secure the object of this right; he sustains fully the right of every obedient subject to the legal reward, though he does not, as he cannot secure the object of this right, because there is no obedient subject to receive the legal reward; he sustains his right to his own highest conceivable blessedness, though he does not, as he cannot secure the object of this right, because the perfect and universal obedience of his subjects is withheld; he sustains the right of his kingdom to its own highest blessedness, though he does not, as he cannot secure the object of this right, because of the disobedience of his subjects on which such blessedness depends. Thus the moral governor sustains every right of the moral universe by sustaining his own right to reign, i. e., his authority, and by securing the object of this right—the actual influence of his authority through an atonement—by sustaining this right of his own, and by securing its object through an atonement, as perfectly as he would by rewarding a perfectly obedient, or by punishing a perfectly disobedient kingdom.

And now if he finds good reasons for pardoning transgression, or rather if by so doing he can accomplish a far higher amount of good than by any other means, then why not pardon, accept and save as many transgressors on certain conditions prescribed by his wisdom and goodness, as the greatest good possible for him to secure may require? By so doing would his perfect moral character be concealed or impaired? Plainly not, for he accomplishes all the good he can. What more can be done? If less were done, who could trust, who adore? Can then his justice be impeached? Plainly not; for while he has violated no right of the pardoned transgressor, he has sustained and vindicated every right of his own and of his moral kingdom. Can his authority as a lawgiver or the authority of his law be questioned? Plainly not; for by the provision of an atonement he has fully sustained this authority. Can it be pretended that he has violated, sacrificed, abandoned any principle of rectitude, of truth, of justice, or goodness? Not surely in granting pardon and justification under the provision of a perfect atonement; for as we have seen, he appears in the full glory of his rightful dominion. Not surely in *providing* a perfect atonement, for there is no principle of rectitude, of law, justice, or truth, which forbids such a provision, nor its effect in modifying the law of a merely legal system, so that it shall cease to be a rule of judgment. The lawgiver in his law under a merely legal system, declares that *under the existing system the transgressor shall die.* But he neither declares nor says aught which implies that the particular system, and with it the law of the particular system, shall not be so changed or modified by an atonement, that while the sanctions of law remain in full force, the specific law itself of a merely legal system shall not cease to be a rule of judgment; and that while *the legal necessity* of executing its penal sanction in case of transgression shall also cease, his right or prerogative remains unimpaired to execute the legal penalty or not in any case of transgression, as it shall seem good in his sight. Otherwise the God of truth could never have provided the atonement, nor any atonement properly so called. Nor can it be pretended that the lawgiver by any influence of an atonement, separates from this perfect law its sanctions, or in any degree weakens their influence; for how does the moral governor in adopting this additional expedient for the purpose of sustaining his authority, take away or weaken the influence of existing sanctions? Is an addition a subtraction? If an atonement annihilates the sanction of law, or in any way renders it unjust to execute the penal sanction on any transgressor, then so far it does not uphold but annihilates law itself. In such a case, no matter how or by what means an atonement is made, whether it be based on a mystical union, on the imputation of sins or of righteousness, still it destroys law by separating sanctions from law, and so exempting the transgressor from a just exposure to penalty. Exemption from the penalty is accomplished by the atonement through the annihilation of law. The act of pardon and justification by the lawgiver and judge is therefore an absurdity and an impossibility. Besides, sanctions are not only essential elements of a perfect law, and as such essential to its authority and its existence, whether in certain circumstances they are executed or not, but in certain other circumstances eternal justice demands their execution. The perfectly obedient subject, if there be such a subject, must according to every principle of law and justice be rewarded. Nothing can divest law of its reward for the obedient subject. The disobedient subject of law, according to the same principle of law, must *without faith* be punished even under the provision of a perfect atonement. The certainty that the elect sinner will believe during his probation, affects not the truth of the proposition, that *without faith* the legal penalty must be executed on him, which shows that the law has the same penalty according to its essential nature as law, which may *justly* be inflicted on both the elect and non-elect, though it will not be inflicted on the former, when both shall be judged by the law of faith.

Nor can the moral governor or his kingdom, acquire a right to the pardon of even a believing transgressor as the necessary and proper effect of an atonement. The atonement is not designed to create, nor can it create any new rights. New rights may indirectly result from it by gratuitous promise to the Redeemer and to others; but the atonement as such, is designed simply to sustain one and only one existing right, and to secure its object—the authority of the moral governor or his right to reign. There is no other existing right in case of transgression, as we have seen, whose object an atonement can secure. The right of the moral governor, and that of his kingdom, to their own highest conceivable blessedness in respect to these objects of these rights are irretrievably marred by sin. To say when sin has taken place, that the atonement secures the objects of these rights in the highest possible degree, and so creates rights which did not before exist, is not true; for both these rights existed in absolute perfection before and without the provision of an atonement—the right to the highest possible happiness conceivable, involving in each case the right to the highest possible happiness *in all circumstances* even when sin exists, while neither of these rights can be acquired as the effect of the atonement, nor could be alienated without an atonement. Besides, that the lawgiver cannot acquire his right to pardon the transgressor as the *true and proper effect* of the atonement, is evident from another consideration. When the atonement as such has fully sustained the authority of law as it must, there is yet another thing necessary to the lawgiver's right to pardon even one transgressor; for the act of pardon must not only be rendered consistent with the authority of the lawgiver, but consistent also with *the general good.* But the pardon of the transgressor *without faith* or personal holiness would not be consistent, but inconsistent with the general good, and the lawgiver can have no right which is inconsistent with the general good. The atonement as such, therefore, cannot result in *the right* of the lawgiver to pardon the transgressor, but must produce its whole effect in sustaining the authority of the lawgiver. Nor can the atonement as such be the ground of pardon, either directly or indirectly, by being a manifestation of the love of God to a sinful world, and as such a manifestation, having a reclaiming tendency or influence; for it is only as a complete and perfect atonement, that it becomes such a manifestation of love as it is, and thus acquires its reclaiming influence. An effect is no part of the essential nature of its cause. The atonement then must be complete in its essential nature, and so fully sustain the authority of the lawgiver, or it cannot manifest the love of the lawgiver to sinful men, or possess the least reforming tendency. Is it then said, that an atonement must be *a designed substitute* for the punishment of the pardoned sinner? But surely a perfect lawgiver can *design* to substitute nothing for this punishment except a complete and perfect atonement; except that which as its full effect sustains the lawgiver's authority. The *design* thus to substitute it, cannot therefore be essential to its completeness or perfection as an atonement, but must result solely from its completeness as an atonement.

Nor yet—and most of all—can an atonement render it unjust, as some suppose, to an elect transgressor to punish *him*. Every transgressor, elect or non-elect, deserves to be punished, and therefore may be as *justly* punished under an atonement as were no atonement provided. He *deserves* to be punished, not on the ground of having the absurd right *to be punished*, but solely on the ground of having violated the rights of the moral governor and of his kingdom—rights which are eternal and immutable, and which, with one grand exception, God's right to reign—a right protected by God, and not by the transgressor—are eternally frustrated in their objects by transgression. Nor can the transgressor be supposed to acquire, as the effect of an atonement merely, the absurd right to be exempted from the legal penalty, according to any principle of law or justice. To suppose this, is to suppose that as the effect of an atonement merely, he acquires and sustains some new personal relation to law, to justice, and to the general good, which renders his exemption from punishment *his due;* for no being, except on the ground of such a relation, can possess a right to any blessing as *his due.* To exempt one then from a *deserved* penalty who has *a right* to such exemption, is not an act of pardon or forgiveness, but an act of rendering to him what is *his due*, what can be justly claimed on his part, what cannot be withheld from him without flagrant injustice to him; in a word, it is an act of justice. Thus to exempt one from a *deserved* penalty who has *a right* to the exemption, is to exempt from punishment one who ought *in justice* to be punished, and who ought not in justice to be punished—who deserves to be punished, and does *not* deserve to be punished—the doing of which defies all power and all prerogative. Besides, the transgressor can deserve punishment simply and solely on the ground that the rights of the moral governor, and the rights of his kingdom—rights which in their very nature are immutable and eternal—that these must with one exception remain violated by the transgressor, and be thus frustrated in their objects for evermore. He has done this deed. He has done what he could to frustrate every right of the moral universe, and to fill this universe with the woes of sin instead of the joys of perfect and universal holiness: he had successfully accomplished the result, had not God by atonement and grace interposed his influence to prevent the dire catastrophe. And now can ill-desert be separated from such an act or from its author? Can the relation of the cause to its effect be separated from the former? Can these momentous rights of God and of his kingdom, thus irretrievably and eternally frustrated in their objects by the transgressor, be looked upon in their ruins, known and thought of by himself and by every rational and knowing being, and the ill-desert of such a deed not be necessarily and infallibly known by all to be *forever inseparable* from its perpetrator? Can such a moral being become sinless, free from ill-desert in the sight of God, of man, of truth? Not while he is immortal. Ill-desert once incurred by the act of the transgressor, is not an appendage which can be laid aside or separated from his act. This is admitted by the doctrine of imputed sin. And if it cannot be separated from the act, no more can it be from the actor. The act when done is in its nature and tendency, and as a cause of its actual effect, all in ill-desert that it ever can be. It cannot be changed by being made a less evil than it is; and however the *full* effect of the act in the destruction of all rights is restricted and limited by the interposition of the lawgiver, the ill-desert of the act or of the actor is not thereby either lessened or taken away. For a perfect atonement enthrones law and the lawgiver, not by rendering it unjust to punish, but by rendering it *not unjust*, that is, consistent with justice to pardon the transgressor. Thus the sanctions of God's law, the terrors of his justice, and the withering abhorrence of his holiness for sin, in their unobscured and awful manifestation, are combined with the full effulgence of his love and mercy in all their attractions and charms to a revolted world. These are the wonders of the cross. It is this vision of God which will make the heaven of the redeemed. The ill-desert of sin will not be regarded as a thing that was and is not, nor yet forgotten or unthought of, in one note of that song to the Lamb who is in the midst of the throne—much less will *a right* to pardon and eternal life be claimed in that song. Will that persecutor and blasphemer, that chief of sinners who said, "God forbid that I should glory, save in the cross of Christ;" and again, "By the grace of God I am what I am;" and again, "I count all things but loss for the excellency of the knowledge of Christ Jesus my Lord;" will this man whose life as an apostle was one halleluiah of praise to his Redeemer here on earth, forget this song on his throne above? Will he ever forget his present ill-desert, or deny that the justice of God as a lawgiver might cast him down from his throne to the doom he deserves? Can such theology be in heaven? The claim of *right* to heaven's reward, no matter on what it were founded, would chill and break every heart and cause the praises of redeeming love to cease. No mystical union, no imputation of sins and of righteousness, no works of law, no legal righteousness, will be set to music in that world. Sinners there appreciate the mercy which confers eternal life on those who deserve eternal death. They wish not to forget their ill-desert. It is the cherished remembrance of it, with its contrition, which inspires their gratitude, their joys and their praises; nor would heaven be heaven to them, could they not cast their crowns at the feet of Him "on whose head are many crowns."*

In confirmation of our present leading proposition, that the law of God is immutable in its sanctions, much more might be said on the authority of the Scriptures. Indeed the proof meets us as it were in every part of the sacred volume. It is so various, so multiform, and so obviously decisive, that while it would be tedious, it is quite unnecessary to attempt any exhibition of it in its particular forms and fullness. What I further propose at present, is in a brief way to call attention to some of the more striking facts of God's providence, in which he must

* Contrition on the part of a sinner against God is so fit, so appropriate, so becoming, and therefore so grateful to the mind, that it is absolutely necessary to his highest happiness. Having sinned, it is impossible in the nature of things that he should be happy in the highest degree possible to him without contrition. The heaven of the sinner is emphatically the contrition of grateful love, ever under the smile of God, singing "Unto Him that loved us and washed us from our sins in his own blood."

be viewed as having begun the execution of the penal sanction of his law.

Man then at his creation was placed under law by his Maker, with the sanctions of eternal life and eternal death.* This law as a perfect rule of action, involved nothing less in requirement than that spirit of loyalty which is due to the all-perfect Being from creatures made in his own image, and of course was nothing less than what our Saviour has called "THE FIRST AND GREAT COMMANDMENT OF THE LAW." This law, considered as a perfect rule of action, was virtually given to God's entire moral creation, and of course thus given as the law of requirement to the whole race of human beings, as binding on them from the commencement of their future moral and accountable existence. God however, had in his high counsels determined not only that our first parents should be the progenitors of a numerous race, but also that this whole race should become the subjects of this perfect rule of action from the commencement of their moral agency and commence their moral character by transgressing this perfect law. Our first parents had no sooner transgressed this perfect law than the promise of redemption was revealed, and they and the whole race of their descendants were placed under an economy of mercy—an economy under which the latter were to commence not only their moral relations to their Maker but also their moral character in sin. Was then the perfect law of God repealed, or its essential sanctions separated from it? Was it thus annulled as an authoritative rule of action by grace? Was the law *as law* impaired in its essential perfection and force, so that the transgressor aside from grace was not fully exposed to its penalty? Then were grace in redemption a solecism—a redemption from a legal penalty when there was no such penalty which could be executed. Redemption then necessarily implies a law with a penalty, which from the very nature of law must be executed on every transgressor, unless its execution be prevented by his compliance with the condition of pardoning mercy.

And now how prominently and impressively is all this presented throughout the whole patriarchal history! Who had not transgressed the law of God? Not one. Who was de-

* I shall attempt to show hereafter that such is the only possible meaning of the language of this law.

livered from its fearful penalty? Abel, Enoch, Noah, Abraham, Lot—those and those only who *in faith* offered sacrifice to God, emblematical of the real and all-sufficient atonement of the promised seed—the Son of God. What became of all other men? Let the deluge answer which engulfed a world; let the tempest of fire which destroyed the cities of the plain. These according to Christ and his apostles, were ensamples "suffering the vengeance of eternal fire."* Thus in the beginning of this world's history, the actual execution of the legal penalty of sin has been averted from those only who by faith have relied on the great sacrifice of redemption, while the execution of this penalty has been begun before the eyes of men in all those innumerable cases in which temporal death in God's vindictive judgments has been known to come upon men in their sins. And now is there no penalty as a legal sanction pertaining immutably to God's law—penalty which can be averted from the transgressor only by accepting the great sacrifice of redemption, with the acknowledgment of the just desert of that penalty? Is the law of God *as law*—I do not say as a particular *kind* of law—modified in the least respect; especially is it not distinctly, and as it were in fact sensibly manifest, enthroned in its full authority by its essential penal sanction? And if we follow the history of God and of man in this world as given by revelation, from the calling of Abraham, in the deliverance of his descendants from Egypt, in the giving to Israel of the law on Mount Sinai, and in his administration of this law itself as their national king and national deity; or rather if we view this theocracy as a system representing God's moral government over men as moral beings—for otherwise it is nothing but a system of beggarly elements—what do we find in this history of God and man but God in sensible manifestation, presenting himself constantly, almost exclusively, in the premature *temporal death* of men as transgressors of the Mosaic law, by war, by famine, by pestilence, every instance of which stands forth as an instance of vindictive wrath, of death in sin—eternal death?† These things were done through

* Christ has clearly taught the general principle that all the signal judgments of God which plainly overtake men in the form of temporal death, *for their sins and in their sins*, are the begun execution of the legal penalty of sin. Thus in Luke, xiii. 15, he enforces the doctrine by an appeal to facts!

† Vide subsequent lectures on Legal Penalty.

many, many long centuries—done not only in the view of Israel, but of all the nations of men. If now we pass to the righteous judgment of God in the destruction of this people who crucified their Messiah—the most signal expression of wrath which God ever made in this world, and view it as we must, the beginning of his vindictive wrath never to end—what do we find but God revealing himself by facts manifest to sense, in the execution of the penalty of his law on impenitent and unbelieving men? And now in view of these facts, will it be pretended that the penalty of God's law is separated or separable from it, so long as it is *law* in its essential nature? Nothing plainly has separated the penalty of the law from the law itself in respect to those on whom this very penalty is executed. Has any thing produced this effect in respect to those who as a further effect, are exempted from this evil through grace? This implies that the evil as a legal penalty, is in respect to this class, separated from the law before their exemption from the evil. Of course such are not exempted from the penalty of law, but from an evil which had before been but has now ceased to be a penalty of law. They are not pardoned; they are not forgiven; they are not justified according to any principles of law, for the law has been annihilated in its sanctions, and of course wholly annihilated that they may be exempted from what was once its just penalty, but is so no longer in respect to them. No matter on what supposed grounds or reasons this is done—whether by mystical union, by imputation, by atonement, by faith, by any one or all these combined—if by the separation of the penalty of law from law itself, the transgressor is exempted from this evil, he is not and cannot be said to be exempted from a legal penalty, for there is no legal penalty from which exemption is conceivable, but forgiveness, remission, pardon, justification by grace in respect to a transgressor of law, are words without meaning.

But it cannot be necessary to dwell longer on this subject. Any view of God's sovereignty, of mystical union, of imputation or atonement, which separates from God's perfect law its penal sanction in respect to a transgressor, annihilates that law for the transgressor's benefit.

Here too it might be shown that the whole system of redemption as revealed in the Gospel in all its grace and mercy, is according to this view of law wholly subverted. For what can be plainer than that if by some mysterious, unheard-of maneuver or process, a lawgiver could and should, in his sovereignty, constitute in reality and truth a multitude of disobedient subjects of his law, and another sinless or perfectly obedient subject of his law, ONE MORAL PERSON, so that the moral character, and with it all the *legal relations* of the former as transgressors should cease to be theirs and become those of the obedient subject, and so further, that the moral character of the latter, and with it all his *legal relations* as a perfectly obedient subject, should cease to be his and become those of the transgressors—I ask if these things were done, where would be the grace, the mercy, the forgiveness, the pardon, the gratuitous justification of the Gospel? So far as acts of grace and mercy to the transgressor are concerned, these consist in some sovereign acts of necromancy called constituting a mystical union, imputation—justly and on grounds of ill-desert inflicting legal penalty on a perfectly obedient subject, by which all personal sins and ill-desert of the transgressor cease to be his own and become another's, and all the perfect personal obedience and merit of another become his. Here cease the acts of grace and mercy toward the transgressor. What more grace or mercy does he need? What more are possible in his case? But in all this there is no forgiveness or remission of sins, no pardon, no gratuitous justification, nor yet the least preparation or ground for the possibility of either, but only a preparation for him who was once a transgressor, to come free from all ill-desert, all guilt, all just exposure to legal penalty, free from sin and perfectly obedient to law, and demand as matter of absolute right and justice, on the ground of personal merit, the acceptance and favor of the lawgiver. Is this *pardoning* or *forgiving* iniquity? Is any such use of language to be found in Hebrew, Greek or Latin in any human language? Did a human being ever ask God or another human being to pardon his offense or his sin, meaning that it should be done by the process of mystical union, imputation, and by so giving him a personal claim—a claim *de merito*, a claim of right and justice—to favor on the ground of his absolute faultiness and the fulfillment of every obligation? Is this "justifying the ungodly?" Is this being justified *freely* by his *grace*, through the redemption that is in Christ Jesus? Or is it the subversion of the entire system of grace and mercy revealed in the Gospel?

LECTURE IX.

THE *NATURE* OF GOD'S MORAL GOVERNMENT AS REVEALED.

Section 2: The law a rule of action and not of judgment.—Error on this point.—Law as a rule of action never called law in the Scriptures.—All men are under it, however.—All men, in fact, condemned by it, but not judged by it as yet.—Objections considered.—Position confirmed by a view of the facts of the Scriptures.—Section 3: The law, in requiring obedience, prohibits disobedience, and *vice versa*.—Distinction made by theologians, untenable from the nature of law.—Impossible to be applied to a subject of law.—Introduced to justify another; viz., that between the active and passive obedience of Christ.—Source in the use of negative terms.—Denied in the Scriptures.

Having, in the preceding section, considered the law of God as immutable in its authority, its claim, its sanctions, I now propose to consider it—

Sect. 2.—As a rule of action, and not a rule of judgment.

My proposition may be more fully stated thus: *That the word law, when applied in the manner now under consideration, though used in the Scriptures to denote God's rule of action, requiring of men their whole duty, is never in this application used to denote the rule of judgment.*

Error in respect to this part of the subject, has, I apprehend, been a source of other errors, and on this account requires correction. In many, not to say in most of those languages into which the Scriptures have been translated, as well as in that in which the New Testament was written, the word *law* may be said to denote *a rule of judgment as well as an authoritative rule of action.* This may be said to be the common and proper meaning of the word with all nations except the Hebrews. Hence it is not to be wondered at, that one peculiarity in the Hebrew use of the word should be overlooked by at least many of the translators and expounders of the sacred writings. Indeed, it is difficult, if not impossible, in some cases to avoid conceiving and speaking of the law of God's moral government over men, without conceiving it as unmodified by an economy of grace. In this use the word denotes—and for aught I see, is and must be used to denote for certain necessary purposes—a universal, authoritative rule of action and of judgment to its subjects; thus requiring of them all that which as moral beings they ought to do, as the only condition of acceptance and favor on the part of the lawgiver. This I shall find it convenient to speak of as *law in the classic sense of the word*, or in other forms of language which shall distinguish it from *law* as including an economy of grace. The reality of such a law, in this full and precise meaning, must be admitted. Its comprehensive nature, what it is not and what it is, I have attempted largely to unfold in preceding lectures. Nor can we even form any just or adequate conception of an economy of grace, without forming this conception of law under such a system of moral government as that which, without an economy of grace, would and must exist over the moral creation of God.

This law of God's moral government, as both a rule of action and of judgment, is the law of benevolent action—that law which the Saviour calls (not law, but) "the first and great *commandment of the law*." "The second," as he tells us, "is like unto it." These for certain purposes may be distinguished from each other as he has distinguished them. They may also be understood as one; the former as including in all ordinary cases the latter, together with such particular precepts for the regulation of subordinate acts and doings as in the variable circumstances of men become *right* and *wrong*, though, as before explained, never *morally* right and wrong. Under this law, God, as we have seen, placed our first parents in Paradise, requiring obedience to the first and great commandment, in instituting the holy rest and worship of the Sabbath, and obedience to the second in their social relations; while the positive prohibition, which they violated, bespoke his supreme and rightful sovereignty, and was clothed, as were the others, with all the majesty of law as a rule of action and a rule of judgment, sustained by eternal sanctions.

But here the question arises, Is this rule of action and of judgment—this law of God's moral government—in this full meaning, ever called *law*, or spoken of as an actually existing law of God, in the Scriptures? I admit and maintain that enough is said of it in the Scriptures to unfold its nature and import, and to render proper the application to it of the word *law*, in this most absolute or fullest import. (Vide Gen. ii. 16; iii. 11; Rom. v. 14; 1 Tim. ii. 14.) The formal enactment in Gen. ii. 16, and the sentence, "unto condemnation," after its transgression, though not a sentence dooming our first parents and their posterity to bear the full penalty threatened, are decisive that our first parents were placed under this rule as *a law* in the most absolute sense of the word. The reason that it is never expressly called *law* as an existing reality, is not that it ceased to be an authoritative rule of action to men; nor that men by transgression did not deserve its full penalty; nor that without redemption through the promised seed they must not incur such a doom. But I would ask, whether the reason of this fact may not be this: that this rule of action and of judgment was no longer what it had been to Adam before his apostasy, nor what it would be to his descendants were they to live and act under a merely legal system, but that as a rule of judgment, in all its fearfulness, it was superseded by that of the Gospel? (Rom. ii. 16; John, iii. 18; Heb. xii. 18; John, v. 22, 27; 2 Thess. i. 8; 1 Tim. i. 11.) Was it not of high practical importance to divest the minds of sinful men of the thought, that they were in the absolute sense under this law as a rule of judgment, and to convince them that "there is forgiveness with God, that he may be feared?" Would this have been easily accomplished, had this law been held up to human contemplation as a rule of judgment? Has it not ever been difficult to possess the human mind of the idea that a rule of action is not necessarily also a rule of judgment?

Whatever opinion we may form upon these points, it seems quite undeniable that the word *law*, since the fall of man and the promise of the Redeemer, cannot be used in divine revelation to denote the law of God's moral government as an actually existing rule of judgment to this sinful world. The reason is, that this law is not nor can it be a rule of judgment under an economy of grace.

On this point let me not be misunderstood. I am not saying that the whole world are not, and have not always been, under the law of God's moral government *as a rule of action*. As such a rule—as a requirement of what ought to be done—it is a rule of constant, universal, unchangeable, and eternal obligation upon every subject of God's moral dominion. Nor is this all that can with truth nor all that need be said of it. It is such a rule that all men, having transgressed it, are already under its just condemnation; so far under its condemnation, that if tried by it and judged by it and by nothing else, they would and must be actually condemned, and sentenced to bear its full penalty. Such a result must follow such a trial that the authority of the law might be sustained. But there has been no such trial of any human being, nor any necessity for it. The authority of this law, which is its whole influence, has been, as we have seen, fully preserved and established by the great propitiation of the Son of God. (Rom. iii. 31.)

While then it is conceded that all men are thus under the law of God's moral government; under it as a rule of action with unimpaired obligation; under it as imparting a knowledge of sin and just condemnation; under it as a rule of judgment so far that they must be doomed to bear its full penalty, unless deliverance comes from some other source than the law itself;—it is still maintained that they are not under it as a rule of judgment, according to which on the great day of account their final allotment is to be fixed. If this were so then none can be justified or saved; for he who is judged and sentenced according to this law, and who has transgressed it as all men have, must bear its penalty. Nor will it be pretended, at least by any Protestant, that this law is a rule of judgment to believers—to them who obey the Gospel. For then how can they be justified? Is it then a rule of judgment to unbelievers—to them who do not obey the Gospel? But where do the Scriptures teach that unbelievers are to be judged and condemned on the last day, by the law of God's moral government? How does this comport with the Saviour's declaration, "He that believeth not is condemned already" [not because he has disobeyed the law], "because he hath not believed in the name of the only-begotten Son of God?" Besides, is any thing more plainly taught in the Scriptures than that all men, Jew and Gentile, shall be judged on the final day according to the Gospel? (Rom. ii. 16.) Nor does this imply that the unbelieving are not under condemnation for the sin and guilt of transgressing the law of God's moral government, so far as they can be without the final and decisive act of the judge; nor that they will not as unbelievers be actually doomed to bear the penalty of this law, when tried and sentenced by the Gospel. Surely the Gospel exempts no unbelieving transgressor of this law from the execution of its penalty. All men come to the judgment-seat in the common character of transgressors of this law, condemned by it as law, self-condemned, not to be convicted of their transgression by trial, but knowing that they are worthy of the death which is the legal penalty. Every mouth is stopped with an overwhelming sense of guilt, and the way fully prepared without trial, or judgment, or sentence, for the execution of the legal penalty. For aught that appears from the Scriptures, God (were there no other fact to be decided except that men are transgressors of this law) might execute its penalty without a judgment-day, and still sufficiently manifest his justice. Or if not, if there would be a necessity that all should be tried by the violated law as a rule of judgment, then all must be condemned to bear its penalty. To say otherwise, or to say all that can with truth be said in the present case, viz., that thus tried by the law, all must be doomed to bear its penalty, unless as tried by the Gospel also, they shall be exempted from this penalty, is to say that this law is not the rule of judgment by which their final allotment is to be determined.

Indeed, how can this law be the rule of judgment to any? In respect to all men, with the common character of transgressors of this law and the common condition of just exposure to its penalty, the sentence of the law is suspended by a gracious economy, or rather has been so set aside, that the connection between transgression and punishment may be dissolved by the subject's own act, and that not a human being need be fixed in his final allotment by this law as a rule of judgment. Another probation than that under law as a rule of judgment has been instituted for all, and another trial than that according to law awaits all under a provision of grace, which nothing can annul. The judge cannot condemn and so doom a transgressor of this law to bear its penalty, according to this law as a rule of judgment, without contravening his own ordinance of grace. The final question is then, not what saith the violated law to all transgressors as a rule of judgment. It has already said one and the same thing concerning all. It has given to all the knowledge of sin and of merited condemnation, and so stopped every mouth. Its decision in respect to men is so far final and needs no repetition. But does the Gospel assume in its provisions and proffers of grace, that this law has thus actually condemned any? What then is its redemption (2 Peter, ii. 1) provided for all men? Besides, if this law has actually condemned any as sinners, it has actually condemned all; and what then is that Gospel which with its provisions of grace is to be preached to every creature?

Is it here said that none will be condemned at last, except those who have transgressed this law? True; but how does this prove that any will be judged by this law, and condemned because they have transgressed it, when all through grace may escape such a trial and its doom; and when not one can or will be thus condemned, nor condemned at all, except he disbelieves the Gospel, or at least the proffered grace of God to both Jew and Gentile? Surely the fact of transgressing law decides nothing in respect to any, either for justification or sanctification, and therefore decides nothing concerning the future allotment of men as transgressors of law. On the contrary, the final decision of the Saviour of the world has fixed the terms of life and death once for all: "He that believeth and is baptized shall be saved, and he that believeth not shall be damned." What can be plainer than that the final, the determining question in respect to each transgressor of this law —a question on the decision of which the eternal issue wholly depends—is, has he believed the Gospel or has he not, has he obeyed the Gospel or has he not? If he has, the non-execution of the legal penalty being conditioned on his believing is arrested—averted; and he being tried and judged is also justified according to the Gospel—that is, according to the principles of a gracious economy. If he has not, the execution of the legal penalty being conditioned on his unbelief, is not arrested or averted, and he being tried and judged is condemned according to the Gospel. And now what is the determining cause or reason of the justification of the one? Plainly his faith in the Gospel! What is the determining cause or reason of the condemnation of the other? Plainly his disbelief of the Gospel! Had the believer not believed, he had been condemned. Had the unbeliever believed, he had been justified.

Is it said that no transgressor of law can be doomed to bear its penalty unless he be tried, judged, and condemned according to law? But the Gospel proceeds on the opposite assumption—that the transgressor of law must bear the legal penalty, unless he be delivered from it when tried and judged according to the Gospel. Besides, the law itself demands no such trial or process as that now supposed for the specified purpose. It demands no execution of its penalty to uphold its authority, which is the only conceivable reason for demanding it. The atonement of the Son of God upholds its authority in absolute perfection, and thus wholly removes the necessity for this legal process by removing every reason for it. The end or object of a trial is, not to determine who can and who cannot be justified consistently with the authority, and with all the principles of law, for all can be; but to determine who can, and who cannot be justified consistently with other interests of benevolence—interests with which the justification of the sinner becomes consistent by his faith or personal holiness. On this condition the Gospel proclaims a complete amnesty to all men in respect to legal penalty; and the question is, whether being as every one is a transgressor of the law, when judged as he must be according to the Gospel, he shall be condemned by the Gospel? If so, the law takes its course, and the transgressor has to bear the deserved penalty of the law with the superadded curse of the Gospel. Nor is there any other way or mode in which he can be sentenced to bear the penalty of the law; for if we suppose him to be judged by the law and convicted of being a transgressor of law, still he could not be doomed to bear its penalty without being also tried and judged by the Gospel, and thus being convicted of having rejected the Gospel by unbelief, and in this way only incurring the penalty of the law.

While all men are then under the law of God's moral government as a perfect rule of moral action, and while none can escape its just penalty except by faith in the Gospel, they are not under it as a rule of judgment by which their future allotment is to be determined. If these things are so, it follows that the word *law* can never be used in the Scriptures to denote the law of God's moral government as both a rule of action and of judgment.

Again, it may be said, as it often has been, that when the subject of God's law transgresses that law, he falls at once under its just condemnation, or that he is at once condemned by the law. Such forms of language are often used by theologians. But is not such language very equivocal—is it not often used in one meaning and then in another meaning by the same writer, without his being aware of the fact—and hence often used in a meaning in which in its proper meaning it is not true? If then it mean that the transgressor of law is justly condemned by the law, so far as he can be without the act of the judge condemning him to bear the penalty of the law; or that he is *exposed*, so far as any principle of law is concerned, to a just or merited condemnation by the judge; or that judged and sentenced according to law, he must be condemned to bear its penalty, the truth of this I have already conceded. But if it mean that the transgressor of law is, according to law, necessarily and hopelessly condemned to bear its penalty, so that through an adequate atonement there can be no authorized hope of escaping the penalty, or so that the proffer of pardon may not instantly follow the act of transgression—this I deny, as contrary to the revealed fact in the case of our first parents, and of all their surviving descendants. According to one of these meanings of the language, if true there can be no economy of grace, while the truth of the other is the only possible ground of such an economy. The difference in these meanings of language is then of fundamental importance. That use of it in which one meaning in the mind of a writer is confounded with the other, or that in which the two meanings specified are not precisely distinguished, is only to begin and end in confusion of thought respecting one of the most material truths on the subject. And yet how few of one large class of commentators on Paul's Epistle to the Romans, especially on the 5th chapter, have not either confounded the two meanings of this form of language, or rather used it to mean the act of God condemning men actually to bear the penalty of his law! If this be so, of what avail is redemption by the Son of God?

Let us now look at the various dispensations of God toward the human race at different periods. From the apostasy of man and the promise of a Redeemer, we find in all the Scriptures no formal express promulgation of the law of God's moral government as a rule of judgment to this sinful world. During the whole patriarchal dispensation, that is, from Adam to Moses (Rom. v. 14), we find Revelation silent in respect to this law, even as a rule of action, and of course as a rule of judgment. We find sin abounding as the transgression of this law, and its prevalence recognized in the severity of divine judgments, or rather in the execution of its penalty begun in the destruction of the world by a deluge, and afterward of

Sodom and Gomorrah by fire and brimstone (Jude, ver. 7). And yet how impressively in both cases is the great truth of Gospel grace unfolded! Righteous Noah and his family are safe in the ark; righteous Lot is delivered in the overthrow of the cities of the plains, and had there been ten righteous there, i. e., *righteous by faith*, these cities had not been destroyed. Here then is a revelation of the doctrine of justification by faith—of the relation of the "obedience of faith" in averting the wrath and securing the favor of God. We find sin also—sin as the transgression of law—not less truly recognized by all the generation of the righteous, as Abel, Enoch, Noah, Abraham, &c., especially in their "offerings and burnt-offerings for sins." We find various divine commands and directions for the regulation of human conduct, but no full, formal, promulgation of the law of God's moral government. Still, we find sin and the knowledge of sin as meriting condemnation, ever distinctly recognized. But we find so far as the language of Revelation is concerned, not the law of God's moral government presented as the rule of judgment, but instead and prominently, the placability and the mercy of God to the guilty. We find this law clearly implied as a rule of action and duty for men as moral beings, who had transgressed it—a law according to which they might be *justly* judged and *justly* condemned; but we find even for such beings, not a rule of judgment in this law, but a rule of judgment provided by grace—provided in "the law of faith," and the question of man's acceptance or condemnation to be, not whether he has transgressed the law of God's moral government, but whether he has obeyed the law of faith. In a word, we find clearly implied the perfect law of God's moral government in all its authority and influence as a rule of action, and we also find an economy of grace. The latter implies sin as the transgression of the former, but wholly precludes it as a rule of judgment.

Accordingly, if we now advert to the most signal event under this dispensation—the calling of Abraham, and especially to the covenant (Gal. iii. 8) which God made with this father of the faithful—we find no promulgation of the law of God's moral government, but the economy of grace more fully disclosed in the import of its conditions, in the superiority of its typical priesthood, and in the riches of its grace: in the import of its condition, for the patriarch's faith is counted for righteousness (Gen. xv. 6*); in the superiority of its typical priesthood, for the name of the priest is "*king of righteousness;*" in the riches of its grace, for its promise is, "I will be a God to thee, and to thy seed after thee." I cannot but here remark, how divinely fitted was this method of God's revealing himself to men, to lead them to a compliance with the conditions of his gracious covenant. Instead of the formal promulgation of law with its sanctions of reward and penalty, and thus destroying hope through conscious guilt, or fostering self-righteousness through the perversion of human pride, that law was known at most as a rule of action written on the conscience, and through the execution of its penalty by terrible judgments on men in their sins, who by faith might have averted this issue. God too, was ever making abundant and decisive manifestations of his tender mercy to men but imperfectly good—men who, though justly deserving condemnation by law, became righteous by repentance and faith. How could the wicked expect to escape the judgment of God? If they did, how must they brave the peculiar terrors of the merciful dispensation of God by despising the riches of his goodness, and after their hardness and impenitent heart treasure up wrath against the day of wrath!

We now pass to another signal change in God's dispensation—a change wrought not by abrogating the Abrahamic covenant or abating aught from its provisions or promises of grace, but by introducing another covenant founded on far inferior promises. The descendants of Abraham with the rest of the world are now wholly given to idolatry. They have been long in Egypt, and are thoroughly Egyptianized. The designs and efforts of God's mercy and grace toward them are apparently baffled, but they are not abandoned. He delivers them from the bondage into which he had carried them for their sins, and by his outstretched arm conducts them through the Red Sea and the wilderness to Mount Sinai. Here he makes with them another covenant (a *διαθήκη—institution*), and under

* The condition in Gen. xvii. 1, is, "Walk before me and be thou perfect." The precept, as I suppose, must be understood to inculcate not absolute but a relative perfection—or perfection as related to the end for which it is required. Thus Abraham was required to be a sincere believer—to obey "the law of faith"—to be what he must be, to be accepted and blessed of God through grace. (Vide Eph. iv. 13; Phill. iii. 15.)

it as a peculiar system, separates this people from all other nations in the land of Canaan, and perpetuates their existence as a nation with various revolutions and changes, until it had served the high purpose of introducing the reign of their Messiah over them and over the world.

This system, as we have seen, was a theocracy—a system of national government, of which God was the national king and tutelary deity, adopted with the comprehensive design of recovering this people from polytheism, and of representing the higher system revealed to Abraham, which it could not disannul—the system of God's moral government over men as moral beings under an economy of grace. Here I have occasion only to call to your remembrance two important things. The one is, that God in establishing this theocracy and assuming the relation of the national king of Israel, did, like every other national king, as became him, require a spirit of loyalty on the part of his subjects—i. e., he clearly revealed the perfect law of his moral government as the rule of action, though not as a rule of judgment. The other is, that as a representative system it taught that God, with the authority of the law of his moral government unimpaired, was still administering that government under a gracious economy, so that with nothing abated of this law as a rule of duty, there was yet another rule of judgment for men revealed in the covenant made with Abraham and his seed forever, even "the law of faith."

Thus we see, that in all the dispensations of God toward men, the law of his perfect moral government has since the apostasy been so modified by an economy of grace, that while its force of obligation is not weakened, it has not lost one iota of its authority or influence as a rule of action, while its penalty will be executed on every unbeliever when judged by the Gospel; still, not this law, but the Gospel, will be the rule of judgment to this sinful world on the last day. In accordance with these things, we find, that while the only rule, which is both a rule of action and of judgment to men, is in the Scriptures called *law*—"the law of faith"—the only possible rule of judgment, and therefore of justifying and condemning sinful men under an economy of grace,—the word *law* is never applied in the Scriptures to the law of God's moral government over men as moral beings, to denote an existing rule of action and of judgment.

Sect. 3.—The proposition next to be maintained is, that the *law of God in requiring obedience prohibits disobedience*, and *in prohibiting disobedience requires obedience.* The importance of presenting this as an essential principle of law does not arise from the unobvious truth of the principle, nor from any want of its admission in practical life, so much as from the assumption and use of the opposite principle in theology. Who but theologians have ever thought that a subject of law could be obedient to law without being *not disobedient*, or disobedient to law without being *not obedient?* Many theologians since the Reformation, modifying the view of Anselm, which in literal language represents sin as *a debt*, have maintained that the transgressor of law incurs *two debts—the debitum pœnæ* and the *debitum negligentiæ.* Their theory is, that the transgressor of law not only transgresses but fails to obey the law; that by his transgression he incurs its penalty, and by his failure to obey forfeits its reward. Hence the advocates of this theory have been led to the distinction between what they call the active obedience of Christ—his obedience to the law, and his passive obedience—his voluntary submission to sufferings and death. Hence again, they maintain that the *debitum pœnæ* incurred by transgressing law, is canceled by the passive obedience of Christ, and the *debitum negligentiæ* incurred by the want of obedience, is canceled by his active obedience.

This view of the nature of law I claim to be wholly groundless and forbidden. The known nature of the subject decisively shuts off this interpretation. The question respects the meaning of the word *law*, *de usu loquendi.* There is not any word better understood by mankind the world over, than this word in its present application. Every one knows that law is such a rule of action, that its subject acting under it either obeys or disobeys it. As a line cannot be conceived which is not either straight or crooked, so a subject of law acting in this relation, cannot be conceived who is not either obedient or disobedient. He cannot be conceived to want obedience without being conceived to be disobedient, nor to want disobedience without being conceived to be obedient. The want of obedience without disobedience, and the want of disobedience without obedience, may be truly predicated of a book, a table, or any thing else which is not a subject of law. But neither the want of obedience without disobedience, nor the want of disobedience without obedience, can, with a shade of truth, be predicated of a subject of law acting in this relation. A man may be either wise or foolish, but he cannot be both. So a subject of law may be either obedient or disobedient, but he cannot be both. If therefore he is not obedient, he is disobedient, and if he is not disobedient he is obedient.

Further, what would be the relation of a subject of law, who, under its ceaseless claim for his obedience, can be viewed as without obedience and yet not disobedient; or as without disobedience and yet not obedient? Should it here be said that neither of these two relations of the subject of law is supposable *in re* or in reality, then I ask, Why is it supposed? If there is nothing in the nature of law nor in the relation of its subject, to hinder his standing in one of the supposed relations without the other, why may he not be supposed in reality so to stand? If the so-called passive obedience of Christ can, according to the nature and principles of law place its subject in the relation of one who is *not disobedient*, without placing him in the relation of one who is obedient, or, as some would say, in the relation of one who is *pardoned* but *not justified*, who shall say that transgressors of law are not often placed in this relation to law? And what shall be said of the condition of such transgressors of law? The law cannot demand their punishment, for they are *pardoned:* it cannot acquiesce in their acceptance and reward, for they are *not justified.* If they are summoned to the judgment-seat in this condition, what shall be their allotment? Does the law of God, in one of its essential principles, recognize a purgatory?

Again: should the subject of law from the beginning, perfectly obey the law, his obedience would secure the twofold effect of a title to reward and exemption from penalty. Should the subject disobey the law, his disobedience would secure the twofold effect of the loss of reward and of exposure to penalty. But now, if the disobedient subject can according to law, be exempted from penalty without being secured in the reward, why may not the obedient subject be secured in the reward without being secured in the exemption from penalty? If it be said that security in the reward of an obedient subject of law, necessarily in the nature of the case involves security in exemption from penalty, I answer, so does exemption from penalty on the part of a disobedient subject of law necessarily, in the nature of the case, involve security in his reward. If then something more than that which is necessary to exempt the disobedient subject from the penalty is necessary to his securing the reward, then something more than that which is necessary to secure the obedient subject in his reward is necessary to secure his exemption from penalty. We cannot indeed, suppose that a stone should be either an obedient or disobedient subject of the law of God's moral government, nor of course, that as either, it should be rewarded or punished. But man is a subject of this law. As such he is either an obedient or disobedient subject, and must sustain all the relations of one or the other. That therefore, which secures to him the reward of this law, must exempt him from its penalty; and that which exempts him from its penalty, must secure to him its reward.

Again: according to the theory now opposed, there are in the justification of the sinner two causes supposed, each resulting in its own distinct effect, while either cause must produce both effects. Thus, according to this theory, *the passive obedience* of Christ results in or is the cause of the justified sinner's exemption from punishment. Here then is one cause, and its own and exclusive effect. Again: the active obedience of Christ results in or is the cause of the justified sinner's acceptance and reward as its own exclusive effect. But according to the essential nature of law, nothing can exempt the transgressor from the penalty of law but his obedience to law, which also secures his reward. The active obedience of Christ then, in gratuitous justification supplying the want of obedience to law or paying the *debitum negligentiæ*, must produce the same effect which the perfect obedience of the sinner would have produced had it been rendered, and must therefore wholly supersede the necessity of Christ's *passive obedience*. So, according to law, the exemption of the sinner from the penalty of law is secured by the absence or want of disobedience, which also would have secured his reward. The passive obedience of Christ then, in gratuitous justification, answering the end of the absence or want of disobedience, or paying the *debitum pœnæ*, must secure the reward, and must therefore wholly supersede the necessity of Christ's active obedience. Thus, instead of a different, distinct single effect peculiar to each cause, each cause produces both effects, or a twofold effect which is the same in both cases. The entire requisite effect being necessarily produced by either cause, the necessity of the other cause is entirely superseded. If we suppose either, not the shadow of a reason so far as the principles of law are concerned, can be given for supposing the other. The inference then from the nature and principles of law is undeniable, that if the subject of law is not obedient to law he is disobedient, and if he is not disobedient he is obedient. Thus all men, in their practical conceptions of the subject, conceive of the relations to law in every subject of law. None of the principles of human intercourse are better or more assuredly understood than those which result from law. The entire influence of law in human society, and all that is comprised in the administration of justice or of government among men, must wholly cease, if men did not regard a legal requirement as a prohibition of its opposite, and a legal prohibition as a requirement of its opposite, on the part of the subject of law. Such being the universal conception of men, such and such only is the universal import of the word *law*, as used in the word of God in its present application. To say otherwise, is to say that the word is not used in the Scriptures *de usu loquendi*, which is to say that the word has no meaning, and that so far as this important word is concerned, the Scriptures are not a revelation.

It may confirm the truth, briefly to refer to the probable source of the error on the subject under consideration. This seems to be the use of negative forms of language in certain cases in which they answer all the purposes of speech, as well, to say the least, as the use of positive forms. Language often derives peculiar force from expressing more than it says. When our Saviour said to the Jews, "I know you, that ye have *not* the love of God in you," instead of implying even the possible absence of the opposite principle, his language in import was a direct and impressive charge of the existence of that principle. Because that it can be said of a stone that it is not either foolish or wise, can it be said of a man that he is not wise, without saying in import he is foolish; or of a subject of law, that he is not obedient without saying he is disobedient, or that he is not disobedient without saying that he is obedient?

But I appeal to the language of Christ, which is still more

explicit: "No man," saith he, "can serve two masters, for either he will hate the one and love the other, or else he will hold to the one and despise the other." How could the truth be more plainly or convincingly taught respecting man, than that if he hates or does not love one of the two great objects of moral affection, he does love the other? And again, he saith, "He that is not for me is against me." Who then shall say, that in man's relation to God's law there is any middle ground, which he can occupy between obedience and disobedience; or that not being for God is not necessarily identical with being against him?—that the want of obedience to law in the subject of law is not disobedience to law?

But we have instruction on this topic, which, it would seem, must terminate all debate. The case of the unprofitable servant (Matt. xxv. 30) is one not of disobedience as distinguished from obedience, but of *the want of obedience.* For this, he is not merely deprived of a reward, but is doomed to outer darkness, in weeping and gnashing of teeth. How can it then be said that punishment comes for disobedience and not for the want of obedience?

Thus the principle of law, that in requiring obedience law prohibits disobedience, and in prohibiting disobedience it requires obedience, is not a merely speculative and harmless principle, but one which common sense determines to be involved in the essential nature of law, and which our Lord deemed of sufficient practical moment formally to inculcate. Why then has this principle of law been denied to such an extent by theologians? Is it not plainly invented for the purpose of carrying a point, in their sectarian scheme of theology respecting the influence of what they call *the active* and the *passive* obedience of Christ in our justification? Whether they can maintain their views of the subject on other grounds than the principle of law on which they claim to rest it, is not now the question. Whether they can or cannot, these views can derive no support from this or any other principle of law. What would be the relation of a subject of law with its claim on him for ceaseless obedience if he can be viewed as without obedience and yet not disobedient, or as without disobedience and yet not obedient?

I have dwelt the longer on this principle of law, because the error in respect to it has been made, as it seems to me, the most plausible basis of a far more serious error respecting *the active and passive obedience* of Christ in our justification—an error which excludes the great sacrifice of the Son of God from its Scriptural and august relation to law, as exclusively sustaining its authority in our justification.

LECTURE X.

THE *NATURE* OF GOD'S MORAL GOVERNMENT AS REVEALED.

Section 4: The law in the sum of its requirements.—The sum of requirements stated.—Measured by human and not angelic capacities.—The law requires supreme love and honor to the extent of man's power.—This love comprehends those great duties that are always binding, and every other duty whenever it is binding.—Mistake of divines in considering "the two commandments of the law" as equal.—Love to God.—Love of benevolence and not love of complacency.—Relation of one to the other.—This love is an elective preference, and supreme.—The law of God is perfect; it is holy, just, and good.—This view important to elevate the standard of Christian piety.—Ought to be enforced by the Christian ministry to stimulate to holiness, and to expose the defects of a godless philanthrophy.

I now proceed, as I proposed, to consider the law—

Sect. 4—In the sum of its requirements.

By *the sum of the requirements* of the divine law I mean that one comprehensive requirement which, in its true nature and tendency, so involves or includes all others, as when obeyed to secure obedience to all others.

I shall now attempt to show that the sum of the requirements of the law of God is, *that man love God in the highest degree in which he is capable of loving him;* or in more simple phrase, *that he love God as much as he can love him.*

Such is the obvious and undeniable import of what our Saviour calls "The first and great commandment of the law," which is so often repeated in the Old Testament and so fully ratified in the New; viz., "Thou shalt love the Lord thy God with all thy heart, and with all thy soul, and with all thy mind, and with all thy strength." No form of language, according to Hebrew idiom, stronger than that which is here employed, can be supposed,for the purpose of expressing man's duty to love God to the extent of his power to love him. To understand the language therefore in any other meaning, is not only gratuitous, but is forbidden by the very terms employed.

The language is also so peculiar, compared with any used to describe love toward any other object than God; it is so manifestly intensive in form and exhaustive in specification, that we at once admit its propriety and truth, and feel the irreverence of applying it to any other object.

We shall, I think, be still more convinced that such is the import of this rule of action by further explanation and reflection.

Man's capacity to love God is comparatively limited. He is not an angel, and with his inferior powers he cannot love God as angels do. His feebler intellect with its necessary feebler apprehension and limited comprehension of God, involves a corresponding weakness of heart and will, so that were he to love God with all his power to love him, his love would not burn and glow with the intensity of a seraph's fervor. This fact should guard the mind against all enthusiastic notions on the very subject, in respect to which they have been allowed and cherished. And further, man's power of loving may be viewed, so to speak, as a given quantity—so much in degree, more or less—in relation to all the objects which he is qualified in his nature to love.

Moreover, he has not only power to love other objects than God, but is under an absolute necessity of loving many other objects. These are fit objects of a degree of affection or love, and man cannot suppress and extinguish all affection in his heart for each and all of them. If he could, and were actually so to do, he could not exercise gratitude to God—he could not sing the song of heaven—for gratitude involves not merely love to a benefactor, but also the love of his gifts. Now if man should love all other objects of affection in as low a degree as he can, or in no higher degree than they are fitted to be loved, the residue of his power of affection would remain to be exercised in loving God; and should he actually and perfectly exercise this power in loving God, he would love God *as much as he can love him*,—i. e., " with all his heart, and with all his soul, and with all his mind, and with all his strength." He would thus perfectly fulfill the FIRST and GREAT commandment.

This perfect love to God is indeed supreme love; but it is also more than supreme love, for man may love God supremely, and yet not love him to the extent of his power. Some however, suppose that the sum of the divine requirement is *supreme love* to God, and nothing more. Indeed, theology is almost silent in respect to any thing more, even as man's duty; as if a creature formed in God's image had no power to place God in his affections, in but a slight degree above the things which are seen and temporal. But can this be true? Can it be true that God has given only powers so diminutive to the creature whom he has made for eternal companionship with himself? Or has man powers of affection, which in the perfect use of them, qualify him to become an associate with angels and archangels, and can any reason be given why man should not love God more than supremely, even to the extent of his powers? or any reason why he does not in fact thus love God, except that he loves something else unduly—more than it is fit to be loved in view of its relative worth? Nor can man love God less than with all his power to love him, and at the same time love him as it is fit that he should love him. But perfect fitness in the degree of affection toward any object, according to the true worth of the object, is essential to, or rather is the perfect rightness of the affection, whether natural or moral. Of course there can be no perfect rightness either natural or moral in any affection on the part of man toward God, in which man does not love God to the extent of his power. This element therefore, whatever be necessary to the *moral rightness* of this affection, is essential to its *perfect rightness* or rectitude in any sense, and of course to its perfect *moral* rightness or rectitude. Besides, why ought God to be loved by us with merely *supreme* love, and not to be loved to the extent of our power to love him? Of what love less than this can a Being of so much greatness, and goodness, and capacity of blessedness, be thought worthy? If in the whole range of existence there is one such being as we call God, then in the infinitude of his attributes, and in his capacity of blessedness, how far must he excel any and every necessarily limited system of creation! If we suppose such a system to be enlarged, and its perfection and happiness—all that can render it beautiful and lovely—to be increased to any extent, so would the blessedness of God as rejoicing in his own work also increase, in the peculiar and higher blessedness of giving instead of receiving. In view of the future, God can never be said to have already made the fullest conceivable expression of himself in the happiness of his own creation, nor to have secured to himself the highest conceivable degree of blessedness. Creation, however vast to our apprehension, is and ever must be insignificant compared with the Creator, save only that it reveals a greatness in him unexpressed in the past, and which never can be expressed in a coming eternity.

If God is a part of the actual universe, then is he inconceivably greater in excellence than all beside. In comparison with him, any created system were as nothing. To deny man's obligation to love with all his power such a being as God, is to deny his obligation to love in the degree proportioned to the work of the object; and if this obligation to love God does not exist, none exists. But better, far better surely were the non-existence or the misery of God's creation, than the non-existence or misery of God himself. Yet either the non-existence or misery of God is the necessary result of a warrant for practical enmity on the part of his moral creation, or, which is the same thing, of denying their obligation to love him to the extent of their power. If God then, in that perfect rule given in the FIRST and GREAT commandment of his Revelation, holds men to the full measure of their obligation as moral beings, then he requires them to love him to the extent of their power.

This affection is, as I maintain, *the sum* of God's requirements of men as their perfect moral governor. It is so in the first place, as it is the whole of that to which, in all circumstances of man's existence, alone pertains perfect moral rectitude. Other action as distinguished from this and not included in it, may, according to variable circumstances, be *right*, or may be *wrong*, but can never be *morally* right. But I have already said enough on the important distinction between *morally* right action and action merely *right*, to show my own views of it, and also how confused and erroneous the views of many moralists and theologians.

In the second place, the affection of which we speak is the *sum* of God's requirements as it fully meets and satisfies every claim of God on man. He who should love God to the extent of his power always and in all circumstances, cannot be conceived to be *morally* delinquent in any respect or degree whatever. If circumstances exist which dictate and demand acts of love and beneficence to his kindred or to other fellow-beings, or if circumstances demand the contrary (Luke, xiv. 26), he will be sure, under the controlling influence of this principle, to conform his subordinate acts to the demand of circumstances, and thus, in such action, to act *right*. But he thereby adds nothing to his own *moral* rectitude, except the manifestation of it, and of course nothing which is necessary to satisfy God's claim on him as a moral being. What God requires of men as moral beings is not subordinate, executive action, but that morally right affection, *and thus* he secures the performance of all *right* subordinate action in all the varying circumstances of their existence. Such love to God is the sum of all God's requirements, as it comprises in its very nature as a *principium* or principle all *right* subordinate action, as the good tree comprises the good fruit which it produces, or the good treasure of the heart the good things which the good man bringeth forth from it.

There is however, another sense in which theologians seem often to speak of what they call *the sum* of God's requirements. They appear to be misled, by misapprehending what the Saviour means when he says, "On these *two* commandments hang all the (Jewish) law and the prophets." The meaning of the Saviour is plain, viz., that all *the instruction* given by Moses and the prophets, for the regulation of human conduct, depends on and is determined by these two commandments. But this is not saying that the FIRST and GREAT commandment is *not* the *comprehensive* requirement of God's moral government. On the contrary, as we have shown in our previous explication of the Saviour's language, he clearly teaches that the second commandment, like all other requirements which respect subordinate acts or duties, is comprised in the first. Nor, as we have seen, is it possible in any sense of the language, that any man should love his neighbor as himself, unless his love of himself be first duly regulated by his obedience to the first. By obeying and only by obeying the first, does or can his love of himself cease to be inordinate, and thus to be inconsistent with perfect love to God, and thus by its due regulation become the measure of love to his neighbor. Besides, a man's love to his neighbor, his fellow-creature, even to his kindred, may be inordinate, or rather will be inordinate, unless he first obeys the first commandment, in loving God to the extent of his power. The sum then of God's requirements of man as a subject of his moral government, in the only proper meaning of the language, is that he love God to the extent of his power. Such is the only supposable meaning of the FIRST and GREAT commandment, "Thou shalt love the Lord thy God with all thy heart, and with all thy soul, and with all thy mind, and with all thy strength."

This view of the sum of God's requirement of man may be confirmed by briefly considering some other essential characteristics of the state of mind required. I remark, then—

That the love to God required in the divine law, is primarily *the love of benevolence.* Some theologians suppose the primary and only form of this affection to be *the love of complacency*,* or the love of God's perfect moral character. This however, in view of the only just distinction between these two kinds of affection, cannot be true. *The love of benevolence* is the love of the well-being, or of the highest happiness of the sentient universe. As God comprises in himself immeasurably "the greatest portion of being," and of course compared with the universe besides the greatest capacity of blessedness, his perfect happiness has more worth than any which can be conceived to come into competition with it. He therefore, who loves God as his law requires, must love God's highest blessedness, which depends on and results from his own perfect character, i. e., his own disposition to produce the highest happiness which he can produce. Now he who loves God's highest blessedness will also love God's perfect character. This love of his perfect character is *the* love of *complacency.* It is loving God's perfect character on account of its *intrinsic loveliness and excellence.* But the *intrinsic loveliness and excellence* of his perfect character consists in its nature and tendency to produce the highest happiness which is possible to God in the nature of things. The mind of man, without *primarily* loving the highest possible happiness, and of course without loving God's highest happiness, cannot love God's character on account of its *intrinsic loveliness* and excellence. The mind cannot love *the means* of an end as such, without primarily loving the end of which it is the means. If then the mind does not *primarily* love the highest blessedness of God and his perfect character as the means of this end, and this on account of its perfect fitness or adaptation as *the means* of producing this end, it does not love his character on account of its *intrinsic loveliness or excellence*—does not love it at all. In other words, unless the mind *primarily* loves God with *the love of benevolence,* it cannot love God with *the love of complacency.* I do not in this use of language mean to say that in *the order of time*

* Vide Bishop Butler's Sermon on the Love of God.

one of these affections is prior to the other; but I intend to express simply the idea of priority in the order of nature, or *the dependence* of one on the other. I do not suppose, nor would I imply, that the two affections ever exist separately in the mind in such a manner, that the love of benevolence can exist without the contemporaneous existence of *the love of complacency.* Though separable by a mental analysis which shows *a dependence* of one on the other, as in many other cases, they are justly viewed as co-existing in one complex state of the mind, properly called *the love of God.*

Again: the love required in the divine law or God's perfect rule of action, is *an elective preference of God.* President Edwards has often said that "the affections are only the stronger and more vigorous actings of the will." And yet it would be easy to show that he often distinguishes them, not only in the Inquiry on the Will, but in his other writings. In his Dissertation on Virtue, he says: "True virtue most essentially consists in *benevolence* to Being in general. Or, it is that consent, propensity, and union *of heart* to Being in general, that is immediately exercised in general *good-will.*" I cite this passage from Edwards to show that its meaning is the same as that which I have so often used on the same subject when speaking of the nature of virtue, and substantially that which, theologically speaking, I express, when I say *the love of God is an elective preference of God.* I adopt this language because it describes *love to God* as both *an affection* and *a choice*—as an act of the will and heart.

As I have elsewhere shown more at length, every act of will not only implies the prior existence of affections toward at least two objects, but the *present* existence of such affections; for the mind in every act of will, electively gives these existing affections supremely to one of these objects rather than to the other. It is equally true, that *affections* can in no form of love, desire or propensity, become *practical,* or prompt or move the mind to subsequent action in respect to one object rather than another, without an act of the will, or the elective act by which the affections are placed supremely on one object rather than on the other. I need not say that love to God as required in the great commandment, is eminently a practical affection,—the moral principle, *principium,* the beginning and source of all other right action. Thus viewed it involves therefore an act of the will—the elective act, which places one object above another in the affections. It is an *elective preference* of God to every other object of affection. Hence as I have before shown, it is in the Scriptures spoken of as an act of choice as well as an act of affection, when the object of the writer or speaker requires him to give prominence to the elective element of the complex act. (Josh. xxiv. 15; Isaiah, vii. 15; Luke, x. 42.)

Again: true love to God must, for another reason, be at least supreme love. God is so far beyond and above not only our fellow-creatures, but any conceivable universe of creatures in all that is worthy of our love, that if he ought to be loved at all, he ought to be loved more than any conceivable system of creatures. This is only saying, that God compared with all things besides, ought to be *supremely* loved, because according to the eternal truth and fitness of things, our affections ought in all cases to be in proportion to the intrinsic worth and loveliness of their objects. To deny this, is to deny the intuitive proposition that it is fit that we should love every object as it is fit to be loved by us; which is to deny that it is fit that we should love the object as it is fit that we should love it. Whether God ought to be loved more than supremely is not now the question. It is, whether he ought to be loved at least *supremely?* And how plain is it, that any lower degree of affection for him would be a palpable violence to truth and a practical outrage on nature;—a practical outrage on our own nature as well as on that of God, and would tend directly to the complete ruin and wretchedness of all. Without at least supreme love to God there can be no degree of that practical affection for him which is his due—no executive doings prompted by such a principle fulfilling his will in the production of actual results—no glorifying God by offerings of praise—no walking worthy of God unto all well-pleasing—no rejoicing on the part of God himself in all his works, even in his moral creation made to reflect his own moral image forever—no condition of his pardoning mercy to a sinful world; for every other condition—any act not involving this—would defeat the grand end of his benevolence in providing pardon for the guilty. Without this affection every *practical* principle of the human heart would be hostility—enmity to God, to his designs, to his highest blessedness and that of his sentient creation—the utter defeat of infinite benevolence in complete and universal misery.

And further: if love to God is not an elective preference, i. e., if it does not involve an act of will, then it can possess no moral quality. If it is not such an act, it must be merely a necessary *constitutional* affection; and can no more possess moral quality than the circulation of the blood or the beating of the heart. Thus destitute of moral quality, it cannot as a moral act be the subject of requirement or approbation by a moral governor, nor yet be dictated or approved by the conscience of the subject. To be a *moral act* and of course to be a *morally right* act, it must be a free act—an act exempt from all necessity—an act done in the exercise of moral liberty. No act of the mind which with the knowledge of the difference between the excellence and worth of God and of all other objects, does not by an act of the will fix the affections in a higher degree on God than on any and every other object, can be the subject of legal requirement by the Supreme Lawgiver, or enthrone him in this high position. If then God in his law requires any affection for himself on the part of men, he requires at least supreme love as an elective preference.

In view of what has been said, it is manifest that supreme love to God, if it falls below loving him to the extent of the powers, is not all that he claims of men in his perfect law. Any and every degree of affection for God as a substitute for this or compared with this, is a low, weak, and unworthy principle of action. God may and doubtless does require of men under the provision of a perfect atonement for sin, a lower degree of supreme love than he requires in his perfect law. But he does not require the former as that which in any respect meets and satisfies the claim of his perfect law. In its relation to this claim it falls utterly short of it, and must be viewed as the transgression of law, and as such justly exposing the subject to its full penalty. Under the relation of satisfying the claim of his perfect law, or as in any sense obedience to this law, God neither requires nor accepts that low degree of supreme love which is the condition of his pardoning mercy. It were entirely consistent with his justice or with his authority as lawgiver, to pardon sin under a perfect atonement without the required condition. Such an atonement would fully sustain his authority, without the imperfect love or faith or repentance of the sinner. The reason for the requirement of these as the condition of pardon is not as some maintain, that they are necessary to sustain his authority in granting pardon to the sinner for the same reason as is the atonement. It is widely different. It is not to uphold his authority, or vindicate his justice as a lawgiver in the slightest degree. This is fully and perfectly accomplished by a perfect atonement. The reason for making faith and repentance—imperfect but supreme—the conditions of pardon, is derived exclusively from his *benevolence* as distinguished from his justice. It is, that having by the atonement removed every obstacle from his justice, he may gratify his benevolence in raising up from this world of sinful beings a holy and happy kingdom. He makes personal holiness, in some low degree, the condition of his acceptance of sinners, that in this way by the discipline of his grace he may perfect the imperfect principle, and so prepare them for that world in which this kingdom itself will be perfected, and into which nothing that defileth shall enter.

Thus God requires far more in his perfect law than he exacts as the condition of his pardoning mercy. These requirements, made for different reasons, harmonize with each other, with every attribute of God, and with every principle of his perfect moral government. Thus law is established, and in every element of its influence. Alike therefore under his system of grace as under a system of mere law, he enforces in all the majesty of his rightful authority, his immutable and eternal claim that men love him to the extent of their power.

REMARKS.

1. How perfect is the law of God's moral government!

According to the view which has now been given of it, man is bound by the full authority of God to absolute moral perfection in all his doings. Thus appears the force of the apostle's commendation of the commandment, that it *is holy, just, and good.* It is "holy." Such a claim of law utterly excludes all sin or moral defilement. As requiring a positive and exactly defined act of the subject, it meets every want or deficiency with the frown of God's prohibition. The claim, in its full form and absolute purity, must be met by the subject. In this respect it bespeaks the purity, the holiness of its author, who cannot look on sin, and casts his withering abhorrence upon the slightest moral defilement! It is "holy," for it requires holiness—holiness in its celestial beauty—that resplendent moral purity which gives to heaven its glories as "the habitation of God's holiness," and awakens the song that makes all its pillars tremble; "holy, holy, holy, is the Lord God Almighty." It is also "just." The love to such a being as God by man to the extent of his power, is but the homage due. The right to require it is based in his infinite perfection, eternally and immutably possessed in his own Godhead. Who shall be found to question the rightful authority of such a being as God, his absolute prerogative to reign, the justice of his legal requirement, or the equity of his administration? The love which he claims on the part of men is the only true and full recognition by them of God's greatness and worthiness compared with any thing in a universe besides. It is this love which alone attests, exalts, and honors the supremacy of God. It is this love which alone by its reverence, its adoration, its submission, its confidence, its universal obedience, gives the throne to Him to whom only it belongs, and thus, recognizing the rightful authority of Him that sitteth thereon, imparts protection and safety to every interest of his kingdom. What less according to the principles of eternal justice, can be done by man *than to obey this law of love;* what less can be claimed by the sovereign and guardian of such an empire? The commandment which is so "holy" and so "just," is also "good." If God has created all things for his pleasure; if he will rejoice in all his works; if he is blessed forever—how is his creature man to contribute to his blessedness except by doing his will, by walking worthy of God unto all pleasing? How is God as a perfect moral governor to be pleased, to be perfectly blessed, except by the obedience and the homage which he requires in his law? The ultimate end of God, in creation and providence is his own highest blessedness. This end is necessarily and emphatically the ultimate end of his moral government; for, as we have seen, all his other works both of creation and of providence are subordinate to his moral government and to its great end. His law is of course perfectly adapted to this end. What higher, better end—what end worthier of himself—what other ultimate end than this can God propose? What law so perfect as that which is perfectly fitted to accomplish this end? It is the necessary and perfect means of God's highest blessedness. How excellent—how absolutely good is such a rule of moral action! But this is not all its excellence. It is based in the everlasting truth—the grand, cardinal fact of the nature of things—the absolute coincidence of God's highest glory and blessedness with man's highest well-being. Thus while it aims,at and uncounteracted, would secure the former, it is not less adapted to secure man's perfection in character and in happiness. As an intelligent preference of God—involving the knowledge of the difference between God and every other object of affection—how must it give the mind the calm dignity of repose in truth—the gladness and the joy of walking in the light of life! How as the governing principle of the mind it secures the end of his being, giving to all subordinate affections their beautiful harmony and to all executive doings their most productive energy! How like the whole armor of God it resists temptation and the tempter! How as the most vigorous health and life of the soul it tends to its own perpetuity and ever-augmenting strength! How it evinces in the mind's own consciousness, the peace and triumph of its own reality and excellence! How it ventures into fellowship with God assured of his love in return! How it delights in doing his will, and in the unfolding and fulfillment of his designs! How it finds its own blessedness in God's! How it adorns the soul with all the beauties of holiness! How it enters, sure of their joyful welcome, into companionship with angels and archangels! How it lives and acts and rejoices under the light of God's countenance—the ceaseless smile of his love! In a word, how it imparts to man God's own likeness in character and in blessedness, while according to its own measure it engages in the service, augments the bliss, and partakes of the glories of heaven! Can such love to God dwell in the heart of man! What else is great; what else is good; what else is godlike; what else is to be thought of but the God whom he loves?

2. This view of the divine law is important, not to say necessary, to elevate the standard of Christian character. It will be generally admitted, that the character of good men in this world is marred by great moral imperfections; vide John, xv. 2; Rom. vii.; Gal. v. 17. Would not such imperfections be greatly diminished by juster—more adequate views of God's

perfect law as the authoritative rule of moral action? It is true, that no child of God may ever attain that perfect love of God which his law so justly demands, till the last hour of probation—even till the moment in which the soul begins to leave the body—a process perhaps, of separation more gradual than is commonly supposed, and which may involve a mental consciousness before unknown. Then, in a momentary but unclouded vision of faith, the soul, aware of its departure, may let go of the world with all its undue affection, and fix its love on God as he is. Until then however, we are constrained to believe that love to God in the heart of good men is at most only a low degree of *supreme* love. Herein consists the imperfection of the saints—their remaining sin as we call it—which is so common and so much to be lamented. Nor must we disparage the principle in any of its relations and aspects. Such love to God as *supreme* is also sincere, and through abundant grace, secures God's forgiveness and favor. But it is not that perfect love which God with the full weight of his infinite authority, in his law demands of all men. Still, as *supreme* love to God, it is vastly diverse from the supreme love of the world. It has a useful tendency and influence, while the supreme love of the world in every substantial respect is wholly destructive. The *one* is destined by use and discipline to attain perfection: the *other* by its own inherent corruption, to grow worse and worse. The *one* being imperfect, according to the law of works, is sin, while in relation to the law of faith it is obedience: the *other* is sin without qualification, or in all its forms and relations. The *one*, through an atonement, renders pardon and acceptance with God not only consistent with justice, but with every other interest of benevolence: the *other* subjects to condemnation and punishment without hope, not only as consistent with but as demanded by justice, and by every other interest of benevolence. The *one* causes sorrow and contrition, more or less, over its own imperfection, and many a struggle and sacrifice, that it may triumph over a tempting and corrupting world: the *other* acquiesces in its own deformity without sorrow and without conflict, and defies and resists external assault. The *one* desires most of all, higher measures of personal holiness: the *other* is indifferent, or rather decidedly averse to any such acquisition. The *one* through grace issues in eternal life: the *other* as the demand of inflexible justice in eternal death. And yet with this vast and ever-increasing difference between the two great practical principles of the righteous and the wicked—with all the worth and excellence of the former when contrasted with the unqualified moral deformity of the latter—still how imperfect, how *sinfully* imperfect according to God's perfect law, is all that can be called, in this world, Christian principle! It is, as I said, *supreme* love to God; but how low *in degree!* How is it chilled, and checked, and weakened, by unduly and sinfully holding the affections of the heart to the world! These affections still linger and play about the former idol of the heart with so much activity and vigor, that the Christian's love to God scarcely acquires the vitality and power which determine its distinctive reality. For the most part, it is but a feeble, fitful, and often an entirely inactive principle, wanting the strength and controlling influence necessary to own distinct visibility to the mind, while its existence is more than doubtful both to its subject and to others. In many sad instances as in those of David and Peter, it betrays its weakness or rather its suspended activity, in overt crimes, as it would in thousands besides under like temptations. Thus one of the only two objects of moral affection to man—a vanity as it is—is loved more than it is fit to be loved: the other, though the all-perfect God, is scarcely loved more than this vanity! Oh, has man no more power of affection for the living God! What a stinted, dwarfish affection, in view of so much greatness and excellence! How unworthy, how inexcusable, I had almost said, how *vile*, were such love to God as this! What cause for humiliation—for shame and confusion of face! How it needs to be washed with the tears of repentance, and these very tears themselves need to be purified with atoning blood!

Now I do not say that perfect love to God has ever been or ever will be attained by the Christian, until the last hour or even moment of his probation on earth. Nor yet do I find, as some think they find, a scriptural warrant for saying that he will not attain to such perfect love, and still less that he cannot. But I do say that he can—that he ought; and that he has no excuse or palliation for the imperfection of his love to God. God's authority is upon him. He cannot throw it off, nor weaken it. He must fulfill or violate the obligation it imposes. The concern of the Christian is not merely to comply with the condition of God's forgiveness, and to be satisfied merely to escape damnation. He must hereafter awake in God's perfect likeness. The work must be achieved before his probation in the strict sense terminates. And sloth and worldliness through life give no security that it will be achieved when the final summons comes. He is called to perfect holiness in the fear of God. The same unbending authority which requires him to set his affections on things above, requires him *not* to set them on things below. He must lay aside every weight. He must press toward the mark for the prize of his high calling of God in Christ Jesus. He who would give the arrow its highest elevation must aim at the sun. So the Christian, in the exercise of holy affection, must aim to give it perfection in view of its object—God, as he is. In every act of worship—in every act of faith, repentance, prayer, he should love and therefore aim to love God to the extent of his power. If he has never done it in the past, the more reason for doing it in the present.

Finally I remark, how important it is that just views of the perfect law of God be entertained and inculcated by the Christian ministry. How else shall they become co-workers with Christ in calling not the righteous, but *sinners* to repentance? How commend the great Physician to any except the sick? How fall in with the mission and work of the Holy Spirit in convincing the world of sin? How show that sin, by the commandment, is exceeding sinful? How render Christ precious to every believer? How magnify the superabounding grace of God? How enforce daily, hourly repentance? How prepare the children of God for a triumphant or even a peaceful death? How present every man perfect in Christ Jesus at the judgment-seat?

There are yet other considerations on this part of the subject which are not to be unthought of. What exceedingly low and superficial views of the full claim of God on the men who are to live and to act under his moral government forever, are entertained by large portions of the Protestant Church, and even by professed Christian divines and moralists! To what an extent is the law of God depressed and obscured! How, as the consequence, are the sinful imperfections and shortcomings of good men, every one of which according to God's law deserves God's condemnation, unseen in their true moral turpitude and unrepented of for their defilement and guilt! How common to infer that because God's perfect law is not a rule of judgment, therefore it has lost all its authority, ceased to be a rule of action and become unworthy of a thought! Or to conceive of *supreme* love to God, and a low degree of it, as if it were *all* the love that God's law requires, and to regard mere compliance with the conditions of his pardoning mercy, as that absolute moral perfection which fits the soul for heaven's purity, services, and joys! How great is the error! And yet who of the best religious teachers, so exhibits that use or exercise of all the powers and capacities of the immortal spirit within us—call them by what names you will—intellect, heart, affections, susceptibility, will, conscience—which is requisite to give to the love of God that absolute perfection, without which there is guilt on the soul! Or if the law is quoted—which is better than nothing—how constantly is it assumed that it is understood without explanation! How is explanatory instruction almost exclusively confined to repentance, to faith, to regeneration, and other conditions of salvation through grace, or to some slight and imperceptible progress in religion, as if man's absolute moral perfection were no concern of his in this life, but the responsibility and the work of preparation for heaven were to be thrown upon God at the moment of the soul's departure from the body, or in some short purgatory during its flight to a better world! Worse than all and in confirmation of all this, how is the full measure of man's *moral* obligation obscured, shaded away into practical oblivion, or rather unequivocally denied by the perpetual asseveration of his utter inability to love God as God's law requires, i. e., his inability to love God with all his ability! What sad views of truth are these for beings whose preparation for heaven must be not only begun, but completed during this short probation on earth! What a complete paralysis is thus imparted to the Christian life on earth, in which, if Christ and his apostles are to be regarded, all, all is action, energy—life in all its fullness of activity and strenuousness of effort—the labor for sustenance, the wakefulness of the watcher, the energizing for the strait gate, the exertion of the race, the vigor of the wrestler, the resistance and onset of battle! And yet the pulpit and the press, theology, preaching, prayer, all join the chant of the sluggard heart—you *cannot*, you *cannot;* i. e., *you cannot love God as much as you can!*

And then again, what multitudes of ungodly men extol, commend, and hold in exclusive esteem, love or kindness to our fellow-men! The good man in the world's estimation, is the man who loves his neighbor, his fellow-men, though he make little or even no account of God. According to this standard of morality and religion, the man who practices a generous liberality or philanthropic beneficence, reciprocates kindness with kindness, and is blameless in the intercourse of business and of social life, fulfills every moral obligation. He may live and die as thousands do, without supreme love to God, and even without one respectful or affectionate thought of God beyond what is necessarily associated with not denying his existence, and still love God as much as he ought. It is enough so far as God is concerned, that man is not a contemptuous atheist. Thus mere philanthropy without supreme love to God—humanity, going forth, uncounteracted, in its instinctive emotions,—kindness to man without godliness or rather with utter ungodliness of heart, is true virtue, true religion. Thus God in all his greatness and his worthiness to be loved, is not to be supremely loved, but our fellow-men; so that if God's will, interests, or designs in any respect come into competition with those of our fellow-men or our own, the former will be as they constantly are, sacrificed to the latter. But as we have said, if the least degree of love is due to God, then *at the least* it is *supreme* love. For why should beings of far inferior worth and therefore of far inferior fitness to be loved, be loved at all, and yet a being of infinitely superior fitness to be loved, not be loved in a far superior degree? Has man no capacity or power to love in degree any object beyond that degree of love which is due to a fellow-worm, or even to this atom world? Has God destined so insignificant a creature to immortality? Plainly, if there is a God and if there is a man, then either God must be loved at least *supremely*, or he cannot be loved at all, as it is fit that he should be loved. What then shall we say of mere philanthropy as virtue—the merely loving man without loving God? Instead of any due recognition of God, it wholly excludes him as an object of affection from the human heart, for it is the love of the creature more than of the Creator. It exiles God utterly from a world of his own,—a world of creatures made in his own likeness—made for high fellowship—high social intercourse with himself. It is practical atheism, for it is a practical denial of every important relation between God and man. It practically denies all the rights of God as the benevolent Father of man's existence, and all the obligations of man reciprocal to these rights. It thus denies the supreme and rightful sovereignty of God's moral dominion over men, and of course the reciprocal spirit of loyalty, with its supreme love, its reverence, its submission, its unqualified devotion in doing all his will. It thus denies God as the constant and bountiful benefactor of his creatures, their all-providing God, for it neither acknowledges with gratitude and praise their dependence on him for blessings in the past, nor for blessings in the future, by prayer and supplication. In the relations of Redeemer and Sanctifier in which God comes closest to sinful man, grasping as it were the very heart with his love, they know him not in the least return of grateful affection, nor in the peaceful repose furnished for human guilt by trusting in his mercy. They know him not in the condescension which brings him from his high sanctuary where he inhabiteth eternity, to dwell with the humble and to revive the heart of the contrite. They know nothing of his invitations and promises, as alluring to heaven, inspiring its steadfast hope, and securing its immortal joys; and nothing of his warnings and threatened terrors in their kind and salutary design to secure safety from impending ruin. They know nothing of the probation he assigns them as a place of preparation for his presence—for that theater of existence, of life and action amid the scenes, the grandeurs, and the glories of eternity. They know nothing of him as the final judge, the supreme and resistless arbiter of all destiny, in the exaltation, purity, and joys of perfect holiness, or in the ever-deepening turpitude and miseries of sin. They are WITHOUT GOD and WITHOUT HOPE.

What is the remedy? The first remedy is that the commandment should come, and come in the fullness of its claim and its rightful authority—come to the conscience and to the heart of every subject of the Lord God Almighty. And how is this to be accomplished, except through the instrumentality of the Christian ministry? And if they will not awake to the summons and rouse themselves to the work of their high calling; if they will not comprehend and unfold God's commandment in its exceeding breadth; if they will not hold up the torch of God's law to the sin-darkened mind, to what purpose can they hope to proclaim the salvation of the Gospel? They will neither save themselves nor them that hear them.

LECTURE XI.

THE *NATURE* OF GOD'S MORAL GOVERNMENT AS REVEALED.

Section 5: *The law in the import of its sanctions.*—The reward.—Proposition stated.—Eternal life not the sanction of the law of Moses.—The reward not directly revealed.—Not frequently repeated.—Made known by inference and representation.—Does this involve *double sense?*—The *proper* and *accidental* sense of words distinguished.—Both authorized by usage.—Allegorical and fantastic interpretations deprecated.—Twofold sense abundant in the Scriptures.—Examples in parables: Gen. iii. 15; xvii. 8.—Application to reward promised in the Mosaic law.—Use of the word *life* in the Old and New Testament.—The law of Eden.

I COME now, as proposed, to Sect. 5,—the law in the import of its sanctions; and first, of the reward.

Concerning this, I state the proposition now to be proved, thus:

The reward promised by the law of God's moral government to the obedient subject is complete or perfect happiness so long as he continues obedient.

For the reasons already assigned, I shall first inquire what evidence is furnished by the Mosaic law.

To prevent misapprehension, I would here say, that although I suppose a future state was revealed under the Mosaic dispensation, I do not suppose that *eternal life*—meaning by it confirmation in holiness and happiness in a future world on condition of perfect obedience in this—was *the sanction of the law of God's moral government* as *revealed through this dispensation.* Such a promise may have been received, but according to principles already stated, I suppose it to be the same promise of eternal life to personal holiness, which the Gospel more fully reveals. But the reward of the law as such, exclusive of a gracious economy, was simply a reward promised during the continued obedience of the subject. Nothing more and nothing less could be inferred.

Again, I need only to advert to the fact which has been so fully explained, that the moral government of God, administered over Israel, is to be carefully distinguished from the theocracy which was also administered over that people. The perfect moral government of God over men as immortal beings, in respect to any *formal* development of its great principles, was but imperfectly exhibited directly by the Jewish lawgiver. The theocracy or civil institute was very fully and minutely unfolded. I am not saying how much this people knew, or had the means of knowing respecting God's moral government, from earlier revelations; but that it was not the primary or leading object of the mission of Moses *formally* and *directly* to unfold the nature and principles of this government. This object was aimed at *indirectly* and through *the medium* of the theocracy or civil government, and was in fact accomplished as has already been explained.

Further: we are not to look for those frequent and formal recognitions and statements of the truth now under consideration, which we might expect to find in the actual administration of a perfect moral government under a merely legal dispensation. The perfect moral government of God which is here distinguished from the theocracy or civil government which God administered over Israel, was administered under an economy of grace as revealed in the covenant with Abraham, which the law—the civil institute that was four hundred and thirty years after—could not disannul. We shall look in vain therefore, for any instance of a legal reward under God's moral government according to the principles of such a government. There was no pefectly obedient subject to be thus rewarded. Nor, viewing the Mosaic code as a mere *national* institution, can we rationally expect the *direct*, *literal* declaration of our doctrine. The promise in that broad and comprehensive import which includes perfect happiness, does not pertain to such an institution. All that we are to look for under this institution in *formal* and *literal* statement is, the promise of a long, prosperous, and happy life to obedient subjects. There is yet another reason why we are not to look for any *explicit*, *literal*, *formal* declaration or development of this great principle of a moral government in the Mosaic economy. The earlier revelations of God were comparatively obscure, and the light which was to be shed on this world was, in the wisdom of God, to be progressive. In accordance with this fact, the Jewish theocracy in the Scriptures, which is often called by way of eminence, THE LAW, was "a *shadow* of good things to come"—a covenant or institution not faultless (not perfect), and therefore to give place to another and a better covenant founded on *better* promises—it was an *example* and *shadow* of heavenly things. (Heb. viii. 5–8; x. 1; Gal. iii. 17, &c.)

How then would the Jew reason in respect to the rewards of that perfect moral government which was represented by the theocracy? Could he derive but one inference, and would not that be the inference which is expressed in our proposition? Were there any facts to bring doubt or uncertainty over this inference? Not the fact that God did not proceed on the strict principles of legal retribution which pertain to a perfect moral government; for, as we shall see hereafter, the clear exhibition of a future state and of an economy of grace forbid such a conclusion. Or rather the fact that he gave a perfect law of a perfect government in connection with these facts, amounted to a full confirmation of the reality of a perfect moral government and the import of its sanctions. Now add to these considerations the truth that God assumed the relation of a national king, with the facts which it involves. As such he shows himself rigidly exact in respect to its every principle and requirement. He promises in the most absolute forms to award earthly happiness to obedience under the civil constitution, and to do this even by a course of extraordinary and miraculous providence. But if God promised to do, and did actually do this—if after proving the reality of a perfect moral government, he subverted the laws of nature in the rigid execution of this lower kind of moral government, conferring earthly happiness as the reward of external conformity to the law, for such *in effect* was the known fact—with how much higher approbation must he regard, and with what richer gifts would he bless the sinless obedience of a perfect heart? In this system of national law it was manifest beyond all denial, that the demand in respect to action went far beyond the condition on which, *in effect*, its reward of earthly happiness was promised and on which it was given. The demand was for spiritual religion—holiness of heart; the *condition* of the promise was *in effect* the mere external appearance of what was demanded. What then but perverseness or criminal stupidity could infer, that by the most blameless external conformity one could satisfy the omniscient King? If men were justified and rewarded on such principles by a national ruler, would not the Searcher of hearts—the perfect moral governor—give a higher reward to him who should fully meet the demand of his perfect law by the homage of a perfect heart? I know that the error, the capital error of the Jew was in thinking that the demand of the law required external obedience only, and that this would secure the favor of God. But which was the most rational inference from the premises—that because the national king awarded earthly good for external obedience for the mere show of obedience, this was the full measure of his demand; or, in view of the express and unqualified nature of the demand as reaching to the heart, and of the facts which showed the reality of his moral government under a gracious economy—that a spiritual obedience would secure a still higher reward? Surely no degree of intellect which makes a man rational, if unperverted, could fail to adopt the latter conclusion. The reproofs and denunciations from God for the want of spiritual service—the homage of the heart on the part of the people—show how he expected them to reason on this subject.

Here the question might arise, whether these views and those like them in Lecture IV. do not require a double sense or meaning to the language of this part of the Mosaic code? This question must be decided by those principles by which we assign to language its meaning. Now one way in which words as the signs of ideas, become precise and definite in their import is by prior use: such import is so definite that there are some meanings which in ordinary use they cannot possess. Thus according to this law the word *tree* cannot denote the same thing as the word *man*, nor the phrase *the land of Canaan* the same thing as the word *heaven*. To admit any other principle in deciding the meaning of language in its ordinary use, would be to introduce confusion into its use, if not to destroy it as the vehicle of thought altogether. No one can assign a higher place or influence to usage in determining the import of language than I do. It is that, and that only which gives to words what may be called their *proper* meaning, and their only fixed or permanent meaning so far as they have any. It is of course the only criterion of deciding what that *proper* meaning is. If then words can never *be properly used* except in their *primary proper* meaning, the question concerning their being *properly used* in a double meaning would be settled at once.

But it is to be remembered that prior use is not the only

criterion of the meaning of a speaker. The meaning of language and the meaning of a speaker are often two things. *The true and only meaning of language* as determined by usage, may be called its *proper* meaning. Any other meaning *which the writer or speaker shows by legitimate evidence to be intended by him in the use of it*, may be called *accidental*. Prior use is only one way of ascertaining this intention of a writer or speaker, or rather it is in all cases a decisive criterion, except the writer or speaker furnishes decisive evidence that he uses language in some other import than that which has thus been assigned it. But if he does furnish such evidence, whether by definition or otherwise, that *he intends to convey another meaning*, then the meaning which he thus shows that he intends to convey is his real meaning. Such a use of words is always an authorized use provided the speaker furnishes some sure criterion of deciding his real meaning. Usage decides *that we must use words in the sense which prior use has given them, or show clearly that we use them in some other sense, and in what sense.*

Let it then be kept in mind, that in determining the meaning of language, as that which the speaker intends to convey to the hearer—that in judging of his intended meaning, prior usage as it fixes the meaning of words is one kind of evidence, and one which, unless other decisive evidence be furnished of another meaning, is ever to control interpretation;—that, nevertheless, prior use is not the only evidence of a speaker's meaning, nor can it by any means set aside other decisive evidence of a different meaning;—that the meaning of language is not lost nor in the least degree obscured on the principle now stated, for in both cases, decisive evidence though different in kind is furnished of the intended and real meaning;—and that when this is done, whether it be the evidence resulting from prior use, from definition, or from a representative system, language is properly used, and is to be interpreted according to the manifested intention and design of him who uses it.

What this evidence is which proves an *accidental* or *acquired* meaning to be the real meaning of a speaker, is an inquiry which deserves the attention of every interpreter of language. I cannot enter now into the consideration of it to any extent. It is however, important to my object to show that what I have called the mode by *inference* and *representation*, constitutes decisive evidence on this point. In regard to the former I remark, that nothing is more easy or common than to use language in such a manner, that in view of known facts and in particular circumstances, it shall, in the way of palpable inference, turn the mind to something beyond the *proper* import of the language used; and this, as certainly and as clearly as any direct and literal phraseology could do. In such a case there can be no doubt of the speaker's design to convey the *inference* itself to the mind of the hearer; and accordingly, we decide by this true and only criterion, the inferential meaning to be a part, and frequently the *principal* part of his real meaning, and often also his only meaning. Nor does this mode of speaking lead to any confusion or peculiar liability to mistake. For it is always attended with *decisive evidence* of the real design of the speaker. It is therefore as easy to distinguish such an inference from one which, though legitimate, is not intended, as to distinguish,(as we always must,)the real from the possible meaning of direct literal expressions by attendant evidence. At all events, let the inference be manifested as I have supposed, and let it involve *personal reproach* and *insult*, and we never fail to regard it as intended.

In connection with this mode, that of representation or of exhibiting one thing by another, may also exist, as has been shown in Lecture IV. When these concur, the evidence of the real meaning of the speaker is peculiarly decisive. The latter however, when existing alone as a common and well-understood mode of conveying knowledge, is scarcely less satisfactory than that by words used in the import which usage has given them.* I am aware that the contrary is extensively supposed to be true, and that the mode of conveying truth by representation is also supposed to be peculiarly vague and peculiarly liable to abuse. That it has been and is still greatly abused, I readily admit. But it is not more abused or perverted than language when used according to the laws of actual usage.

* It admits of a question, I think, whether this mode involves any peculiar obscurity in itself considered, compared with that of literal language, and whether what we call the obscurity of the Old Testament on some subjects does not consist rather in the less frequent repetition of some truths, as that of a future state; and in less specific statements of others, as that respecting the office and work of the Messiah. It may be in a given case more obscure than literal language, but the question is, can it not be made as clear?

I need not say that the abuse of it furnishes no reason against the use of it. Nor do I admit that it is especially liable to abuse. True indeed, it would be so if we might, as some actually do, regulate, limit or extend our interpretation of such language by the mere fact of *resemblances*, and this by giving the reins to fancy and conjecture; or if we might discard all those principles and laws of evidence which are to guard and limit and guide the interpretation of such language. And so the same disregard of fixed principles, the same lawlessness in interpreting other language, would lead and I may say has in fact far more frequently and extensively led to similar results. The question then is, not whether this mode of interpreting language has been in fact perverted and abused—for what mode has not been?—the question is, whether it is not as strictly and definitely and plainly guarded by certain principles and laws of interpretation as any other? I could not well express more abhorrence than I feel for any mode of eliciting the import of the sacred oracles which dispenses with the severe logic of interpretation, suffers the imagination to run riot in tracing resemblances and analogies, and sanctifies its results by the pretense of some second sight or sense as a peculiar prerogative of the interpreter. It is true indeed that the natural man, the man enthralled by groveling appetite and passion, discerneth not the things of the Spirit, neither can he know them. Such a man under such mental tyranny must be a miserable interpreter of the lively oracles of God. His very intellect by the bad dominion of this state of mind, is not only unfurnished with the first principles, the very elements of successful interpretation, but is stupefied and cramped as to all vigorous action on such subjects. The soul's constitutional discernment is peculiarly blunted in respect to the beauty, and weight, and excellence of divine realities, and disqualified for that perception which is necessary to give them their practical influence. In this state of sinful enthrallment the man cannot appreciate, nor apprehend, nor successfully judge of the things of God's revelation. But then this same man, as truly as any other man, has those powers and properties of the soul which may be roused from this state of dormancy and inaction; his susceptibilities to other objects than those which now engross him may be touched and excited; his intellect may be awakened and directed to those matters of unwonted attention; and then he must and may learn what is the meaning of the Spirit, by the self-same mental process, and by the self-same laws of interpretation, as those by which the most privileged saint must learn it. To talk of any other mode of discovering the import of God's revelation than the healthful and earnest use of the mental powers, influenced indeed in some cases by the Spirit of truth, but employed with honest intention on the materials of discovery, and directed by the sober well-known laws of interpretation, is enthusiastic dreaming.

These principles I shall now attempt to illustrate and confirm in respect to scriptural language, having a special reference to the general subject before us. I remark—

1. That the Sacred Scriptures abound in instances in which language has a *proper* and *accidental* meaning, i. e., *a double sense.* Here I wish it to be remarked that I do not attribute *two proper meanings* to the same language, i. e., two senses, *both of which are acquired by usage.* When words by a change of import acquire by usage a further meaning than their original meaning, then the whole comprehensive import is not *two* meanings, but *one* comprehensive *proper* meaning, because *usage* now assigns this as the meaning, and there is therefore no longer any distinctive mark by which *the parts* of the meaning can be distinguished and pronounced *two* meanings. One part is decided to be included in the *proper* meaning on the same ground as is the other, viz., that of usage. But when words are used in a meaning not acquired by usage, and this in addition to the meaning which is acquired by usage, then there is a distinctive mark or characteristic in these meanings by which they may be distinguished and regarded as two meanings. Now if I mistake not, it has been simply and solely from overlooking this fact, that some have become so zealous in contending against *a double sense.* They have seen with great clearness that words can have but one *proper* meaning; that whether it be more or less comprehensive, still as a *proper* meaning, a meaning acquired by usage, it is but one; that the parts of it cannot be distinguished as two by any distinctive characteristic, both being determined to belong to the language on the same ground, viz., usage. But while they have seen this on the one hand, they have *not* seen on the other, that words may be used, and if their meaning is ever enlarged or extended *must* be used, in an *accidental* meaning, i. e., a mean-

ing not acquired by previous usage; that this meaning, though as *real* as the *proper* meaning, is still arbitrary in this first instance, and must remain so till subsequent usage shall render it the *proper* meaning, and that still it is that which is *intended* by the speaker as really as any meaning can be. What therefore they contend for is very true, viz., that no language can originally possess *two proper* meanings or senses. In other words, terms have in no instance two *primary* meanings. To this of course I fully subscribe. But what I maintain is, that words may have two senses, the one being a *proper* sense, the other an *accidental* sense, i. e., the one being the sense of prior usage, the other a sense or meaning *which the speaker intends to convey to the mind being manifested by some other evidence than that of prior usage.* If these remarks be just, then the controversy about *a double* sense, as I before intimated, is a mere dispute about words, or rather a controversy resulting from the want of correct definition.

In proof of my position as I have explained it, that much of the language of the Sacred Scriptures has *a double sense*, or is used to convey two distinct meanings, I refer to *the parables* of the Scriptures, and what I maintain is, that the language of these has both a *proper* and *accidental* meaning as I have explained these terms. Take as an example the parable of the prodigal son. "A certain man had two sons, and the younger of them said unto his father," &c. Now the question is not whether this is not a fictitious or false narrative, nor whether our Lord is to be justified in giving a false narrative in such a case. Both are admitted. But a *real* meaning belongs to false propositions as well as to those which are true. The falsehood of the narrative therefore, instead of precluding, implies a *real meaning* which is false. Falsehood or fiction can be predicated of nothing else but of some real meaning of the terms. What propositions then are false in the present instance? Why that "a certain man had two sons," and every proposition in the parable. Every proposition in the parable therefore has a meaning which is false. And if this were not so—if the language had no meaning which is false, it can have none which is true; for divest it of all meaning according to the usage of terms both true and false, and it becomes absolutely destitute of all meaning and wholly useless in its design. As another test, I ask, can any one read this parable and not bring the image of the returning son and the glad father distinctly before the mind and home to all its sensibilities? Do we not find this touching, melting family scene possessing our thoughts and feelings in spite of ourselves; is it not necessary that it should be so to secure the ultimate effect of the parable; and was not this intended by the speaker? What brings these thoughts and feelings into the mind but the language of the parable? Here then is one meaning, viz., the proper meaning of the words—their meaning according to usage actually and clearly conveyed, unavoidably conveyed, and *designedly* conveyed to the hearer. And if this is not a *real* meaning of the language, nothing can be. But will any one say that our Lord intended to convey no meaning by the language of this parable except that which is *false?* Did he not also intend to convey one which is *true*, and a meaning too not pertaining to the language of the parable according to any prior usage? Is it not most manifest that by the phrase *two sons*, our Lord intended to designate Jews and Gentiles, and by the word *father*, God himself; and thus to turn the minds of his hearers as truly and intently on these objects as objects of thought, as had he used these words themselves? This will not be denied. It is manifest then that in this parable, and the same is true of every other, the design of the speaker is to use language in its *proper* meaning, and *through this* meaning which is justifiably *false*, to turn the thoughts of his hearers to a substantial reality, which is therefore another and a very diverse meaning of his language. And I flatter myself after what has been said, that these meanings are justly distinguished as two.

But if language may have two distinct meanings when one of them is false, it would seem *a fortiori*, that it may have two meanings when both of them may be true. As examples of this I refer to the following:

(Gen. iii. 15.) "And I will put enmity between thee and the woman, and between thy seed and her seed; it shall bruise thy head and thou shalt bruise his heel." That this language has what I have termed a proper meaning, and describes the aversion of mankind to serpents and their practice of destroying them, I cannot doubt. Indeed to deny it, seems to me to involve the rejection of the most decisive evidence of the meaning of language which can exist in any case; I mean the exact agreement between the meaning of words as fixed by usage, and known facts or things—e. g., that horse is black. Who that knows the meaning which words have acquired by usage and has eyes to see, can doubt in such a case the meaning of the speaker.*

That the passage also conveys another meaning, which the words according to usage do not express, is placed equally beyond doubt by the *known* facts in the case, as well as by apostolic allusions. Our first parents could not be ignorant of him by whom their ruin was accomplished, nor fail to understand from this assurance, that this enemy of man was to be vanquished by one born of a woman. The allusions of the apostle to this destroyer under the name of the serpent, and as the introducer of sin and death into this world, with their declarations that the Son of God was manifested to destroy him that hath the power of death, and that Satan should be bruised under the feet of his followers, are sufficient to convince us of the reality of the second and improper meaning of the passage under consideration.

As another example I refer to Gen. xvii. 8. That this language had its *proper* meaning, and that God did here truly promise to Abraham the literal country of Canaan, is evident not only from the agreement between words and things, but from the undeniable facts that the promise was both understood and fulfilled in this import. That this language possessed another, and what I have called a *representative* meaning, is also placed beyond a question by many considerations as well as by the context. Abraham, it will be admitted, had some just knowledge of God. He had also a knowledge of a future state. He had been expressly told that in him all the families of the earth should be blessed. The Almighty had promised to be his exceeding great reward. Such a man must have known how to estimate the favor and friendship of his covenant God; how to trust his grace and to measure his promises. Could this friend of God then have heard this covenant repeated again and again; could he have listened to this promise of an earthly country, and know as he did that he was a stranger and a pilgrim on earth and was to live forever be-

* To say that here was a mere allusion in the way of allegorical expression, will not help the matter in respect to the fact that the words have this as their *proper* meaning, for otherwise no allusion could be conveyed to the mind by the language.

yond the grave, and doubt the design of his Maker to carry his thoughts and his hopes upward to a better country, even an heavenly? Let us look also at the accompanying assurance, *I will be thy God.* Had this friend of God then confined his expectations to mere earthly good, would he not have degraded this great and precious promise in a manner altogether unworthy of its import and its author? What it was for God to be the God of Abraham in the days of Christ, we know. He was not the God of the dead but of the living. He was the same when the promise was made. How then could Abraham, how could any one hear the promise of the land of Canaan, made in such circumstances and in such a connection, and fail to look for a city which hath foundations whose builder and maker is God? Without then adverting to the declarations of the apostle that the *Gospel* was preached unto Abraham, and that this covenant with him comprises that Gospel in all its promises of grace and of glory, it is sufficient to settle the question before us, that I have stated the fact as stated by the apostle, and adopted the same argument to prove it. (Vide Heb. xi. 8–16.)

But I proceed to consider the language of the Scriptures, particularly that of the Old Testament. I refer—

First, to the language used to express *the legal reward of obedience* under the Mosaic law. Whenever the *legal reward* of the Mosaic law is described, I suppose the language has what I have called a representative meaning, and as it teaches that obedience to the national law (this being decided on according to the principles before stated) is entitled to the specified reward while continued, so it as clearly teaches or asserts that obedience to the law of God's perfect moral government while continued, is entitled to its reward. This view of the subject shows with what decisive conclusiveness Paul, when discussing the subject of justification under the perfect government of God, cited the passage from the Mosaic code, "The man that doeth them, shall live in them."

Secondly, I refer to the use of the word *life* to denote the reward to be graciously given to the imperfectly holy. As the national government of God was administered under a gracious economy, so was his perfect moral government. As the word *life* was used in some cases to denote the gracious reward under the former, so it would *at first* in such a use and in the case of the true penitent, denote also the reward promised to such under God's perfect moral government, i. e., eternal life. This would of course be a *transferred* meaning. Now as I said, words often change their meaning, and a transferred or representative meaning by usage becomes the more usual meaning, and may even exclude the literal meaning altogether. This change, by which the latter meaning is wholly excluded, is especially natural and common when the new meaning respects what is by far the most important and prominent relation or truth, and more especially when it is that in which there is most occasion to use the word, and still more especially when there is no occasion to use it in any other meaning. As then the doctrine of a future happy life to the truly penitent was compared with a life of mere earthly good, pre-eminently important, and as this doctrine in the progress of divine revelation was more extensively understood by the people, and more frequently alluded to or dwelt on by their religious teachers, the word *life* was not only the term most naturally adopted to express this truth, but it lost, occasionally at least, its former and inferior meaning, and at length when the national law ceased, it lost it altogether. Of this the following examples will be sufficient (Ps. xvi. 11): "Thou wilt show me the path of *life;* in thy presence is the fullness of joy; at thy right hand are pleasures for evermore." Nothing can be plainer than that the Psalmist here had no reference to earthly good; and surely he was not looking to these pleasures for evermore as the reward of sinless obedience. Prov. xii. 28: "In the way of righteousness is *life*, and in the pathway thereof there is *no* death." If any further proof of the fact before us respecting this Jewish usage were necessary, it would be sufficient to refer to the language of the Saviour and of his apostles: "He that hath the Son hath *life*," &c.

The above examples are not referred to, to prove that *in every instance* in the Old Testament in which *life* is promised to the penitent, it is not to be understood as having at the time a double import, instead of this exclusive import, acquired by usage. In Ezekiel, xviii., for example, it may have a double, i. e., a *proper* and a *transferred* meaning. This remark is of importance, because it shows how entirely unessential it is in such cases to decide this question, in order to justify us at this age of the world in quoting this class of passages in the Old Testament, as having exclusively the latter meaning. For if they had a double meaning at the time, then they had the latter meaning, and this to us is strictly their only important meaning; or rather, in respect *to us*, they have lost their former meaning, but retain fully and perfectly the latter, and are therefore to be quoted accordingly.

In respect to the law of Eden, I observe that it clearly teaches that so long as our first parents were obedient they should not die, i. e., should live; and what the *life* promised is, is inferred with entire satisfaction from what we have said of the Mosaic law in connection with the fact that the law of Eden is given in the language of Moses and is Jewish language. For if the principle of reward was developed by the Mosaic law in the manner supposed, it must have been understood, if justly understood by Moses and by those for whom he wrote, to have been the same in Eden.

LECTURE XII.

THE *NATURE* OF GOD'S MORAL GOVERNMENT AS REVEALED.

Section 5 continued, viz., The law in the import of its sanctions.—2. The penalty of the law.—The *nature* of the penalty, viz., temporal death and eternal suffering.—The penalty originally denounced, *general* and *indefinite*.—Temporal death, as it now occurs to all men, not penal.—The sentence in Gen. iii. 19 not a part of the legal penalty.—Spiritual death not penal.—Proof of Prop.—The temporal death of the Mosaic law taught eternal death without mercy.—External obedience clearly shown not to suffice.—The words *to die* and *death*.—Illustration from the double or extended meaning of *exile* under certain supposed circumstances.—*Death* and *to die* used in the Old Testament with this additional meaning.—Additional considerations. Book of Ecclesiastes.—Enoch and Abraham.—Prayer of Balaam.—Destruction by the deluge, and of Sodom and Gomorrah.—Argument from the New Testament.

THE object is first to state and explain what I understand to be the penalty of the divine law, and secondly, to justify the statement by proof. I propose—

I. To state and explain what I understand to be the penalty of the divine law.

I suppose this penalty to consist *in the cessation of existence here on earth, and the greatest possible misery forever in a future state.*

I here use language which is in some respects indefinite, in order to comprise all that the penalty included, as originally denounced. It is supposable that the language or *the mode* adopted of conveying knowledge on this subject should not *specify minutely* all that the penalty in fact included; and it is quite possible, not to say probable, that we should be able to show from a subsequent revelation, that it did comprise specific things, which it was not understood to include, either by our first parents or by Moses. Nor does the use of such general phraseology involve the lawgiver in reproach; for the language may be broad and comprehensive enough to cover all that is made known by a subsequent and more specific development of its import.

By this mode of presenting the subject, I avoid what seems to have occasioned perplexity and not a little discussion. For example, were we to say that the penalty in its original form included and expressed the destruction of both soul and body (considered as the language of Moses), it might be difficult to prove our position; for the resurrection of the body and its future union with the soul in a state of suffering may be regarded as not very clearly revealed in his time. Still, this may have been actually comprised in the penalty; the form of promulgation may be sufficiently comprehensive to include it, and subsequent revelation fully disclosed it.

Again: when I say that the penalty included the cessation of existence on earth, I do not mean that temporal death as it now takes place among men, is *in every instance*, and as an event common to all men, a penal evil or legal sanction. In the case of those who die in their sins, it is doubtless a real part of the evil, which constitutes the legal penalty as a whole. It is doubtless so regarded by God, and in those cases in which we have proof of the one fact we have proof of the other. Thus the signal destruction of Sodom and Gomorrah by fire and brimstone was regarded. (2 Peter, ii. 6, and Jude, ver. 7.)

Temporal death, considered as an event to which all men are subject, is a very different thing from temporal death inflicted on the finally impenitent as the commencement and a constituent part of the legal penalty. As an event common to all, i. e., both Jews and Gentiles, it is the consequence of Adam's sin, though not without their being sinners. Accordingly, the inhabitants of the old world and of Sodom and Gomorrah, would have died, had they not died by signal judgments. Although then temporal death when it comes to the impenitent, is in fact a part of the penalty; although when brought on men by the signal interpositions of God in vindictive judgment it is to be *so regarded by us;* and although in all cases it is to be regarded as an expression of God's displeasure in some degree toward sin, yet it is not in all cases to be regarded as an evil sustaining the penal relation. It may be properly said to be part of the penalty, or a part of the evil which penalty includes, but as a part it is not a *penal* evil. Aside from the inconsistency of this supposition with the death of those who by faith are delivered from the curse of the law, and with the fact that temporal death in respect to them is destroyed and is strictly not an evil, it is evident from the account of the introduction of death into the world, that considered as the inheritance of all men, it does not sustain the relation of a penal evil. Nor is this at all inconsistent with the fact that it does constitute in some cases a part of the legal penalty. Whatever may be the *parts* of that evil called penalty, the whole and not the parts are the penalty. The peculiar relation or characteristic which we call *penal*, or which constitutes it a legal penalty, is predicable of the whole and of none of the parts. If forty stripes save one constitute the penalty of a law, then in a case of the actual infliction, every stripe is a part of the penal evil. But as a part it is not *penal*, since that cannot be truly affirmed of a part which is true only of the whole. Nor is this inconsistent with the fact that one stripe should be inflicted under some other relation in another case, even as the dictate of kindness. Indeed, nothing can be plainer to my mind than that the original sentence, "Dust thou art and unto dust shalt thou return," was not pronounced in execution of the penalty of the law, "Thou shalt surely die." I shall have occasion to resume this topic hereafter. I only remark now, that temporal death here denounced on the whole human race, was one among other evils to which they were doomed under an economy of redemption from sin and its curse, and was not therefore the curse itself, nor as a part of the complex evil which constitutes the legal penalty, does it sustain a penal relation.

Further: I remark here that I do not consider *spiritual death*, or continuance in sin, as properly any part of the legal penalty. It may be that he who once sins against God will with absolute certainty continue to sin, and it is unquestionably true that the threatening of complete misery from the lawgiver, must prevent all effectual interposition on his part to restore a transgressor to holiness, under a merely legal dispensation; it may even require that he place the transgressor in circumstances that will result in continued sin. The natural evil or misery attendant or consequent on continued sin may be a part of the penal evil. But it does not follow that *the sin itself* is therefore specifically threatened, or that it exists as an evil under the relation of legal penalty. The threatening may in a similar manner imply the *continued existence* of the transgressor, since otherwise its execution would be impossible. There may be as real a ground of the certainty of continued sin as there is of continued existence, and the former may be as necessary to the full execution of the penalty in the complete misery of the transgressor as the latter, and yet it would be far from correct and precise phraseology to speak of either as a part of the legal penalty. Similar remarks apply to the sinner's capacity of suffering, to his condition and circumstances, so far as these are necessary to the full execution of the penalty.

Further: it has been shown that nothing but natural evil, and this only as it is an expression of the lawgiver's disapprobation of sin, can constitute legal penalty. But sin considered merely as sin, is not a natural evil, i. e., it is not itself pain or misery. The choice of the inferior good viewed abstractly from the knowledge or conviction that the good chosen is the inferior good, and also from the effects which we ascribe to conscience, and from fear, regret and other similar states of mind, is not painful. It is true that pain or misery may be the invariable attendant of such a choice, because the appropriate causes of the pain may always co-exist with the choice. The intellect may always perceive the folly of it and this will occasion painful regret; and conscience may always operate in the production of painful self-reproach. But the *operations* of the intellect and conscience are not the pain felt, but the cause of it. So the act of will or the choice is not the pain, but only that which with these operations of intellect and conscience, is necessary to the existence of the pain felt. Or if we regard sin as a complex thing made up of acts of intellect, conscience and will, still it is not itself painful, but simply the cause or occasion of pain to the mind, the pain being the effect of the complex acts which constitute the sin. There is of course no more propriety in pronouncing sin, whether we mean by it the act of the will simply or the complex state of mind just described, to be in itself pain or natural evil, than there is in pronouncing the operations of the intellect and conscience which produce pain the pain itself; nor of course in pronouncing the sin a part of the legal penalty, than in so pronouncing the operations of intellect and conscience; and of course no more in pronouncing either a part of the legal penalty, than there is in pronouncing a cause an effect. It is true that in the looseness of popular language this is often done—it is often done in this very case. Nor have I any objection to the use of the language now referred to for popular purposes; as, for example, when sin is said to be in itself unhappiness or misery, and even the greatest of evils. But my objection is, that such popular propositions, which in terms are loose though not ambiguous in import, should be applied (for such is the fact) out of their true import to the analytical inquiry before us. The truth is, that misery is so associated with sin as its consequent, that in popular language it is itself according to abundant usage pronounced misery. Being thus *in words* pronounced a natural evil in itself, the way is prepared (for what on a superficial view of the matter seems like entire consistency), actually in thought, to distinguish sin itself as natural evil from all the natural evil of which it is the cause or occasion, and on the ground that all natural evil enters into the penalty of the law, to pronounce it thus distinguished, a part of the legal penalty. Now who does not see the fallacy of this process of reasoning? The popular proposition that sin is itself unhappiness, has not the meaning which this reasoning gives it. The popular proposition is not intended to separate the sin from the unhappiness connected with it, and to make the one distinct from the other, as they obviously are distinct. And hence in this reasoning, the proposition that sin is itself unhappiness is applied as if they were not distinct. Thus it is that the revolting conclusion is obtained, that God threatens sin with sin—threatens the violation of his law with its violation—threatens the acts of a free voluntary agent with the acts of a free agent.

Such a law among men would be regarded as a burlesque on all legislation. And when we reflect that all our views of the moral government of God must be derived and modified by an ultimate reference to our views of human governments, it must I think be regarded as incredible, that what would be regarded as so preposterous an enactment in a human legislature, does in fact find place in the perfect moral government of God. The first sin of any being is a punishment of sin,—i. e., sin is punished before it exists—punished for his holiness, or at least for his innocence!

If any should say that all this is refined metaphysical speculation, I will not deny it. I have however, this reason for it: that the argument for the doctrine that spiritual death is a part of the penalty, derives its entire plausibility from the metaphysics of its premises, and that it is impossible to unfold its fallacy except by the same mode of reasoning. Thus the argument takes a popular proposition and turns it from its true import into one of a minute metaphysical import, assumes the truth of this import and rests its conclusion upon it. This is undeniable. For let the popular position be understood to mean simply what it does mean in popular usage, viz., that sin and misery are inseparably associated as cause and effect, and it is at once seen to be very different from that which asserts that sin is itself misery viewed abstractly from its effects; and thus the conclusion built on this position is overthrown.

Again: according to the principle that nothing can constitute legal penalty but *natural evil*, and this only as it becomes *an expression* of God's disapprobation of sin, sin itself can be no part of the legal penalty. For how can the fact that God renders sin certain, express his disapprobation of sin? Indeed what is more palpably absurd than to suppose that God should inflict sin as a punishment of sin—should cause sin to exist forever, to show his disapprobation of it? Nothing is plainer than that God, on the present supposition, must be regarded as giving existence to sin in such a manner that its existence may answer the end of legal penalty. But who does not see the gross incongruity of the supposition, that God should give a perpetual and eternal existence to that which he supremely hates and abhors, as the method of showing his abhorrence to it?

Again: sin cannot with the least propriety be regarded as an event whose existence so depends on God, as its relation to law as a legal penalty requires that it should. Sin in its very nature is the act of a free moral agent. It is not a thing *suffered* from the hand or agency of another; but an *act done* by the accountable agent himself;—a thing entirely within the power and at the disposal of the transgressor himself. It can therefore never be regarded as an evil coming from the hand of God, in such a manner as to become a part of the legal penalty. Nor is this all: the supposition that God renders sin certain as a part of the legal penalty, makes it the necessary means of the greatest good, and thus annihilates its nature. But according to the views which I may consider as satisfactorily established, God does not, and cannot as a consistent moral governor, purpose sin as the necessary means of the greatest good, nor purpose its existence in any respect whatever, except as incidental in respect to his prevention to the best system, and therefore purposes it in no sense which is inconsistent with an unqualified preference of holiness to sin, in every instance in which sin does exist. So every subject of God's government with just views of his purposes must regard them. How then can the existence of sin be regarded as purposed of God to subserve the end of upholding his moral government, or as the necessary means of this end? And if not, how can it be supposed to be a part of the penalty of his law?

Should it be said that as continued sin is necessary to the complete execution of the penalty (since none but a sinful being can be completely miserable), God must have purposed its continuance as the necessary means of executing the penalty. I should deny the premises. It is not true that the complete execution of the penalty requires the complete misery, but only the highest possible misery. So that if we suppose a transgressor to reform under law, and God to make him as miserable as possible, the penalty is fully executed. It may be and doubtless is a fact that complete misery is threatened, not on the supposition that he who once sins will afterward become holy, but in view of the fact, that the character which the subject of law voluntarily assumes in an act of sin is an unchangeable character. For aught that can be shown to the contrary, it may be assumed, that he who sins under a given influence of moral government will never under the same influence reform, and that that degree of moral influence which God, as a moral governor and under a merely legal dispensation, brings upon every subject at a given time, is as great as the perfection of this system demands or allows. In this view of the subject, not only the sin but the perpetuity of it are both incidental to the best system. The perpetuity of sin therefore, cannot be regarded as purposed of God as the necessary means of inflicting complete misery; but the penalty is to be viewed as made to consist in complete misery in view of the perpetuity of sin when once committed. Indeed the difficulties and objections pertaining to any other view of the subject lead me to the belief, that a subject of God's moral government is by the very nature and circumstances of it when existing in its perfection, called upon to choose God or an inferior good as his portion *once for all;* and that choose which he may, if there be no change in the system there will never be a change in his character. His act of choice will be for once, and immutable forever. Being made with the knowledge that it is a choice by which he becomes, in the lowest degree of it, a decided enemy of God and of all good—a choice which will continue one and the same during his immortality, which will strengthen by continuance, and which remaining one and the same choice or purpose of heart, will lead to open acts of malice and blasphemy against God. I say with this knowledge, the transgressor does in his first act of sin become, *ipso facto*, an eternal rebel against God. There is in the first act a real and virtual consent to all sin. Nor is this in principle any excessive refinement. For says an apostle, "Whoso shall offend in one point is guilty of all." He who in heart violates one precept of the law does really violate every other, for the thing and the only thing which the law in fact forbids, is that state of heart which violates the supposed precept. ("Cursed is every one," &c.; "He that hateth his brother is a murderer.") Nor is this view of the subject inconsistent with the fact that the guilt and sufferings of a transgressor should increase. As the same disease may increase in virulence and in anguish, so may the self-same sin. And here I would remark, that I regard that as an erroneous view of the subject, which represents the wicked in a future world as committing a succession of separate sins, each having its own appropriate measure of ill-desert, and the sinner as suffering the punishment for one and then for another in similar succession. The Scriptures and reason present another view, viz., that *the commission of sin* brings the curse, the full penalty, and warrant us to assert that although the wicked hereafter grow worse and worse, and suffer more and more, they never cease to suffer for sin as one act or purpose of rebellion done here on earth. With this act all that ill-desert commenced which is the basis of their continual and complete misery; there pertains to it, when committed, this amount of guilt. And if it be said that it could not incur this amount of guilt were it not to be perpetual, I answer that this depends on what the act of sin involved when committed. And if it could not exist under a merely legal dispensation and be what it is without being perpetual, it involved all this guilt when committed. The continued sin of the transgressor is not to be viewed as the necessary means of inflicting the amount of suffering implied in the penalty, but the amount of suffering in the penalty is to be considered as threatened and determined on in view of what sin is, as an act of perpetual revolt from God. I conclude therefore, that sin cannot, according to any just principles of reasoning, be viewed in any manner or respect whatever as a part of the penalty of the divine law.

Having stated in what I suppose the penalty of the law to consist, I now proceed—

II. To justify that statement by proof. Here, for reasons already assigned, we resort again to the Mosaic law.

The argument founded on the Mosaic law, viewed as a representative system, would be this: that as the penalty of that law, considered in its relation to man as its subject and as having an earthly or temporal existence, was *premature temporal death without mercy;* so the penalty of the perfect moral law of God, considered in its relation to man as an immortal being, was *eternal death without mercy*, or the highest degree of *misery* forever.

No truth stands out more conspicuously in the Old Testament, than that mere external conformity to the law, though it averted the civil penalty and secured the civil reward, did not avert the wrath and secure the favor of God as a moral governor. It was most clearly taught, that all such sacrifices and all such doings without a holy heart were an offense and an abomination. When God conferred national blessings on the Jews in view of an external reformation, he distinctly declared that it was not for their righteousness, but for his own name's sake and for the love he bore to their fathers, and that they were continually a stiff-necked and rebellious house. The truth was made conspicuous, that they were not all Israel who were of Israel, and that as children of the flesh they were not children of God. God ever set himself before this people as the searcher of the heart and the judge of all the earth, according to the great principles of a moral administration which were to be illustrated and vindicated in a future state of being. Indeed, in view of the high and holy requirements of God, and especially in view of the acknowledged fact of a future existence, and a future retribution under the government of the true God and the living Jehovah, the Jewish theocracy must have been regarded by every enlightened, honest inquirer after truth, as a most impressive representation of God's more perfect dominion over accountable immortals. Viewed as a merely legal dispensation, the sanctions of the one in all their rigor of application, must have exhibited and illustrated the sanctions of the other according to the unbending principles of eternal righteousness. Viewed in its connection with a gracious economy, the gratuitous proffers of earthly good to apparent penitence and through typical sacrifice, must have been regarded as adumbrations to the truly pious of the higher joys revealed by Christian promise, and the solemn threatenings of temporal calamities and death to the perversely wicked, as distinct denunciations of the wrath to come.

Here it would be in point to support, from the New Testament, the view which I have taken of the Mosaic law. To this I have before referred sufficiently to show the decisive nature of the argument.

To see the nature of the argument as furnished by the Mosaic institution itself, is to my own mind alike interesting and important, as it shows not only what that institution was as a revelation of divine truth to Israel, but also develops its utility to us. The force of the reasoning will indeed scarcely be appreciated without more attention to the Old Testament—a more accurate estimate of its facts and of the character and condition of the ancient Jews—than is commonly given to the subject. With these in the mind, and by transferring them to ourselves, we should I think be prepared to appreciate the evidence of the point under consideration. Suppose, for example, a similar system to that of the theocracy adopted in respect to this people; suppose our present knowledge of God and of his relations (for though there would be a modified difference between them and us in this respect, it would not be such as ought to affect the conclusion); suppose also the same reasons to exist in our case as in theirs for understanding the national institute as a system of representation; could we easily conceive of any mode so fitted to impress the mind with the great truths concerning God, and man, and eternity? Suppose we were to witness what they did—the miracles of Egypt and those at the Red Sea! or were to see and hear God in Sinai!

From this view then of the Mosaic law as a system of representation, I derive my doctrine respecting the legal penalty of God's moral government, as before stated, that as the penalty of the one was temporal death, the penalty of the other was eternal death.

I now appeal also to the language of the penalty, i. e., to the words *die* and *death*, as used to describe it both in the Old and New Testament. This import of these words I shall attempt to unfold according to the principles before stated, respecting the language of words and the language of things, as suggesting and representing more than their literal meaning. That I may be the better understood on this part of the subject, instead of repeating the principles already stated, I shall attempt to illustrate them by an example, which shows that these principles are those of constant use and decisive authority.

Let it then be remembered that my object is to illustrate the various meanings of the word *death*, as descriptive of the legal penalty in different cases as facts and circumstances varied, assuming the primary meaning of the word death to be *the cessation of existence on earth.*

Suppose then a king, whose empire is *visibly* confined to a single island—a rich and happy country—should make *the loss of residence in that country* the penalty of his law against treason. Of this single expression, were no facts known in the case beyond what the language itself conveys, the import would be very indefinite. Were the subjects so ignorant as not to know whether there was or was not any other country, they would regard the penalty as involving at least the loss of a residence where they would wish to live—a departure from their native land. Whatever also they might conjecture as the further consequence, they would regard this evil unmitigated, and in its full extent as the penalty of the crime. This, estimating their guilt and the displeasure of their sovereign by the magnitude of the interests opposed by the crime, would be the only positive definite conception which the language of the law would authorize or require.

Let us now suppose the subjects to know that their king reigns not merely over the small empire of an island, but over a vast continent of empires; that there is a remote and dreary desert which is specified as the place of banishment, and that the king estimates the crime of treason by its true tendency to destroy his extensive empire. Now the same language of the penalty conveys far more than it did before. It necessarily conducts the thoughts to this desert, and though little comparatively might be known of it, a residence there would be unavoidably supposed to be wretched in such a degree, as to express the sovereign's displeasure for the crime of treason against his great and happy kingdom.

Suppose again, that more extensive and minute information respecting the place of exile should be given; that it should be known as a place where existence could be barely sustained, and sustained under continual suffering from cold and hunger, from nakedness and disease, and amid all the miseries of a community of unrestrained maniacs. Now how expressive and how full of meaning does the language of the penalty become, compared with the case in the first supposition, or that in the second? The single word *exile* or *banishment* used to designate the penalty of treason, would unavoidably convey to the mind the full conception of all the known facts in the case, in their appalling combination.

Let us now suppose that all the subjects of the king unite in one universal conspiracy and revolt, and that the sovereign, instead of an immediate execution of the legal penalty, provides a plan of forgiveness and restoration to his favor, proffering both on condition of returning to duty, but declaring nevertheless that all, whether they comply with the terms of forgiveness or not, *shall be exiled from their country;* that those who do comply shall dwell in a city prepared for their residence, where they shall enjoy a far more happy existence than they can enjoy in their native land; and that those who do not, shall suffer the entire penalty of the law. Now when the word *exile* or *banishment* is used, it will unavoidably be seen how diverse its meanings are in different connections. To speak of the exile of those who have complied with the terms of forgiveness, is, in fact, to speak of the happiest event of their earthly being; but to speak of the exile of the perverse and unsubdued rebel, is to speak of all that is dreadful.

I shall now attempt to show, that what I supposed respecting the language of the king's law against treason, is true of the language used to describe the penalty of the divine law.

Here then I begin with the primary literal import of the word death, as denoting the cessation of existence on earth, leaving all beyond it so uncertain and dark that even faith has no concern with it. Now whether any of the human race to whom the penalty of the divine law was ever made known were thus ignorant or not, need not here be decided. If they were, and *necessarily* so, then this restricted view of the import of the penalty was in fact the only penalty to them. But we know that it was not so. (Vide Rom. i. 32.) Even the heathen who do such things as are here specified by the apostle, know that they are worthy of that death which includes "indignation and wrath, tribulation and anguish."

But the question first to be decided according to the proposed method of inquiry is, what facts were known or believed by the ancient people of God when the Mosaic law was given, which would control and determine their views of the import of its penalty. They knew or believed that man was an immortal being: they, like the Egyptians and other nations, believed in future rewards and punishments, and that the law of God did and must respect them under other relations than those of a mere earthly community. Now I maintain that the knowledge or belief of these facts must, except we suppose the grossest perversion of evidence, have controlled their interpretation of the language of penalty, and that they could not but understand the death threatened, as involving the cessation of existence on earth under the hopeless displeasure of God, and of course as including future endless misery. The only possible question is, whether this people did know or believe, or which is the same thing in respect to our argument, might have known the facts specified. But there can be no question on this point. It was the universal doctrine of all nations as well as of the Egyptians, inculcated and enforced on the popular belief, that their gods would reward the good and the bad in a future state. Of course, as I have before said, all that was really necessary to prove to the nation of Israel that the God of Israel will execute such sanctions, *was to prove that he was the true God.* The question therefore in regard to the knowledge or belief of these great facts can no longer be a question. But with this knowledge or belief, it is utterly impossible that by the laws of correct interpretation this people should not have understood the legal penalty to be what I have stated it to be. The use and the import of language are always determined by the known facts of the case. And that the penalty of the Mosaic law should not denote what I have supposed, is as impossible as that in the example supposed, the word *exile* or *banishment* should not have the meaning supposed; or as that the phrase *Solomon's temple*, to one who had seen it, should denote the wigwam of an American Indian.

Such we shall see was the fact in regard to its import, as understood and exhibited by those who understood it correctly.

Now it will be admitted that Ezekiel and David and Solomon knew no more on this subject than what was revealed under the Mosaic dispensation. The question then is, what did they mean when they spoke of *death* as the punishment of sin? And this question is answered by one incontrovertible fact, viz., that this death was a death which in its full import at least, the righteous *should not die*. But the righteous did die a temporal death. Thus Solomon, for example, while he declares in many and different forms that the wicked shall die as the reward of their iniquity (Prov. v. 4, 22, 23; viii. 35, 36; xi. 19), also asserts that "in the way of righteousness there is life, and in the pathway thereof there is *no death*." (Prov. xii. 28; vide also x. 2; xi. 4; xiii. 14; xiv. 27.) Ezekiel also asserts with peculiar directness, that *the soul that sinneth shall die*, that the wicked shall *surely die*; and yet he no less unequivocally asserts that the righteous shall live, and *not die*. (Ezek. xviii. 21; compare Isa. lxvi. 16, 24; vide also Prov. x. 2; xi. 4; xiii. 14; xxiv. 27.) Now the death from which the righteous are delivered is the death which the wicked suffer. But the righteous are not distinguished from the wicked by exemption from temporal death. The death therefore which the wicked suffer is something compared to which the temporal death of the righteous is *not* death. Was it natural death in circumstances of peculiar suffering? The righteous often died in such circumstances (vide Heb. xi. 37), being stoned and sawn asunder. The righteous died prematurely or in early life, even "perished in his righteousness" (Eccles. vii. 15). Besides the difference supposed is not such as the case obviously requires, to exhibit the displeasure of that God toward sin, who had adopted such a course of providence to prevent it. Was it then annihilation? But they acknowledged the doctrine of a future state, and therefore could not so understand it. It was death then as the wages of sin; it was death which excluded from the rewards of the righteous and from the favor of God; it was the cessation of existence on earth, under the frown of the Almighty—death as an expression of his displeasure as a lawgiver, and death to an immortal being, without one ray of hope, of favor, or of happiness from his offended God.

Many other considerations confirm this view of the subject. As to temporal death and calamities, the wise man declares that there is no substantial difference in the state of the righteous and the wicked, all things happening alike to all. By this we are not to understand that he esteemed the penalty of the Mosaic law as not an evil peculiar to its transgressors, but that in view of their future allotments, which was the theme of his discourse, the difference is not deserving of consideration. As if he said, This world is not, but a future world is the place of just retribution. Again, natural death was without terror to the righteous; they welcomed the event—they hailed it often with joy. But to the wicked this event was replete with unqualified terror. Now keeping in mind their belief of a future state, what must have been their views of this event as one so appalling? Further, the promises of eternal life to the righteous throw a strong and clear light on the nature of that death which was the penalty of sin. The only condition of such promises was personal holiness, and therefore in every one of them the truth was clearly revealed that "without holiness no man shall see the Lord." Beings then who were known to exist forever, dying in sin, were never to see God—never to enjoy good in the least degree; were to be excluded from it under his severest displeasure. For here also, let it be remarked, the fact of God's unqualified and extremest displeasure against the wicked was fully revealed, and what evil could immortal beings fail to expect from the wrath of God against sin as exhibited in the Old Testament?

I might here refer to the book of Ecclesiastes, as written in the opinion of some learned men, for the purpose of proving from the light of nature a state of future rewards and punishments. (Vide Graves on Pentateuch, Vol. II., p. 255, *note.*) If this was so, how striking a disclosure of the principles of our argument and the conclusion founded on them! But I only refer to some facts which are no less decisive—I mean those which doubtless were well known in the time of Moses; and first those which exhibit God's dealings with his faithful servants. Take for example those which respect Enoch and Abraham. Now we may assume, as it respects the present argument, that it was a known fact, that these men on the ground of personal holiness were rewarded with the favor of God and everlasting happiness in a future world, one of them being conducted thither by God's miraculous interposition. What is the inference but that there was such a future world—that without holiness the inheritance of its joys could never be obtained—and that the wicked, as the object of God's hopeless displeasure, were doomed to a future existence the very opposite of these holy men?

Such was in fact the view of the wicked themselves, at least in one instance. For what could the prayer of Balaam, "Let me die the death of the righteous, and my last end be like his," import, if there had been in his view no difference between the state of the righteous and the wicked after leaving this world? We know, and he knew, that the most desirable consideration in the death of the righteous was the hope of future joys. To suppose this prayer to be prompted merely in reference to any general providential difference between the attendant sufferings of the one and those of the other, or by any thing, while he believed the prospects of both for futurity were alike, is to me incredible.

Again: I appeal to the destruction of the old world by the deluge, and of Sodom and Gomorrah by fire and brimstone. That these are properly regarded as decisive instances of the departure of the wicked from this world to one of endless misery, we are assured from the New Testament. But let us look at the facts themselves, and ask what instruction these must have furnished to God's ancient people on the subject before us. With the knowledge that those destroyed were immortal, of the distinction made between them as wicked on the one hand, and Noah and his family and Lot as righteous on the other, who could suppose that these signal judgments of God terminated in mere temporal death, and this too when Noah and Lot must so shortly die? Could it be supposed that in these cases the legal penalty of the Jewish theocracy, a merely temporal institute, was executed? But this law had no existence. Under such a law therefore they could not have died. But they died under the most signal and awful proofs of God's displeasure. They died too as immortal beings. They died, as the apostle reasons, under another law than that of a theocracy. If the very heathen know that they are worthy of death for their crimes, what must be the conclusion in respect to those whom God destroyed by the deluge, and by fire and brimstone? What must be in store for those who were ushered into eternity under such tokens of the wrath to come?

I might here refer to many passages in the Old Testament which *in words* describe the penalty of sin to be *everlasting*.

(Vide Isa. lxvi. 24; Daniel, xii. 2.) "Many that sleep in the dust of the earth shall awake; some to everlasting life, and some to shame and everlasting contempt." In view of the acknowledged fact of the soul's immortality, there is not only no reason for limiting the language of this class of texts, but decisive reason for not doing it.

In conclusion, I appeal to the New Testament, not to prove the fact that the penalty of sin is endless, but to prove that it was so understood under the Mosaic dispensation. Here we shall not only find this fact established, but a striking illustration of those principles of using language which I have stated and exemplified. It is then undeniable that our Saviour did assume the doctrine of future endless punishment, and used Jewish phraseology to describe it. So also did the apostles. This they did when the national law with its temporal sanctions had ceased. Nor is this all; it was a doctrine of the popular faith, the Sadducees excepted, and their error our Lord exposed by an argument from the Old Testament. Now let these things be accounted for, unless the Old Testament taught the doctrine of a future state with its retribution in eternal life and eternal death. And in view of the acknowledged fact of the theocracy with sanctions of temporal life and death, let the above usage of language by our Saviour and his apostles be explained, except on the principles which have been stated respecting the change of meaning.

Cor.—It follows that all those passages in the Old Testament in which life and death, good and evil, blessing and cursing are set before men to induce to holiness and to deter from sin, are properly quoted by us in the New Testament import.

LECTURE XIII.

THE *NATURE* OF GOD'S MORAL GOVERNMENT AS REVEALED.

Section 6: The law expresses God's preference of obedience to disobedience, all things considered.—Two opposite views on this subject possible.—The first, inadmissible by the language of the law; opposed to the dictates of common sense; self-contradictory and absurd; mistakes an involuntary state for a preference; converts sin into holiness and holiness into sin.—The second view supported by the language of the law; by God's sincerity, &c., &c.; by his own solemn assurances in the Scriptures.—No texts teach the contrary.

I PROCEED now to consider the law of this government in—

Sect. 6.—As an expression of God's preference of obedience to disobedience, all things considered.

We have consulted the dictates of reason on this subject, and now propose to consider it in the light of Revelation.

Before I proceed to show what the Scriptures teach on the subject, I remark that there are two different, and only two different views, in respect to which we need direct our inquiries:

One is, *that God expresses in his law simply a preference of obedience to disobedience in themselves considered, or when each is considered in its true nature and tendency; while he also expresses in his revelation, a preference of disobedience to obedience, all things considered,* or, *of the former to the latter in every instance in which the former takes place, as being the necessary means of the greatest good.*

The other is, *that God in the circumstances, or under that perfect system of moral government under which he addresses his law to men, expresses a preference of obedience to disobedience, all things considered, i. e., considered in every respect and in every instance of moral action.*

I propose to consider these different views of the divine law in the order in which I have now stated them.

I. Concerning the former, I remark—

1. That the language of the divine law not only does not *admit* of the meaning now expressed, but forbids it. There is not a word in the language, which expresses or implies, or in the remotest manner intimates that God prefers *disobedience*

to his law to obedience, or sin to holiness, *all things considered.* Much less is there any thing in the language which shuts it down to this meaning. On the contrary, the language of this law in its form or manner of use, is the direct, unqualified, and decisive form which lawgivers have ever employed, and subjects have ever understood to express an absolute preference, *all things considered*, of obedience to disobedience to law. Such language, therefore, requires this meaning, *de usu loquendi*, the only umpire of *propriety*, and admits of no other. It is absolutely incredible that the lawgiver should use this language in any other meaning, and not intend to deceive his subjects, especially if he employ it to mean that he prefers disobedience to his law *all things considered*, to obedience in its stead. If therefore, there be any reason for this interpretation of the divine law, it must be found elsewhere than in the language of the law. And further, it is worthy of remark, that none who thus interpret the divine law pretend to derive their interpretation from the language of the law; but simply and solely from certain peculiar and false notions of Scriptural language as employed on another subject—the decretive will of God. The argument is this—that without the interpretation of the law now opposed, its just meaning would be *inconsistent* with the meaning of the Scriptural language respecting the decretive will of God. Be it so. If just interpretation gives inconsistency or contradiction in the language of the Scriptures, we must admit the inconsistency or contradiction. But we shall see there is no pretense for this alleged inconsistency; and if this be so, then there is not even a pretense that the law of God expresses his preference of obedience to disobedience *all things considered*, and in all instances in which obedience takes place.

2. The interpretation of the divine law now opposed, does violence to the plain and incontrovertible dictates of common sense, and ascribes a peculiarity to the moral government of God which is incredible. It will not be pretended that the law of any other moral government was ever understood to express such a preference of obedience as that now supposed. And to show how revolting to the common sentiments of men such a law would be, we have only to suppose its import fully and precisely developed. Suppose then a parent or civil legislator should, in the absolute and unqualified form of a law,

require any given act of duty, and should at the same time unequivocally declare that in every instance in which the law should be violated, its violation would be the necessary means of the greatest good, and as such be preferred by him to an act of obedience in its stead. Now I do not ask merely whether such a law thus explained by the lawgiver, would not be regarded as something unheard of; but whether it would not be considered as furnishing decisive proof of either insanity or falsehood, and be pronounced by the unhesitating decisions of common sense and sound reason to be worthy either of contempt or execration? When we reflect that God in revealing himself to men as their moral governor, does in fact assume that men are prepared to understand the nature of this relation, and leaves them to the obvious dictates of reason and common sense as the medium of understanding the language of his law, can we suppose that he intended that his law should be understood in a meaning which all the world would regard as absurd and revolting in the law of a human legislator? Is such a peculiarity in the government of God credible? Who made this discovery? Not the people, but theologians; and how were they led to give the law such an interpretation? Simply to maintain its consistency with other errors about decrees.

3. This scheme is self-contradictory and absurd. It is here necessary to advert to the different phraseology used by the advocates of this scheme. Some of their language I regard as unobjectionable, only when used as synonymous with that which I regard as entirely false. Thus they often say that God purposes sin, or the existence of sin, *all things considered.* This is undoubtedly true. But then it is by no means synonymous with the position that God purposes sin *rather than holiness, all things considered.* God doubtless purposes the existence of sin rather than its prevention (and this is the true meaning of the elliptical statement under consideration), it being *considered* that the prevention of sin by God required the nonexistence of the best system. This however does not imply a preference of sin *to holiness* for any *consideration* whatever, when the existence of one is compared with the existence of the other under the best system. The doctrine to which I object is that which represents God as preferring sin *to holiness*, all things considered, under the present system of government,

and *the thing* considered in sin as the ground of the preference, is its relation as *the necessary means of the greatest good.*

But that I may not misrepresent this doctrine, I would still more minutely exhibit it in the language of its advocates.

It is said then that holiness and sin, or obedience and disobedience, are what they are in their true nature and appropriate tendencies, and that they are nothing more: that whatever good sin may be made the occasion of under the government of God, decides nothing in respect to its true nature and tendencies, i. e., nothing in regard to the thing itself: that although its existence may be NECESSARY, as the occasion by which God can produce greater good than would be the result of universal holiness in creatures, yet its true nature and tendency are only to evil, while the true nature and tendency of holiness are only to good; that therefore the estimate expressed by the Moral Governor simply respects holiness and sin as they are in their own nature and tendencies, i. e., in themselves abstractly from the good which he may bring out of the evil, and that therefore the law of God is a proper expression of his preference as a lawgiver for holiness to sin, although the existence of sin is preferable to holiness in reference to the good of which it is the *necessary* means.

Upon this I remark, that it contains a palpable inconsistency; in other words, that it comprises two positions, both of which cannot be true. Thus it asserts that sin is what it is in its own nature and appropriate tendency, and that it is properly nothing more; and that it is, thus viewed, wholly evil: and yet it also asserts that in the circumstances in which it exists, it is *the necessary means* of the greatest good. Now I ask, what is the import of this last position but this, that God being what he is and man being what he is, the moral government of God being what it is and holiness and sin being what they are—in short, the nature, relations, and reality of things being what they are, sin in the circumstances in which it exists, is the necessary means of the greatest good? But if this be the meaning of this position, then its meaning is that sin in *its true nature and tendency* is the necessary means of the greatest good. I assert on high authority, that of President Edwards,* "That *tendency* is truly esteemed to belong *to the nature* of any thing, or to be

* Works, vol. vi. p. 150, 1st Am. ed.

inherent in it; that is the *necessary consequence* of its nature, considered together with its proper situation in the universal system of existence, whether that tendency be good or bad." If then sin in the circumstances in which it exists will produce and is *the necessary means* of producing the greatest good, according to the real nature and relations of things, or "in its proper situation," &c., then it is the *true nature and tendency of sin* to produce the greatest good. But this palpably contradicts the position in the same scheme, that the true nature and tendency of sin is only to evil. Both cannot be true.

Notwithstanding the plain contradiction and inconsistency of this scheme, we can be at no loss which of the contradictory positions essentially belongs to the scheme itself. It is unquestionably that which affirms the *necessity of sin* to the greatest good; for the moment this position is separated from the scheme, its real or its professed object fails. That object is to give an intelligible and satisfactory explanation of the existence of sin, and of the purpose of God in regard to its existence. The explanation is, that it is the necessary means of the greatest good. But if this be denied and rejected from the scheme, it fails utterly to give satisfaction on the question why sin exists, or to show in what respect it is an object of the divine purpose. The scheme *itself* by such a denial would be denied and abandoned.

If I be asked whether God may not bring greater good out of the existence of sin and the system with which it is connected, than WOULD HAVE BEEN the result of the obedience which *would* have been *actually* rendered under any different system, I reply that there is no doubt of it. But this does not prove that he will or can bring more good out of sin, than would have resulted from the obedience which SHOULD AND MIGHT have been rendered *in this system.* Of course it does not show that sin in this system is necessary to the greatest good.

It may be said that God is able and will in fact bring greater good out of the existence of sin, than COULD have resulted from the universal obedience of his accountable creatures, and that thus sin may be desirable, not as having in itself any tendency to good, but as the necessary means of the greatest good. It may be urged as decisive in favor of the distinction between a thing as thus good in itself, and good as the necessary means of good, that as the means of good it has no inherent property in itself, but is entirely dependent on the will and agency of God, and that on the supposition that God brings greater good out of it, than could have resulted from universal obedience, then it is good not in itself, but only as the necessary means of good. I answer that this supposition is inconsistent with itself. For while it asserts that sin is the necessary means of the greatest good, it also asserts that it has no inherent property which fits it to be such a means. But if sin has no inherent property in its own nature that fits it to be the means of good rather than any thing else, then it cannot be *the necessary means of good*, rather than something else; and therefore to say that it has no such inherent property, and to say that it is the necessary means of good, is to assert a plain contradiction.

Again: sin either has inherent in its nature that property which fits it to be the necessary means of the greatest good through divine agency, or it has not. If it has not, then something else through the divine agency might answer the proposed end as well. If it has such an inherent property, then it is *in its own nature* fitted to be the means of the greatest good in a respect in which nothing else is, and is therefore in its own nature or tendency better than any thing else as the means of good.

Again: if there be nothing in the nature of sin which fits it to be the means of the greatest good, and if it be true that the supposed result, viz., the greatest good, is not to be ascribed at all to the nature of sin but solely to divine agency, then for aught that appears, divine agency might use any thing else as the means of that good as well as sin. Of course sin is not the necessary means of that good, for the same divine agency might have produced the same result without the existence of sin as well as with it. A case referred to in illustration of the opinion which I am opposing, will demonstrate the error of that opinion. I mean the crucifixion of the Saviour by wicked hands. It is assumed that in order to the good which results from the atonement of Christ, it was necessary that he should be put to death by a murderous act. Whether it be so or not must depend on the question, whether there was any thing in that sinful deed as such, which was necessary to the fact of an atonement. If there was, then the act may be said to be necessary to the good resulting from this work of divine mercy. But if there was not, then his death, allowing that to be necessary, would, though accomplished in any other manner—for example, by the direct agency of God, or in the way in which the Saviour suffered in the garden—have possessed the same atoning efficacy. And to make the error of the above theory still more apparent, let it be supposed that there was that in the act of the murderers of our Lord which was in the nature of things indispensable to the redemption of a fallen world, and that benevolence required that this redemption should be accomplished, and would not the moral quality of the act be at once changed? It would indeed be malice toward an innocent man—it would be in direct violation of a divine command; but the moment that such malice becomes in its true nature and tendency, and according to the true nature and tendency of things, indispensable to the greatest good, it becomes a matter of duty, and ought to be a subject of precept, according to the only principle that benevolence itself can be decided to be a proper subject of precept.

But it may be said still further, that it may be necessary, in order that sin may be the necessary means of good, that it should be a violation of a divine command, since otherwise it *could* furnish no occasion for the display of the divine mercy in its remission. I answer, that sin is what it is, independently of the law which forbids it. It is not made sin by being forbidden. That the law is given by a perfect being, may be *proof* that the act forbidden is sin; but the mere fact of violating a *good law* does not, strictly speaking, constitute the sin of the act. The act is in its nature sin or it is not, and no law can alter its nature. If it is not in its nature sin, then it would furnish no occasion for the display of mercy, since there can be no display of mercy in forgiving sin which is not sin. If it be in its nature sin, then it cannot be in its nature the necessary means of the greatest good; for to suppose this, is as we have shown, to suppose that concerning it which wholly changes its moral quality.

4. That which this scheme denominates a preference in the divine mind of holiness to sin, is not and cannot in the case supposed, be a *preference*, but can be only *an involuntary state* of mind. I need not say that we properly decide what is possible and what is impossible in respect to volitions, preferences, &c., in the divine mind by the known laws of our own mental

operations. I affirm then, that it is absolutely impossible according to these laws, that I should really and truly prefer one object of choice to another viewed in themselves, and at the same time *prefer* the latter to the former as the necessary means of the greater good. In every act of choice we take into consideration the entire amount of good inherent in and connected with each object, and form our choice or preference in view of the whole. In other words, we never prefer or choose an object because in *one respect* we esteem it better than another, while yet in another respect we esteem the other as so much better than that, as to possess on the whole a superior value. Let us take an example. Rich fruit and a bitter medicine which is necessary to life are proffered. Now I may desire, i. e., be *involuntarily* inclined to choose the fruit as better in one respect, or if you please, better in itself than the bitter medicine. It may be true that I *should* choose the fruit IF my life were not in danger. But is not this all that can possibly be true respecting my state of mind toward the fruit? Can there be a real preference or choice of it in such a case? There is according to the supposition, an actual preference of the medicine as the means of the greatest good. Is there also an actual preference of the fruit? If so, which will be taken? Both cannot be. Which will be when each is actually preferred to the other? But the point is too plain for controversy. Precisely however like the supposed preference for the fruit, which is not preference and can with no propriety or truth be called a preference, is the preference of holiness to sin which is imputed to the Divine Being, and which he is supposed to express in his law, which is no preference. It is merely an *involuntary* desire or inclination which in all cases precedes choice or preference, and is as truly diverse from an act of the will as any one mental act or state is from any other. All therefore that can be said with truth on this scheme is, that God has an *involuntary desire* that men should be holy when holiness and sin are considered in themselves; but instead of preferring holiness to sin on this account, he *prefers* sin as the necessary means of the greatest good, to holiness. The scheme therefore which represents God as preferring sin to holiness as the necessary means of the greatest good, does ascribe that to God which necessarily implies that he neither has nor can have in any sense whatever, a preference of holiness to sin; that his law, interpreted as it must be, is an absolute falsehood, and himself the unqualified approver of sin.

5. This scheme converts the act of man which the Scriptures pronounce to be sin, into duty or moral excellence.

This it does in two respects. (1.) As it asserts it to be the most useful; for, as we have already shown, if sin be the necessary means of the greatest good, then it is such in its nature and tendency, and of course is in its nature and tendency the most useful. But we hold that there is not a plainer truth in morals, than that virtue or moral excellence is founded in its tendency to good. As we have before had occasion to say, it is not the law which *makes* an action right in a moral sense, but only proves it to be so. The action is right or wrong independently of the law which prescribes it, and is morally right simply and only as it is as a voluntary act which in its nature and relations tends to produce the greatest good. Such according to this scheme is sin. Sin therefore is morally right as the best act of man.

It is so (2.), if we appeal to the known will of the Lawgiver, for according to this scheme God has expressed no will but one, and that is a preference of sin to holiness. Even if we admit the opposite and inconsistent preferences, which this scheme ascribes to the Supreme Lawgiver, still we know at least in respect to all the sin that has been and all that shall be committed, that he prefers it to obedience in its stead. So also as we are told that all men who come into the world will commit some sin, it follows that *some sin* in every man even before its commission, is known to be preferred by God to perfect holiness. Indeed if we reflect how long the world has stood, and how much sin there has been in it, how few and solitary are the exceptions furnished by individuals to the universal sinfulness of our race, and that all the sin which has existed has, as the necessary means of the greatest good, been preferred by God to holiness in its stead, the probability is not slight but preponderating with respect to an individual, that he will better please God by disobedience to his law than by obedience. Rather I may say it is matter of absolute *certainty*. For if God has in one instance preferred sin to holiness—and surely if he has in all instances in which sin has existed—then his law is no expression of an opposite preference, and cannot furnish a particle of evidence that he has any other preference than that of sin to holiness. If his law furnishes no such evidence, none is furnished. We are left simply to the known and declared expression of his preference of sin to holiness as the rule of duty.

Many other consequences might be legitimately derived from the scheme now opposed, which are equally revolting and absurd. It might be shown that repentance on the part of a sinner is not only not a duty, but in view of the divine will as the standard of right, is impossible. It might be shown that benevolent action also is not right action, &c., &c.

II. I shall attempt to show the truth of the second view of this subject as before stated, viz., *that God in the circumstances or under the system of moral government, under which he addresses his law to men, expresses a preference of obedience to disobedience in every respect and in every instance of moral action.*

This I argue—

1. From the language of the law.

I have already remarked that the language of the law is the direct and unqualified language used by men in all legal enactments to express an unqualified preference. I now say that it *must be* understood to express such a preference. In proof of this I allege the principle that the language used in this instance must be interpreted as it is interpreted when used in similar cases and in a similar form. If not, then how can it convey any meaning to the mind? I admit there may be cases in which *reasons* may exist for limiting the ordinary import of language; but no reason can be assigned for such limitation here. If it be said that otherwise the Bible is contradictory, and this is all that can be said, I answer, first, that this according to principles before advanced, is an insufficient reason; and secondly, that the Bible is not made contradictory by this interpretation.

2. This being the true interpretation of the language of the law, it follows that if the meaning now given is not the real meaning, there is no sincerity in God's commands.

This is sufficiently obvious from a single illustration. If I invite a friend to my house, or command a child to perform a certain act, and should connect with such an invitation or command the declaration that all things considered I preferred the invitation should not be accepted, or the act should not be performed, should I be counted sincere? How then can God be so accounted? Surely it makes no difference whether the fact is uttered in connection with the command or is capable of being known from other sources of evidence. It is the fact and not the method in which it is learned, that makes God sincere or false—that binds man to take him at his word, or releases him from the obligation.

Several other considerations might be urged; such as the moral perfection of God; the nature of the thing required of man; his hatred of sin; the character of the law as holy, just, and good; the essential nature of law as involving an honest and sincere preference of holiness to sin; the design of law as fitted to make men believe the lawgiver sincere, &c. It is sufficient to refer to the frequent and strong assurances which are made by God himself. "As I live, saith the Lord God, I have no pleasure in the death of the wicked, *but that the wicked turn and live.*" "O Jerusalem, Jerusalem! how often would I have gathered thy children together, even as a hen gathereth her chickens under her wings, but ye would not!" "If thou hadst known, even thou, at least in this thy day, the things which belong unto thy peace!" "Not willing that any should perish, but that all should come to the knowledge of the truth." "How shall I give thee up, Ephraim? how shall I deliver thee, Israel? how shall I make thee as Admah? how shall I set thee as Zeboim? Mine heart is turned within me, my repentings are kindled together." Last of all we have God's own vindication from the charge that is urged by this theory: "What could have been done more to my vineyard, that I have not done in it? *wherefore when I looked that it should bring forth grapes, brought it forth wild grapes!*"

Again: I urge that no valid objections can be derived from opposing texts. If there are texts which, when properly interpreted, teach the contrary, then we are forced to admit that there are contradictions in the Bible. The declarations ought to be very explicit and precise, to lead us to doubt that the law expresses God's preference of holiness to sin. Neither are true.

Acts, iv. 28, and ii. 23, are often referred to. But in these texts nothing more is declared than that God purposed the wicked act by which Christ was crucified. This I cheerfully admit. But the question is, in what respect did he purpose it?

Did he purpose it as the necessary means of the greatest good? Is this distinctly asserted? Is it implied? It is not to the point to say that great good followed the act. The question still returns, whether all this good might not have been secured without the act. Who knows that it could not? And if no one, who shall say that it could not?

(Gen. i. 20.) Here nothing more is said than that God meant or purposed the wicked act of selling Joseph into Egypt to be the occasion of good, as he doubtless does design in respect to all sin. But it is not asserted that sin, or this sin was preferred as the necessary means of the greatest good.

(Ps. lxxvi. 10.) The meaning of this passage is exhausted by saying that God will cause sin (wrath) to praise him and prevent all that he cannot render subservient to this end. But how does it follow from this that the wrath—the sin—is the necessary means of the greatest good?

(Exodus, ix. 16, and Rom. ix. 17.) These passages declare only that God purposed Pharaoh's existence and his acts. But they do not declare that these acts of sin were the necessary means of the greatest good, or of any good.

(Matt. xiii. 14; Mark, iv. 12; Luke, viii. 10.) Christ did not choose to change the system of influences that he had purposed, nor to add to it influences which would secure the conversion. This was for wise reasons; but among these reasons it is not said that their continuance in sin was preferred as the necessary means of the greatest good.

END OF SECTION III.

APPENDIX—No. I.

ESSAY ON JUSTICE AS THE ATTRIBUTE OF A PERFECT MORAL GOVERNOR.

PART I.—CONCEPTION OF JUSTICE ANALYZED AND EXPLAINED.

Justice defined.—1. Justice a benevolent disposition.—Manifested in subordinate purposes and executive doings.—Relation of one to the other.—2. Justice is a disposition to render to every one his due.—What is it to render to every one his due?—Difference between *what is due* and *what is "his due."*—Executive acts divided into two classes, and each of these subdivided into two.—The cases arising under these classes considered in order.—*What is "his due"* arises from a special relation, and involves a right.—Inalienable rights.—What is a right?—Right involves obligation.

There is perhaps no one of the particular moral attributes of the Deity of which accurate views are more important, in both natural and revealed theology, than his attribute of justice. *What is justice as the attribute of a perfect moral governor?* The inquiry is intimately connected with the discussion of many theological questions, as well as of the nature of a perfect moral government.

The word *justice* has, as we commonly say, a variety of meanings in different applications. It is often applied to mere executive acts or doings, as these occur in the various forms of intercourse and business among men. It has however another important application, and one with which we are now more directly concerned, viz., that in which it denotes a virtuous or morally right state of mind. The general import of the word, in this use of it, I propose to ascertain before I enter on the investigation of the present leading inquiry—*what is justice as the attribute of a perfect moral governor?*

I proceed then to say, that

Justice, in respect to sentient beings, is a benevolent disposition or purpose of mind to render to every one his due;* more particularly—

Justice is a benevolent disposition or purpose of mind to ren-

---

* We sometimes speak of doing justice to *a cause, to an argument,* &c.

der or to do to every one what ought to be rendered or done, the obligation to which arises from some peculiar relation of the object of the act, which creates and implies a right reciprocal to such obligation.

In defining a general complex term, like the term *justice*, it is convenient to employ such general terms in a leading definition as shall be more obvious and familiar, though for certain purposes they may need themselves to be defined. In this way, by a progressive analysis, we may successfully unfold the elementary ideas comprised in the complex idea. Accordingly I now propose to show the correctness of the above definition of *justice*, in both its general and particular forms, by a progressive analysis and explanation.

The definition of justice by the civil law is this: "*Justitia est constans et perpetua voluntas jus suum cuique tribuendi.*" This as a definition in moral philosophy, whatever may be true of it in political philosophy or civil jurisprudence, is defective in omitting the elementary idea denoted by the word *benevolent* employed in the definition. This elementary idea is obviously essential to the true conception of justice as a morally right act or state of the will. Nor is this definition as one in political science, or as a definition of justice on the part of men considered as simply members of the body politic, an adequate definition, since in this relation, justice on the part of both ruler and subject must include benevolence toward the body politic, or a disposition to promote the welfare of the State. Again: in this definition of the civil law, the phrase *suum jus* must denote, not *his right*, as distinguished from *that to which he has a right*, but the latter only. Even in this sense of the phrase, the definition does not by any means include every instance of justice. The will or purpose to punish a criminal, in certain cases, is an act of justice. But it is plainly not a will to render to the criminal *his right*, or *that to which he has a right.* It is only by understanding *suum jus* to mean *his due*, in the specific sense of this English phrase, as used and explained in the foregoing definitions of justice, that the definition of the civil law, in this respect, is unobjectionable. But more on this topic hereafter.

Premising then, that I speak of *justice* only in its general meaning, when used to denote a virtuous or morally right state of mind, I remark—

In the first place, that *justice is a benevolent disposition or purpose.* Here it is important to advert to the difference between benevolence, considered as that primary moral affection which is the sum and essence of all virtue, and that which may be called *benevolence*, although viewed abstractly from the former, it is not virtuous. Benevolence then, as the primary morally right affection, is an elective preference of the highest happiness of all—the sentient universe—to every conflicting object. In this sense of the word, benevolence is to be distinguished from other and very different states of mind, which are often and properly called *benevolence*, viz., from any merely constitutional affection, which includes no act of will; and also from any affection which, though voluntary, directly respects only some *limited degree* of good to others, and which may be prompted either by benevolence or selfishness. This general or universal benevolence—benevolence as an elective preference of the highest happiness of sentient beings—must then be distinguished from all those limited forms of kindness or good-will with which it is so often confounded by philosophers. Benevolence which respects merely one's country, or one's circle of friends and acquaintance, or an associate company of highwaymen, is not a virtuous or morally right state of the mind. Such benevolence is prompted by selfishness, and is of course a selfish affection.

Again: general or universal benevolence—benevolence as merely an elective preference of the highest happiness of all—must be distinguished from all subordinate action, in the form of volitions, dispositions, or purposes, and in the form of executive doings, to which it may lead. This state of mind, as first arising in the mind, and as a mere moral preference (Ps. lxxiii. 25), may be conceived as a mental state in which the mind has no reference to any specific or subordinate action whatever. But if we suppose, which seems to be uniformly true, that the mind in making this preference, knows that the attainment of its object depends on subsequent subordinate action, then this state will be something more than the mere elective preference of the object specified. It will involve another act of will, viz., a purpose or a disposition of mind to perform all such subordinate action as may be known to be necessary to attain the object. It is this complex mental state as including the elective preference of the highest happiness of all, and a purpose or disposition to perform all such action as may be necessary to attain its object, which is properly called benevolence, or general benevolence, universal benevolence or good-will. By President Edwards it is called *the love of being in general.* Though this state of mind is one in which no particular subordinate action is *directly* willed or chosen, nor properly included, it is in a most important respect a practical principle, inasmuch as it is not only a disposition or purpose of heart, but a permanent governing principle, which in its true nature and tendency prompts to, or, etymologically speaking, *arranges*, or directs all those subordinate volitions, dispositions, or affections, and those executive doings, which are necessary to the attainment of its object. This state of mind is morally right, and the only act which, viewing other acts as not including it, is morally right. Being in an important sense a permanent state of mind, whose tendency is to prompt to other mental states, it is combined with them, and the various combinations are properly called benevolent affections, dispositions, and purposes. These are the particular forms or modifications of general benevolence, or universal good-will. Each of these, for the sake of distinguishing it from others of the same class, and from *general* benevolence, we distinguish by a particular name. One of these particular forms of general benevolence in which the mind wills a limited degree of the well-being of another we often call *benevolence*, relying on the connection to show the meaning of the word. In this case there is *a particular* disposition or purpose to perform beneficent action prompted by *general benevolence*, which particular disposition or purpose, though properly called *benevolence* or *kindness*, differs from general benevolence. In another case there is a like disposition or purpose to speak the truth, which is properly called *veracity.* In another, there is a like disposition or purpose to render to every one his due, which is properly called *justice.* Any one of these particular forms of general benevolence, contemplated as including this principle, is truly and properly said to be *morally* right, and is properly called a virtue. But then its *moral rectitude* consists exclusively in the element of *general benevolence*, since if we conceive the particular disposition, affection, or purpose to exist, as it may, without this element of *general benevolence*, we necessarily conceive of it as a form of selfishness. If again we conceive of the element of general benevolence as existing in the same degree without the particular disposition, affection, or purpose, we necessarily conceive of the same degree of moral rectitude. In like manner, when benevolence is conceived as combined with any particular disposition, &c., and these as going forth in executive action, we properly speak of the entire combination as morally right action.

When however we contemplate justice or veracity, or any particular disposition, purpose, volition, separately from, or as not including either the benevolent or selfish principle of the heart, it is neither morally right nor morally wrong. At the same time it must be admitted that justice, veracity, &c., each being conceived as a particular subordinate purpose or disposition without general benevolence, and including its appropriate executive action, are in some sense *right*, but not *morally right.* They are *right* as they are fitted to promote some limited good necessary to the general good. It may be truly said of any of these particular acts, that it *ought* to be done. But its *rightness* or *oughtness* is not *moral* rightness or *moral* oughtness, for this is a predicate only of (general) benevolence, or that which includes it. The *rightness* or *oughtness* of any particular subordinate disposition or purpose and its executive action, without including benevolence or selfishness, is the same kind of rightness or oughtness in relation to the end of action which is predicable of the structure of a watch or a pen in relation to the end for which it is made—that is, a mere *natural fitness.* The particular virtues of justice, veracity, &c., differ from benevolence considered as the governing principle of the heart, not as excluding it, for as virtues they necessarily include it; but as including something more, viz., particular subordinate dispositions, purposes, to perform the particular actions which are necessary to the production of the general good. Benevolence, as the term is employed in this connection, is a governing, practical principle—a controlling disposition or purpose to secure the highest well-being of all by all those subordinate particular affections, &c., and executive doings which are necessary to accomplish this end, while each particular virtue of this class consists in the benevolence which prompts the particular affection, purpose, &c., and in the particular affection, purpose, &c., which is prompted by it. In accordance with this classification, it is now maintained that justice, when the word is applied to denote a virtue—a morally right state of mind, in the general import of the word, is *benevolence in the form of a disposition or purpose;* or *it is purposing with benevolence;* or *it is a benevolent purpose or disposition—to render every one his due.*

In the second place, I now propose to explain and confirm the other part of the general definition given of the word *justice.*

The inquiry here is, what is it to render to every one *his due?* I answer, *it is to render to every one what ought to be rendered to him, the obligation to which arises from some peculiar relation of the object of the act, which results in some right reciprocal to such obligation.*

In further explanation I remark, that an act of rendering to another his due, is *executive* action, and that when we speak of such an act as an act of justice, we speak of it as dictated by a benevolent disposition or purpose. Again: an act of justice may respect as its object an individual or the public; and by *the object of the act,* I mean not one who is the object of the act merely as an act, but one to whom it is an act of justice, whether an individual or the public, in respect to whom it is an act of justice; even including one's self, as we do, in speaking of one as doing what justice to himself requires, thus making him both the agent and object of his act. Again: the obligation to render to another *his due,* arises from some peculiar relation of him who is bound to perform the act. This implies a peculiar relation on the part of him to whom the thing to be rendered is due, as the ground of the obligation to render it. The relation of the debtor, which is the ground of his obligation, implies a relation of the creditor, which is also a ground of the same obligation. The latter relation is so plainly implied in the former, as equally the ground of the obligation in all cases under consideration, that I have chosen not to burden the definition with its specification.

Further: we now inquire concerning the phrase *his due,* when it is said that *justice is a benevolent purpose to render to every one his due.* It will be readily admitted that whatever justice dictates and demands should be rendered to another, is *his due.* It is then important in the present investigation, to ascertain if possible the precise import of the phrase *his due.* Some moralists suppose that to render to another what ought to be rendered, or to do to another what ought to be done, or to render or to do to another what *is due*, is the same thing as to render to another *his due*, or what *is due to him*. The error it is believed will be obvious, if we accurately determine the meaning of these different forms of expression. That to render to another what ought to be rendered, or to do to another what ought to be done, is to render or do to him what *is due*; and that to render or to do to another what *is due*, is to render or do to him what ought to be done, is undeniable. It is equally so, that to render or to do to another what ought to be rendered or done, or what *is due*, is *in many cases to render to him his due*. But that to render or to do to another what ought to be rendered or done, or what *is due*, is *in all cases* to render what is *his due*, cannot be pretended. How often the act of conferring a favor on a neighbor, or a friend, or a stranger, ought to be done, and *is due*, e. g., in relinquishing a debt, or forgiving an injury, when the favor conferred can with no propriety be said to be *his due*. This part of the subject claims a more particular consideration.

I remark then, that there is an obvious difference between rendering to another *what is due*, and rendering to another *what is his due*. This difference may be presented in a classification of executive acts, which will show that in rendering to another *what is his due*, is only one species of those acts which are properly called rendering to another *what is due*.

Acts or doings then, which generally speaking constitute rendering to another WHAT IS DUE, *are those which ought to be done as fitted and necessary to the highest good of the whole.* It is obvious that by another is meant one or many, as the case may be.

This general class of executive acts may be divided into the two following classes or kinds, viz.:

I. Those which ought to be done as fitted and necessary to the highest good of the whole, and also of an individual.

II. Those which ought to be done as fitted and necessary to the highest good of the whole, though fitted not to promote but to impair or destroy the good of the individual.

These two classes of executive action may each be subdivided.

I. The first class may be divided into the two following classes:

(1.) Those which ought to be done as fitted and necessary to the highest good of the whole, and also of an individual, considered *merely as sentient beings*, and therefore not on account of any peculiar relation on the part of the objects of the act. Examples of this particular class are acts of forgiving an injury, showing kindness to an enemy, remitting a debt, acts of hospitality and generosity, with other forms of beneficent action.

(2.) Those which ought to be done as fitted and necessary to the highest good of the whole, and that of an individual, considered not merely as sentient beings, but on account also of *some peculiar relation* of one or both of the objects of the act —the public and the individual—which gives rise to the obligation of such action. Examples are acts of protection, care, and kindness to children, fulfilling contracts and promises, paying the laborer his hire, rendering an equivalent for what is received, rewarding an obedient subject of law, &c.

II. The second class may be divided into the two following classes:

(1.) Those which ought to be done as fitted and necessary to the highest good of the whole considered *merely* as sentient beings, though fitted not to promote but to impair or destroy the good of the individual who is an object of the act, when no peculiar relation on his part gives rise to the obligation of such action. Examples are acts of imposing taxes, pulling down one's house to stop the progress of a fire in a city, compelling men to fight the battles of their country, &c.

(2.) Those which ought to be done solely as fitted to the highest good of the whole considered not merely as sentient beings, and though such action is fitted not to promote but to impair or destroy the good of the individual, *when some peculiar relation* on his part and on the part of the public gives rise to the obligation of the act. Examples are acts of inflicting punishments or penal sanctions of law.

This classification is sufficient to show, that every act of rendering to one what ought to be rendered, is rendering *what is due*, but not what can be properly called rendering to one *his due*. It is true that between rendering to one what *ought* to be rendered or *what is due*, and rendering to one what is *his due*, there is an important resemblance. Both are acts of rendering to one *what is due*. But every act of rendering to one *what is due*, is not an act of rendering to one *his due*. Both are acts which *ought* to be done—acts of obligation, and of obligation which rests ultimately on one common basis, the fitness and necessity of action to the general good. But between these kinds of action there is an important difference. The fitness and necessity of the two kinds of action to the general good depend on very different relations, which determine such fitness and necessity, and so determine the obligation in respect to the different kinds of action. This will appear if we consider the subordinate classes or kinds of executive action above specified.

Let us consider those which ought to be done, as fitted and necessary to the highest good of the whole and that of an individual, when viewed as sustaining the relation of sentient beings. Take the act of forgiving one who has injured us. While it is admitted that the obligation to such action arises from the relation of the objects of the act as sentient beings, it is plain that it arises in no degree or respect from any *peculiar* relation of either. It will not be pretended that it depends on any peculiar relation of the public. Nor does this obligation depend on any *peculiar* relation of the offender; that is, on what he is or has done as an offender. The supposed act of kindness ought to be done, or would be *due*, had he not offended. The obligation is simply not taken away, and therefore is in no respect created or increased by the offense. For these reasons it is plain that the act cannot be properly said, in respect to the offender, to be *his due*, nor in respect to the public, to be *their due;* in other words, to be an act of *justice* either to *him* or to *them*.

Let us now recur to that class of cases, in which the obligation to action arises from the fitness and necessity of the action to the good of the public and the good of the individual, considered not merely as sentient beings, but as sustaining some *peculiar relation*. We see at once by referring to the examples, that the obligation to any one of these acts arises out of and is determined by the *peculiar relations* of the objects of the act. Every one sees that *a peculiar* relation exists between the laborer and his employer, which is the ground of the obligation of the latter to pay the hire of the former; and another peculiar relation between the public and the employer, by which the latter comes under obligation to the public to the same act. Similar remarks apply to the act of fulfilling a contract, and to the act of obedience to law. In the latter case, the lawgiver or government, as a guardian of the public good, is brought by the act of the obedient subject under a peculiar obligation to him, and also to the public. Thus the act of rewarding the obedient subject of law is rendering to him *what is his due*, and to the public what is *their* due. The same is true of the acts of paying the laborer and fulfilling a contract. It is rendering *his due* to the individual who is the object of the act, and it is also rendering to the public *their* due. As such, the act in each instance is properly called an act of *justice* to the individual who is its object, and an act of *justice* to the public.

Let us now recur to that class of acts which ought to be done *solely* as fitted and necessary to the highest good of the whole, though they impair or destroy the good of the individual who is the object of such action.

In respect to an act which falls under the first subdivision of this class, we see at once that the obligation depends on no *peculiar relation* of the individual who is the object of the act. For example, the obligation to pull down one's house to stop the progress of a fire in a city, while it results from the fitness and necessity of the act to the highest good of the whole, depends on no *peculiar relation* of the owner of the house, since the obligation would be the same were the house without an owner. Hence while this act is rendering to another *what is due*, and to the public what is *their* due, it cannot be properly said to be rendering to the individual what is *his* due.

Again: in respect to an act which falls under the other subdivision of this class, the obligation arises from a peculiar relation of the individual who is the object of the act, by which the act becomes fitted and necessary to the highest good of the whole; and from a consequent peculiar relation of him on whom the obligation rests. For example, the obligation of a lawgiver or moral governor to punish the disobedient subject of law, arises not at all from his relation as a sentient being, since this would imply an obligation to inflict suffering for its own sake; but it arises from his peculiar relation as a transgressor of law, and the peculiar relation of a lawgiver or moral governor to the public, which render the act of punishing the transgressor necessary to the highest good of the whole. Hence this act is not only rendering to another what is due, but what is *his* due, and what in respect to the public is *their* due.

Again, as I have already said, while the obligation to render to another *his due*, or the obligation of an act of justice, arises from some peculiar relation of the object of the act, this peculiar relation results in and implies *some right* reciprocal to this obligation. This *right* however does not always vest in him who sustains the relation which is the ground of the obligation. As the act of justice can never respect merely an individual as its object, but must respect either the public only or both an individual and the public, so the *right* which is reciprocal to the obligation of the act can never vest merely in an individual, though in some cases it may vest merely in the public, and in others there may be a right to the act on the part of an individual, and also a right to the act on the part of the public. This right can never vest merely in an individual, that is, no one as an individual merely, can possess a right which does not imply a right to the same thing on the part of the public. Such rights of individuals seem to have been claimed by some under the denomination of "*inalienable rights*," e. g., the right to life, to liberty, and to the pursuit of happiness. Without here affirming what can scarcely be questioned, that the rights here specified, or at least some of them, would become in some circumstances inconsistent with the highest good of the whole and therefore could not exist,* one thing is plain, that if they exist at all, they must exist on the ground that they are consistent with and required by the greatest good of the whole. The public therefore must possess the right to secure, as far as may be, the individual in the possession of the blessings which his rights respect, for the possession of these blessings by him is as necessary to the highest good of the whole to which the public has a right as it is to the good of the individual. I said that in some cases *a right* may vest only in the public. The *right* to pull down a house by the police of the city, to arrest the progress of a fire, vests not in the owner of the house, but only in the public or in the police as representatives of the public. The peculiar relation of the public, which is the ground of the obligation of the act, and which results in the reciprocal right

* Did not our fathers, for the independence and liberty of their country, pledge life, property, sacred honor—all? What "inalienable rights" had these patriots when their country, the general good, demanded this total self-sacrifice?

of the public, is the relation of the greatest number whose highest good depends on and requires the act. The act of a moral governor in rewarding an obedient subject of law is an act of justice both to the subject and to the public. In this case there is a twofold obligation and a twofold corresponding right: there is an obligation to the obedient subject with a corresponding right on his part as an individual, and there is an obligation to the public with a corresponding right on their part. The peculiar relation of the obedient subject considered as an individual, which is the ground of the obligation to reward him, and which results in his corresponding right to a reward, is the relation of one whose highest good by his obedience is rendered necessary to the highest good of the whole; and the peculiar relation of the public, which is the ground of the obligation to reward the obedient subject, and which results in the corresponding right of the public that he be rewarded, is the relation of the greatest number whose highest good depends on the act. The act of punishing the disobedient subject of law is an act of justice both to the subject himself and to the public. In this case the obligation is not an obligation to him, but to the public only. The right which corresponds to the obligation to punish him does not vest in him, as the right to a reward vests in an obedient subject. A right always respects some good; or in the language of Burke, "men have no right to what is not for their benefit." As punishment then, or a legal penalty, is only an evil to the subject, the right which corresponds to the obligation to punish him, does not vest in him but in the public only, whose benefit only it respects. The obligation to punish him arises indeed from his *peculiar relation* as a disobedient subject, and on this account the act of punishing him is an act of justice to him. It is an act, the obligation to which is created by his disobedience, but it is not an obligation *to him*, nor does it imply a right on his part corresponding to the obligation. The legal penalty is not inflicted on the transgressor as a personal benefit to him or as the means of good to him; and since every obligation of one to another respects the good of the latter, it follows, that although in the present case there is an obligation on the part of the moral governor to punish the transgressor; although this obligation in one respect arises from the peculiar relation of the transgressor; although he deserves punishment; although punishment is his due; although the act of punishment is an act of justice *to him* as well as to the public; yet the obligation to punish him is in no sense an obligation *to him*. To him punishment is only an evil; and as no one can be said to have a right to an evil merely for evil's sake, so no one can be properly said to be under obligation to another to inflict evil upon him merely for evil's sake. Legal penalty is inflicted on the transgressor as the necessary means of sustaining the authority of law or of the lawgiver, and so as the necessary means of the general good. The transgressor by his act of transgression creates on the part of the lawgiver an obligation to punish him, and also a corresponding right to his punishment on the part of the public. Hence punishment is *his due* or an act of justice to him, inasmuch as he has brought the moral governor under an obligation to punish him, not to himself, but to the public; by creating *a right* not on his own part to be punished, but a right on the part of the public to his punishment, which corresponds to the obligation to punish him. The peculiar relation of the transgressor, which is the ground of the moral governor's obligation *to punish him*, and of the right to his punishment on the part of the public, is the relation of one, who by his transgression has made his punishment necessary to the public good. Thus it appears that the obligation to an act of justice always implies a correspondent right somewhere, either in an individual and in the public, or at least in the public, and that the obligation of the act, and the consequent right to its performance depend on some peculiar relation of the object of the act.

But *what is a right?* The answer to this question will serve still further to explain and establish the present definition of justice. I proceed to say then—

In the third place, that the word *right*, in its most general import, when we speak of one as *having a right*, denotes *the fitness to the general good which arises from some peculiar relation of the possessor of the right that some good to him which the right respects as its object should be, which also creates or implies a corresponding obligation.*

After some explanation of terms which I deem important, I shall attempt to show the correctness of the above definition of *a right*.

A *right* may be that of an individual, as the right of a ruler, a subject, a parent, a child, a creditor, &c.; or it may be the right of the public, a community, a state or kingdom. As a matter of convenience in the use of language, we may conceive of the public or a community as a moral person. I shall so use the words *one and another* that they may be applied either to the public, to a community, or to an individual, as the case may require.

Again: a right always respects some good to its possessor as its object; that is, happiness, or the means of happiness, or both. It may be a right *to be* or a right *to do*, in the broadest sense of the word—as a right to act or to forbear acting, a right to possess or to relinquish, to think, to judge, to will, to execute one's will or to have it executed by another, to confer good or to inflict evil, &c., &c.

Further: when I speak of the thing which a right respects, or the object of a right as that *which should be*, the propriety of the language in certain cases may not be obvious. For example, we say that one has a right to an estate, but who would say that the estate ought to be. We have however only to remember, that in this case, as in many similar cases, the popular form of expression is elliptical, and that the meaning fully expressed would be, one has the right to the possession and use of an estate. The propriety of saying that one's possession and use of an estate is that which should be, is at once apparent. At the same time this form of expression, or some equivalent form, is the only one which is applicable to all cases. For example, the public has a right to the punishment of a criminal as truly as one has a right to an estate, or as an obedient subject has a right to a reward. But while we may properly say in respect to *the object* of the right in the former case—and so in respect to *the object* of every right—that it should be, we cannot properly say of this object that it should be possessed by the person holding the right, as we may properly say this in respect to many other objects of a right.

Again: when I speak of the fitness to the general good, &c., that the object of the right should be, I do not mean to imply that a right or every right is inalienable, nor that it may not be relinquished in a change of circumstances, or on the ground of that which is an equivalent to the object of the right. The contrary is undeniable. One may alienate his right to property on the ground of an equivalent in money, or in the happiness which he finds in imparting good to others. A moral governor may abandon his right to punish a transgressor, and the public may abandon their right that he be punished, on the ground of an atonement, which is an equivalent in respect to the end of punishment; provided that the abandonment does not involve in any respect the sacrifice of public good. But no one can voluntarily alienate or relinquish a right, consistently with the principles of moral rectitude, knowing that the alienation or relinquishment involves a sacrifice of the general happiness.

Further: we often speak of one as having a right of which he is deprived, or of his not having, or of being deprived of *his* right. The incongruity of the language does not however obscure our meaning. We mean that he *has* a right, or that a right is *his* so far forth as *having* it or its being *his* is determined by that relation on his part which is the ground of a right, while he has not the actual possession or use of the object of the right. Thus in one sense one may be said to have a right, which in another sense he may be said not to have, or to be deprived of, and the possession of which he may have occasion to seek by force or by a legal process.

Once more: in common language we speak of one as *having* or *possessing* a right, or of *one's right*, or of a right as being *another's*—being *his* or *your* or *my* right, and the question may naturally arise when it is said *that a right is the fitness to the general good, which arises*, &c.—with what propriety or truth can this *fitness*, when called a right, be said *to belong* to one or to be *his?* I answer, that nothing is more common than to say that a thing *belongs* to one or is *his*, or to use other forms of expression, to describe him as its possessor when it pertains to him as inseparable from what he is or has done, or results from any relation which he sustains. In this manner we speak of one's obligation or of one's necessity, meaning an obligation or a necessity which exists in respect to him as inseparable from his circumstances, or results from some relation on his part. In the following passage from Shakspeare we have this use of the word:

> "Were it *my fitness*,
> To let these hands obey my blood,
> They are apt enough to dislocate and tear
> Thy flesh and bones."—*King Lear*.

This is obviously equivalent to saying—were it in respect to the true end of action (which is no other than the general good), fit or proper in my case, or in view of what I am or the relation I sustain, "to let these hands," &c. The fitness here spoken of, whether it be that which constitutes *a right* or not, is the fitness which arises from the relation which one sustains, and on this ground is spoken of as *his*. The fitness in such a case is the fitness that an agent *should act* in a given manner, and the fitness which constitutes *a right* is the fitness that one should be the object of an action on the part of another as already described. Indeed, should one affirm in analytic language that there is a fitness to the general good arising from the peculiar relation of the laborer, that his hire should not be withheld by his employer, and this creates a reciprocal obligation on the part of the latter, what would it be but to say that the laborer has a right to his hire?

With these things in view, I will now attempt to show that the particular or elementary ideas specified in the above definition constitute the complex idea of *a right.*

I remark then, that we cannot form the common and familiar idea of a right without the idea of *the fitness to the general good, that the particular object of the right should be.* This will be obvious from reflecting on any familiar instance of a right. We say one has a right to life, that is, to have or possess life; and so in respect to liberty, property, &c., &c. But who can conceive of the existence of *the right* without conceiving of the fitness to the general good, that the particular good which is the object of the right should be? If we conceive the particular good, which is the object of the right, *not to be fitted* to the general good, we necessarily conceive it to be inconsistent with the general good, and of course that the individual has, and can have no right to the particular good. The moment we conceive of one as having a right to any particular good, we necessarily conceive that the being of that thing is right—that it is *right* that it should be—that it is what in the case *ought* to be and should *not be prevented by any other.* But it is plainly impossible thus to conceive of it without conceiving it to be *fitted to the general good;* or which is the same thing, if we conceive it to be inconsistent with the general good. What possible right can one be conceived to possess to life, or liberty, or property, when his possession of the particular good is inconsistent with the general good? Or to take an example of a right of the public. What possible right has the public to the punishment of the criminal, except his punishment is fitted to promote and of course not inconsistent with the public good? Punishment is in no respect a good to the criminal himself, and if we suppose it to be in no respect a good to the public, or the means of the public good, what possible right can exist on the part of the moral governor to inflict it, or on the part of the public that it should be inflicted? Such a right would be a right to inflict evil merely for evil's sake. The act of infliction could in no respect be good to him who should inflict the evil, or to him on whom it should be inflicted, or to the public. There could be no motive to the act, and the act itself would be impossible in the nature of things. Or if we suppose the act to be possible, still it can be supposed to be possible only to unqualified malice; while the right to perform the act or the right that it should be performed, would imply that the act would be morally right. And if it be morally right to inflict evil merely for evil's sake—to act with unqualified malice—then I ask, what is it to act morally wrong? It is then plainly impossible to form the universal and familiar idea of *a right* without the idea of the fitness to the general good that the object of the right should be.

Again: in conceiving of a right, we necessarily conceive of the fitness of the particular good which is the object of the right, to the general good, *as resulting from some peculiar relation of the possessor of the right.* This may be seen in a few examples. The fitness to the general good of one's paying a debt, the payment of which is the object of *a right* on the part of the creditor, results from the peculiar relation of the creditor—the relation of one who has imparted a good to another, on condition of receiving an equivalent. The fitness to the general good that a moral governor should reward the obedient subject, so far as the right to a reward on the part of the latter is concerned, results from his peculiar relation—the relation of one who, by his obedience, has rendered his reward necessary to the general good; while this fitness, so far as the rewarding him is the object of a right on the part of the public, results from the peculiar relation of the public—the relation of the greatest number to the highest well-being as depending on the act. The fitness to the general good of punishing the disobedient subject under a merely legal system, the punishing of whom is the object of a right, not on his part, but on the part of the public, results from the relation of the public—the relation of the greatest number to the highest well-being so far as it depends on the act. Thus in conceiving of a right, whether it be that of an individual or of the public, we necessarily conceive of some peculiar relation of the possessor of the right, from which results the fitness to the general good of that which is the object of the right.

The same thing may be shown by familiar cases, in which no right can be conceived to exist, because the peculiar relation, which is one necessary ground of a right, does not exist. There are many cases in which there is a fitness to the general good, that one should act in a given manner toward another, but in which the latter has *no right* that the act should be done. There is a fitness to the general good, that one injured by another should forgive the offender—that one's house should be pulled down to arrest the progress of a fire, &c., &c. But it is impossible to conceive that the offender has a right to forgiveness, or the owner of the house a right that his house should be pulled down. And one reason is, that it is impossible to conceive of any peculiar relation on the part of either from which the fitness of the supposed act arises. The relation of each is indeed such, that the supposed act done to him will subserve the general good. But the fitness of the act to this end does not arise from his peculiar relation, as the ground or reason of it. Kindness toward an offender is fitted to the general good, and would be so were he not an offender. It is so, notwithstanding his offense, and therefore does not become so by his offense. The ownership of the house does not occasion the fitness of pulling it down,to the general good. Neither the offender nor the owner of the house can appeal to any peculiar relation on his part as the ground or reason of the fitness of the supposed act in respect to him, to the general good, nor as a reason that it should be done. The one cannot say, I have injured another, and therefore I have a right to kindness from him; nor can the other say, I own the house, and therefore have a right that it be pulled down. These examples are sufficient to show that we cannot conceive of *a right* without conceiving of the fitness of the object of the right to the general good, *as arising from some peculiar relation of the possessor of the right.*

Nor is this all. We cannot conceive of a right without conceiving of that peculiar relation of its possessor of which I have spoken, as creating and implying a reciprocal obligation on the part of another. By this reciprocal obligation I mean an obligation which corresponds to the right in its foundation and its object. Thus there is an obligation to the laborer on the part of his employer to pay him his hire, and a right on the part of the laborer to the payment, and both this obligation and this right are founded in the peculiar relation of the possessor of the right. What the obligor is under obligation to do or to avoid doing, the obligee has a right that he should do or avoid doing, and this obligation and this right arise from one and the same relation on the part of the possessor of the right and respect the same object: so that the obligation and the right are reciprocal; that is, they correspond in their foundation and their object. I say then, that we cannot conceive of a right without conceiving of the peculiar relation of its possessor as creating and implying an obligation to him in respect to the object of the right. As the laborer has a right to his hire, that is, to the payment of his hire by his employer, there is a correspondent obligation to pay it on the part of the latter. As the laborer has a right that none should prevent the payment of his hire, others are under a corresponding obligation not to prevent it. The same things are obviously true in respect to every other right.

The same thing is further obvious from the nature of obligation. Obligation is the necessity one is under, or the being bound by a necessity to do (either by acting or forbearing to act) that which is *fitted* to the great end of all action, the general good. As then there is a fitness to this end that the object of one's right *should be*, arising from some peculiar relation on his part, so from this fitness and therefore from this peculiar relation arises a necessity, i. e., an obligation on the part of another, even of every other, to act so that the object of the right shall be. Right and obligation are therefore reciprocal. If there is a right on the part of one, there is a corresponding obligation on the part of another. An essential idea or conception of a right is the idea of it, as that which in the manner explained creates and implies a reciprocal obligation.

It is this characteristic which constitutes the difference, or as logicians say the *differentia*, between a case of fitness to the general good on the part of one that a particular good to him should be, which is *a right*, and that which is *not* a right. There are, as we have seen, many instances of fitness to the general good which imply an obligation to confer good on others, or not to prevent or hinder the existence of such good, but which are not cases involving corresponding rights. But wherever we find a case of fitness to the general good arising from some peculiar relation of one that a particular good to him should be or should exist, which peculiar relation on his part creates and implies a consequent obligation on the part of another to secure or not to prevent the existence of that particular good, there we find *a right*. That the particular good which is the object of the right *should be*, is emphatically and in a peculiar sense right in respect to the possessor of the right. It involves *a rightness*, i. e., a fitness to the general good, not merely as such fitness exists in many other cases, irrespective of any peculiar relation on the part of him to whom the particular good is a good, but a fitness to the general good, which arises from some peculiar relation on his part, appropriating it to him and creating an obligation to him on another or on all others to secure or not to prevent the existence of that particular good. This fitness is thus with great propriety appropriated to him from whose peculiar relation it results, and on this account is called *his right*, while as creating in the manner explained a corresponding obligation, it is *par excellence* called *a right.*

Having thus attempted to specify the several elementary ideas which constitute the complex idea of what we call *a right*, the question naturally arises whether any other element is essential to the complex conception. On this point I can only say that I am unable to discover any other, or at least any other which is not fairly included in the specification.

According to what has been said, *justice*, considered as a morally right state of mind, may be said, in general terms, *to be a benevolent disposition or purpose to render to every other his due; or more particularly, justice is a benevolent disposition or purpose to do to every other what ought to be done, the obligation to which arises from some peculiar relation of the object of the act which creates and implies a right reciprocal to such obligation.*

That this definition of justice may be more fully apprehended

I have defined by progressive analysis and explanation the leading terms used in the above forms of definition, and particularly the term *right*, and shown, if I mistake not, that *a right is the fitness to the general good, which arises from some peculiar relation of its possessor, that its object should be, thus creating and implying a corresponding obligation.*

With this import of the word *justice* in view, I next propose to consider some of the kinds or species of justice.

PART II.—DIFFERENT SPECIES OF JUSTICE WITH APPLICATION TO THEOLOGICAL ERRORS.

Justice commonly classified as commutative, distributive, and general.—This erroneous.—Theological errors founded upon it.—In opposition to these views three propositions vindicated, viz.: 1. Justice in a moral governor not general benevolence; 2. Not distributive justice; but, 3. A benevolent disposition to maintain authority.—These propositions defended from a consideration of various instances of justice, and from the fact that it is not exposed to the theological errors specified.

THE leading inquiry before us is still, *what is justice as the attribute of a perfect moral governor?* On this subject diversity of opinion has existed among theologians, and occasioned corresponding diversity of opinion on other topics of equal or greater moment. Differences of opinion on the subjects of atonement for sin, of justification before God, and of a future retribution, may be traced in many cases to different views of the justice of God as a moral ruler. To the theological student we can hardly present a theme more worthy of his attention, from its relations to other subjects which demand investigation.

Justice as the attribute of a perfect moral governor is obviously a particular kind or species of justice. Hence writers on the subject, both philosophers and theologians, who have professed to give precise and accurate views of it, have often attempted to classify and thus to distinguish the different kinds of justice. These they have commonly comprised in three classes, viz.: *commutative*, *distributive*, and *general justice*.

By *commutative justice* they mean a disposition to fulfill contracts.

By *distributive justice* they mean a disposition to confer

legal rewards and inflict legal punishments, according to the personal character of the subjects of law.

By *general justice* they (erroneously) mean general benevolence, or a disposition to promote the highest happiness.

This classification I deem erroneous, inasmuch as it confounds general justice with general benevolence. It thus, as I claim, gives a false view of general justice, and wholly omits any precise and adequate view of justice as the attribute of a perfect moral governor.

To present these errors in their true form, and to show the importance of correcting them and of ascertaining the exact truth, it is necessary to consider some of their theological applications.

Some prominent New England divines hold principles on this subject, which, in connection with other views also maintained by them, have been supposed to lead by direct inference to the doctrine of universal salvation. Though these divines reject this inference with abhorrence, I cannot doubt that it is fully authorized by certain premises which they furnish. Thus while they have maintained that general justice is the same thing as general benevolence, they have also maintained that the atonement is made for all men, and renders it consistent with general justice—that is, according to their definition, with *general benevolence*—to pardon and to save all. The proposition is unqualified, that the pardon and salvation of all are consistent with general benevolence. From these premises it follows that God will actually pardon and save all men. It would be to no purpose to say that the atonement has rendered it consistent with general benevolence to pardon and save all on condition of repentance. This is to modify, and thus to change the proposition controverted. Besides, these divines maintain that God can bring all men to repentance. If then the atonement has rendered it consistent with general benevolence *in all respects* to pardon and save all, it has rendered it consistent with general benevolence to bring all to repentance. Of course as God can, he will bring all men to repentance, and all will be pardoned and saved.

I need not say that the premises thus furnished by the New England divines are adopted by at least one class of Universalists, as a sufficient basis for their peculiar doctrine.

Another large class of divines however, who charge on their

New England brethren the doctrine of universal salvation as a legitimate consequence of their views of the justice of God and of the atonement of Christ, and who agree with them and with Universalists in maintaining that God can bring all men to repentance, not only deny a universal atonement, but also that view of justice in God as a moral governor which the New England divines have maintained.

What then, in the view of this class of divines, is justice as the attribute of a perfect moral governor? Perhaps it would be regarded by them as a just and satisfactory answer to say, that justice as the attribute of a perfect moral governor is *distributive justice* as defined in the above classification. This definition however, of justice in the present application of the term, I regard as in a high degree objectionable, whether the language be understood in its proper import or according to the views of the divines referred to. In what I consider the proper meaning of the language, the definition presents only one specific meaning of the word justice instead of its general import; for as it may appear hereafter, a perfect moral governor may be as truly just when he forgives a transgressor through an atonement, as when executing legal sanctions according to the merit and demerit of his subjects. But this definition, as the language is explained by that class of divines to whom I have referred, is still more objectionable. They maintain that there is *an inherent or intrinsic merit* in obedience to law, and an *inherent intrinsic demerit* in disobedience to law, aside from and to the entire exclusion of any relation in either to the general good of the kingdom, or to the authority of the law or of the lawgiver, as this is the means of the general good;—that on account of this *inherent merit* of obedience and this *inherent demerit* of disobedience, viewed in this restricted and narrow sense and irrespectively of any other relations, the moral governor is disposed to reward the one and punish the other—and that this disposition is his attribute of justice. In explanation of these views they are careful to insist that it is *right in itself* to execute legal sanctions for the reasons assigned, even right in itself to inflict penal evil on a transgressor, though no good result would or could be accomplished by the infliction. In accordance with these views of *merit and demerit, of desert and ill-desert or guilt*, they form their peculiar views of atonement, imputation, and justification, maintaining the imputation of the sins of a believing transgressor to another as his surety or sponsor, and the imputation of the surety's righteousness to the transgressor, so that his *demerit*, *ill-desert*, or *guilt* is wholly removed from him and ceases to be his and becomes another's, and so that he becomes as perfectly righteous as had he perfectly obeyed the law; and a just lawgiver does and must regard and treat him as being perfectly righteous, and thus justice requires that he be rewarded and forbids that he be punished. I need not say that these views of atonement, imputation, and justification, together with the view of justice as the attribute of a perfect moral governor on which they are founded, are regarded by another large class of divines as highly erroneous.

I have thus specified supposed errors in the foregoing classification of the different kinds of justice, as the language is defined and explained by different classes of theologians, and some of the more serious errors in theology which result from them. I have done this that we may better appreciate the importance of these errors of classification, and of ascertaining with precision the nature of that attribute which we call justice in a perfect moral governor. In opposition to the errors of the foregoing classification I now propose to show—

1. That justice as the attribute of a perfect moral governor, and which is properly called general justice, is not the same thing as general benevolence.

2. That justice as the attribute of a perfect moral governor is not distributive justice, especially as defined by some theologians; and,

3. That justice as the attribute of a perfect moral governor, is a benevolent disposition to maintain his authority as the necessary means of the highest good of his kingdom.

1. Justice as the attribute of a perfect moral governor, and which is properly called general justice, is not the same thing as general benevolence.

This is evident at once from the nature of both. So different is one from the other, according to our necessary conceptions and to every proper use of language, that nothing but those confused conceptions and that improper use of terms which result from the want of due reflection, could occasion the confounding things which are so different. This I claim to have shown abundantly in what I have already said for the purpose of unfolding the nature of general benevolence and the nature of justice. According to what has been said, general or universal benevolence is an elective preference of the highest happiness of the sentient universe to every object that can come into competition with it. As such a preference merely, it includes no disposition or purpose to other volitions, choices, dispositions, or purposes; and therefore it is not justice, or a disposition or purpose to render every one his due, nor a disposition or purpose to speak truth, nor any other specific disposition or purpose. Or if we include under general benevolence a disposition or purpose to all those subordinate specific dispositions or purposes which respect executive action, still it is not the same thing as any one of them. It is no more the same thing as a disposition to render to every one his due, than it is a disposition or purpose to speak truth, or than it is a disposition to relieve the suffering, or than it is a disposition or purpose to show favor to the guilty. In these particular subordinate purposes, the mind wills certain different kinds of executive action. But in the mere exercise of general or universal benevolence, it forms no such particular purposes. Of course, in the elective preference of the highest good of all, the purpose or disposition to render to every other his due, which is *justice* in the most generic import of the word, is not included, and therefore that particular kind of justice which is an attribute of a perfect moral governor cannot be included.

I proceed to say—

2. That justice as the attribute of a perfect moral governor is not distributive justice, especially as defined by some theologians.

When we speak of justice as the attribute of a perfect moral governor, the language means an attribute under this name, which is essential to and inseparable from the character of one who sustains this high relation. But distributive justice, that is, a disposition or will to confer legal rewards and to inflict legal punishments according to the personal character of subjects, is not in the proper meaning of the language essential to the character of a perfect moral governor. In one respect indeed, viz., as a disposition or will to confer rewards on obedient subjects, it is essential to his character. No being can sustain the character of a perfect moral ruler who is not disposed to confer and who does not actually confer the merited reward on every perfectly obedient subject. But a disposition to inflict merited punishment on disobedient subjects is plainly not essential in all cases, e. g., in a case of an adequate atonement to the character of a perfect moral governor. If so, his character for justice must be forfeited by every act of pardon, even under an adequate atonement for transgression. Distributive justice then, properly so called, is not the attribute which in all cases is essential to, and inseparable from the character of a perfect moral governor.

Nor is this true in respect to distributive justice, as it is defined by the class of theologians to whom I have already referred. According to this view, justice in the form of distributive justice requires that the legal penalty be inflicted on the transgressor, though no good can be produced and no evil be prevented by the infliction; and this on the ground, as it is called, of the *intrinsic demerit* of transgression. How entirely unwarranted this view of the subject is, has been perhaps already sufficiently shown. It has been shown that justice always implies a correspondent right somewhere to some good or benefit which is the object of the right. What sort of justice would that be which proposed to accomplish no good to any one? And what sort of *a right* would that be which had no good or benefit for its object on the part of the possessor of the right? It has also been shown that the right to some good or benefit which corresponds to an act of justice, must either vest in both an individual and in the public, or at least in the public; that as punishment is in no respect a good to the transgressor, it can in no respect be the object of a right on his part, and therefore cannot in this respect be an act of justice to him nor an act of justice to him in any sense, except that he by his act of transgression has created a right to his punishment on the part of the public; that if we suppose it to be in no respect a good to the public, it can in no respect be the object of a right on their part, and therefore cannot be the object of any right whatsoever. It cannot therefore in such a case be an act of justice in any sense whatsoever. It was further shown that such an act would be inflicting evil merely for evil's sake, which is physically impossible on the part of a voluntary and moral being, and is even beyond the capacity of infernal malice. Such a representation of justice as the attribute of a perfect moral governor is in the last degree preposterous.

Again: these divines would do well to ask what they mean by the *intrinsic demerit* of sin or transgression. Every one who reflects at all on this subject must know that the ideas denoted by the terms *merit* and *demerit*, whether applied to a being or his acts, are *relative* ideas. Hence what may be called the absolute nature of obedience, or of disobedience to law, aside from *all relation* to some being or thing, or rather to both, is neither good nor evil, deserving nor ill-deserving. That in transgression or sin, which we call its *demerit*, is not its nature considered as *absolute or positive*, and so aside from, and exclusive of any relation to any thing else, but it is its absolute or positive nature conceived as related to something else. Particularly it is *that relation of transgression to the penalty of law which renders its infliction on the transgressor, under a merely legal system, the fit and necessary means of upholding the authority of the lawgiver, and of thus securing the public good.* Hence, if we separate this conception of the relation of sin or transgression from our conception of its nature, and so conceive of its nature as absolute, without being thus related to punishment, there can be nothing in our conception of that nature, which can be conceived to be or which can be called its *demerit.* It is to no purpose to say that transgression or sin is evil *in itself*, and therefore a fit object of the expression of abhorrence from a moral governor. There are only two possible senses in which sin or transgression, or any thing else, can be properly said to be *evil in itself*, viz., either as unhappiness or suffering is *evil in itself*, or as that which is the means or cause of unhappiness or suffering is *evil in itself.* But transgression cannot be truly said to be *evil in itself* in the first sense. If therefore it is not *evil in itself*, in the second sense, as now supposed, it is in no sense *evil in itself.* To talk therefore of the *demerit* of transgression as an *evil in itself*, and exclusive of all relation to evil as its consequence, is to talk without ideas. Plainly, sin is an evil only as in its nature it is related to evil consequences. The annihilation of this relation would be the annihilation of all that which constitutes its evil nature; all that on account of which it deserves punishment, or which can be called its *demerit.* What kind of justice would that be which should inflict punishment for transgression, to which pertains no ill-desert or demerit, or which inflicts punishment when no good can be produced and no evil prevented by its infliction? Who will on due reflection ascribe this kind of justice to a perfect moral governor?

I now propose to show—

3. That justice as the attribute of a perfect moral governor is a benevolent disposition to maintain by the requisite means, his authority as the necessary condition of the highest good of his kingdom.

What has been said in our previous discussions concerning the relation of a perfect moral governor to his kingdom, is sufficient to show that as a perfectly benevolent being he must be benevolently disposed to maintain his authority, as the necessary means of the highest good of his kingdom. This benevolent disposition or particular form of benevolence is not only an essential condition of his right to reign, but to accomplish its end or object—to maintain his authority by the various means which in the varying circumstances of individual subjects and of his kingdom may be demanded or dictated by perfect benevolence,—is the grand, peculiar, sole function of his office. All that he does as a moral governor, he does for the purpose of maintaining his authority, and all that depends on his relation as a moral governor, depends on the maintenance of his authority. This maintained, all his responsibilities as a moral governor are fulfilled. Otherwise he betrays his trust and forfeits his throne. Otherwise he defeats the end of his administration, and all that depends on his rightful moral dominion is sacrificed and lost.

Now it is claimed that this benevolent disposition on the part of a moral governor to maintain his authority as the necessary means of the highest happiness of his kingdom, is what is truly and properly called his justice. Or thus, I maintain that in the generic import of the word, when applied to denote the attribute of a perfect moral governor,

Justice is a benevolent disposition on his part to maintain by the requisite means his authority as the necessary condition of the highest happiness of his kingdom.

This I shall attempt to show—

In the first place, from a comprehensive classification of the different kinds of justice.

I recur then to the *summum genus*, that is, to the most generic or general meaning of the word *justice*, as already defined, viz.:

Justice is a benevolent disposition or purpose of mind to render or to do to every one what ought to be rendered or done to him, the obligation to which arises from some peculiar relation of the object of the act, that creates or implies a right corresponding to such obligation.

Assuming on the ground of proof already given, the correctness of this definition of justice in the most general import of the word, I proceed to say that justice may be divided into two kinds, viz.:

1. Justice as it pertains to the high relation, or is an attribute of a moral governor, which is general justice properly so called; and,

2. Justice as it pertains to moral beings in other relations than that of a moral governor.

This second kind of justice, it is obvious, includes very many kinds or forms of justice; so many, that to frame subdivisions which should include the whole and accurately distinguish them would be difficult, and on this account has not often been attempted. What has been called *commutative justice* is one prominent and very comprehensive subdivision under this kind of justice. It is manifest however, that in the most comprehensive import given to the language, it cannot with propriety be so extended as to include all the subordinate kinds which belong to this general class, e. g., so as to include the justice on the part of parents to afford care, protection, and support to children, &c. Without therefore attempting any further classification of this kind of justice than merely to say, that commutative justice is one prominent subordinate kind of it, I recur to the first of the two subordinate kinds above specified, viz.:

Justice as the attribute of a perfect moral governor, which may be properly called general justice.

That what I have now defined justice to be, as an attribute of a perfect moral governor, is one kind or species of justice, is at once manifest by comparing its definition with that before given of justice in the most generic import of the word. Thus justice as the attribute of a perfect moral governor, according to the present definition as given in somewhat general terms, may be defined thus, viz.: *a benevolent disposition to do what ought to be done by a moral governor to his kingdom, in the specific form of maintaining by the requisite means, his author-*

ity as the necessary condition of the highest happiness of his kingdom, the obligation to which arises from the peculiar relation of his kingdom to him as depending on him thus to guard and secure its highest happiness, which relation implies a right on the part of his kingdom corresponding to such obligation on his part. That such a disposition on the part of a moral governor is properly and truly called justice, I cannot suppose will be denied or doubted by any one who has ever reflected on the import of the word justice, in its present application. What less or what more can the word denote, according to usage? Should a moral governor refuse that protection and security to the highest happiness of his kingdom which he owes them, by upholding his authority as the ruler and guardian of all—should he suffer all that can be called the authority of law, or government, or his own authority, to be utterly subverted—should he thus utterly annihilate this peculiar and essential influence on the subjects of his dominion, what shadow of that which is called justice on his part could remain? What would such an act on his part be, and what would it or could it be called, but an act of the grossest injustice? On the other hand, what more is or can be necessary to the absolute perfection of this attribute on his part, than a perfectly benevolent disposition to uphold, and the actual upholding of his authority as the necessary means of the highest happiness of his kingdom? As a moral governor, he is not bound either to secure the obedience or to prevent the disobedience of his subjects; but simply and only to maintain his own *authority as the requisite means* of securing as far as may be the one, and preventing the other. Whatever acts benevolence on his part may dictate in other relations—whatever acts of kindness, or of commutative justice, or other kinds of justice it may dictate or demand, they can never conflict with or set aside his obligation to maintain his *authority* as a moral governor, nor abrogate the right of his kingdom, which corresponds to that obligation. To maintain his authority is the entire function of his office. Whatever else be supposed which is supposable in the case, the necessity is absolute and immutable, that as a perfect moral governor he maintain his authority. On this the highest happiness of his kingdom depends. To this every thing else supposable mnst yield. This can be yielded to nothing. *Justice, then, as the attribute of a perfect moral governor*, is nothing more and nothing less than *a benevolent disposition on his part to maintain, by the requisite means, his authority as the necessary condition of the highest happiness of his kingdom.*

Again: this will still further appear if we pursue our classification, as we may, into the particular kinds of justice as the attribute of a moral governor. Justice then as the attribute of a perfect moral governor is not only one kind or species of justice; it also includes particular kinds of justice under itself.

(1.) *Distributive justice;* or justice as the attribute of a moral governor, which involves the particular disposition to maintain his authority by means of legal sanctions.

(2.) *Atoning justice;* or justice as the attribute of a moral governor, which involves the particular disposition to maintain his authority by means of an atonement.

In both these cases it is evident that the generic import of the word justice, as the attribute of a perfect moral governor, is preserved, viz., a benevolent disposition to maintain, by the requisite means, his authority as the necessary condition of the highest happiness of his kingdom. In both cases also, there is a further meaning. In the one, it is a benevolent disposition to maintain his authority by *legal sanctions;* in the other, by *an atonement.*

One of these particular kinds of justice as the attribute of a moral governor is, according to usage, called distributive justice. For the other, it occurs so rarely as an actual existence or fact, that usage has furnished no name. I know not why it should not be called, as I have called it, *atoning justice.* It is really a disposition to maintain the authority of the moral governor in the circumstances in which an atonement is provided, as is that disposition to do the same thing in other circumstances, by executing the legal penalty. The act of providing an atonement is as really the act of the moral governor, done for the purpose of manifesting his justice, as the act of inflicting the legal penalty on transgressors.* His justice, that is, his disposition to maintain his authority, is seen not less clearly through an atonement than it would be in the infliction of the legal penalty.

Further: distributive justice may be subdivided into two

* This is evidently the view which the apostle gives of the great propitiation in Rom. iii. 25, 26.

subordinate kinds, viz., a benevolent disposition to maintain authority by a legal reward to obedience, and a benevolent disposition to maintain authority by a legal penalty for disobedience.

The difference between these two subordinate kinds of distributive justice needs to be more fully unfolded. In respect to the former, viz., a benevolent disposition to maintain necessary authority *by a legal reward to obedience*, there is a twofold obligation and a twofold right. There is an obligation both to the obedient subject and also to the public to reward him, arising from his relation as an obedient subject; and there is a reciprocal right on the part of the subject, and also on the part of the public, that he should be rewarded. In respect to the latter, viz., a benevolent disposition to maintain necessary authority *by a legal penalty for disobedience*, there is but one obligation and one right. There is an obligation to the public to inflict the penalty on the disobedient subject, but none to the subject himself; and there is a reciprocal right on the part of the public to its infliction, but none on the part of the subject himself. The importance of this difference between the two subordinate kinds of distributive justice, as showing how distributive justice toward an obedient subject can in no case be dispensed with, and how distributive justice toward a disobedient subject can in a certain case be dispensed with, will more fully appear hereafter.

I have thus attempted to classify the different kinds of justice as a morally right state of mind, for the purpose of clearly distinguishing from all other kinds, that kind which constitutes justice as the attribute of a perfect moral governor. If this classification comprises all the different kinds of justice as a morally right state of mind, and if it correctly exhibits the genus and the species of justice which in different circumstances and cases can be predicated of a perfect moral governor, then it is evident that justice as the attribute of a perfect moral governor, in all circumstances and cases, is what I have defined it to be, viz., *a benevolent disposition on the part of a perfect moral governor to maintain by the requisite means his authority as the necessary condition of the highest happiness of his kingdom, the obligation to which arises from the peculiar relation of his kingdom, and implies a right on the part of his kingdom corresponding to such obligation on his part.*

It will not be pretended that what is thus defined as the attribute of justice which is peculiar to a perfect moral governor, is not properly and truly called justice on his part. What is now claimed is, that nothing different from this, either less or more, can in all cases and circumstances constitute this attribute. It cannot, as we have seen, be synonymous with general benevolence, since general benevolence is concerned for, and committed to secure the highest happiness of his kingdom in all respects, or in respect to every thing on which this happiness depends; while justice as the peculiar attribute of a perfect moral governor is concerned for and committed to secure the highest happiness of his kingdom in only one respect, or in respect to only one thing on which this happiness depends,—the support of his authority. His authority must be maintained or all is lost. Again: justice as the attribute of a perfect moral governor, being one particular form of benevolence, cannot include other particular forms of benevolence, as veracity, compassion, mercy. Nor can it include various other particular forms of justice which arise from other relations of moral beings; such, for example, as commutative justice; for then it could not be that kind of justice which is peculiar to the relation of a moral governor. Nor can it include in all cases the particular kinds of justice as the general attribute of a moral governor, either distributive justice, or what I have called atoning justice. In giving forth the law of his government with its requisite sanctions, and prior to all acts of obedience and disobedience, the moral governor makes a full and decisive manifestation of his justice. But this is not the manifestation of a disposition, will, or purpose actually to reward an obedient subject; for as yet there is no obedient subject. If the moral governor is omniscient, then he may know that there never will be a perfectly obedient subject to be rewarded. Nevertheless he may be perfectly just, and most decisively prove his perfect justice, without an absolute will or purpose to reward an obedient subject by proving his will or purpose to maintain his authority. So likewise, in the case now supposed, there is no decisive manifestation of an unqualified absolute will or purpose to punish a disobedient subject, and this for two reasons,—one is, that there is no decisive proof that there will be a disobedient subject to be punished, or that he as an omniscient ruler does not know that there will not be; and the other is, that if there should be a disobedient subject, there is no decisive proof that he will not be pardoned through an atonement to be provided. Even in case of universal disobedience on the part of subjects, and under a perfect atonement, it is possible that the moral governor should be perfectly just and wholly dispense with distributive justice by the forgiveness of all. Nor can justice as the attribute of a perfect moral governor in all cases include what I have called *atoning* justice; for it is quite possible that, in case of transgression, the moral governor should be perfectly just and provide no atonement, either by rewarding the obedient and punishing the disobedient, or by rewarding all if all are obedient, or punishing all if all are disobediént. I am not saying that the hypothetical proposition, that *if there should be a perfectly obedient subject justice would not reward him*, is not true. It is most undeniably true that he would. I am not saying that the hypothetical proposition, that *if there should be a disobedient subject, there is not good and sufficient reason to believe, under a merely legal system, that he will be punished.* There is such evidence. But I am saying that neither of these particular forms of distributive justice is essentially involved in the attribute of justice as an attribute of a perfect moral governor, and that, as the case may be, he can be perfectly just, though this attribute does not include either of these particular forms of justice, or any other particular form of general or public justice, as distinguished from another particular form. A benevolent moral governor, in promulging the best law with its requisite sanctions, fully evinces, prior to all obedience or disobedience on the part of his subjects, his perfect justice. But what is this perfect justice which he evinces by the supposed act? Not the perfect justice of a perfect moral governor in any one of its specific forms or kinds before specified. He rewards no one, he punishes no one; nor from the nature of his attribute of perfect justice merely, can it be inferred that he actually willed or purposed to do either in distinction from the other; or rather the nature of this attribute does not imply an absolute disposition or purpose to adopt any one particular mode of maintaining his authority, either by rewarding an actually obedient subject, or by punishing an actually disobedient subject, or by preferring an atonement to the adoption of another particular mode. There is however decisive proof, even all the case admits of, of an unqualified determination or purpose to maintain, by the requisite means, his authority as the necessary means of the highest happiness of his kingdom. It is obvious therefore, that the only sense in which justice can be conceived to be a permanent immutable disposition or attribute of a perfect moral governor in all cases, is that in which this attribute has now been defined. In every case it must be all that which is included in the definition, and in every case is perfect justice though it include nothing more. The only sense therefore in which the word justice can be defined as applicable to all these cases, or as denoting that which is common to them all, is a benevolent disposition of the moral governor to maintain by the requisite means his authority as the necessary condition of the highest happiness of his kingdom.

I proceed to say—

In the second place, that the view now maintained of justice as the attribute of a perfect moral governor, is strongly confirmed by the consideration that it is exempt from important errors which pertain to other views of the subject, and is consistent with other great and acknowledged truths.

1. It specifies one essential kind or form of justice on the part of a perfect moral governor, which in the view maintained by a prominent class of divines is entirely omitted.

Justice as now defined—justice as a disposition to maintain the authority of a perfect moral governor—is surely one kind of justice on his part. Indeed, if what has been said be true, it is the only kind of justice which is peculiar to this relation. But this kind of justice, in that classification of all kinds of justice into commutative, distributive, and general justice, is entirely omitted and unknown. Thus the class of divines now referred to, fail to recognize the existence of that attribute of justice which is peculiar to a perfect moral governor in all cases, and which he alike possesses and manifests, whether prior to all action on the part of subjects he simply gives the best law with the requisite sanctions, whether subsequent to action on the part of subjects he rewards the obedient or punishes the disobedient, or whether he pardons the latter on the ground of the atonement.

2. The view now maintained avoids the error of confounding general or public justice with general benevolence.

This is done, as we have seen, in one mode of classifying the different kinds of justice. According to what has been said, general benevolence is concerned for, and is committed to promote the public good in all respects, and is of course concerned for, and committed to the securing and employing all the necessary means of the public good. Among these necessary means of the public good, one is the maintenance of the moral governor's authority, and general benevolence as committed to secure this is general justice. General benevolence and general justice differ, as general benevolence is concerned for, and committed to secure the public good in all respects and by all the necessary means, and as general justice is concerned for, and committed to secure the public good in one respect and by one necessary means, viz., the maintenance of the moral governor's authority. General or public justice—justice as the peculiar attribute of a perfect moral governor—stands as the guardian, not of the public good, as this depends on every necessary means necessary to it, but as it depends on one means of it—the authority of the moral governor.

3. This view of justice as the attribute of a perfect moral governor, which is now maintained, avoids the error of those who represent an atonement as rendering pardon consistent with general benevolence.

Dr. Edwards and others maintain that the atonement of Christ satisfies justice in the sense of general benevolence—that it not only supports the authority of law, but renders it consistent with the glory of God and the good of the whole system to pardon the sinner.* We have already shown that from this view of the subject, in connection with the doctrine of universal atonement and other views of a large class of divines, the doctrine of universal salvation follows as an unavoidable consequence. According however to the view now maintained, an atonement does not render the pardon of the transgressor consistent with justice in the sense of general benevolence, which Dr. Edwards admits to be an *improper* sense of justice,† but with justice as the peculiar attribute of a moral governor, *properly* so called, viz., with justice as committed

* Vide Dr. Edwards on the Necessity of Atonement, pp. 95, 98.

† According to this view of Dr. Edwards, when the apostle teaches the consistency of pardon with justice, he means justice in an *improper* sense of the word, which is incredible.

to uphold the authority of the moral governor as *one* indispensable means of the public good. Now it is obvious that many things besides an atonement may be necessary to render the *pardon* of the transgressor consistent with general benevolence. For example, to render the pardon of a transgressor consistent with general benevolence, it may be necessary that he should return to obedience by faith and repentance, since otherwise the act of pardon might produce more evil than good. But such an inconsistency between pardon and general benevolence can be removed, not by an atonement but only by faith and repentance on the part of the transgressor. So we may suppose that to pardon a transgressor under an atonement on condition of his faith and repentance, might be followed with his apostasy or occasion the revolt of other subjects, and so be inconsistent with benevolence. In neither case can pardon be rendered consistent with benevolence simply by an atonement. If we suppose the facts so changed in these cases that pardon shall be consistent with general benevolence, still such consistency in no respect depends on an atonement, but solely on the conduct of the subjects. It is plain therefore that an atonement cannot render the pardon of a transgressor consistent with general benevolence *in all respects*. On the contrary, while it must be conceded that an atonement can render it consistent with general benevolence in *one respect* to pardon the transgressor, viz., as general benevolence in the form of general justice is committed to uphold the authority of the moral governor, it is obvious that this is all that it can do to render pardon consistent with general benevolence.

If the pardon of the transgressor on condition of repentance would be consistent with general benevolence in all respects under an atonement, then he could be pardoned without an atonement, were it not for the inconsistency of his pardon with maintaining the authority of the moral governor. Without an atonement, this inconsistency would be indeed an insurmountable but still the *only* obstacle. To remove this inconsistency, that is, to render it consistent with benevolence, in one respect to pardon such a transgressor, viz., as benevolence is committed to uphold the authority of the moral governor, is therefore the only and the whole effect which need be or can be produced by an atonement. In other words, the only and the whole effect of an atonement is to render the pardon of a transgressor consistent with general or public justice—justice as the peculiar attribute of a perfect moral governor.

Should it here be said that the act of requiring faith and repentance as the condition of pardon, is as truly necessary to uphold the authority of the moral governor as an atonement, this may in some respect be admitted. The act of the moral governor in requiring repentance and faith, may be *indirectly* necessary to the maintenance of his authority as is every other act of benevolence, viz., as the proof of his benevolence, or as the want of it would prove his want of benevolence, and thus indirectly necessary to evince his right to reign, that is, his authority. But this requirement has no *direct* tendency in its own nature to uphold the authority in pardoning a transgressor. For if the requirement and compliance with it be supposed, the act of pardon without an atonement would involve the subversion of authority as absolutely as it would without such requirement; while were it consistent with the public good in other respects than that of supporting authority to pardon without repentance, an atonement would fully support authority. The requirement of repentance may be necessary to manifest the moral governor's benevolence in some respect, so far as this may depend on the reformation of the pardoned transgressor; but it cannot manifest his benevolence in another respect, viz., as absolutely committed to uphold his authority as the indispensable means of the public good. This is the exclusive effect of an atonement.

What has been said to show that an atonement does not render it consistent with general benevolence, but only with general or public justice to pardon the transgressor, may be illustrated by a supposable instance of commutative justice. Suppose that A owes B a sum of money, and that the obstacle to B's remitting the debt is, that commutative justice requires, as the dictate of general benevolence, that A makes the payment. But C becomes A's sponsor, giving ample security for the payment of the debt to B, if he will consent to exempt A from the payment; and thus, so far as commutative justice is concerned, B may relinquish his demand on A. Now it does not follow from this that B can do this consistently with general benevolence. For it may be true that to relinquish his demand on A, while it will in no respect be inconsistent with commutative justice, will only encourage A in idleness and profligacy, and conduct him and many others to irretrievable ruin. So a moral governor may by an atonement remove every obstacle to the pardon of the transgressor arising from the attribute of justice, or from benevolence as committed to uphold his authority, and yet there may be other reasons why general benevolence requires that he withhold pardon and punish the transgressor.

4. The view of the attribute of justice in a perfect moral governor now maintained, shows the error of supposing that an atonement renders pardon consistent with distributive justice.

Distributive justice is a disposition to treat, and in overt action does treat, subjects according to their personal deserts. But surely an atonement does not, and cannot render pardon consistent with treating the transgressor according to his personal deserts. In whatever form of justice pardon is rendered consistent with justice by an atonement, it cannot be that particular form of justice which is properly called distributive justice. This is to say, that to pardon the transgressor is consistent with treating him according to his personal desert; that is, that pardon and punishment are consistent—that is, a subject may be both pardoned and punished, which is absurd. An atonement cannot render the pardon of the transgressor either consistent or inconsistent with distributive justice. An atonement can render pardon consistent with general or public justice. But pardon and distributive justice—pardon and punishment at the same time—are necessarily in their own nature palpably inconsistent, and therefore cannot be rendered either consistent or inconsistent with each other by an atonement or by any thing else.

And yet palpable as is this absurdity, many divines have maintained that an atonement renders the pardon of the transgressor consistent with distributive justice. The expedient by which this conclusion has been obtained, is the theory or doctrine of imputation—a theory which seems to have had its foundation in the assumption, that justice as the attribute of a perfect moral governor is distributive justice, and that of course an atonement in rendering pardon consistent with justice, must render it consistent with distributive justice. Hence the theory or doctrine of imputation, as we have already described it, was evidently adopted as furnishing the only possible method of explaining what obviously needed explanation—how a transgressor could be pardoned, and at the same time be treated according to his personal deserts—that is, how he could be both pardoned and punished at the same time. My object here is not to examine a theory which I deem palpably preposterous as well as unscriptural; but rather to trace it to its origin and to show how one error leads to another, or rather to many others, and especially how wise and good men, when they have combined error with truth, will, for the sake of the truth, not only maintain the error, but in order to vindicate it plausibly, will do the most palpable violence to reason and common sense.

The class of divines now referred to, evidently saw and felt bound to maintain the truth, that an atonement must render pardon consistent with justice as the attribute of a perfect moral governor. But their error, their first error, was, that justice as the attribute of a perfect moral governor is in the case of transgression necessarily *distributive justice*, and thus obliges to a retributive punishment, or the infliction of the legal penalty according to personal demerit. Hence the imputation of sin to the sinner's substitute, with the supposed corresponding result of pardon, and full and exact retribution according to personal demerit. Now this theory with its connections and results vanishes at once, not merely as absurd and impossible in the nature of things, but as founded in nothing but a false view of the justice of the perfect moral governor. This is not as we have seen in all cases, nor in the case now under consideration, necessarily distributive justice. It is simply a benevolent disposition to uphold the authority of the moral governor by the requisite means; and this, whether in the present case by the infliction of penalty on the transgressor or by an atonement. If this be not so—if justice require in the absolute sense the infliction of penalty in the case of transgression—then an atonement and pardon on the ground of it would be impossible. All that justice requires is, that the authority of the moral governor be maintained; and since this can be done by means of an atonement as well as by inflicting the legal penalty, pardon through an atonement is consistent with justice. Without distributive justice, and without imputation and its palpable and manifold absurdities, and with an immense diminution of misery and a vast increase of happiness in the universe, the throne of justice stands in all its majesty—for mercy and truth are met together—righteousness and peace have kissed each other.

Thus an atonement, while it renders pardon consistent with *general or public justice*, does not and cannot render it consistent with *distributive justice*. Pardon under an atonement is consistent with the full authority of the lawgiver, this being sustained by the atonement, and also with the public good so far as this depends on the support of this authority. The transgressor may be pardoned without the sacrifice of one item of the influence which is peculiar to the law or authority of the moral governor, and without the least violation of his obligation to the public to maintain, or the least infringement of their right that he should maintain that authority unimpaired. But pardon under an atonement is not consistent with distributive justice, for it is not consistent with treating the transgressor according to his personal deserts. The atonement does not remove his personal ill-desert. If it did, then pardon or forgiveness would be an absurdity and a solecism, for there would be nothing to be forgiven. On the contrary, his personal ill-desert remains under an atonement, and though the public good as this depends on the support of the lawgiver's authority, does not demand the punishment of the transgressor as it would without an atonement—that is, his being treated according to his deserts—yet if the public good demands in any other respect or for any other reason that he be so treated, there is nothing in the nature of an atonement nor in any thing else to prevent his being so treated—that is, to prevent his punishment. The justice of the lawgiver is fully manifested, for his authority is fully maintained by an atonement. By this provision he is neither obliged to pardon nor to punish, but is free to pardon or to punish, as the public good shall require, without violating the right of the public or any right of the transgressor. If we suppose an atonement for all, then not only might all be pardoned so far as safety to the authority of the law or of the lawgiver is concerned, but all who will believe may be pardoned, with safety to every other interest of the kingdom.

APPENDIX—No. II.

ESSAY ON THE PROVIDENTIAL GOVERNMENT OF GOD.

PART I.—RELATION OF PROVIDENTIAL TO MORAL GOVERNMENT.

Providential and moral government defined.—Moral government included in providential.—All events fall under providential government.—Grounds of the certainty of different kinds of action differ in their nature and their design.—In what sense does God purpose wrong moral action?

THE government of God is both providential and moral. I shall attempt to describe and show the difference between them so far as they relate to the purposes of God.

The providential government of God consists in that system of influence by which he secures the accomplishment of his providential purposes; i. e., those purposes which respect the certainty of the events purposed.

According to this definition the providential government of God directly respects all his own acts, as these are the objects of his providential purposes; i. e., he employs his power in performing all those acts which he purposes to perform. It indirectly respects all the acts and agencies of creatures, as these fulfill his purpose that they shall take place. It thus comprises his own direct agency in performing those acts of his own by which he produces effects as their proximate efficient cause, and those acts also by which he produces the grounds of the certainty of the acts and operations of all created beings and things.

The moral government of God consists in that influence which is *designed* and *fitted to secure right moral action* in moral beings rather than wrong. This influence I have already described as consisting in the simple influence of authority on moral beings through the medium of law. It respects only one single purpose or will, viz., that right moral action *should* (not shall) take place rather than wrong. It consists not in any act or acts of God, but simply in that influence which arises from the full expression of his will in the form of law. While it is designed to produce right moral action rather than wrong, and is adequate to produce, and if uncounteracted by its subjects would produce the former, still it does not necessarily imply, as we have already shown, an influence which will actually secure right moral action. It is an influence on beings who have power to counteract it, and thus to defeat the direct end which it is designed and fitted to accomplish through their agency. It may indeed, in entire consistency with its nature, actually secure right moral action; and yet there may be a perfect moral government, under which not right but wrong moral action on the part of subjects is certain, even universal.

The purpose or will of God which is expressed in his law is not a purpose that its object—viz., right moral action—*shall take place*, but a preference that it *should take place* rather than wrong; a preference of the manner in which he would that his moral creatures should act. This preference does indeed imply a providential purpose actually to secure the highest amount of obedience on the whole, which he can secure by furnishing the necessary means of this end, or the ground of its certainty. The purpose however which respects the certainty of right action and the means of it, is not the same as the purpose or preference that right action should take place rather than wrong. The latter preference must, in the order of nature, precede the purpose to secure the actual existence of the former.

While therefore moral government implies an influence which, considered in relation to the powers of its subjects, is adequate to produce right moral action, and implies a preference of right moral action rather than wrong moral action—while it implies also every kind and degree of influence that will secure the highest amount of obedience which the moral governor, if benevolent, can secure—and while in some cases, or even in all, it may actually secure and be intended to secure right moral action, still it is not essential to its nature that it secure right moral action even in one instance, much less in all instances.

To mark clearly this distinction between the providential and moral government of God, it is necessary further to remark, that the influence which I have called moral government may, without losing its peculiar character, become also a part of his providential government, although that influence which we call providential government cannot become a part of his moral government. The former is true, when the influence called moral government is used with a design or purpose actually to secure right moral action. This influence would be complete and perfect considered as that of moral government, though it were used with no other preference than that the subjects *should* obey rather than disobey the law, and though all should rebel. But when, as the case may be, the moral governor can secure right moral action, knows he can secure it, and purposes actually to secure it by the influence of moral government, then this influence, without losing its distinctive character, becomes an influence of his providential government, being used not only with the preference that the subjects *should* obey rather than disobey, but also with a further design or purpose actually to secure their obedience. Thus this influence, considered as used with the simple preference that subjects *should obey* rather than disobey, is the influence of moral government, and when also used with the further design or purpose actually to secure obedience, it is an influence of providential government. It is obvious however that the influence of providential government, being designed merely to secure the certainty of the event which is its object, can never be used *merely* with the preference that the event which is its object *should* take place, and therefore cannot become the influence called moral government.

If these remarks be just, then that influence which we call moral government, when it is used actually to secure right moral action, becomes also, without losing its distinctive character, a part of that influence called providential government. Hence if we assume that God's providential purposes extend to all actual events, it will follow that all actual events are brought to pass by his providential government. Here however there is one grand peculiarity in respect to right moral action. When this actually occurs, although the influence by which it is brought to pass is an influence of providential government, and designed to accomplish the purpose that the action *shall take place*, yet this same influence is also called moral government. It is still the simple influence of authority, and as such is the same influence, whether right moral action be secured by it or not, or whether there be any providential purpose to secure it or not. Nor is this all. It is that peculiar influence by which alone as the proximate influence, obedience to a moral governor can be secured. All other providential events, except such obedience and its results in happiness, may be secured without this influence as their appropriate antecedent. But voluntary submission to the will of a lawgiver can be proximately secured by no other influence than the authority of a lawgiver.

According to the preceding view of the subject, it follows that *all actual events*, considered as events—even the existence of that peculiar influence called moral government—fall under the department of providential government, inasmuch as they are all the objects of God's providential purposes, and brought to pass by that influence which we call providential government. This universal fact however, does not exclude or conceal the peculiarity of that influence called moral government, as the great influence to whose existence and efficacy all other influences are subservient, for the sake of its results in character and happiness.

That those influences which result in events in the material world fall under the department of providential government, will not be doubted. A question however may naturally arise whether some other influences which, according to the present view of the subject, would belong to providential government, do not more properly fall under moral government. I here refer to the influence of motives, and to any other influences which may be supposed directly to reach the mind and secure obedience; particularly whether the acts of giving a law to moral beings, and furnishing motives to obedience, are not properly a part of *moral* government? The answer to this question depends on the principle of classification we adopt, or on the views we form of the two departments. If we include under the department of moral government those acts of God, or those events directly consequent on his acts, like the act of giving a law, which have a direct bearing on moral action in creatures, then indeed these acts fall within the department of moral government. To this mode or principle of classification however there lies, if I mistake not, one serious objection, if no more—viz., it utterly confounds the two departments. For example, the trials of life and the gifts of divine bounty have as direct an influence on moral action as the giving of a law, or the furnishing of motives to obedience in any other mode. But the former, by universal consent, are denominated *providential* events. Indeed all that God does in all the varying modes of dispensation, has a bearing, more or less direct, on moral action in creatures, as we shall have occasion hereafter to show. Nor do I believe it possible, on the principle of such a connection of events with moral action, to draw any clear line of demarkation between the two departments of the divine government.

The principle now proposed seems to me at least, to be the only one on which any correct classification of events under the two departments can be made. Moral government is an influence on moral beings; an influence to produce simply right moral action in moral beings. It is designed, so far as there is any purpose formed in the divine mind in regard to the moral quality of actions, to produce those which are right and no other. But the acts of God in giving a law, supporting it by sanctions, and providing means of conveying truth to the mind, &c., are not this influence, but are acts from which this influence results. It is this influence only, resulting from these acts, which can affect or move moral beings as subjects of a moral government. The acts themselves can produce no such event as their proper and proximate effect. The acts therefore of giving a law, sustaining its authority by sanctions, providing means of conveying truth to the mind, are not constituent parts of moral government, but are *providential* acts which are necessary to that *influence* which constitutes moral government.

If the preceding remarks be just, then the certainty of all moral action results from the government of God, and the question naturally arises, why is not all moral action to be placed under the same department? God, it may be said, provides alike for the certainty of every right and every wrong moral action, and why is not this provision one and the same, and to be known by the same name? I answer, while it is true that God provides for, i. e., furnishes the grounds of the certainty of every right and every wrong moral action that takes place, these grounds are widely diverse in the two cases. They differ in their *nature* and in their *design*.

They differ in their *nature*. The influence which is the

ground of the certainty of right moral action, is in its appropriate tendency fitted to produce right moral action in every being on whom it operates, and has no other tendency in respect to him. In case it fails to produce its appropriate result, i. e., in the case of certain wrong moral action, this failure or this wrong moral action can in no sense be ascribed to this influence. It is always sufficient for its end, viewed in connection with the powers of the subject. Wrong moral action therefore cannot be ascribed to this influence, even on the ground of its imperfect degree, because if it fails of its end, the failure is not owing to its deficiency as means or influence, but to the counteraction of it by the agent who is its subject. When wrong moral action is certain, it is to be traced either to the strength of propensities to natural good in the subject, or to the degree of temptation which assails him—an influence widely different from that which we have denominated moral government—an influence so different, that to yield to it implies the direct counteraction of the other. Now things so different are properly distinguished by different names, while to make no distinction between them, is to annihilate right and wrong in the actions of moral beings. While therefore the government of God furnishes the grounds of the certainty of every right and every wrong moral action, the grounds of this certainty in the two cases are widely different in their nature —the one we denominate moral government, the other providential government.

Again: they differ widely in their design or purpose. We shall hereafter see some of the different respects in which God may be said to purpose different events. This difference has an important application to the present subject. Thus God, in the character of a moral governor, purposes right moral action and not wrong moral action; i. e., he prefers in every instance that moral agents should act right and not wrong, so that wrong moral action compared with right moral action is never an object of the divine purpose or preference, while right moral action is always the object of his preference compared with wrong moral action in every instance in which the latter occurs. Such is the only purpose or preference which God has in relation to moral action. He knows no other. Now we say that the influence which he provides for the accomplishment of this single preference for moral actions as such, deserves a name. We say the purpose itself is distinct from every other purpose of God, and the influence appointed and designed for its fulfillment is in its design also distinct from every other. It is true, as we have already said, that this influence is provided by providential government. But then by this influence, viz., moral government, a design or purpose is to be answered which no act or influence of providential government is designed directly to answer—viz., a purpose that there should be right moral action rather than wrong. This is a preference that moral agents *should*, and not that they *shall* act right. The only design of the providential acts which result in this influence is, that they shall result in it. Here their design terminates; and when these acts have produced the degree of influence that will result in right moral action, the purpose which respects the moral quality of actions is not gratified, but simply the purpose to furnish the means of gratifying it. In a word, the providential governor furnishes, in fulfillment of his purpose, the moral governor with the means of fulfilling *his* peculiar purpose. Thus the purposes of the providential governor are wholly subservient to the grand purpose of the moral governor, and obviously distinct from it. Of course providential government and moral government differ widely in their design.

This difference will appear still more clearly if we inquire in what respect God may be said to purpose wrong moral action. Does he purpose it in a moral respect? does he prefer its existence in any case to right moral action? has he put into operation any system of influence which bespeaks such a preference? If he has established a moral government, the law of which requires right moral action, then he has no such preference, and has done nothing to gratify it. But if God does not prefer wrong moral action to right—if he has no preference for the former in respect to moral qualities—in what sense can he have a purpose that wrong moral action should exist? I answer, he can be conceived to have such a purpose only in one respect, namely, that wrong moral action is to him unavoidably incident to the necessary means of the greatest good. It falls into the system aside from his main design, and in opposition to that design. It is therefore itself designed only as an evil, incidental so far as divine prevention is concerned, if the system be adopted. The system itself is not designed to produce it rather than right moral action, but the contrary. But either the system must not exist or sin must exist. The existence of the system with this inseparable evil, God purposes; i. e., he prefers the existence of the system to its non-existence with this inseparable evil. Such a purpose that sin shall be, is perfectly consistent with another purpose, viz., that compared with obedience, sin should not be. God, instead of a purpose that sin should be when compared with obedience, has an unqualified purpose that it should not be. To prevent its existence and to secure obedience, he has in fact done all he could do in the circumstances in which it exists. It results only from that which is the necessary means of the greatest good, as a consequence which God cannot prevent without the sacrifice of these means.

Let any one then compare the purpose of God that obedience should exist in preference to sin, with the only purpose which he can be supposed to have in respect to the existence of sin, and he will see that as moral acts, on the one the heart of God is supremely fixed, and that the other he only wills in the form of acquiescing in an unavoidable evil. Let any one compare the influence which is provided to secure, and actually does secure obedience when it exists, with that which is the direct occasion of the existence of sin, and how widely different is all that God designs and does in reference to the existence of one, from what he designs and does in its relation to the existence of the other. While then the certainty of all moral action results from the government of God, yet this government in relation to one class of these actions is so diverse from it in relation to the other, that truth and propriety both require that this diversity should be marked and described. This diversity, for aught I see, is accurately defined by dividing his government into moral and providential, and whether I have succeeded in drawing the line of demarkation between them or not, I am satisfied that the distinction is real and important. I am fully convinced that as the consequence of not making this distinction, or making it but imperfectly, the theology of many has tended directly to conceal that character of God, in which above all others he would be known and recognized by his intelligent creatures, and that instead of a moral governor willing the obedience of his children, with the most unqualified sincerity and most solicitous affection, God has appeared only or chiefly as an omnipotent disposer of all things, whose pleasure can in fact be known only by actual events, and whose decrees render nugatory the purposes and agency of his dependent creatures.

PART II.—THE PROVIDENTIAL PURPOSES OF GOD.

Topics to be discussed.—Remarks on the terms *decrees*, *predestination*, &c.—I. Nature of the divine purposes.—II. Their extent; they include every event.—III. The certainty of their accomplishment. IV. The mode of their accomplishment: 1. As they respect events in the material world; Question argued at length in respect to the efficiency of second causes; 2. As they respect the acts of moral agents.—These determined by the constitution of man and his circumstances.—Objections considered.

According to the views given of this subject in the preceding discussion, the providential government of God consists in that system of influence or control by which he secures the accomplishment of his providential purposes.

The topics which next claim consideration are the *universality* of his providential government, and *the mode of its administration.* And here it is obvious that every question on these topics must depend on the *universality* of his providential purposes, and the mode of their execution; since it is undeniable that God's providential government must be *co-extensive* with his providential purposes, and the *mode* of its administration must be identical with the *mode* in which he executes these purposes. This then brings us to the consideration of what has been commonly called *the doctrine of God's decrees.*

Here again, as I have often done before, I take occasion to notice the language or phraseology commonly employed on this subject. And I must say that in my own view, the principal terms employed have occasioned much of the controversy respecting it, and that the use of them, if not unjustifiable, ought on the ground of expediency, at least in many cases, to be relinquished. The words to which I allude are *decree*, *predestination, and the like.* These words are of heathen origin and of heathen import. They were used originally by those who believed in fate and destiny, and who applied them, not merely to denote the certainty of events, but to denote also the still further notion or idea of the most absolute natural necessity. If then these terms are to be understood according to their original meaning and use, they surely convey a meaning, or express ideas which are false. With such a meaning they ought not to be adopted, at least in many cases, by the translators or the expounders of the Word of God. I do not intend by this to censure our translators in the instances in which they may have employed some of the terms now referred to; for in my own view, the context in those instances in which the objectionable idea ought to be excluded, does exclude it, as in Rom. viii. 29, the event spoken of is moral conformity to Christ, a conception inconsistent with the heathen notion of *destiny*.

Nor do I intend to censure those theologians for an unjustifiable use of these terms, who have been careful to define them and to exclude, by their definitions, the objectionable import. I only say that the use of these terms to convey the idea of absolute natural necessity, is a use unjustifiable and ought to be exploded.

Conceding the unquestionable right of any speaker or writer to use terms as he pleases if he defines them, and also the propriety of using terms which in themselves are ambiguous, provided the context limits and defines their meaning, still even in such cases there is room for considerations of expediency. For if after all (and the fact is notoriously common in controversial discussions), the terms will not be understood in the sense in which they are used, it becomes a serious question whether if other terms can be used that will convey to others our real meaning instead of that which we do not intend to convey, we ought not to reject the former and to adopt the latter. Or rather there is no question, for as the object of the use of language is to convey to others the real ideas of our own minds, we are bound, if we can, to use such language as shall accomplish this end. On this principle, I would either exclude the terms *decree*, *predestination*, and *kindred terms*, from discussions of the truth under consideration, or explain them so that they cannot be misunderstood. I should not indeed expect in this way to prevent all controversy, but I am confident that men of evangelical sentiments may be brought by it to agree in *words*, as they do actually agree in *things*. There is not one of these men who will not admit that under all providential events, however evil, and whether they be viewed as natural or moral evils—we are bound to exercise cheerful resignation to the will and government of God. But yet in the view of many of these persons, to speak of God's *decreeing* or *predestinating* moral evil, is to utter a sentiment deserving the severest reprobation. And why? Plainly because they attach very different ideas to these terms, from those which the former phraseology conveys. And yet that phraseology conveys the whole truth, while their ready admission of the truth thus expressed is decisive that the parties agree in things and dispute only about words,—a sort of controversy that should be left to philologists and grammarians, rather than agitate the Church of God. For these reasons I adopt, instead of the phrase, *the decrees of God*, the phrase, the providential purposes of God, and now proceed to consider—

I. Their nature;

II. Their extent;

III. Their certainty; and,

IV. The mode of their accomplishment.

I. Their nature.

To this part of the subject our attention has already been directed. The providential purposes of God as they are distinguished from his purpose as a moral governor, are *those purposes of God which respect the* CERTAINTY OF EVENTS, *or purposes that events* SHALL BE, or SHALL TAKE PLACE.

That God has formed such purposes in regard to *many events*, and even in regard to all events which *directly* depend on his own agency, no Theist will deny. Whatever God does, he always designed or purposed to do; is a position too plainly true to need argument for its support.

II. Concerning their extent—

I maintain that the providential purposes of God apply to all actual events. The meaning is, that God has from eternity purposed that every event which takes place shall take place. The proof may be thus stated. God as an omniscient and immutable being forms no new purposes respecting actual events. His purposes therefore are eternal. God also as an omniscient being must foreknow all events. He must therefore purpose either that they shall take place, or purpose that they shall not take place, or be indifferent whether they take place or not. A heathen philosopher would say, "*Magna Dî curant, parva negligunt.*"—(*Cic. de Nat. Deorum*, 66.) But that God is indifferent to any actual event, however trivial it may appear to us, cannot be justly affirmed, unless it can be shown to have no connection whatever with any other important event. On the contrary, that he is not indifferent to any event, however trivial in our view, is satisfactorily inferred from manifold such events, and those of the highest moment. The cackling of a goose saved Rome. The showing of a fig in the Roman senate caused the destruction of Carthage. Who will pretend that the apostle unjustly appreciated the reality or importance of such connections in his exclamation, "Behold, how great a matter a little fire kindleth!" so true in the case to which he applies it, and so applicable to cases innumerable? Who shall tell us the effects on this material system of the annihilation of its least particle, or even of its occupying another place than it does at any moment of its existence? Indeed the connection of which we speak, is so often and so decisively manifested to us, as to warrant the conclusion that the ultimate design or end of God, in the creation and government of this world, may depend on events which in themselves would appear to possess no importance. Hence the inference is authorized, that God can no more be indifferent to one event than to another—to the floating of an atom than to the ruin of a world. Besides, to suppose God to be indifferent to any actual event, is to suppose him either *directly* or *indirectly* to give existence to that event without a reason, which is plainly impossible.

God then must purpose that every actual event shall take place or that it shall not. But to suppose that he has purposed that an event shall not take place, and does not prevent it, is to deny his power to prevent it. But since nothing can exist except in dependence on God, it were as absurd to say that he could not prevent its existence, as to say he could not abstain from acting. It follows therefore that no event takes place which God has not purposed shall take place; in other words, that God has purposed the existence of all actual events.

It is common to present an argument on this subject founded in the assumption that God cannot foreknow that an event will take place, unless he has purposed that it shall take place. The question is not, whether God can as a matter of fact foresee any event which he *has not* purposed, but whether, in the nature of things, it is conceivable that he could foresee such an event, supposing it to take place. If by this assumption it be meant that it is inconceivable that God should foreknow that an event will take place which he has not purposed shall take place, or which is contrary to his purpose, allowing the possibility of such an event, I cannot admit it. For since events which are contrary to my purpose are possible, and since I may know that they will take place, so if we suppose any event contrary to God's purpose to be possible, he may also foreknow that event. I may foreknow that my friend who is sick with a fatal disease will die, and it is plain that my knowledge of the fact no more depends on a purpose that it shall be, than my knowledge of any present event which is contrary to my pleasure. It is true however that if it were in my power to prevent such an event, then it would be impossible that the event should take place contrary to my purpose. On this account it is impossible that any event should take place contrary to God's purpose, and therefore we cannot suppose him to foreknow an event which is not in some respect the object of his purpose. Having the power to prevent it he would prevent it, if for some reason or another he did not purpose that it should take place. But then the impossibility that God should foreknow an event which he has not purposed, results not from the fact that he could not foreknow such an event allowing it to be possible, but from the fact that it is impossible that he should foreknow that an event will be which is contrary to his purpose, when we take into consideration his power to prevent it. But this is the same argument with the preceding; i. e., such is the knowledge and such the power of God, that he will suffer no event to take place which is in every respect contrary to his purpose.

III. The certainty of their accomplishment.

As every actual event fulfills a purpose of God, so no event whose actual existence he has purposed will fail to take place. This is conclusively argued thus. If an event be not within the power of God he cannot purpose that it shall take place. No being can purpose that an event shall take place, the existence of which he knows to be impossible. But such impossibility, so far as it exists, is perfectly known to omniscience. No event therefore whose actual existence God cannot secure can be the object of his providential purpose. Of course every event whose existence God purposes, he can bring to pass, and therefore will bring to pass.

IV. The mode of their accomplishment.

It is the philosophical doctrine of some theologians, that all events are brought to pass by the direct efficiency of God; in other words, that neither matter nor mind possesses efficiency in itself or is in its own nature an efficient cause, but that all material phenomena and mental acts are results of divine efficiency, as directly and truly as the existence of any created thing. To this philosophical doctrine, in its full extent at least, I cannot subscribe. My views of it and of the subject now before us, will be given by considering the mode in which God accomplishes his providential purposes.

1. *As these respect events in the material world;* and,

2. *As they respect the acts of created moral agents.*

1. As the purposes of God respect events in the material world.

Laying aside miraculous events as not properly belonging to the present inquiry, the topic of discussion is—

Whether second causes in the material world are efficient causes, or whether the phenomena connected with them are to be ascribed to the direct agency of God? This a question which, if I mistake not, it is difficult for us to decide with any high degree of confidence, and the decision of which is of no great doctrinal or practical importance; still, as a topic frequently investigated, it may be well to devote to it some consideration.

In support of the doctrine of direct divine efficiency, in opposition to that of the efficiency of material causes, the following things may be alleged:—First, that the efficiency of such causes is impossible. This has been often asserted as an axiom, a self-evident proposition, the truth of which no sound mind can doubt, and which no argument is necessary to support. All efficiency, it is said, must exclusively pertain to the Great First Cause. It is enough to say, in reply to this assumption, that it is wholly gratuitous. Others who hold the truth of this position rest it on a different basis. On the ground that matter is incapable of intelligence, and that most if not all effects in the material world are marked with design and bespeak intelligence in their cause, they infer that matter cannot be the efficient cause of these effects. The correctness of this conclusion, admitting that matter is incapable of intelligence, depends on the assumption that an efficiency cannot pertain to second causes, which without possessing intelligence shall produce effects which bespeak intelligence. To pronounce this impossible to an omnipotent Creator, seems to be an assertion entitled to no very high degree of confidence.

In opposition to the doctrine of the efficiency of material causes, it may be still further said that it greatly impairs, if it does not wholly destroy the argument *from this part of the creation* for the divine existence; for he who can believe that a flower comes into being through an efficiency inherent in matter, can believe that a world or a universe might come into existence in the same way; that there is no greater absurdity so far as the thing itself is concerned, in supposing the eternal uncaused existence of that substance which we call matter, than in supposing the eternity of that which we call spirit; and that since, if matter actually possesses such efficiency, it is in its own nature capable of it, it will follow that no good reason can be assigned, why the present material system is not the result of such efficiency. For it may be said, if this doctrine be true, then it is proved either that intelligence in the cause is not necessary to the manifestation of contrivance in the effect, or if it be necessary, then matter being proved to be the efficient cause of effects that manifest contrivance, is proved to possess intelligence; so that since matter by its own inherent efficiency produces such effects, preserving the regularity of the material universe and giving existence to all its phenomena, it might by its own inherent energy have disposed itself into its present form, and be the independent cause of all the changes and results which occur.

To all this it may be replied, that although we ascribe real efficiency to matter, it will not follow that matter possesses intelligence, nor that there is not an intelligent being from whom the efficiency ascribed to matter is itself derived. There may be an efficiency in the particles of matter which shall dispose them in given circumstances into the form of a crystal or a rose, and still this efficiency may be derived from an intelligent Creator. The design manifested by a watch in the division of time, may be traced to the efficiency of the mainspring, and yet we cannot avoid on the one hand, the conviction that intelligence has been employed in the production of the machinery and its results, nor on the other, that such intelligence does not pertain to the materials of which it is constructed, but is exclusively the attribute of its contriver. The supposed efficiency of matter then, is not inconsistent with the existence of an intelligent being as its author by direct agency, and thus indirectly of all its results. But this is not all; the legitimate evidence on the subject conducts us unavoidably to the conclusion that there is such a being. As we have before shown, from the manifestation of contrivance the mind unavoidably infers the existence of an intelligent being, i. e., of a contriver. The fact or principle on which this inference rests is this, that in all cases in which we *know* the cause of adaptation, we *know* it to be either directly or indirectly an *intelligent* cause. Although therefore there are instances of adaptation which our knowledge does not enable us to trace *directly* to an intelligent cause, yet we are obliged as sound philosophers to conclude that there is no such instance, which is not to be ascribed either *directly* or *indirectly* to an intelligent agent. We do not therefore destroy or weaken the argument from the design or contrivance manifested in material phenomena in support of the existence of an intelligent Creator; for though we ascribe an efficiency to second causes, still that efficiency implies the existence of such a Creator.

It may however be further said, that all the power or efficiency of which we have any decisive evidence pertains to spirit, and that therefore as the phenomena of the material world are effects which are beyond the power of any finite spirits which we *know*, we are led to the simple but sublime doctrine, that they are produced by the direct and ceaseless agency of the Infinite Spirit.

The reply which may be made to this reasoning, which I think must be admitted to be plausible, brings me to the arguments on the other side of the question.

It may here be said that although all the efficiency or power which *we know*, pertains to spirit, yet according to analogy we should be led to believe from this very fact that power or efficiency pertains to other causes. Finding in our own consciousness that certain changes are produced by our own powers or efficiency, and thus that God has created finite agents, the possibility of the fact can no longer be doubted that he can create such agents; and witnessing changes without us connected with what we term causes, precisely as they would did efficiency pertain to them, it may be said that the dictate of philosophy is, that efficiency does actually pertain to these causes. Whether this be the dictate of philosophy or not, what we have already said on the subject in our previous discussions, will satisfy us that such is the actual process of the human mind, and such are its actual conclusions almost without exception.

It is further said, that if efficiency does not pertain to these causes, the creation of the material world is useless. In this I see no force. For it may be replied that all the ends to be answered by giving efficiency to second causes would, so far as we can discover, be accomplished by the regular direct agency of God through the medium of these causes.

It is further said, that the efficiency of second causes is obviously the dictate of common sense, as evinced by the universality of human belief. To this it may be replied, that the universality of human belief may be accounted for, without supposing it to be founded in evidence, by tracing it to the acknowledged propensity of the human mind to exclude God from all its thoughts; and it may be said as a strong confirmation of this, that men of piety are wont to see God in every thing. It may however be doubted whether men of piety derive their views and impressions respecting the presence of God from their belief of his direct agency, for God is as truly presented to the view of the mind which contemplates his power manifested by the efficiency of second causes, as by direct agency through the medium of those causes. He is still brought before the mind as the author of all. Nor can it be doubted that the human mind finds it peculiarly difficult not to believe that there is in the nature of material causes, something which is the ground or reason of their appropriate effects —something for example in the nature of fire, which constitutes it an efficient cause of certain effects, which there is not in water, and *vice versa.* Indeed no philosopher can decide that God could create such a thing as fire is, and not impart to it such a nature and such an efficiency.

It may be still further alleged, that to deny all efficiency to second causes is to deny the reality of material things. For it may be said, what are they, if they have not a nature or properties—and what is nature and what are properties, if not a real *esse*, a real existence? For example, who will say that if you suppose the peculiar property of the loadstone to be taken from it, it would not become a different thing from what it is; and that if you were to go on abstracting one property after another, till all its properties or all its efficiency were taken away or annihilated, that any thing would be left? And so of every thing else. If there be then no efficiency in these things, there are no real existences without us; and what then are the senses which our Creator has given us, with their inseparable *inferences*, if you please so to term them, but organs of deception and error? To suppose that our Creator has so constituted the mind, as to lead us into error and mistake in regard to the reality of things, is hardly to be admitted.

On the whole, the specific question before us is perhaps one on which, if confident conclusions are authorized only by demonstrative evidence, we ought not to come to any confident conclusion. I would however say that my own mind inclines to the belief of the efficiency of second causes. The possibility of the fact cannot be denied. The fact evinced by our own consciousness of the existence of created agents of one sort, not unnaturally leads us to infer, on the principle of analogy, the existence of created agents of another sort. The universality of human belief in some degree corroborates the doctrine, while the apparent necessity either of admitting it or of denying the reality of material things, and thus implicating our Maker in the charge of deceiving his creatures, goes still more strongly to confirm my belief.

Be this however as it may, the preceding remarks show that the intelligent Creator of the material universe is its providential governor. If he is the author of all material phenomena by direct agency, and as truly so as he is of any created existence, then surely all these events take place as the expression of his will and as the accomplishment of his providential purposes. Nor is this conclusion weakened at all by the supposition that he has imparted efficiency to second causes. For still that efficiency is the result of his power, and we may be confident that an omniscient and omnipotent God will no more create such causes of such a nature, or arrange them in such a manner that they shall fail to fulfill his designs, than were his direct agency employed in producing their results. Still therefore, all events in the material universe are the expressions of his will and proofs of his dominion throughout this portion of his works.

It was proposed to consider the mode in which God accomplishes his providential purposes—

II. As they respect the acts of created moral agents.

If what we have already said on other occasions be true, men are free moral agents; and if what has now been said be true, the providential purposes of God extend to all the actions of men; in other words, God has purposed that every human action which takes place shall take place. The present inquiry is, *how* does God secure the certainty of the actions of free agents? The more common doctrine of Orthodox divines is, that he does this by motives. In this however, if we would state the whole truth with metaphysical accuracy, we must include the nature or constitution of man; and our meaning must be, that the constitution of man and his circumstances are such as to be the occasion of the certainty of all his actions. Perhaps however this answer to the inquiry may be considered as differing from that which ascribes the certainty of human action to motives, at least in one respect; viz., as it may include a divine influence, which secures in some cases a result which would not be secured simply by the essential constitution of man, and by what we commonly term *motives.* On this account I prefer it, and for the sake of giving precision and comprehensiveness to the statement of my views on this topic, I choose to say that God secures the accomplishment of those of his providential purposes which respect human action, *through the constitution of man and the circumstances in which he acts.*

When however I make this statement, I do not question the propriety or truth of that popular phraseology which is often used, and which in words ascribes the certainty of human action in particular instances to some single cause; as for example, to the nature of man, or to temptation, or to divine grace. For as I shall have occasion to show elsewhere, the real meaning of such popular phraseology as authorized by usage comprises all that I mean in the statement which I have made. I would here only observe, that when the actions of man are traced to the nature of man, the meaning cannot be that his nature is the cause considered apart from his circumstances or from the objects of choice; nor when human action is traced to motives or temptations can it be meant to exclude the nature of man; nor when divine grace is spoken of as the cause, can the object be to exclude the nature of man and the motives to holiness. So that the popular statement, when taken in its true meaning, whatever be its form, comprises all that is included in the more precise and comprehensive statement now made.

To the inquiry, how does God accomplish his providential purposes which respect human action, I answer—

Through the constitution of man and the circumstances in which he acts. In support of this position I observe—

1. That considered simply as an hypothesis it adequately accounts for the certainty of human action.

Who can doubt that physical propensities may be so strong toward a given action or course of action, and the motives or temptations so powerful, that such action will be certain? But if this may be so in one case it may be in all; and unless it can be shown that such is not the ground or reason of the certainty of human action in all cases, then it cannot be asserted that such is not the sufficient ground or reason.

2. Such substantially must be the ground or reason of the certainty of voluntary action in God.

None will deny that the voluntary acts of the Divine Being are certain, nor that the divine nature is a ground of such certainty. But is it not equally undeniable, that there is in the nature of things a ground or reason why a being of such a nature as God, chooses and acts in every instance as he does choose and act? If so, then the real ground or reason of the certainty of his acts is substantially the same with what we affirm to be the ground or reason of the certainty of human action. The question is, whether it is not so in fact? I answer, there is no absurdity in the supposition that such is the fact, for if such is the ground of the certainty of divine action, it may be of human action. God can in this respect make beings in his own image.

But further, we have no warrant to assert that such is the ground of the certainty of divine action, unless we first assume that such is the ground of the certainty of human action; for we can in this respect reason concerning God only from what we know of ourselves. We know nothing of the nature of voluntary action except from ourselves: so that our decision, whatever it be in regard to the ground of the certainty of such action in God, must rest on the previous decision that the same thing, i. e., the same thing in its nature as a cause, is the ground of the certainty of such action in us. I say then, that from the universal concession of those divines with whom we dispute on this point, viz., that the nature of God and the nature of things are such as to be the ground of the certainty of his acts, it follows that the true dictate of reason is, that the nature of man and the circumstances in which he acts are the ground of the certainty of his acts. I further say, that they do and must admit this to be the fact before they come to their conclusion respecting God, and that this conclusion shows that whether they are aware of the fact or not, and that however inconsistent they may be with themselves, they do admit our present doctrine in regard to the certainty of human action, since it is the only possible basis of their conclusion respecting the certainty of divine action.

3. It is the dictate of common sense, and what all the world believe.

In any inquiry into the reason of any human action, who ever in the exercise of common sense thinks of tracing it to any thing except the constitutional propensities, the objects of choice and other circumstances in which man acts? I speak here of the ultimate cause, ground, or reason of human action. It is common indeed to trace specific action to the governing purpose, yet if we pursue the inquiry, whence is this governing purpose, we are carried back to the constitution and circumstances of the being. Nor do I appeal here to what must be conceded to be a matter of fact in regard to mankind generally, but to the very philosophers and divines who adopt a different theory. They too, when they would speak to the conviction of their fellow-men, are obliged to trace and do in fact always trace, human action to the cause now assigned. Look into their popular sermons and discourses for example, and see to what cause they trace human sinfulness. It is *to the nature of man*, or it is to the *influence of the world*, or to temptation, or to the strength of passion and appetite, and so on, all of which causes are resolvable into the cause which we assign.

4 The same thing is evinced by the consciousness of every human being.

Every one who acts voluntarily or as a free agent, knows why he acts as he does. But whatever be the reason why one acts in a given manner is the reason of the certainty of such action. Now, that this is a matter of human consciousness supersedes any further argument. Nor can we from the nature of the case make any other appeal except to every one's own consciousness. In making this appeal however, strange as it might seem if facts did not confirm it, we are not always sure of a true answer even from honest men. Their philosophy blinds them to the operations of their own minds. Still there is a way to settle the question of consciousness in cases in which a mere appeal to consciousness results in a false answer. I ask then, what is an act of choice? Consciousness must answer that it is a preference of one kind of good to another. I then ask why is there a given choice or preference? Consciousness must answer that such is my known or conscious capacity of good from the object chosen, such are my propensities toward it, such are the views which I take of the adaptation of the object to my happiness, that I choose it. Now I say that there is not a human being that is not in every act of choice conscious of all this. To be more particular, take a sinful choice as an example. What is it, and why is it? Is there a human being who knows what duty is who cannot tell from his own consciousness what the act is which is sin, and also the *why* and the wherefore of the act? Does he not know that the act is a preference of worldly good, and does he not know why he prefers this good? Does he not as a matter of consciousness, trace this act of choice to his estimate of the comparative value of the object as an act of his own, and to other inseparable preliminary acts of his own? And does he not trace this act and those connected with it, to his susceptibilities to that good, to the adaptation of the object to his happiness, and to the circumstances, perceptions, and so on, which resulted in this estimate? Does he not know that these things being as they were, he chose as he did? I say if man is conscious of any thing he is conscious of this, and that he is conscious of the reason why he acts as he does in every case. But as we have said, the reason why he acts as he does is the reason of the certainty of his act; i. e., with this antecedent this consequent would certainly follow. It is then out of place here to resort to philosophical arguments drawn from any other source than human consciousness and which contradict its decision. They are false, for consciousness is the highest evidence. Nor do I admit that there are any such arguments whose fallacy cannot be exposed. This is the next topic of inquiry.

To the view which has now been given the following objections deserve notice:

Obj. 1. It may be said that it is inconsistent with one fact, viz., divine influence in the production of holiness. I answer, that when human action is secured by a divine influence, the *circumstances* of the agent are changed, so that this case is properly included in the theory or doctrine now advanced. True it is, if this be an influence that secures holy action independently of and abstractly from the nature of man as a moral agent, and of motives, then indeed it will follow that God secures one kind of human action in a manner not recognized in the present theory. For there would be no truth or propriety in saying that all human action is secured through the nature and circumstances of man, including in these circumstances the motives to action, provided there is in fact one kind of action which is secured, without having any relation or connection with either man's nature or motives. But if this influence of God does not dispense with the nature of man as a moral agent, nor with the influence or relation of motives to moral action, but is an influence which is actually coincident with both—an influence which results in or secures this event, viz., that such a being as man is, yields to the motives to a given action which are presented to him, when without such influence he would not yield, and when with it he is not obliged to yield by physical necessity—then it is true in this case that the certainty of holy action is justly traced to the nature of man and to the circumstances in which he acts. For then this divine influence is as really one of the circumstances in which he acts, as are the motives in view of which he acts.

Obj. 2. It is said that independent action in creatures is a physical impossibility. This is argued first, from the nature of creatures as necessarily dependent for their actions on their Creator; and secondly, from the nature of their actions, considered as *effects* which must have a cause.

In reply to the first of these positions I remark, first, that it assumes what cannot be proved; viz., that God cannot create an agent, i. e., a being with powers to act. This argument, as presented by those who adopt it, wholly overlooks the distinction between the dependence on God *for the power* to act and dependence *for action* itself. Now let it once be admitted that man is an agent, and it is admitted that he has the power of acting. And although he is dependent on his Creator for the power to act, yet when it is conceded that he has received this power, it is the very perfection of absurdity to say that he is necessarily dependent for action; it is to say we have a power to act and yet cannot act, i. e., have power to act and have not power to act.

Again: the admission that *man acts* is inconsistent with the principle now under consideration. For what is action but power acting on the exercise or exertion of power? For example, what is an act of volition but an act of the power to will? If this be so, then it is plainly impossible that God or any being should be the author (in the sense of absolute efficiency) of any volition except his own. If it be admitted that there is an influence of one being upon another which causes or occasions the certainty of action in the latter, still the thing caused or occasioned is action, and is therefore in its own nature an event whose existence as truly and properly depends on the agent or actor as on him who occasions it, and of which, strictly and properly speaking, the agent is the author or efficient cause.* To suppose him to be the agent, and a moral agent, is to admit that he has adequate power to act not only as he does, but to act otherwise. Of course, to suppose that the event—viz., action—is necessarily dependent in the sense of natural necessity on an influence or efficiency *ab extra*, is to deny the power of acting to one who confessedly acts, and has the power to act as he does and otherwise; i. e., it is to admit and deny at the same time, that he has the power of acting. So that if we admit that *man acts* in the exercise of a power to act, it follows that instead of its being physically impossible that there should be independent action, i. e., instead of its being thus impossible that there should be action except it be produced by divine efficiency as its physical cause, it is impossible that there should be any such action thus produced in such an agent. For the very nature of action implies that it exists independently of *any physical efficiency* from without the agent who acts. Or thus:

To suppose action to be produced by an efficiency *ab extra*, as its physical cause, destroys the essential nature of the action by ascribing it not to the power of acting as its efficient cause;

* Vide Edwards' Miscellaneous Observations, p. 176.

for we have no conception of action, except that it is power acting. So that instead of its being impossible that there should be action independent of efficiency, *ab extra*, as its physical cause, it is impossible that there should be action which is not thus independent.

The proposition that man from his nature is necessarily dependent on God for his actions, is then not only inconsistent with the fact that man acts at all in any sense of the term, but the only argument used to support the doctrine rests on what may be confidently affirmed to be a false assumption, viz., that God cannot create an agent. And here I would add, that so far as I know, all who have maintained the doctrine of divine efficiency in the production of human volitions, have rested it on this gratuitous and false assumption.

In reply to the second principle on which the present objection rests, and which assumes that actions are *effects*, I remark—

First, that this language is objectionable, because it is liable to convey a meaning in which it cannot be applied to human action. The word *effect* as used in the present argument, in order that the least plausibility may pertain to the argument, must be used to convey a false meaning. The meaning must be that human actions are *physical effects*, i. e., events which exist by natural necessity, and of course the existence of all power adequate to their production except divine power, and of all power adequate to any other event, is denied by the terms of the proposition. Thus there is a *petitio principii* in the very outset of the argument. There is also an assumption, which if what we have been saying be true, is inconsistent with the essential nature of an action, while yet the reality of action is conceded. It is an assumption also equally inconsistent with the power of acting in man, since to suppose that actions are physical effects of divine efficiency, and of course that they take place by a natural necessity, is to deny the powers of moral agency to man, and thus to assert that a being acts who has no power to act, i. e., that a being who has power to act has no power to act.

It is to no purpose to say here that man has power to act when acted upon by divine efficiency or power. For still it is saying that he has not natural or physical power to act, that not being power to act, which cannot act without power or efficiency *ab extra* to aid it. Besides, when this power or efficiency is exerted, a given action not only will but must by a natural necessity follow ; none other can take place. But the freedom of human action is destroyed by the natural necessity of human action, and confessedly so by those whose scheme is now opposed.

PART III.—THE DIFFERENT KINDS OR SPECIES OF PROVIDENCE.

Kinds of providence incorrectly divided.—Providence considered as *mediate*, *particular*, *universal*, *ordinary*, and *extraordinary*.—Question of *special* providence discussed at length.

THE providence of God has been divided into *ordinary* and *extraordinary*, *common* and *special*, *universal* and *particular*, *mediate* and *immediate*.

1. *Ordinary* providence denotes that which is exercised in the common course of events through the medium of second causes. *Extraordinary* is that in which He departs from the common course of events, as by miraculous interference.

2. *Common* providence, that which pertains to the world; *special*, that which pertains to the Church.

3. *Universal* respects a general superintendence of all things; *particular* respects each individual being and event.

4. *Mediate* providence is that which is exercised in the use and by the efficacy of means; *immediate*, that which is exercised without the efficacy of means, though there may be some medium, as *a word*, &c.

This classification of the modes of God's providence is objectionable, as it makes distinctions without a difference, applies terms in a peculiar sense without definition, and affirms that to be of which there is no evidence.

First, it makes distinctions without a difference. Thus the ordinary providence of God is not distinguishable from that which is *common* in the true import of this term; ordinary providence as administered through the medium of second causes is *mediate;* and since the purposes of God extend to every event, his providence is both particular and universal, as these terms are commonly used.

Secondly, in the above classification terms are used in a peculiar sense without definition and without conveying a distinct meaning. Thus the terms *common* and *special*, as they are applied to the providence of God toward the world and toward the Church, are either used simply to denote the different objects of his providence, which is an unreasonable principle of classification, or they are used to designate some difference in the mode of his providence, without specifying what that difference is.

Thirdly, the above classification asserts that to be of which there is no evidence. Thus there is no evidence from the light of nature of a *common* in distinction from a *special* providence in the sense intended, or of an *immediate* providence, nor of a *universal* providence as distinguished from a particular providence.

For the purpose of simplifying this subject, I remark that the providence of God, or that government of God which we term providential, may be considered as *mediate*, as *particular* and *universal*, as *ordinary* and as *extraordinary*.

First, *as mediate*. That God has acted since the creation of the world *immediately* in the production of any event, that is, without the intervention of second causes, there is no evidence. That he has acted through the medium of second causes in such a manner as to preclude the belief of *the efficiency* of second causes and to command the belief of *his own direct agency*, natural religion cannot deny and revealed religion may fully establish.

Secondly, as *particular* and in the strict sense *universal*. This has been already proved in considering the extent of the divine purposes, and the certainty and manner of their accomplishment. There is however a sense in which it has been maintained that the providence of God is *not* particular, that he only exercises a general superintendence over the affairs of the world, without extending his purposes and his government to every event.

This theory is not only contradicted by what we have already proved respecting the extent of God's purposes, but is most obviously inconsistent with itself. So intimately connected are the events of this world; so entirely in many cases do events the most important in reality depend on the most trivial in appearance, that it is impossible to conceive that God should act as the governor of the world at all, unless his superintendence extend to every event which happens.

Thirdly. The *ordinary* providence of God is that which is

exercised according to certain stated regular laws of operation. The proof that God exercises such a providence is furnished by experience and observation.

Fourthly. The *extraordinary* providence of God is that in which he dispenses with, or departs from the stated regular laws of operation in the production of events. Thus admitting the facts on the authority of historical evidence, the deliverance of Israel from Egypt, and the conducting of them to the land of promise, is an instance of extraordinary providence. So also is every miraculous event.

Besides these kinds of providence another has also been supposed, commonly termed *special* providence, which, though not producing events strictly miraculous, is deemed extraordinary. It is supposed to differ from that kind of extraordinary providence by which miracles are wrought, as marking less decisively the mighty agency of their author, and to differ from ordinary providence, as satisfactorily evincing a departure from the regular course of events in reference to some special individual purpose.

Of this view of *special providence* I remark—

1. It cannot be proved to be impossible.

There is no inherent absurdity or impossibility in such an occasional mode of divine interference, and the assertion of its actual existence is to be received or rejected as the result of the examination of evidence.

2. There is no argument *a priori* which will support the doctrine. For no necessity for such special interposition to accomplish the purposes of God can be shown. He can arrange the succession of events in that luminous and exact order, from eternity, which shall supersede the necessity of the least variation, and so direct all, that each shall fall in at its appointed time and place.

3. There is no decisive proof of this doctrine from any actual phenomena.

Second causes do not in many cases so clearly and fully come under our observation, as to authorize us to believe in every case in which we cannot assign the particular cause of an event, that it was not produced in the regular way. In those cases in which we possess what we deem satisfactory knowledge of the whole combination of causes, we find no evidence of special interposition from the phenomena themselves. We never see a stone projected at another's head, arrested in its progress lest a wound should be inflicted, nor a falling tree upheld in its descent to furnish time for the escape of one beneath it. It is true that the want of such evidence is not decisive proof against the supposed special interposition. There *may* still have been a retardation in the motion of the falling tree for the purpose specified, which is not discernible by us. In such cases we cannot say positively that there has *not* been a special divine interposition; but we can say that any *decisive evidence* of such interposition is not furnished by any known phenomena.

4. There is a degree of presumptive evidence against this doctrine, from what we know of actual phenomena.

That there is a general continued uniformity in the phenomena of the world is an acknowledged fact. That such uniformity is designed and is even necessary to the creatures of God for the purposes of existence—that it is maintained regardless of particular consequences—must also be confessed. But such extensive prevalence leads to the belief of entire universality, so far as any reasoning from the nature of the subject can effect belief. At the same time it must be admitted that this extended uniformity is not decisive proof against the doctrine of special providence; for the maintenance of general uniformity with all its advantages is not inconsistent with occasional special interpositions. The more extensively however we explore, and the more minutely we are able to analyze the phenomena around us, the more are we confirmed in the belief that the regularity and uniformity of cause and effect pervades the whole system, and that a more extended and accurate acquaintance with what is now unknown would fully evince such regularity and uniformity to be universal. Such is the actual influence on our belief when we listen to a narrative of wonders, while to pronounce absolutely that any exception to this general course of providential events is an impossibility, would be a confidence of decision unauthorized by evidence. Should a wave next succeeding to that which had plunged the mariner into the boisterous ocean, bear him again to the place of safety at the very instant of his exhaustion and despair, it might be impossible to say the event was not the result of special divine interposition. But on the other hand, did we know all the causes which in their regular operation resulted in the event, we should feel no surprise on finding it explained by their ordinary influence. So far from it, if we reasoned as we do in similar cases of ignorance, we should confidently expect that such knowledge would furnish such an explanation.

The argument which probably has the greatest influence to conduct the mind to the belief of a special providence, is taken from the supposed peculiar tendency of the doctrine to awaken devotional feelings. It cannot be doubted that the tendency of the doctrine is to excite devotional feelings. The mariner preserved in the manner supposed, would doubtless find reason for devout gratitude to his deliverer in the supposed peculiar interposition of the Divine Hand. Nor would it be strange if in his ignorance of the second causes which were connected with his deliverance, and in the vividness of his joy while yet sensibly alive to the danger he had escaped, his reasoning should be governed more by his feelings than by a calm and dispassionate estimate of evidence.

The question however, is not whether the belief of this doctrine tends to awaken the delightful and amiable feeling of gratitude to our Divine Benefactor, but whether this tendency pertains to the belief of no other doctrine of providence.

It is undeniable that the view of Divine Providence which supposes special divine interpositions, has a tendency to gratitude superior to that which proceeds from some other conceivable theory of this agency. To suppose for example, that the ordinary events of providence are no expressions of the divine will, that they are merely results of a general providential machinery which produces effects regardless of the individual interests of men, is certainly to remove every ground for this virtue. Nor is it to be doubted that some such plan of providential dispensation as this with respect to all ordinary events, is that which is assumed, and with which is compared that of special interposition, when the superior tendency to awaken gratitude is so confidently assigned to the latter. The mind first removes from its conceptions, every such view of the ordinary providence of God as would tend to produce gratitude at all for blessings received, then imagines one which has indeed a direct and powerful tendency to such an effect, and on this assumption pronounces this tendency peculiar. But such a mode of ordinary providence is not properly introduced into the comparison. The doctrine of *ordinary* providence supposes a particular purpose of God respecting every event, and that while all events are brought to pass through the intervention of second causes, and as it may be, through a long and connected series of successive causes and effects, the plan in all its minuteness of arrangement lay in the Eternal Mind, and contemplated each event as the result of an eternal and unchangeable purpose. With such a system then, let the doctrine of special providence be compared in respect to practical tendency.

Two ministers were conversing together: one said he had met with a remarkable providence; for his horse had stumbled on the brink of a precipice, thrown him upon the very verge, and yet he was saved.

The other said that his life had also been preserved by a providence also remarkable; for his horse had not stumbled at all.

1. There is nothing in the scheme of an *ordinary particular providence* to render our gratitude less under the reception of blessings, than it should be on the supposition of a *special* providence.

That we may make a just estimate of the comparative practical tendency of the two schemes, we must suppose the value of the blessing in a given instance the same, for the inquiry respects not the value of a gift but simply the *mode* of conferring it. Now the real and the only foundation of gratitude to a benefactor is the manifestation of kindness *to us*, and the measure of gratitude we owe is in proportion to the measure of kindness manifested. In either of the cases under consideration, it must be admitted that there is a real manifestation of kindness, and of course a real foundation for gratitude. The question is, whether the measure of kindness manifested according to the scheme of special providence, is greater than that manifested according to the scheme of ordinary providence. If there be any difference in this respect, it must result from the mode of conferring the blessing. What then is there in this which bespeaks the difference? The one involves no greater sacrifice on the part of our Benefactor than the other; the blessing is the same in value to us in either case; it comes from the same hand, it is dictated by the same benevolence; that benevolence is shown to be equally intent on our welfare.

The blessing therefore bespeaks the same kindness in our Benefactor in one case as in the other, and therefore lays a foundation for equal gratitude.

It may be true that the belief of a special divine interposition in our own favor, may greatly heighten our gratitude when compared with the influence of our faith in an ordinary particular providence; but the reason may be, not in the different schemes of Providence, but in the weakness of our faith in that which we profess to believe, or even a measure of atheism that mingles with our faith or annihilates it, and thus excludes or nearly excludes from our conceptions the benevolent purpose and the agency of God. Indeed that the supposed, and it may be the real diversity of practical effect is wholly owing to these or other similar causes, will appear from an example which implies an equal measure of faith in the different methods of conferring benefits. Should a human benefactor, foreseeing our future wants, devise and put into operation a train of causes for our relief; should he steadily pursue his benevolent purpose, and should the designed benefit reach us at the very moment of our extremity, every one would feel his obligation to gratitude to be the same as had the blessing come by direct communication.

2. On the scheme of special providence there is far less reason for gratitude on the whole than on the scheme of an ordinary particular providence.

The real ground of gratitude in either case can be nothing more nor less than the manifested kindness of our Benefactor. But if such manifestation be *peculiar* to the scheme of special providence, it cannot pertain at all to that of ordinary providence. Thus the scheme of ordinary providence furnishes no foundation for gratitude at all, and thus that extended and uniform system of arrangement by which the Author of all is ministering his providential bounties to his dependent creatures is overlooked in our praise for some particular blessing imparted by an occasional and unfrequent interposition of kindness. It need not be told how inferior that tribute of gratitude to God must be which is produced by considering him as only the occasional benefactor of his creatures, compared with that view of his providence which in the whole of this beautiful system of things, makes it a ministration of particular and universal bounty.

3. On the scheme of ordinary particular providence there is a foundation for a higher and a purer gratitude than on the scheme of special providence.

In proportion as we discover the disinterestedness and strength of benevolent affection will our gratitude be augmented in intenseness and in purity. One may confer a kindness on us from sinister motives, and we shall not, we cannot feel real gratitude. He may do it from real affection, and yet that affection be evinced by the mode of its manifestation to be fitful in its nature or to be a mere matter of favoritism. In either case it might not unnaturally be regarded as unworthy of any thing more than a lawful joy in the advancement of our own well-being. But how much stronger and purer would our emotions be when called for by that disinterestedness and enlargement of affection, which should as it were, continually watch and promote our happiness in almost ceaseless acts of communication!

There is no reason to doubt that a belief in a special providence has a tendency to produce a sort of selfish congratulation and self-importance, as if we were objects worthy of that kindness which departs from the common course of things for our benefit, and to cherish within us the fond conceit that we are heaven's peculiar favorites. In the imagined special interpositions of his providence, God appears to us as peculiarly provident for us in some circumstances of peculiar necessity; but in that extended and yet minute communication of good which flows from the uniform laws of providential operation, while he is not less but more provident for us as individuals, he appears also in the unmistakable character of the benevolent provider of all. It is surely in the latter character that he pre-eminently manifests the purity and intensity of his benevolent regards for his creatures, and becomes pre-eminently worthy of their grateful adoration.

The conclusion is, that if it be too much to assert that there never has been any special interposition of Divine Providence in behalf of individuals, there is no decisive proof that there has been; that it is far more philosophical to believe that there has not been than to pronounce positively that there has.

APPENDIX—No. III.

ESSAY ON THE QUESTION—IN WHAT DIFFERENT RESPECTS MAY GOD BE SUPPOSED TO PURPOSE DIFFERENT AND EVEN OPPOSITE EVENTS?

PART I.—QUESTION EXPLAINED AND DISCUSSED.

Importance of the question.—Confused and unsatisfactory views in respect to it.—Question stated hypothetically.—Three suppositions.—Vindications of the propriety of arguing from the purposes of man to the purposes of God.—Supposition of a father.—Application to the present question.—Illustration to show the use of language.

To give the true answer to this question is of the highest importance, if we would form precise and correct views of certain controverted topics in theology. For if I mistake not, imperfect and false,or rather confused notions on this subject are the chief source of error and dispute. In the controversy between Calvinists and Arminians, some of the most important questions in debate turn upon accurate distinctions in regard to *the different respects* in which, or the *different reasons* on account of which, God may be supposed to purpose different and even opposite events. It is undeniable that events take place under the government of God, which are of a directly opposite nature and tendency. How this is consistent with the perfection of his character and government, especially if we suppose that his purposes extend to all events, has been deemed one of the most difficult of theological inquiries. Indeed nothing is easier than to present views of the purposes of God which are in the highest degree perplexing, for there seems to be hardly any subject on which truth and error can be so plausibly combined, through the ambiguity of language, or rather those elliptical forms of speech which usage sanctions. Nor is it too much to say, that apparently contradictory and inconsistent views of this subject, have been not unfrequently presented and zealously contended for, even when the best intentions have been shown.

No two events can be more opposite in their nature and tendency than holiness and sin; and to say that God purposes the existence of both, is *in words* at least to assert a contradiction. Whether such a *verbal* contradiction fairly involves a real contradiction, or a contradiction in ideas according to the true principles of interpreting such phraseology, may be doubted, or rather denied. In such cases of verbal contradiction, and they are not uncommon,* we are bound to inquire whether the language may not *according to usage* have different meanings when applied to different things, and whether by giving it different meanings, the writer is not exempted from the charge of contradiction. If so, the charge is not valid. Still, in my own view the use of such language without qualification or explanation, should be carefully avoided in subjects of controversy where advantage will be taken of merely verbal ambiguities, to misrepresent, or to become the occasion of misapprehending the real meaning of a writer. I would as far as may be, prevent the perversions of dishonesty, and force even prejudice to see. It is not however always true that dishonesty occasions contradiction on such a question. For there may not be—commonly there is not—that familiar acquaintance with the true method of using and interpreting such language which will in fact prevent misapprehension. Be this however as it may, when it is said that God purposes holiness and God purposes sin, the language is often interpreted in a manner which overlooks the fact that God may purpose opposite events in different respects or for different reasons. With such an interpretation, to say that God purposes sin, is equivalent to saying that he does not purpose holiness, and to say that he purposes holiness, that he does not purpose sin; and to say both, to saying that he purposes and does not purpose one and the same thing. But this is absurd and impossible. Since therefore these events are of such a nature that a perfect God cannot be supposed to purpose both for the *same reason* or in the *same respect*, then so to use language as to convey in fact such a meaning, is to leave the subject in inextricable embarrassment. On the other hand, if there can be *no different respects* in which God can be supposed to purpose these opposite events, then the universality of his purposes must be abandoned.

Similar remarks apply to natural good and natural evil when viewed as objects of the divine purposes.

---

* Gen. xx. 1; Josh. i. 13.

Now whether it be possible or not to relieve this subject of all embarrassment and difficulty, it is plain that the only way in which we can hope to succeed in such an attempt, is by showing that God may be supposed to purpose or rather to will different and opposite events in different respects. If the subject cannot be freed from absurdity and contradiction in this way, there is no way in which it can be. Indeed this is the only way in which Calvinists have ever attempted thus to relieve it. The question in respect to them therefore is, not whether God purposes holiness and sin in different respects, or for very different reasons, but what these reasons are.

It ought here to be remarked that absurdity and contradiction are charged in many forms upon the universality of the divine purposes, and that to exempt the subject from inconsistency in one form, is not of course to exempt it from inconsistency in another. What therefore we have to do is, to show that inconsistency is chargeable upon the doctrine in no form or manner whatsoever.

It ought also to be noticed that the present question is stated hypothetically, and that in answering it we are only making suppositions authorized by the known nature of the mental acts which are the subject of inquiry. This course is adopted not only because mere suppositions are sufficient for the purpose at which we ultimately aim, but also because we do not suppose any facts to be established in respect to the moral perfection or government of God. We are simply inquiring then what facts may be *supposed*, judging from the nature of things, so that these may be shown to be consistent with facts actually proved. For example, it is true that the purposes of God extend to all actual events both good and evil, and that nevertheless his character and his government are perfect. The design of the present suppositions is to show the entire consistency of these important doctrines.

I proceed then to specify several different respects in which God may be supposed to purpose different and even opposite events.

1. God may purpose an event as the means of a further end, —e. g., a moral system,—which has no value in itself or considered abstractly from its relation to consequences, because it is the necessary means of the greatest conceivable good, and

because he knows that though the greatest conceivable good will not be, yet that the highest degree of good which he can possibly secure will be the actual result.

It is here supposed that the highest conceivable good, or greater good than is possible in any other way, would result from the combined agency of God and his creatures directed to the production of good, and that some less degree than this, is all that is possible to God.

2. God may be supposed to purpose or to prefer, that an event which he knows will not take place *should take place* rather than its opposite, because it is good in itself as the necessary means of the highest conceivable and highest possible good, and because he knows that he can secure its existence to such an extent that a higher degree of good can be secured by it than by any thing else in its stead.

3. God may be supposed to purpose an event—i. e., to purpose that it *shall be* and to prefer that it *should be*—which is not the necessary means of the greatest conceivable good, but which is wholly evil in its nature, tendencies, and relations, because the evil is unavoidably incidental (so far as his power is concerned) to that system which is the necessary means of the highest conceivable and highest actual good, it being true at the same time, that he can bring so much good out of the evil, that the actual result will be the greatest good which he can secure.

Now it is believed that these three suppositions may be so illustrated and applied to the doctrine of the universality of God's purposes, as to remove all the difficulties and objections which have been supposed to encumber it.

With this view I shall attempt to illustrate the propriety of these suppositions. For this purpose I remark, that since we can reason concerning the consistency of God's purposes with one another, or with other things only from what we know of our own purposes, and since in this manner every possible question on the subject must be determined, it will follow, that *if man may purpose in different respects very different and even opposite events, so may God.* In other words, the existence of such purposes in the divine mind is possible, so far as the nature of the purpose is concerned. To this last remark, as expressing the fundamental principle on which our subsequent reasoning depends, I request particular attention. I do so, not only because it is desirable that a principle on which so much depends, should not if false be assumed to be true, but because its correctness in this particular application is denied by some, and because it is important that in respect to it the mind should be put entirely at rest. Here then permit me to turn your attention to the precise form in which the principle is stated. It is *not* then, that because man may and does purpose different and opposite events in the different respects or for the different reasons described, that therefore God *must*. Though I may have occasion to show hereafter that such is the fact in respect to God's providential and moral purposes, still in the present instance I do not assert this. The position which I *now* take is not the assertion either that such *is* or that such *must* be the fact, but simply that what is true of man in respect to the purposes in question MAY BE true of God. In other words, I assert not the *reality* or the *necessity* of the fact, but merely its POSSIBILITY. That I am justified in taking this position, or assuming the truth of the principle as now stated, on *a priori* ground, or from the nature of mental operations, is evident for the following reasons:

1. There is no proof that the principle is not true, nor that it is not applicable to the case under consideration.

If this be denied, it belongs to him who denies it to support his denial. And this he must do by showing from the nature of the subject, that what is true of man in respect to his purposes either is not or cannot be true of God in respect to his. This, on *a priori* grounds of argument, it may safely be said cannot be done. And this, as the subject is now presented, is the only ground proper to be taken by an opponent. Other modes of reasoning will be examined hereafter.

2. If our principle be denied, then it will follow that we can know nothing of the divine purposes, and of course nothing of God as a voluntary being.

For it is only by our knowledge of volitions, purposes, &c., in our own minds, that we know or can know what these are in another mind; and of course this knowledge is the only possible foundation of all our reasonings respecting God as a voluntary agent. If our principle be denied then, we not only cannot reason respecting what God is, but we cannot prove that there is a God.

3. Our principle, or rather the most absolute form of it,

viz., what is true of man's purposes *must* be true of God's purposes, has been constantly assumed in all reasonings on the subject.

The principle as I have stated it, *ever has been*, *is*, and *must* be assumed by the very men who oppose the views which I adopt. For whatever theory they adopt respecting God's purposes, they must assume the *possibility* of its truth, and this simply and solely on the ground *that it can be true in respect to the purposes of man.* For example, if it be said that God purposes sin as the necessary means of the greatest good, this must be assumed as possible with God solely, on the ground that similar purposes are known to be possible with man. By what mode of fair controversy then is it, that a principle is denied to us, which *is* and must be reasoned upon by our opponents?

4. If they deny the propriety of reasoning from human purposes to the divine, they must give some reason for it.

I know of none which can be even plausibly assigned, except that God is an infinite being, and that therefore it is rational to suppose that some things *may* be, and are widely different in respect to God's purposes from what are true in respect to those of man. That some things may be predicated of God's purposes which cannot be of man's, is undeniable. But it is equally undeniable that some things may and must be predicated of both, as common to both. It cannot therefore be just or true, on account of diversity in *some* respects, to affirm diversity in *all* respects, and thus to maintain that nothing is true of one which is true of the other. This would be to talk of the purposes of God without the least idea or notion of the things so called. The question then is, by what principle are we to be governed in determining this diversity and agreement? I answer, the principle and the only principle is, that so far as any known truth respecting the nature of either God or man obliges us to predicate any diversity of their purposes, so far it is to be done, but no farther. This principle must be admitted, or it must be said that we may predicate diversity and agreement without a reason, and at our own option. According then to this principle, the question is this: is there any known truth respecting God or man that obliges us to say that we cannot reason from the purposes of the human mind to those of the divine; that God *may* not, as man does, purpose different and opposite events in different respects or for different reasons—any thing which obliges us to say that God as a moral and providential governor *may* not or *cannot* purpose obedience and disobedience to his law, in the same sense or manner, and for the same diverse reasons in which man in these relations is ever regarded as purposing these different and opposite events? I leave this question to be answered by those who adopt the opposite view.

5. The consequences of denying our principle and of the course taken by those who deny it.

Some of the consequences of denying the principle I have adverted to, such as that it puts an end to all reasoning respecting God and his character. To this it may be added, on the supposition that we may reason on the subject, that it authorizes any premises and any conclusions. We have no knowledge of truth by which to test the premises; none to forbid the most monstrous conclusions. Whether God be benevolent or malevolent, just or unjust, sincere or insincere, fearful as are consequences of doubt on these points, we have no means of deciding. Without regarding him as the subject of those acts or states of mind which *in kind* are the same which under these names we ascribe to men, what are the things meant when these terms are applied to God? Any thing or nothing. Besides, purposes are what they are, as right or wrong, good or bad, just or unjust, according to *the reasons* in view of which they are adopted. If we deny this in respect to God's purposes—what can we know or believe in respect to them? Any thing or nothing.

But what is the course of our opponents? While they deny to us the right of reasoning from the purposes of the human mind to those of the divine, they do and must adopt this mode of reasoning themselves. They tell us, for example, that God purposes sin as the necessary means of the greatest good. Suppose I deny the possibility of this, as they do the possibility of the truth of my position; how can they show it to be possible that God or any being *can* purpose any event or this event for such a reason? Solely by appealing to the phenomena of our own minds. How came they to know that a purpose may respect its object, as the necessary means of greatest good, rather than as the necessary means of greatest evil? Plainly they never could have obtained the idea itself which their language expresses, except by their own mental operations. While then they reason on this principle, how do they apply it? They apply it to prove, and this by their own concessions, that what they call benevolence, justice, truth, mercy, and sincerity in God, are not what these terms designate in men! Here then we may ask, what do they mean? The answer is, nothing. But this is not all. They apply it, as can easily be shown, to prove that what is esteemed malevolence, injustice, insincerity, falsehood, cruelty in men, is benevolence, justice, truth, sincerity, and mercy in God!

I am then fully authorized to assume that if man *may*, for different reasons or in different respects, purpose different and even opposite events, God MAY also.

Suppose then a wise and good man agitating the question whether he shall enter the marriage state: suppose him to know that if he enters this state, he shall become the father of children whose highest usefulness and happiness he shall greatly desire: suppose him to know that his children will be sons, and that to give them a liberal education at a public seminary would result in their *highest conceivable* usefulness and happiness, provided they should maintain in every respect a virtuous deportment during the period of their education: suppose now that much as he desires their exemplary conduct, the parent knows that placed in these circumstances, these sons will, beyond his power to prevent it, be led into a temporary course of gross iniquity: suppose, however decisive and strong as the reasons are to regret their misconduct, that nevertheless greater evil would result from any other course of education or way of life than from this, while he can also counteract in such degree the appropriate consequences of their vices, and bring so much good out of the evil, that the actual result will be immeasurably greater good than he can accomplish by remaining single, or by placing his sons in any other possible circumstances;—now it is easy to see what would be the purposes of such a man, and how perfectly consistent they would be with each other and with the principle of true benevolence.

Let us apply the example to the illustration of the foregoing propositions.

1. To the first proposition.

It is obvious that such a parent would prefer a married to a single life, and the education of his sons to any other means of their usefulness and happiness in his power, because both events are the necessary means of the greatest conceivable good in the case, and because, though the highest conceivable good will not, yet the highest degree of good which he can happily secure will be, the *actual result.*

So God may purpose a system of moral government, i. e., to create moral beings with a given constitution and to place them in given circumstances under such a government, rather than to adopt any other means of good, because though such a means will not result in the highest conceivable good, it is still the necessary means not only of the highest conceivable good, but also of the highest degree of actual good which he can secure. For in the first place, it may be a very strong reason for adopting such a system, and other things being equal,it may be a decisive reason for adopting it, that it is the only means of the highest conceivable good. Not to adopt such a system might prove a source of great self-dissatisfaction, since he would not do what he could to put it in the power of creatures to secure their highest happiness; and though from the nature of the system it is within the power of creatures to prevent, and though they should actually prevent, through their own disobedience, the result preferred by their Creator, still there would remain to him one substantial ground of self-satisfaction. For were we to suppose the amount of actual good to others from some other system *equal* to that which results from this, still the fact that this only is fitted to secure the highest conceivable good, would be a decisive reason for adopting it, since in this case its author would have the happiness of reflecting, not only that he had secured as much actual good to others as he could secure in any way, but had also adopted that system which was perfectly fitted to secure the highest conceivable good. Other reasons might also exist for adopting such a system, viz., to evince his benevolence and thus to support his authority as a moral governor. But secondly, such a system God would prefer to every other because it would actually result in the highest degree of good which he can secure. This system then would have a double recommendation, viz., that it is fitted to produce the highest conceivable good,and also will result in the highest degree of actual good which God can produce. More decisive reasons for adopting it cannot be conceived.

2. In regard to the second proposition, it is obvious that the

parent would prefer that his sons should practice virtue in every instance instead of perpetrating crime, *because the former would be valuable or good in itself, and also the only means of the highest conceivable good in the case.*

In like manner God may be supposed to prefer holiness to sin in every instance in which sin takes place, i. e., to purpose holiness rather than sin in its stead, as good in itself and as the only means of the highest conceivable good.

3. In regard to the third proposition—

It is obvious that the parent would purpose the existence of the vices of his sons, and prefer it to the non-existence of that system from which they are inseparable. According to the case supposed, the vices are not *the necessary means* of the greatest good, since virtues in their stead would result in greater good. They are however unavoidable so far as the power of the parent is concerned, if he would secure the greatest actual good which he can secure. Now as he knows these vices will take place as the consequences of what he does if he adopts the course supposed, he purposes in this sense that they *shall take place;* and to say this in this sense, would accord with the common usage of language. This purpose also implies a preference that these vices should take place, when their existence as a necessary consequence of the best system is compared with the non-existence of that system.

Thus God may be said to purpose sin, i. e., to purpose that it *shall be* and to prefer that it *should be.* Here however we should fix our thoughts on the respect in which God may be said to have such a purpose in regard to sin. He does not then purpose its existence as good in itself; for by the supposition it is wholly evil in its nature, tendencies, and relations: not as the necessary means of the greatest conceivable good, for holiness is by our suppositions the means of the greatest conceivable good. In what respect then can God purpose the existence of sin? I answer, he purposes that it *shall be* as he purposes that system,—or to do that—from which he knows it will follow as a consequence, and he prefers that it *should be*, rather than not adopt that system.

The propriety of saying that God purposes sin in such a case and in such a sense, cannot be doubted. Nothing is more common when one designs a given action or course of action, knowing the necessary consequences, to regard him and to speak of him as designing those consequences. It were easy to show that the Scriptures abound in this use of language.

In Proverbs, vi. 8–36, to hate wisdom, knowing death to be the consequence, is said to be *loving* death, i. e., choosing it. An example may be given from common life. The good of a community requires the erection of a mill and a dam; but the water overflows and destroys my neighbor's land, and I knew that it would do so. He charges me with designing it, and it may be said and would be said, that knowing the consequences, I did design it or purpose it. But is this a malevolent or benevolent purpose? Plainly the latter. A thousand similar cases might be given to illustrate the principle that *a man is considered and said to design or purpose every known consequence of his actions.* Otherwise no proof from action of intention is impossible. Whether the action admits of a good intention or not, still it is regarded as *designed* or *purposed* for some reason. It is not in the above case to injure my neighbor, but as incidental to that which was the means of public good. To show that this language is authorized by usage, how natural in such a case would be the following dialogue: Says A to B, "You have erected that dam to destroy my fine meadow, and you meant (purposed) to injure me." "Oh, no," says B, "I did not mean—my object was not to overflow and destroy your meadow." "But you did," says A: "it was your object; for you knew if you built the dam it would be so." "True," says B, "I knew it would be so." "But," says A, "did you know it would be so and yet not mean it should be? Can you thrust a dagger into my heart, knowing that it will kill me, and say you did not mean to kill me?" "Why, no," says B, "but then I did not wish to injure you,—that was no part of my purpose." "But," says A, "how could you know that the meadow would be spoiled if you built the dam, and yet not mean to injure me by doing it?" "Why," says B, "the end for which I built the dam was the public good, and if I could have secured this and not injured you, I should have been glad of it with all my heart." "No," says A, "you knew the meadow would be spoiled, and yet constructed the dam, knowing this; and you *meant* it should be so, and that I should be a sufferer."

It is most easy to see that this controversy is founded wholly in words, and that the only reason why the controversy can be perpetuated is because the words *meant*, *purposed*, &c.,

may according to usage be applied to that which is a known consequence of what any one does? It is from this fact only that A's charge has any plausibility. For make now the distinction between purposing an event as the known consequence of what one does, and as an event which he regards as desirable either as good or the means of good to himself, and there could be no plausibility in the reasons assigned by A as a proof of B's *unkind* design.

The purpose of God that sin shall be, and the preference which the purpose implies, by no means alters the nature or tendency of sin. It is in no respect a better thing in its nature or tendency, because God cannot prevent its occurrence in the best system; for man can prevent it by personal holiness, and holiness in man when compared with sin and viewed as the act of man, is as far preferable to sin in the divine mind, as that which tends to the highest conceivable good is preferable to that which tends to the destruction of all good and the production of absolute misery. Nor is sin the better because God can counteract its proper tendency and bring good out of it; for this neither makes it good in itself nor good as the *necessary means* of good, since there would be more good without it if man would do what he can to prevent it. There would be more good without it than with it in every instance, if God could prevent it in the precise circumstances in which it *will take* place. But he cannot. While therefore God, like the parent in the example given, prefers in the most unqualified manner holiness to sin, and while universal and perfect holiness on the part of men in their circumstances would result in the highest conceivable good, and while by holiness on their part no purpose of God whatever would be painfully defeated or crossed, but God's will would be done, still as God is under the necessity either of not adopting that system which is the only means of the highest conceivable good, as well as of the highest amount of good which he can possibly secure, or of adopting that system with the existence of sin as its certain consequence, he may be said, having adopted the system, to purpose the existence of sin. So that as God is not disappointed or crossed by the existence of sin,—neither would he be painfully crossed by the existence of holiness.

Sin then, on the present hypothesis respecting its existence, is an event which God has in one respect purposed shall take place and prefers should take place; and this in perfect consistency with an unqualified preference in another respect that it should not take place. For what two purposes are more perfectly consistent with each other in the same mind, than a preference for right action on the part of others and a purpose of wrong action on their part, differing in the respects now supposed? What parent does not know that if his children live to years of accountability they will do wrong, and yet what parent does not prefer that they should in every instance do right? and yet what parent does not prefer at the same time the existence of wrong action in the case rather than to prevent it by the murder of his offspring?

What legislator in giving a system of laws to subjects, doubts whether there will be frequent instances of transgression, and knowing this, does not by the act of giving law (for where there is no law there can be no transgression) design that transgression *shall be* rather than not adopt a course which the general good demands? And yet who supposes that these facts are any proof that he does not prefer obedience to his laws in every instance? Whoever thought that discrepancy pertained to such purposes in a civil governor, or supposed that to prove his sincere preference for obedience to law, he must either give no law or resort for the prevention of crime to the indiscriminate massacre of his subjects?

So God's unqualified preference of holiness to sin is perfectly consistent with that purpose that sin *shall be*, and preference that it *should be*, which has now been supposed. Were he to resort to the necessary means of preventing sin in any case in which it does or will exist, greater evil would result from the change in the circumstances which would be requisite, than from permitting it to take place in present circumstances; for according to our hypothesis, greater good will be the actual result of the present system than would result from any change in it or from not adopting it.

PART II.—OBJECTIONS CONSIDERED.

1. To suppose that the highest conceivable good is impossible with God, is inconsistent with omnipotence.—2. God could have prevented some sins which he has permitted, and thus caused a less amount of sin.—3. The theory requires that less than the highest conceivable happiness should exist, and less glory to God.—4. Also that the glory of God as a moral governor should be diminished, so far as this depends on the obedience of his subjects.

The following objections may be made against the views maintained in the preceding discussion:

1. It may be said that the greatest conceivable good is possible with God; that so far as it can be supposed to depend on the prevention of sin, as an omnipotent being he must be able to prevent it; and that it is highly dishonorable to God to suppose otherwise.

The question is not, whether it be possible for God to prevent sin. This he might certainly have done by not creating moral beings who are beings capable of sinning. But the question is, whether it may not be impossible on the ground that it may involve a contradiction, that God should give existence to free moral agents and prevent all sin. Or thus, whether if it be possible for an agent to sin, it may not be impossible to prevent his sinning. I am aware that in the estimation of some, such an inquiry savors strongly of irreverence and presumption. I must however be allowed to ask, whether it is not equally irreverent and presumptuous to affirm that God could have prevented all sin in his accountable creatures but *would not;* or that a moral universe comprising the endless guilt and woes of hell is more desirable to a benevolent God, than one in which the purity and joys of universal holiness should reign without measure and without end? Surely it were no very palpable dishonor to God, to suppose him to prefer the universal holiness and consequent perfect happiness of his moral creatures, and that he should do all he can to secure such a result, and yet that some would rebel.

I here wish it to be distinctly noticed, that I do not affirm that God could not prevent all sin in a moral system, but simply that its prevention in such a system *may be* impossible to God. I shall have occasion further to consider this topic hereafter, and propose therefore briefly to reply to the present objection by showing that—

It cannot be proved that God could give existence to free moral agents and prevent all sin.

It will then be admitted that there are but two possible sources of argument on this point, viz., *facts* and *the nature of moral agency.* But facts furnish no evidence; for there is no instance in which there is a known certainty that sin will not exist in moral creatures, which certainty *may not* depend on *the system* with which all the sin that exists was certainly connected.

I ask, who can show that the continued holiness of elect angels and redeemed men does not depend on *the identical system* from which sin, in respect to divine prevention, is inseparable? Now it will be admitted that *the system* remaining exactly the same, i. e., the nature and circumstances of the beings remaining the same, all the sin which has taken place certainly would take place. The principle that the same causes or antecedents, in the same circumstances will be followed with the same effects or consequents, our opponents admit. It is then a matter of absolute demonstration, that to prevent the sin there must have been some change in the system in which it has taken place. But who can determine all the consequences of even the least change in the system? Even supposing God to have done that which would have prevented the sins of one individual, who can affirm that the requisite interposition for the purpose had not resulted in a vast increase of sin in the universe, even in the apostasy and augmented guilt of the individual himself?

Such is the universal attraction which unites the worlds which are scattered through infinite space in one system, that the annihilation of a single particle of matter would *instantly* cause some change throughout the material system; nor can it easily be told how long before the whole would rush to chaos.

Who can say that had God changed the moral system in one iota, that all heaven long ere this had not been in revolt? or that the consequence of any possible change had not been universal and endless sin in all moral creatures? No one. To what purpose then, is it to allege instances of the prevention of sin under a given system of influences, to prove that God could have prevented all sin under some other system? Facts then do not furnish a particle of evidence that God could have secured more holiness in a moral system than he has secured.

It is often inconsiderately supposed and asserted, that if God can prevent one moral being from sinning, he can another and all. This mode of reasoning, conclusive as it may be in respect to physical phenomena, has obviously no application to the actions of free moral agents. The very interposition which would be requisite to prevent the sin of one, might become the occasion of a universal and hopeless revolt.

I now remark, that *the nature of moral agency* not only furnishes no evidence that God could prevent all sin in moral agents, but precludes such evidence. It is not to be forgotten that whatever influence God may be supposed to use to prevent sin in moral agents, it must be consistent with the fact of moral agency and leave *the power to sin* unimpaired. How then can it be proved *a priori*, or *from the nature of the moral agent*, that he will not sin under any supposable influence, when he can do either right or wrong? These facts remain as premises to be reasoned from in the case. But what is plainer than that while these things are so, no inference can be drawn from the nature of the agent in respect to what he *will do.* The fact that he *can* do right is no proof that he *will* do right; for he *can* do wrong. And surely the fact that he *can* do wrong is no proof that he *will not* do wrong. How then can it be proved *a priori* that a being who can do wrong in counteraction of all that God can do to prevent him, will not do wrong?

But this is not all. The nature of moral agency precludes all proof that God can prevent sin in a system of moral agents. For as we have conceded, although it may be true that God by a given system of influence may render it certain that *some* moral agents will never sin, yet it does not follow from this that he could do this by any other system than exactly that with which the sin of others is certainly connected.

In any other system of an equal number of moral agents than that which God has adopted, it *may be* true so far as any evidence to the contrary can be adduced, that there had been more sin than in the present. Of course it may also be true that God in that other system could not have prevented this greater degree of sin. How then can it be *proved* that he could have prevented it? This would be supposing that what *may be true* in view of all the evidence in the case, i. e., that what *cannot* be proved to be *false*, *can* be *proved* to be false.

Again: it *may be true* so far as any evidence to the contrary is concerned, that God has prevented sin in the present system so far as he can prevent it in any. Of course it *may be true* that to suppose that he could have prevented it beyond what he has, would be to suppose that he could do what it may be true he could *not* do. When will it be proved that God could have done that which it may be true he could not have done?

Further: it *may be true* that to suppose God to have prevented sin in moral beings would involve a contradiction. For it *may be true* that he has done all he can do to prevent sin in these beings without destroying their moral agency. And to suppose him to prevent sin in moral beings by destroying their moral agency, is to suppose him to prevent sin in moral beings who are not moral beings.

But it may be said that God could foresee every future cause of sin, and could have so arranged events as to prevent the occurrence of every such cause: for example, he could foresee and could have prevented the existence of that particular temptation which was the cause of the sin of our first parents; and if it be supposed that some other occurrence would have led them into sin if this had not, that he could have prevented this also, and so on, and thus have kept sin out of the world—I answer, that in preventing the occurrence of such causes of sin he must either remove or prevent every thing which can be a cause of sin, i. e., every thing of the nature of inducement or temptation, or he must not. Should he remove every such thing, he would destroy the possibility of moral action in man, since if there were no good which man could choose rather than God, there could be no preference of God to other good; and of course no moral action would in such a case be possible. Should he on the other hand not remove or prevent every such cause of sin, then he would leave that which might in the event prove the cause of sin beyond his power of prevention. If it here be said that he might have permitted some inducement to sin to remain, yet so trivial in itself and so nearly nothing compared with the inducements to holiness that it should in no instance prove the occasion of sin—I answer, that the objector does not know nor can he prove that it could be done. For how can he know or prove *a priori*, that a being who can sin will not sin, however trifling the inducement? The susceptibilities of man to good, be the source of that good what it may, or the degree of good which he is capable of deriving from it what it may, are capable of indefinite excitement, or of such as shall prove the occasion of sin; and how such a being will act depends more directly on the degree of excited propensity toward an object than on the real or comparative value of the object. If it be said that God might have given different susceptibilities to man—I answer, that this supposition only turns us back to a similar alternative to that just stated, viz., that man's susceptibilities must be such that he can or that he cannot sin. If he cannot sin he cannot be holy; and if he can sin, who can prove *a priori* that he will not?

Besides, facts are altogether against the theory of the objectors; for both angels and men have sinned in circumstances in which the inducements to sin were comparatively slight. It was certain beforehand that they would sin in these circumstances, and that God could not have rendered it certain that they would not sin, for this would involve the absurdity of rendering the sin certain and not certain at the same time. How then can it be proved that by any change of circumstances such beings would not sin? If insignificance of motive would render the prevention of sin certain, why did it not in these cases?

After all, the objector may still insist that the supposition that God could not prevent all sin in a moral system is highly dishonorable to God—it is to limit the Holy One of Israel. I answer, it is not dishonorable to God to suppose that he cannot accomplish contradictions; that he cannot perform impossibilities in the nature of things; nor is it dishonorable to God to suppose that it *may be* impossible to him to do what *may* involve a contradiction. And I challenge any one to show that it is not an impossibility—that it would not in fact involve a contradiction to suppose that God could prevent all sin in free moral agents. Such as we have shown may be the fact. Our opponents cannot show that it is not. Must we then, to honor God, assert that he can do that which for aught can be shown to the contrary, may involve contradiction and absurdity? Is God to be honored by the assertions of mere ignorance? Is it essential to render him that homage which is his due, that we assert that to be true of him which for aught that can be shown to the contrary may be utterly false?

It ought here to be further remarked, that such a view of the subject does in no respect limit the power of God. In the assertion that *it may be* impossible that God should prevent all sin in a moral system, I refer merely to an impossibility which may exist in the nature of things, and of course not to the want of any conceivable power in God; to an impossibility to which power bears no relation, and with which it has no concern. If greater power existed it would not remove the supposed impossibility, and to talk of the want of power or a limitation of power in God as the reason why he does not prevent sin, is, on the present supposition, like talking of a limitation of his power as the reason why he does not make a part equal to the whole.

But further, if it still be insisted that my supposition does limit the power of God, so does the theory which I oppose, and in precisely the same manner. It supposes that God *cannot* secure the greatest good without the existence of sin. On both schemes there is an impossibility involved, and an impossibility founded in the nature of things. And why is it more dishonorable to God to suppose an impossibility resulting from the nature of moral agency, than to suppose an impossibility resulting from the nature of sin? Why is it more dishonorable to God to suppose that he cannot prevent a free agent from sinning, than to suppose that he cannot produce the greatest good without sin? Why is it more dishonorable to suppose that God cannot do what it may be true is impossible in the nature of things, than to suppose that that may be true or is true which cannot be true, viz., that sin is better than holiness?

Once more: the theory opposed dishonors God not only by limiting his power, but according to a concession which must be made, by limiting *his goodness.* If it be true that the more holiness the more happiness, as I shall attempt to show hereafter, then God, who according to the theory opposed could produce universal holiness, could also produce universal happiness, or more than he has produced, but *would not.* But it is essential to the perfect goodness of any being that he produce all the happiness he can produce. How directly then and unequivocally does the theory now opposed impeach the *goodness of God!*

It is then an assumption wholly gratuitous, that God could have prevented all sin and secured universal holiness in a moral system—an assumption far more dishonorable than the supposition that he could not, and a mere supposition is all that I now present, and all that my purpose in the present discussion requires.

Obj. 2. It may be said that God could have prevented at least some sins which he has not prevented, and that thus there had been less sin than actually exists; as for example (for I here concede to the objector the privilege of an appeal to Revelation), if the mighty works done in Capernaum had been done in Tyre and Sidon, they had repented. I answer, that the supposition which I have made does not imply that God could not have prevented each and every sin which has taken place or which shall take place. But it is supposed that he could not have prevented any sin which has taken place or which shall take place, in the *precise circumstances* of its actual occurrence; and it will be granted that it was certain that all the sin which has taken place would take place. It is further supposed that God could not have prevented all sin; for although it be admitted that he could have prevented by a change of circumstances each and every sin that has taken place, it is no proof that he could have prevented other sins in their stead. And if it be said that he could have brought sinners to repentance, and thus have prevented subsequent sins, this may be admitted; and yet the change in circumstances necessary to such prevention might have been immeasurably for the worse, since the effect might, beyond his power of prevention, have been a hundred-fold more sin on the whole. Had he brought Tyre and Sidon to repentance by miraculous interposition, it might have occasioned a revolt in heaven; yea, these very individuals might have apostatized, and the result to them have been immeasurably greater evil. Indeed, had the circumstances of men and angels been such that they had continued holy to the present hour, there is no proof that the final result had not been universal sin and hopeless impenitence. It may have been, so far as God's power to secure the result is concerned, indispensably necessary to the perpetuated holiness of elect angels and redeemed men, that they should encounter exactly that degree of temptation and trial, with all its results and circumstances, through which they and their ruined companions shall have passed. It is therefore supposable not only that God could *not* have kept all sin out of his moral creation, but that to have changed the circumstances of men or angels in the least respect would have resulted in immensely more sin than has resulted from their actual circumstances.

Obj. 3. It may be said that according to the theory now advanced, less happiness than the highest conceivable will exist, and that therefore less glory will accrue to God from his works than the highest. I answer, that the glory that will accrue to God from his works depends not on the degree of happiness actually secured, but on the fact that *he* has secured the greatest amount which he *can* secure. Now, according to our supposition, God has done all he could do to secure the greatest conceivable good, and this so far as it depends on the agency of creatures; and not only so, but he has done that which will secure the greatest actual good which he can secure. And in what way could God make a fuller display of his benevolence —in what way appear more glorious? Must he secure more good than he can secure to make a perfect display of his benevolence, and to bring to himself the highest degree of glory?

But, says the objector, if according to the present theory creatures had done what they ought to have done and could have done, there would have been more holiness and more happiness, and thus greater glory to God: I ask how? In that case God had done no more than he has now done, and as the degree of his glory depends on what he does in manifestation of his benevolence, and as he would have done nothing to manifest his benevolence in that case which he has not done already, the degree of his glory could have been no greater.

If for the sake of giving force to the objection, the objector should suppose another being able to secure and actually securing the highest conceivable happiness, and ask whether such a being would not be more glorious in consequence of such a result, than the God whom I suppose, I answer, undoubtedly. But why? Because he would show himself possessed of power which does not belong to the latter, and not because he would show himself possessed of greater benevolence; for to secure the highest happiness the latter shows himself disposed if he could, and the question wholly respects his glory as this consists in the display of his benevolence. Besides, the objection proceeds on a supposition which is inadmissible, viz.: that greater power may pertain to another than that which I suppose to belong to God; for the present theory implies that infinite or the greatest conceivable power cannot prevent sin in the moral creatures of God. Of course his glory cannot be diminished by the fact that he does not display greater power. Indeed the greater power supposed in the objection is power to effect impossibilities, which can add nothing to the glory of one who is supposed to possess it.

But I ask the objector, on what ground or principle the highest glory accrues to God, according to his scheme? He says, on the principle that God produces the highest conceivable good. I then ask, how does he secure this result? And here he must admit that he does not secure it by the perfect holiness of creatures, and of course that the glory of God suffers in this respect as much on his scheme as on mine. But he will say, God produces the highest conceivable good, by the existence of sin, which is the necessary means of that good. But I ask, why does this bring the highest glory to God? He says, because he produces the greatest good that can be produced. But I ask again, why does producing the highest degree of good that can be produced, bring to him the highest glory? The only answer is, because he produces all the good he can produce; for it is plain that if we suppose him to produce all the good he can, and other agents to add to that amount, this would not add to his honor or glory. So that on the objector's scheme as well as on mine, the highest glory accrues to God on the principle that he secures all the good he can. On this point the only difference between us is, whether the highest conceivable good is possible to God, though we may differ so far as the present objection to my theory is concerned. And on the supposition that the highest good is not possible to God, which is implied in my theory, I only ask who can imagine the glory of God to be the less because he does not secure it, i. e., because he does not perform impossibilities?

Obj. 4. It may be further said, that God as a moral governor is glorified by the intelligent voluntary homage of obedience to his law on the part of subjects, and that so far as such obedience does not exist, so far his glory is diminished. In reply, I would remark, that this objection differs from the former in assigning a different reason why the highest glory does not accrue to God according to the present theory, the former assigning the diminution of happiness, the latter the diminution of the homage of obedience. In answer to this objection, I would say that while it is to be admitted that the obedience of subjects honors God as a lawgiver, it is also true that equal honor or glory accrues to him in this character from the execution of the penalty on transgressors, or from sustaining his authority in any other way. Now as all the honor or glory of God as a moral governor depends on the simple fact that his authority is sustained, and as this is the only respect in which they can be affected by the obedience or disobedience of subjects, so if they disobey and thus do what they can to dishonor him, he has the remedy in his own power. He can still sustain his authority either by punishment or in some other way, as he pleases. And since to sustain his authority by his own acts is equally honorable to him as to sustain it by the obedience of subjects, disobedience cannot lessen his authority, and of course cannot lessen his glory.

PART III.—ADDITIONAL OBJECTIONS.

5. According to this theory God cannot be as happy or blessed as if there were no sin.—6. That sin is the necessary means of the greatest good is proved decisively on two grounds.—Otherwise God could not purpose its existence.—By mercy he can produce greater happiness than had there been no sin.—7. A high degree of temptation necessary to the highest degree of holiness, and of course to the highest happiness; and this is the reason why God has permitted sin.

Obj. 5. It may be said that according to the present theory, God cannot be as happy as he would be were there no sin.

Ans. This depends on what according to the present theory would be, were there no sin, or on what the non-existence of sin necessarily involves. And here it is obvious, that according to the present theory the non-existence of sin involves either the non-existence of the present system or the prevalence of universal holiness. If the objection contemplates the non-existence of the present system, then it has not the shadow of plausibility. For, according to our theory, the very reason why God prefers that sin should be rather than not be, is that its prevention by him involves the non-existence of the present system. And surely God cannot be rendered unhappy by the being of that which, all things considered, he prefers should be rather than not be. If God prefers that sin should be and purposes that it shall be rather than not create that system from which it will unavoidably to himself result, he cannot be unhappy that he did not prevent the sin, by not creating the system.

But I ask the objector on what scheme he can show that God is as happy as he would be were there no sin? His answer is, that sin is the necessary means of the greatest good, and is therefore, all things considered, really desirable, and of course cannot lessen the happiness of God. But the theory now maintained assigns as good and sufficient a reason why the existence of sin does not lessen the happiness of God compared with its non-existence. According to the objector's theory, God purposes the existence of sin, rather than its non-existence because it is the necessary means of the greatest good. But if God can purpose the existence of sin rather than its non-existence on any other account or for any other reason than as being the necessary means of the greatest good, then its existence will be equally remote from impairing his happiness. But as we have shown, an event which is neither good in itself nor good as the necessary means of good, may be truly purposed of God on another account, viz., that it is to him unavoidably incidental to that which is the necessary means of the greatest good. Sin then, viewed as thus incidental to the best system, would be as truly purposed of God, all things considered, as were it the necessary means of good. There is therefore as good a reason assigned why the happiness of God is not impaired according to the theory now maintained, as according to that which is opposed to it. Indeed the general reason is the same according to both theories, viz., that the existence of sin, the non-existence of which would impair his happiness, is truly desirable, all things considered. This must, it would seem, settle the question. For it is conceded that the happiness of God depends on the fact that all things are as he purposes they shall be, all things considered. The specific things given as the supposed reason for willing the existence of sin are indeed different: *the thing considered* in the one case being the relation of sin to good *as the necessary means of it*, and *the thing considered* in the other being *the existence of the best system.*

But it may be said that according to the present theory, if the non-existence of sin be supposed to involve the existence of perfect and universal holiness *under the present system*, then

God would be more happy than he now is. I answer, that so far as God's happiness depends on or results from, or is any way affected by the moral conduct of creatures, he would unquestionably derive more happiness from their holiness than from their sin; and would therefore, as the present theory maintains, greatly prefer their holiness under the present system to their sin. It is further admitted that there is no sense whatever in which God can be properly said to derive happiness from the existence of sin, any more than a benevolent physician derives happiness from the disease which he cures; although it be true that he can bring good out of the evil, and that the only proper and legitimate consequence of it to him is an actual and great diminution of his happiness. Nor can this conclusion be avoided according to the scheme of our opponents; for they maintain that sin is truly contrary to the divine will; that God is exceedingly *displeased* with it; that he abhors it as the worst of evils, &c., &c. But how can this be and yet God be as *well pleased* with sin as with holiness? Say what they will of it as the necessary means of the greatest good, if they also say as they do, that it is contrary to his law or his revealed will, then it is contrary to a real preference or choice of God; and it belongs to them as well as to us to show how the will of God can be violated and he be perfectly happy. If they say he can be, then they have answered their own objection to our theory. If they say his law is not an expression of a real preference of holiness to sin, it is asserting that God has given no law. If they say that this will or preference of God cannot be violated without impairing his happiness, then they admit our conclusion; viz., that so far as the happiness of God depends on the moral conduct of creatures, his happiness is greatly impaired by their sin compared with what it would be were they holy.

This objection may be presented in another form. It may be said that according to the present theory, God must be *defeated* or *crossed* in *some* of his purposes, and thus his happiness must be impaired; for that a being should be really *crossed* in his purposes without suffering that which is disagreeable to him, or that which is contrary to joy and happiness—even pain and grief—is impossible. In proof of this it may be further said, that as God, according to the present theory, prefers holiness to sin in man, and also purposes the existence of sin, it must follow that if holiness does not and sin does take place, his preference of holiness to sin is crossed, and that if holiness does and sin does not take place, his purpose that sin shall take place is crossed; and that as either sin or holiness must take place, God must be crossed in some of his purposes and thus be made unhappy.

This objection thus stated, is presented with so much plausibility derived from the form in which it is put, that I choose to examine it as thus presented. I answer then in the first place, that God is not and cannot be *painfully* crossed in his purpose that sin shall be, by the non-existence of sin and the existence of holiness. God's purpose that sin shall be, and his preference that it should be, are in view of its inseparable connection with the best system; i. e., he prefers the existence of sin to its non-existence, as the latter involves the non-existence of the best system. The real object of desire and preference then—that is, the good thing on which the happiness of God depends and in view of which he forms the purpose that sin *shall be*, is the existence of this system. If therefore the system exists, God is not painfully crossed, whether the consequence be holiness or sin in creatures. It is true, if sin did not follow he would be in one sense disappointed; that which he knew would follow as the consequence of the system, would not in fact follow. Still, in such disappointment there would be nothing painful, since all that is necessary to the full gratification of his purpose respecting sin is, that *the given system exist.*

But, says the objector, if sin does not take place, God is not only disappointed in the unimportant respect now admitted, but his purpose that sin shall take place is certainly defeated and crossed; and how can this be and he not be unhappy on this account? I admit that if sin does not take place, his purpose that it shall, is in one respect defeated and crossed; i. e., the thing purposed does not take place. But the question is whether, if this were to be so, it would mar the happiness of God at all? Whether it would or not depends wholly on another question, viz.: whether in regard to the real reason or object of the purpose he is or is not gratified; for if the object of the purpose is secured, there can be no unhappiness resulting from the defeat of the purpose in any other respect. Here then is the turning-point. Now I readily concede that if God purposes that sin shall take place, either because he esteems it good in itself or as the necessary means of good, then if it does not take place, he must be painfully crossed and defeated in his purpose. But on the other hand, if he does not purpose that sin shall take place in either of these respects, i. e., if he does not purpose it either because it is good in itself, or because it is the necessary means of good, but purposes it in view of good which does not depend on the existence of sin, then he is not painfully crossed if sin does not take place. How can he be? There is in sin nothing that is good or desirable in any respect or sense whatever. It is neither good in itself nor good as the necessary means of good; he does not so esteem it. And I ask in what other respect any thing was ever esteemed or called good? But according to the present theory, God has not purposed sin as good in either of these respects now specified, and of course has not purposed it as good in any respect whatever. How then can he be painfully crossed, if in the present system sin does not take place? The reason then why God is not and cannot be painfully crossed by the non-existence of sin in the present system is obvious, and is this, viz.: *he does not purpose sin in view of any good dependent on its existence.* He purposes sin only for the sake of the present system, of which it is to him an unavoidable consequence. If then this system exists, all that exists which he regards as desirable in forming the purpose respecting sin. But the system does exist, and whether sin or holiness follow, God cannot be *painfully* crossed in any purpose respecting the existence of sin. In the amputation of a limb, would the patient be painfully crossed by the disappointment of suffering no pain?

I now proceed to examine the other part of this objection. It is said, that if holiness does not exist, God according to the present theory is painfully crossed in his purpose or preference that it should exist. Here then I admit (nor can I well suppress the pleasure I feel in uttering what I regard as truth so honorable to God and so important to man) that God, so far as his happiness is or can be effected by the moral conduct of his creatures, is painfully crossed in his purpose respecting holiness by the existence of sin in the present system. According to the theory which I advocate, God purposes that sin *shall be* and prefers that it *should be* rather than not create and perpetuate the present system; and this is the *only* reason of his purpose respecting sin. Since therefore the system does exist, there cannot be a reason why he prefers sin to holiness in the present system. On the contrary he must, so far as his happiness is or can be affected by the moral conduct of creatures, prefer holiness to sin in the present system. Nor is it necessary, speaking in the manner in which usage in analogous cases would authorize us to speak, to qualify this position as I do. For it is always assumed in common parlance, that when a lawgiver expresses his preference of moral action, it is in view of the manner in which such action will affect his happiness in the circumstances in which his law is given. Assuming these things then to be fairly implied, it may be said with exact truth, not that God does not purpose sin, rather than the non-existence of the present system, but that he prefers holiness to sin—that he has no purpose or pleasure at all that men should sin rather than be holy—that he would that all should be holy rather than sin—and that he regards every transgressor with anger, with indignation, with grief; or that when holiness does not and sin does exist, God in the language of the objection is painfully crossed in his purpose.

But let not the objector triumph in this concession, as if the perfect blessedness of God were marred by the existence of sin. True it is, according to the present theory, that a source of real unhappiness to God is created by sin; of unhappiness as great as a perfectly benevolent mind can feel in view of the worst of evils. The feelings of God toward every object are such as accord with the nature of the object, and that he should have any other feelings toward sin than those now ascribed to him, would be alike inconsistent with his holiness, his benevolence, and his immutability. When sin actually exists, God would, so to speak, rather cherish these emotions than any other, in view of its nature. He would be more unhappy in any other than in these, *for* these are the only emotions toward sin which he can regard in himself with self-complacency.

These remarks may appear to some strange and paradoxical. The subject which they respect is one which appears to me to have claimed too little consideration from those who have attempted to develop the nature of our pleasurable and painful emotions. I cannot here digress to a discussion of this topic. I would ask however, whether it be possible that a holy, benevolent mind should feel complacency toward sin or be merely indifferent? And if not, what must the feelings of such a mind be on any scheme toward an object so hateful, except those which are opposite to joy and happiness, and which are truly spoken of as painful and unhappy? Doubtless the fitness of all such emotions to the nature of their objects and a consequent approbation of this fitness in such a mind, alleviates their painfulness; and while every such mind would prefer to be the subject of these emotions rather than their opposites in view of the object of them, still who can suppose that here is not a choice of evils or that the emotions awakened by witnessing the beauties of holiness were not immeasurably more delightful? But while I maintain that the happiness of God is affected by the moral conduct of creatures and painfully impaired by the existence of sin; while I might say that no language can too strongly describe his painful emotions toward it when compared with holiness, even that which represents him as *abhorring* iniquity and *shuddering* at the sight of it, still it will not follow that God is not perfectly blessed according to the true import of this language.

I say according to the true import of the language. For it must be granted by my opponents, that by the *perfect blessedness* of God cannot be meant that which excludes every thing of the nature of regret and sorrow in every sense of the terms. It is even admitted on the scheme which I oppose, that God *wills* or *prefers* holiness to sin in themselves considered. The error is not in this statement, but in saying that also which amounts to the position that he prefers sin to holiness, by saying that sin *is the necessary means of the greatest good.* Of course this will of God is crossed and *painfully* crossed by the existence of sin. Of course God's *perfect blessedness*, if the phrase denote that which excludes every thing of the nature of regret or of painful feeling, is unavoidably impaired. In other words, God is not and cannot be perfectly blessed in this sense of the phrase. There is no avoiding this while the principle in the present objection is assumed, viz., that no being can be crossed in his purposes without painful emotion. Nor is this all. It must be admitted that sin is *an evil* in some respect and in some degree. But so far as it is an evil it must be regarded and felt to be an evil by that Being who views things and feels toward them as they are. And further, if the objector should insist that God is *perfectly blessed* to the exclusion of all painful emotion in view of sin, then again he denies the principle of his objection; and if God is in no respect made unhappy in view of evil, then this principle relieves from his objection my theory as well as his own. It will not then be pretended that God is perfectly blessed, in the sense which excludes every thing of the nature of regret or unhappiness. So far from it, that on every possible scheme it must be confessed that the perfect blessedness of God cannot be what it might be conceived to be, were there no impossibilities in the nature of things. Else why did not God create a universe of beings, each of whom should be in nature, character, and blessedness, the nearest possible image of himself? All therefore that can be meant by the *perfect blessedness* of God, is *that degree of blessedness* which is possible in view of the impossibilities in the nature of things, or the highest degree of happiness which in the nature of things it is possible to God to secure to himself.

In this sense, and it is the only proper sense of the phrase, it is maintained that while the purpose of God in respect to holiness and sin is painfully crossed, God is perfectly blessed. For in the first place, according to this theory, sin which is a source of real unhappiness to God, is to him an unavoidable consequence of the best system. The gratification of having given existence to the best system, the best even with sin as the certain consequence, is that of having adopted the best means for the best end in his power to accomplish. God therefore must be happier in the adoption of this system than by not adopting this or any other. Though holiness does not exist, or rather though God *cannot* secure the existence of holiness to that degree which he prefers, still having adopted the best system—that which will result in the most holiness and happiness which he can secure—God has accomplished all the good he can, and must of course be as happy as a benevolent God can be; in other words, *perfectly blessed* according to the true import of this language.

The principle will be seen by illustration to be one of the most familiar and universally admitted.

There is such a thing as happiness from one source, which, though it does not annihilate the attendant pain which results from another, may be such in degree, that the happiness of the subject on the whole may be far greater than if the pain were to be prevented by the necessary means of prevention; such that a percipient being would prefer that the two sources of pleasure and of pain should both exist, on account of the superior degree of pleasure from the former, which would not exist if the latter did not; i. e., in a change of circumstances. Thus the martyr who, with the earnest of heaven in his soul, sings amid the fires of persecution, though the anguish of the burning is felt, may be happier than at any previous hour of his life. Thus too the benevolent physician who feels the pain he inflicts in amputating the limb of a patient, may also feel a pleasure in performing the operation as the known means of life and happiness to one whom he loves, which shall render it the happiest act of his life. The happiness of a benevolent being depends *not merely* on the happiness which *exists*, but greatly on the fact that he has produced it; and still more if he has produced it by direct instead of indirect agency.

So too the Divine Being in establishing the present system of things, with sin as its known consequence, may contemplate his works with higher joy than he could have known had he adopted any other system or not adopted this, though by not adopting any system of creation he had been freed from the positive unhappiness which sin occasions him. And though he had been happier in the present system of things had holiness existed instead of sin, yet it is easy to see that in its establishment he has a source of higher happiness on the whole, than had sin been prevented by not adopting the system. At any rate God is as happy as he can be, so far as his power to render himself happy is concerned, and the deficiency of his happiness resulting from the existence of sin or non-existence of holiness is one which he could not prevent. And I ask on what theory it may not have been so; i. e., on what theory may not the happiness of creatures be less, and of course the happiness of God less, than we can imagine he might have secured were there no impossibilities to him in the nature of things? Suppose that God had created a universe of moral beings each of whom should have been in his constitution the nearest possible image to God himself; and suppose now that each should fulfill the benevolent design of his creation, had not this been a happier universe than the present? But to have given existence to such beings might have been to produce a system the worst possible, since in the nature of things there might have been an absolute impossibility that God should prevent the fearful perversion of powers so nearly like his own. Now I ask would not God have been more happy in a universe of such exalted beings, were each to direct his powers to the production of good, than in any other? And is he therefore, on the supposition that he could not prevent the perversion of their powers, not completely blessed because he did not create such a universe? But if God, though he did not create it, may be completely blessed although such holiness and happiness as we suppose, do not exist, why may he not be completely happy in the present system, although all the good does not result from it which might, had creatures done their duty? It may be, for nothing surely appears to show that the evil which is incidental to the present system,is not immeasurably less than would in fact have pertained to any system, and the amount of good greater than would in fact have pertained to any other which God could have established. All therefore that we can say is, that real imperfection or evil may in the nature of things, so far as his power is concerned, pertain to the creation of God. If then God has given the highest perfection to the present system which he could give, and thus secured to himself the highest happiness which he could secure, and yet there is not as much happiness in the system as there might be, and God not as happy as he might be had creatures been holy, then we are obliged to conclude, either that God cannot in the nature of things secure to himself perfect and complete happiness, or that he is perfectly and completely happy by securing to himself the highest happiness which he can secure. If it be said that according to the present theory the former is true,—viz., that God cannot secure to himself perfect and complete happiness,—so it is according to every other. For though we suppose sin to be the necessary means of the greatest good, yet if holiness be good in itself,God is not perfectly happy, since on this supposition there is an impossibility in the nature of things,—viz., that that which is good in itself should also be the necessary means of the greatest good. Both cannot be. There is therefore real evil in the system. If the latter be true, the present objection is groundless. Here then the question turns wholly on what is meant by perfect happiness in God. If that and that only is perfect happiness in God which is the greatest that we can conceive of on the supposition that there were no impossibilities in the nature of things to hinder or prevent happiness in any degree, then God is not completely happy, for there are such impossibilities, and of course it is not within the power of God to render himself thus happy. But if the highest degree of happiness which God can secure to himself, without effecting impossibilities in the nature of things, is perfect happiness, then is God perfectly happy according to the theory now maintained. The only ground of what can be called imperfection in the happiness of God on this scheme, are the impossibilities in the nature of things; and such imperfection in his happiness is no more inconsistent with his godhead, than not to effect any other like impossibility. We might as well ask, why is not every creature as great and perfect as God himself? Not then to argue about words, we come to this conclusion, that the happiness of God, so far as it depends on the conduct of creatures, is impaired by the existence of sin, and though not in a manner dishonorable to himself, yet really and truly impaired, while the dread responsibility which such a fact involves rests on them.

Another theory has been proposed, viz., that God can fully supply from his own resources the loss or deficiency in his happiness which is occasioned by the existence of sin—e. g., by acts of mercy in redeeming the guilty and the lost; and that therefore there is no necessity for supposing that the happiness of God is on the whole impaired by the existence of sin. To this supposition I reply, that while it would relieve the present theory from the present objection, it is obviously inconsistent with the theory in other respects, as well as with the nature of moral government. Particularly it is inconsistent with the principle, that the perfect and universal holiness of creatures is necessary to the highest conceivable good, and that God, all things considered, should prefer holiness to sin. For if God can render himself as happy by saving those whom he will save,—i. e., a part of mankind,—as he would have been had there been universal holiness on the part of his creatures, then since it is possible that those who will not repent should repent and be saved, and since God would be more happy than he now is should they repent, it is also possible that God should be more happy in consequence of the existence of sin, than he could be were universal holiness to exist. Hence it would follow that it is possible that sin should be the necessary means of the highest possible happiness to God, and of course that he should prefer it to holiness in its stead.

Besides, it cannot be shown that God can supply in the manner supposed the loss of his own happiness occasioned by sin; for the happiness lost to him by the existence of sin and its miseries, together with that which was sacrificed in making the requisite atonement, may overbalance that which is supposed to result from his acts of mercy, though all should be saved. It is utterly impossible so to measure and compare the happiness lost in one way with that gained in the other, as to decide that the latter can be an equivalent for the former. Indeed the contrary is capable of complete demonstration. For evidently there cannot be as much happiness on the part of creatures, if sin exists, as there would be in case of the perfect holiness of all. Perfect holiness involves the perfect or highest happiness of its subject. Sin therefore involves a real loss to every subject. But while it is admitted that there is a peculiar happiness in acts of mercy, the amount of that happiness depends entirely on the happiness or good which acts of mercy impart, or which at least they are designed to accomplish. But it is impossible that God by acts of mercy should actually impart or design to impart more happiness to creatures than the highest, or even happiness which is equal to the highest. Of course it is impossible that God should be as happy by his acts of mercy and grace, as he would be, were all his creatures to be perfectly holy. Nor is this all. The supposition subverts the law of God as a sincere expression of his will. It implies that the perfect holiness of creatures is not necessary to the highest *conceivable* happiness of God, since according to the supposition it is possible for God to secure to himself an equal degree of happiness by means of sin.

What then men have done to impair God's blessedness, though their efforts have not failed to diminish it when compared with what it would have been had they done their duty, has not after all resulted in its full and appropriate consequences. God has opened to himself a new source of happiness. He has made that very conduct which is so odious in his sight, the occasion of a joy and blessedness to himself, which in this specific form he had otherwise never known. He has opened the treasures of his grace, and rejoices with new and peculiar joy in the work of delivering from sin and woe the very objects of his abhorrence—has secured to himself and to the universe, though not the highest amount of happiness conceivable, yet the greatest possible to him to effect, and has thus, according to the only true import of the language, secured his own perfect blessedness. I need not say how remote this view of the subject is, from that which exhibits God as purposing the sin and ruin of a world as a source of *higher* joy to himself, than had such an occasion been prevented by perfect obedience to his perfect law. According to one scheme, God purposed and by providential arrangements secured the existence of sin, and thus plunged his creatures into ruin, that he might have the happiness and the glory of bringing them deliverance; nor could the perfect holiness and consequent perfect happiness of his creatures satisfy his infinite benevolence. According to the other, God though he purposed sin as incidental to the best system in respect to his power of prevention, still preferred the existence of holiness to sin as the necessary means of the highest conceivable good, both to himself and to the universe; and when men had done what they could to impair his joy over the work of his hands; when they had in very deed forever shut off one source of immeasurable delight to their Maker, by revolting from his government, then he devised and adopted the grand expedient of showing mercy to them as in some degree a reparation of the loss—the best redress of the injury of which they are the guilty authors.

But it may be further said, that in the preceding remarks it is admitted that sin is the necessary means of good, as it is the means of that happiness which God derives from his acts of mercy. I answer, that it is admitted that sin is the necessary means of that peculiar happiness which results from forgiving sin. But this does not prove that sin is the necessary means of good or happiness to God, since it may still be true that God would be happier had there been no sin. His happiness from the gratification of his benevolence might be far greater had there been universal holiness than that which now results from his acts of mercy to the guilty.

Obj. 6. It is claimed that the position that *sin is the necessary means of the greatest good* is capable of complete demonstration, and that therefore the theory which is now advocated must be wholly groundless.

This has been claimed on two grounds: one is, that sin actually exists, and that a perfect God could not have purposed its existence unless he had regarded it as the necessary means of the greatest good. This reasoning we have sufficiently answered by showing that God could and may have purposed sin for a very different reason. For to say that he must have purposed sin because it is the necessary means of the greatest good until it be shown that he could not purpose it for any other reason, is simply begging the question.

Another ground on which the above position has been maintained is, that God by acts of grace and mercy toward the guilty and the lost, can produce more happiness than by acts of mere benevolence toward the perfectly holy. I have already sufficiently refuted this assertion by showing that perfect holiness secures the highest happiness of the subject. But even this is denied by our opponents. It is therefore necessary to examine the present assertion more minutely. I remark in the first place, that it cannot be proved that more happiness can be produced by acts of redeeming mercy than could or would exist were all perfectly holy. The truth of this position has been assumed on the supposed authority of Revelation, and argued also from the nature of things.

The passage of Scripture relied on is Luke, xv. 7: "I say unto you, that likewise joy shall be in heaven over one sinner that repenteth more than over ninety and nine just persons that need no repentance." There is no word for "*more*" in the Greek. The passage is supposed to imply, that the evil escaped and the happiness obtained by the penitent sinner is a good of greater value than the happiness enjoyed by a much greater number of perfectly holy beings. By comparing this passage with Matt. xviii. 13, we see that the true rendering is, "that there shall be joy in heaven over one sinner that repenteth *rather than* (*μᾶλλον ἤ*) over ninety and nine," &c. The text is thus a recognition and application of the familiar truth, that a lost blessing when found, occupies the mind with joy rather than other blessings of equal or even greater value which have not been lost. This view of the passage shows that the design was not to compare and estimate the real value of the blessing found with that which had not been lost, but to show that inasmuch as to retrieve a loss is a real good, so it is a good fitted to awaken a peculiar and high degree of joy. That this is the whole import of the language is evident from the consideration that the truth taught by our Lord is illustrated by appealing to our own common experience in cases which directly contradict the supposed import of the passage. Is the owner of the lost sheep happier on the whole by finding it, than if it had not been lost, or glad on the whole that it was lost? Is the father of the reclaimed prodigal glad on the whole that the son was lost because he is found; that he was dead because he is alive again? These questions every one can answer without mistake; and the answer shows that the supposed comparison and supposed estimate are not even alluded to in the passage. It is impossible that we should be happier in the one case than in the other, since it is a matter of consciousness, that the happiness of continued possession, had it not been interrupted, and the unhappiness occasioned by the loss, more than outweigh the happiness of finding that which was lost. I need not say how much stronger the case is when the blessings not lost are many instead of one.

But I will concede the construction put on the passage so far as to admit, that it is a case of comparison in respect to the relative value of two objects. What then are the precise objects compared? Is the recovery then of the lost blessing compared with the entire non-existence of the blessing not lost, or is it compared with it *merely* as a present safe possession? This is a material question; for it is obvious that this blessing contemplated merely as a present safe possession, is far less fitted to awaken joy, than to think of it at the same time as having no existence. For an example, take the case of the hundred sheep. To contemplate the blessing of the ninety and nine as never possessed, and to think what it would be to be wholly destitute of it, would greatly increase its value in our estimation compared with contemplating it merely as a present safe possession. This may be seen by asking whether we should prefer the recovery of that which was lost to the past, present, and future possession of the ninety and nine? This question is easily answered by every one that knows that ninety-nine sheep are of more value than one, though the latter had been lost and found again. This shows at once, if we suppose a comparison in the case, what is and what is not the object of the comparison. It is simply on the one hand the ninety and nine contemplated as a present safe possession without taking into consideration the loss involved in their non-existence, compared on the other with the simple recovery of that which was lost; and this too without taking into account the deduction to be made by the loss itself. So it may be safely conceded, that in a like comparison of a penitent sinner and of ninety and nine just persons, there is more joy over the former than over the latter. But if the question be, whether the existence of one penitent sinner with the evil and the good which it involves, be preferable to the existence of ninety and nine perfectly holy and happy beings, no benevolent mind can thus judge.

This brings us to the second ground of argument.

Secondly: The doctrine now questioned is argued from the *nature of things*. Here the estimate is commonly made in the form and even with the supposed certainty of an arithmetical computation. We have such a computation by Dr. Bellamy in his Sermons on the Wisdom of God in the permission of sin. Unfortunately however for this computation, it depends on the gratuitous and false assumption that the happiness of each sinner saved is "a hundred times greater" than it would have been had he never sinned. Nor is this all. The doctor supposes the damned to lose one degree of happiness and to suffer an increase of misery in proportion to the supposed increase of the happiness of the righteous, viz., a hundred degrees. Now here is one main item left entirely out of account, viz., the misery of the lost, which is supposed to be increased a hundred degrees. The question is, how much is this aside from the supposed increase? It is something more than the loss of one degree of happiness—it is a great amount of positive misery—so great that it were good for the unhappy subject not to have existed. Now the supposed loss of one degree of happiness is a balance for one degree enjoyed, and what scales has Dr. B. or any other man by which to decide how much positive misery is a balance for a given amount of happiness? Who can decide that if in one case the happiness is increased to a hundred degrees, the misery of a lost soul aside from the supposed increase is not so great an evil as not to outweigh both together.

Obj. 7. It may be said that the present system is the best, as it will result in the highest degrees of holiness on the part of the holy, inasmuch as it includes that high degree of temptation which is necessary to the highest degrees of holiness, and of course of happiness, and that therefore the reason that sin is not prevented, is not that God cannot prevent moral agents from sinning. To this I reply, first—That if it may be so, it is also true that it may not be so, and that on this supposition there is no reason for saying that *it is so*, or that it *may not be true* that God cannot prevent sin under a moral system. Secondly: There is no proof that in all cases the degree of holiness of a moral being will be as great as the degree of temptation overcome. This may be true in *some* cases, particularly on the part of those who are imperfectly holy; but how does it appear that a being who loves God *with all his strength* can love him *more*, in consequence of increased temptation and of surmounting such increased temptation? On the contrary, it is plain that in the case of a perfectly holy being, to increase temptation must lessen the degree of his holiness. Perfect holiness in a moral creature consists in loving God as much as he can love him, while he is under a necessity of loving an inferior good in some degree. At the same time, he has but a limited power or capacity of loving all objects of affection. Suppose this capacity of loving in a perfectly holy being to be the capacity of loving fifty degrees, and that being under a necessity of loving the inferior good ten degrees, he loves God with forty degrees or with perfect love. Let us now suppose the temptation to be increased, in other words, the value of the inferior good increased, so that it becomes necessary to love the inferior object fifteen degrees. The consequence is that he must love God so much the less as he loves the inferior object more, and is necessarily less holy as the consequence of increasing the temptation; that is, if the degree of his holiness is determined by the degree in which he loves God more than he loves every other and all other objects. Thirdly: Supposing the system, with the degree of temptation necessary to secure the highest degree of holiness on the part of the holy, actually to exist, and that God, by the direct exertion of his omnipotence, without any other change in the system of influence, can secure the perfect holiness and of course the perfect happiness of all, the question is, why does he not thus secure this result? Having given that perfection to the system which is requisite to secure the greatest degree of holiness on the part of those who are holy under it, can a reason be conceived or imagined why, if by the mere exertion of his power he can make *all* who sin perfectly holy and happy, he should not do it? Which is the most reasonable to suppose, that he cannot by his *mere power* prevent the sin of those who do sin without destroying their moral agency, or that he can do this and refuses to do it without any conceivable reason? If it be said that the sin of those who sin under the supposed best system is the necessary means of the greatest good, this as we have seen is impossible. If it be said that by the supposed interposition of power the system would be changed, and changed for the worse, then I ask, how changed for the worse? Every influence supposed to be necessary to the highest degree of the holiness of those who are holy is preserved, and what the supposed interposition of power would effect, is the perfect holiness and happiness of those who sin. And would such a change in the system be for the worse or for the better? If for the better, then why is it not adopted by perfect benevolence? If for the worse, how can this be conceived; or rather do we not know that if this view of the case is all that is to be considered, it would be for the better and not for the worse, that all were perfectly holy and happy forever? If it should now be said that the supposed interposition of power to make all holy might be for the worse, because it might result in more sin at some future period than it would prevent; but how so, if God can keep all sin out of his moral kingdom, by securing the perfect holiness of all, through the mere exertion of his omnipotence?

The present theory then not only admits that God cannot prevent all sin under the best moral system, but it does not furnish even a plausible vindication of God in not preventing by his power the existence of all sin under a moral system, forever. And further, it is plain that no theory can furnish such a vindication; for when we have supposed the most perfect system of influences conceivable, except omnipotence should secure universal and perfect holiness and happiness, the question still returns, why not so exert his Omnipotence as to secure this result? Can human ingenuity devise an answer, or even be authorized to say there can be any other reason, except that a perfect God cannot prevent all sin, even under the best conceivable system, or in other words, cannot prevent all sin forever without destroying moral agency?

APPENDIX—No. IV.

ARE ANY OF THE PUNISHMENTS OF CIVIL LAW LEGAL SANCTIONS, EXCEPT THE PUNISHMENT OF DEATH?

(VIDE LECTURE VII., SECT. I., VOL. I.)

Prevalent errors to be considered.—All evil employed in punishment not penal sanction of supreme law.—How to decide what is the supreme law.—Civil government does not require virtuous benevolence.—Overt action cognized.—Assumption in favor of every subject.—Reward given by the State.—How viewed as a sanction.—Penalty how considered as a sanction.—*Malum in se* and *malum prohibitum*, in one respect no transgression of civil law.—*Malum in se.*—Many overt acts which are prohibited, not considered as violations of the supreme law.—Burglary and robbery.—Falsely assumed that civil law assigns punishment according to a just moral estimate of offences.—Diversity in degree of penalty.—The enactments under consideration not enforced by legal sanctions.—Punishment of death.

Before I proceed to the argument on this point, there are several errors in respect to the nature of civil law, its requirement and sanctions, which I deem it important to correct. That which I regard as the most serious, and which is occasioned by others, consists in confounding the *penal sanction* of the supreme law of the State, with that kind of natural evil which civil legislation employs, in the form of punishment, to prevent the violation of certain particular legislative enactments. The assumption is common, that this kind of evil, called the punishment or penalty of the particular law, is a *legal sanction*, and as it is employed merely as *so much motive* to secure conformity to the particular law or enactment, the inference is, that the same thing is true in respect to the *penal sanction* of the supreme law of the State, and indeed in respect to the *legal sanctions* of every moral government. To this error as their source, I cannot doubt that the peculiar views of the Universalist and the Infidel respecting the sanctions of God's moral government are to be traced. It is then of essential importance that we form just views of the supreme law of the civil State, if we would clearly discern the difference between this law, which as I maintain is the only law of the State that has legal sanctions, and those particular legislative enactments which have no legal sanctions.

By the supreme law of the State, I mean that law which

is essential to the government of the State as a moral government, and the sum of whose requirement of every subject is disinterested benevolence to the State, or an elective preference of its highest happiness for its own sake. Or to speak more particularly, I mean that law which claims disinterested benevolence to the State from every subject, on the authority of the governor or government, and which on the same ground forbids the opposite disposition or principle of action.

In deciding what the supreme law of the State or of its government ought to be, we may view every one as a distinct and separate community. It is true that every State with its government is in fact one of many great communities in the empire of God, and under his rightful dominion. Contemplating it under this aspect, and supposing its highest happiness to be inconsistent with that of the whole, the great law of benevolence to the universe would require such sacrifice of its well-being as would be necessary to the highest happiness of the whole. But if we suppose its highest happiness to be consistent with that of the whole, then the governor ought, without qualification, to aim to secure its highest happiness by requiring every subject to prefer this end to every other that can come into competition with it as an object of preference. This supposition, at least as a general principle, with its consequence, is undoubtedly, as it ought to be, universally assumed as just. We may therefore view the State, for our present purpose, as a distinct and independent community, and its moral governor in deciding on the supreme law, as sustaining no other or higher relation than that of the guardian and promoter of the highest happiness of this temporal community. This law must be that which we have described as requiring of its subjects disinterested benevolence to the State.

This benevolence must be distinguished from that higher principle toward God and his sentient creation which is the sum of all virtue or moral excellence. The latter is in no respect the subject of civil legislation. Civil government is indeed an ordinance of God, nothing being more manifest than that it is his will that men should exist in society, and be controlled by that influence which we call civil government, as the necessary means of their highest temporal well-being. But civil government, like the institution of marriage, respects the interests of earth and time. It is no part of the function of the civil ruler to make or to attempt to make his subjects *religious* by law. He has in this relation no concern with claiming or enforcing benevolence to God or to the sentient universe. The entire function of his office is, by his authority, to bring every subject to conform to the law of benevolence to the State, and thus to secure its highest happiness as a temporal community. It is true indeed that every subject who is disinterestedly benevolent toward the State, knowing his higher relations toward God or the sentient universe, may also be so toward the latter; and he who is disinterestedly benevolent toward the latter, is so toward the former. But the civil ruler, as such, has no concern with the conduct of his subjects in this higher relation.

Again: the governor, in deciding the question of obedience or disobedience to this law, takes cognizance of overt action—not indeed, as many seem to suppose, as constituting obedience or disobedience, but only as the decisive *proof* of obedience or disobedience to the law. This law, in the estimation of the civil ruler, is obeyed by the subject who by overt action furnishes no proof that he is actuated by the principle opposite to that which the law requires. It is disobeyed, in his estimation, by him only who shows that he is actuated by the principle opposite to that which the law requires. Hence in deciding the question of obedience or disobedience, we have this important principle:—*Every subject who cannot be proved by overt action to be governed by the principle of hostility to the State, which is forbidden in the supreme law of the State, is to be considered and treated as an obedient subject:—or thus: no subject who cannot by overt action be proved to be actuated by this principle can be considered and treated as a disobedient subject.*

With these views of the supreme law of the State, we now recur to its *sanctions*. And first, to *its reward*. This may be said, in general terms, to consist in the protection of the life, liberty, and property of the obedient subject. By this I do not mean to imply that the subject of the civil law has what some call an *inalienable* right to life, liberty, and property, in such a respect that the State by law may not require the voluntary sacrifice of these blessings, when such sacrifice is, as it may be, demanded by the public good. Such laws may not only be made, but may in some cases be enforced by penalties which shall deprive the transgressor not only of property or liberty, but of life also. When therefore I speak of the obedient subject, I speak of one who is obedient to law in every form which involves a spirit of loyalty to the State. The true doctrine on this subject is, that civil government is bound to the extent of its power, so far as it shall be for the general good, to protect the life, liberty, and property of the obedient subject, with every other blessing of his earthly existence.

If now we contemplate the nature of that reward, which is annexed to the supreme law of the State, and the condition on which it is conferred, we cannot fail to see its peculiar characteristic as a legal sanction. As good in itself, and as the means of good, it is obviously the highest good which a civil government can confer on each obedient subject. It is conferred solely on condition of the subject's obedience to the supreme law of the State. It is therefore a plain and unequivocal expression of the moral governor's highest approbation of obedience to this law. No subject can fail to regard it in this light; nor can he do so without considering it as a decisive manifestation of that character in the lawgiver which alone becomes him as the guardian of a nation's welfare, and which alone gives him the right to rule. He may indeed view it as so much natural good, and as such, a motive to conformity to the claim of law. But he must regard it also as something more; as that which, by manifesting the lawgiver's design to secure the highest welfare of the State, gives majesty to his law, and inspires reverence for his authority. Otherwise all that we call the majesty of law, or the authority of civil government, is reduced to a mere contract or stipulation of so much hire for so much service. But can any man of common sense view a wise and faithful administration of civil government under the simple aspect of such a contract? Is there no reason for submission to the supreme law of the State except to secure the personal benefit of the reward as the fulfillment of a contract made solely for the subject's personal advantage? Plainly, if civil government, or the supreme law which it necessarily involves, is nothing but a stipulation to confer so much good for so much good received, let it be called by its right name. To call it government or law, or to speak of its authority or of its influence as law, is to talk of what has no existence. Who is so ignorant, as not to know that the influence of law, of government, is a peculiar influence—that when we speak of a king or moral governor as having the influence of authority, we speak of an influence which is fitted and designed to command respect and reverence, to secure confidential and cheerful submission to his will, and to determine and enforce the obligation to obedience; an influence which emanates from the sanctions of his law, as manifesting that character which alone becomes him as the guardian and promoter of a nation's happiness; an influence which gathers around and clothes him with majesty as with a garment? Viewed under this relation, as manifesting this character in the governor, the legal reward is necessarily something more than merely so much natural good as a motive. It necessarily carries with it to every mind the conviction of that character which gives him a right to rule, and thus ratifies, sanctions his authority. Viewed in any other relation, or under any other light, it can produce no such effect. Viewed, as many are wont to view it, merely as so much natural good designed to influence only as a direct motive to secure obedience, it can sanction nothing which can be called authority; it can produce nothing which can be called obedience, and can no more be viewed as *a legal sanction*, than a stipulated equivalent in traffic, or than any other benefit conferred as the mere dictate of selfishness. But enough has already been said on this point. I only ask, how, without manifesting through this reward his highest appropation of obedience to the supreme law of the State, the governor could manifest a disposition to govern in the best manner, or be regarded as doing any thing to establish or ratify his authority in the lowest degree?

I now proceed to show the same thing in respect to the penalty of the supreme law of the State, as this is distinguished from the penalties annexed to other laws. Here we have the same general error to encounter and to remove—the error of supposing that the penalties annexed to certain particular legislative enactments, especially to those which forbid such crimes as theft, robbery, burglary, &c., have the same design and are of the same nature as the penalty annexed to the supreme law of the State—the penalty of death.

I have already had occasion to show, with respect to the penalties annexed to some of these particular enactments, that they cannot be regarded as *legal sanctions*, but must be considered as simply so much direct motive in the loss of liberty or property, to deter from transgression. And here I might ask, if the fine or pecuniary punishment imposed for the neglect of military duty, or for failure to render an annual account or list of one's taxable property, are not legal sanctions designed to sustain the authority of the government; if the transgressor in these cases is not, in the eye of the law, an enemy of the State? If these penalties are designed simply as so much direct motive to deter from transgressing the statute, why are not the same things true in respect to the short imprisonment which is the penalty for petty larceny, or the longer one for forgery, robbery, and burglary? What is there to show that the government esteems one class of these cases as involving hostility to the State rather than the other; or the penalties of one class as legal sanctions rather than the other; or that the penalties in both are not designed simply as so much motive to deter from transgressing the specified enactments? It is true, these penal inflictions differ in the degree of evil which they involve. In some cases the penalty is merely a pecuniary punishment or fine; in others, a fine and a short imprisonment; in others, a short imprisonment only; in others, a longer imprisonment, but limited to a term of years; and in others, imprisonment for life. But all this is consistent with the design that each several penalty should influence, as simply so much motive to prevent transgression. At the same time, in each of these cases the essential reward of obedience, the protection of life, is secured to the subject not less than had he not transgressed the particular statute. He is still treated as obedient to the supreme law of the State. How then can he be regarded as an enemy of the State? How can the punishment be designed to express the supreme disapprobation of the government toward such a subject? What can the punishment in every such case be, except so much natural evil in the loss of liberty or property, or of both, designed simply as motive to prevent transgression?

But in order to form correct and satisfactory views of this subject, in opposition to what are deemed common errors respecting it, it is necessary to examine these errors; at least so far as to bring if possible before the mind the precise question at issue.

In respect to the transgression of civil law, a distinction has been made between a *malum in se* and a *malum prohibitum*.

Some have maintained a difference between the two kinds of transgression denoted by this language, and others have denied it. As some however have meant one thing by this distinction and some another, the one class has not always denied what the other has maintained. Some have maintained the guilt or moral turpitude of all crimes against the State, who yet have denied that this is the ground on which the State inflicts penalties, at least in all cases. Others, with the same view of the nature of crimes against the State, have maintained that it is the ground of penal inflictions even in all cases. Others, asserting in words the guilt or moral turpitude of all such offenses, but meaning by this merely their tendency to injure the State, have maintained that the ground of all civil penalties is the guilt or moral turpitude of the conduct punished. In view of these different opinions, with no one of which am I satisfied, it is desirable if possible to expose what is erroneous, that we may the more clearly see what is true.

For this purpose I remark, that in one important sense of the language, no transgression of civil law is a *malum in se*. By the moralist who considers man's relations not merely to the State but to the sentient universe, and his consequent subjection to the great law of benevolence toward all, not to love one's country or the highest happiness of the State, is justly viewed as implying the selfish principle, or a principle of hostility not only to the State but to God and his sentient creation; and as such, a *malum in se*. There is on the part of the murderer or the traitor such a palpable violation of this great law—there is so much moral wickedness in the case as distinguished from the mere tendency of the act to impair or destroy any mere interest of time, that it is natural to feel strongly the moral ill-desert or guilt of the transgressor, and to conclude without due reflection, that the civil penalty in the case is threatened and inflicted chiefly if not wholly in relation to such ill-desert. But as I have already shown, with the conduct of his subjects in their high relation to their Maker and his sentient creation, the civil ruler has no concern. This law does not require the subject to love the State and to seek its happiness from a principle of disinterested benevolence to all sentient being. He has no right to require such a principle of his subjects, nor to forbid the opposite. The prohibition of the crime of blasphemy, as an offense against God, by civil law, is obviously inconsistent with religious liberty, and transcends the prerogative of the civil ruler. He can require nothing beyond disinterested benevolence to the State. The transgression of this law therefore, cannot be esteemed by him as involving the violation of the great law of benevolence toward the sentient universe, and in this sense a *malum in se.* It may, and for the most part probably does, involve the violation of this great law, and is, as such a violation, a *malum in se.* But the civil ruler can know nothing of its nature or relations in this sense. His only concern with it as a civil ruler, is as a *malum in se* in another relation—*in its relation to the State.*

In this view of the subject the present question is not, whether he who violates any law of the State, either a law which forbids murder, or one which forbids petty larceny, or one which forbids turning to the left when meeting another on the highway, acts *morally wrong* in the sight of God, or in the court of conscience—in other words, violates the great law of benevolence toward all sentient being. The civil law has no concern at all with this question. Further, the present question is not whether the executive or overt act involved in the violation of every enactment of the State tends in some limited degree to impair the well-being of the State; that it has this tendency is readily conceded. But the present question is, whether the lawgiver or moral governor of the State considers the subject, whatever law of the State he violates, as therein violating the supreme law of the State, and thus guilty of a *malum in se in relation to the State.* When one violates a law whose penalty is death, as the law which forbids treason or murder, the government confessedly considers him as transgressing the supreme law of the State. Does the government form the same estimate of him who violates any other law, or any law whose penalty is not death? The violation of the law which forbids treason or murder, or of any law whose just penalty is death, it is conceded is a violation of the supreme law of the State, involving a principle of action fatal to the well-being, and even to the existence of the State, and is therefore in the view of the government a *malum in se in relation to the State.* But is this the view which it takes of the violation of any law to which it has not annexed the penalty of death? Does it view the executive or overt act involved in the violation of any such law as proof of a principle of hostility to the State? or does it view it merely as a *malum prohibitum*—a violation of a rule designed by some penal evil annexed as simply so much motive to prevent the forbidden action as in some limited degree injurious to the State, and this without the least reference to, or implication of a principle of hostility to the State on the part of the violator? This is obviously the question at issue; and to show that the violation of a civil law not having the penalty of death, is not in the view of the government a violation of the supreme law of the State, is to show that it is simply a violation of such a rule of action as I have now described: to show that it is not a *malum in se* in relation to the State, is to show that it is merely a *malum prohibitum.*

I remark then, that the bare statement of the fact carries its evidence on the face of it. It is one of the most obvious and familiar facts, that the overt act forbidden by any such civil enactment as we now speak of, is not considered by the government either as the violation, or as the proof of the violation of the supreme law of the State. What civil government entitled to respect ever esteemed such an overt act as evincing the same malignant principle of action toward the State which is evinced by the overt action involved in treason or murder? The principle which refuses to perform military duty, or to turn to the right as the law directs, or which steals a melon from a garden to gratify the appetite, or a ribbon from the shop to adorn a head-dress, is not in the eye of the civil law the same that would spread anarchy and death through the State. It may be indeed—probably often is—in the view of God and of truth, such a principle. But the civil law—the government of the State—does not, nor is it authorized so to esteem it; nor does it intend that its subjects should so esteem it. Nothing plainly would be more abhorrent to the universal sense and reason of men than that it should be so considered. Nothing would more justly provoke revolution than such a practical estimate of these offenses by the government of a State. These acts then are not in the eye of civil law *mala in se* in relation to the State, but simply *mala prohibita.*

But it may be asked, is it so in respect to the violation of all this class of legislative enactments; particularly is it so in respect to the act of robbery or of burglary? I answer by asking why it is not so in these cases? Is it that these acts involve a peculiar degree of *moral turpitude* scarcely less than the overt acts involved in treason and murder? Be it so; but with this the civil law has no concern. It has no right to prohibit it or to require its opposite as such. Here lies the great imperfection of civil government compared with a moral government, administered by omniscience. It has no unerring insight into the human heart, and is therefore utterly disqualified to determine so great a question, as whether a man is benevolent or selfish in his high relations to his Maker and his sentient creation; or whether one according to this standard is a good man or a bad man. If its decisions respected this question, it would be obliged in some supposable cases to determine that to be murder which would not be murder. For who shall say that the good man (as many believe David to have been when he killed Uriah) may not, in the eye of the civil law, commit murder? If this be so, then even the crime of murder, as viewed by the civil law, does not necessarily involve the opposite of the benevolent principle toward God and his sentient creation. It can be viewed as involving at most the opposite of the benevolent principle toward the State. Benevolence toward the State as a limited affection may be perfect; that is, it may be a disposition to sacrifice every thing which can come into competition with its object—in a mind, which in relation to the universe, is perfectly selfish—just as benevolence in a parent, or in one of a company of highwaymen toward a limited community, may be perfect in a perfectly selfish mind. And yet such benevolence toward the State would be, and must be regarded by the government as perfect obedience to the supreme law of the State. The civil law therefore can require, in respect to the principle of action, nothing but benevolence toward the State, and this may be either that which is dictated by that higher principle of benevolence to all sentient being, or it may be merely a limited and therefore a selfish principle—a merely selfish benevolence toward the State. Of course civil government in annexing its penalties to the laws against robbery and burglary, and indeed against treason and murder, has no concern with *the moral turpitude* of these crimes. The only thing which it knows and contemplates as crime, is crime against the State; and the only crime against the State which is a *malum in se*, is one which involves a principle of action hostile to the welfare and existence of the State, and is proved to be such *by overt action* which tends to destroy the State. The only question then is this—does the overt act in robbery or burglary evince in the eye of the law this principle of hostility to the State? Does either of these crimes in the view of civil government involve the same principle of action in relation to the State, which is involved in treason or in murder? This we think will not be pretended in regard to the neglect of military duty, nor in regard to an act of petty larceny. But how does robbery or burglary differ in this respect from either of these violations of law? Only as they tend to diminish the public good in a greater though still in a limited degree; a degree however which still falls immeasurably short of that in which the principle involved in treason or murder tends to diminish it. The direct mischief of petty larceny, of robbery, and of burglary is in one respect the same—the loss of property by its rightful possessor. Robbery and burglary in some cases may be justly regarded as tending indirectly to greater evil, especially as awakening a reasonable apprehension of the loss of life. Neither however, correctly defined, involves an intent to kill. Neither, in the view of the law, involves a principle of hostility to the State, nor is inconsistent with that benevolence toward the State which constitutes obedience to its supreme law. The law still throws its protection around the life and the property of the transgressor, thus giving to him the essential reward of an obedient subject to the supreme law of the State. It may deprive him of liberty for a term of years, or for life, and thus properly inflict upon him a severer penalty than it inflicts for minor offenses of the same class. Still he is considered and treated as essentially an obedient subject. He is not considered as actuated by a principle hostile to the welfare and existence of the State, nor as disobedient to the supreme law of the State. There is no proof, nothing which can be regarded as proof, that he is. His offense is not viewed by the government as a *malum in se* in relation to the State. The penalty he incurs is not designed as a legal sanction—designed as a direct proof and ratification of the authority of the government. On the contrary, his offense is plainly viewed by the law simply as a *malum prohibitum*. Its punishment is designed to deter from transgression merely as so much motive. Nor is there any principle by which the civil law can form any other estimate of either of the crimes under consideration, or of any other of the same class, which would not require that it should form the same estimate of an act of petty larceny, or of neglecting to perform military duty.*

But it may be said, that the violation of any law of the State involves a principle of action equally remote from a spirit of loyalty to the government, and equally hostile to the welfare and even to the existence of the State, with that involved in treason or murder. I have no occasion to depreciate the evil tendency of the principle or of the overt act involved in any of the violations of civil law. Let it then be admitted, that in a just moral estimate—in that estimate which truth makes and which God will make—forgery, robbery, burglary, petty larceny, and all other offenses against civil law, violate those civil rights on which the security and well-being of human society depend; that as the legitimate consequence, all industry and trade must decline, the sources of subsistence fail, the authority of law and with it the only foundation of society be subverted, and the country be deserted and reduced to desolation; that as he who is unjust in the least is unjust also in much, so he who commits any, the least offense against the State, is actuated by a principle which tends to lay waste human society and human existence;—I say let it be admitted that in a just moral estimation all this is true; but the question returns, does the law—does the government of the State form this estimate of things; or rather, are they authorized to form this estimate of it? Is the overt act proof of such a principle? If so, why are not all these offenses placed on a level in respect to penalty? If the object of penalty is the same, and this object is to support the authority of law, why is not the same penalty which is necessary for this purpose in one case necessary in every case? If such is the estimate of any of this class of crimes, then it is the estimate of all of them, and the petty thief and the burglar in the eye of the law, and according to the only just estimate by the civil ruler, deserve the same penalty,—nay, more; he who pilfers the most trivial article from a shop-door is in the

* The Spartan law authorizing theft, the patriarchal permission of polygamy, and the Mosaic permission of divorce, show that these things are not deemed hostile to the State as are acts of treason, in their own nature as overt acts, and that they are forbidden by civil law, not as *mala in se* but as *mala prohibita*, or being in some degree injurious to the State.

eye of the law as truly an enemy of the State and proves himself to be so, as he who betrays his country to a conqueror to be desolated by his armies. The government of course which does not visit every diversity of offense with equal penalty, even with that which is necessary to sustain its authority, is recreant to its trust. And yet, plainly no government that should do this could command the respect and confidence of its subjects, or be regarded by them otherwise than as in the highest degree oppressive and tyrannical, and as having no authority.

But the error we are opposing rests entirely on the assumption, that civil government proceeds in annexing its penalties to laws according to a just moral estimation of offenses; for in no other estimation can these offenses be equalized in their evil tendency. Viewed in their tendency to bring detriment to the State, as this tendency pertains to the overt action or to the principle involved, it is obvious that they are not equally injurious. That they are so in the tendency which pertains to overt action will not be pretended: that they are so in the tendency which pertains to the principle, is no more credible according to the mode in which civil government judges and must judge of the principles of action. It can judge of these, only as they are manifested through the medium of executive or overt action. It can decide that a principle of hostility to the State exists, only when the overt action is such as to be the decisive proof of such a principle; and they can decide that the overt action is the decisive proof of such a principle, only when the overt action cannot be accounted for by being traced to any other principle. Can then the overt acts of neglecting military duty, of pilfering from a shop, of taking a man's purse on the highway, or of entering his house by breaking a window or a door and plundering it of its plate, be traced to no other principle than that of hostility to the government and the State? Do such transgressors of law manifest the same deadly principle of hostility to the happiness and the existence of the State, as that of the traitor and the murderer? Is such the estimation of the principle formed by an enlightened civil government or community? Would not such a judgment be wholly unauthorized—flagrantly unjust? Cannot the overt action involved in any of these minor transgressions be accounted for consistently with a principle of obedience to the supreme law of the State, from the weakness of the principle and the force of temptation? Does not every enlightened government thus account for them? Do not the penalties for such offenses inflicted by every such government place this point beyond all dispute, by showing that nothing is aimed at by these penalties except the mere prevention of crime?

Again: this view of the particular enactments is further confirmed by the diversity in the degree of their penalties, and the grounds of this diversity. Were the design of these punishments to uphold the authority of the government, no reason can be given why the same penalty should not be inflicted, however diverse the cases. On the contrary, the most decisive reason exists why the penalty should be the same in degree in all cases; for the degree of penalty necessary to this end in one case is necessary in all cases. Instead of annexing these penalties on this principle, every wise civil government greatly diversifies them, and without the remotest reference to this principle, and entirely on other grounds. One ground is the tendency of the offense to bring detriment to the State; another is the facility with which the crime can be perpetrated; and another is the facility of escape by the perpetrator. These things are consistent only with the supposition, that the principle which regulates these punishments, is their necessity for preventing the violation of these statutes by the influence of motive only. Accordingly, in some cases the violation of one of these statutes, which is far less injurious in its direct result than the violation of another, is visited with a severer penalty. No enlightened civil government in annexing a penalty to any one of these statutes, proceeds on the principle of preventing absolutely its violation and the mischief which in a single instance it brings to the State; but is guided also by the frequency with which the violation is likely to occur, increasing the severity of the penalty as may be requisite to diminish the frequency of the offense. In some cases it even proceeds on the principle of not punishing at all, especially when the crime can be prevented by other means with greater success. In other cases these punishments are designed chiefly as reforming influences. Such are the principles which pervade the whole system of penal jurisprudence in respect to the class of statutes under consideration; and they show that their violation is not regarded by the government as a violation of the supreme law of the land or as a *malum in se* in relation to the State, but as a *malum prohibitum;* that the design of these penalties is not directly to sanction the authority and sustain the majesty of law, but merely to prevent the violation forbidden by so much motive.

Once more: these particular enactments are not enforced by any thing which can be properly called legal sanctions. No reward whatever is promised to obedience to this class of enactments, either directly or indirectly, which can be properly called *a legal sanction.* It cannot be said that the protection of life, liberty, and property is made to depend on conformity to any one of them, for the subject who disobeys any one of them is entitled to this reward in every substantial respect. He is as fully protected in respect to his life, the essential legal reward of obedience to the law of the State, as had he not transgressed the statute; while he is deprived of liberty, or property, or both, only in some limited degree, which is requisite to create a suitable motive to obedience. The degree of liberty or property which he loses by transgression, is all that he would possess and enjoy by obedience, and all that can be called the reward of obedience in the case. But this merely cannot be regarded as sufficient to give, nor as designed to give authority to the law of a State. It cannot have nor be supposed to have any other influence than that of so much motive to secure obedience, and therefore cannot be a legal sanction. That reward which has the influence of a legal sanction is given, in every substantial respect, to the transgressing subject. It is given virtually, given in principle, so given to every subject, that he is truly esteemed a rewarded subject who, whether he has violated one of these particular enactments or not, cannot be proved to have violated the supreme law of the State. Every other subject is considered by the civil law as an obedient subject, and rewarded accordingly. Unless he can be proved to have violated this law, he is considered and treated as an obedient subject, whatever other law he may have violated. Obedience therefore to any one of these enactments receives no reward which can be called a legal sanction. Again: no one of these enactments is enforced by any punishment which can be properly called a legal sanction. This will not, we think, be pretended in respect to those whose penalties consist in some slight pecuniary punishment, or even in a few weeks of comfortable imprisonment. If it be claimed in respect to any of the punishments under consideration, it will be in respect to imprisonment for life. This penalty to a man who loves liberty, and who has possessed and enjoyed it under the institutions of a free government, and especially who has learned to form those lofty notions of it which so much pains is taken to cherish and to exaggerate—notions in which one identifies himself and *his* liberty with the millions of his country and *their* liberty through all generations to the end of time—to such a man imprisonment for life would be a grievous penalty. Liberty to him has afforded its rich and manifold blessings—blessings which need no exaggeration to be highly prized. It is a blessing greatly increased in his estimation by habitual enjoyment, and the loss of it is justly ranked among the sorest calamities of earth and time. For these reasons however, the penalty of imprisonment for life is seldom, perhaps never, incurred by such a man. For the most part at least it is incurred only by those who, by its loss, scarcely incur an evil to deplore, but rather make a change for the better. Their food, their lodging, and their raiment—all essential supplies of their wants, are more sure, more comfortable, more abundant; their society more congenial, their friendships more intimate, their real character and reputation less burdensome, their standing so nearly that of equality as to be no longer irksome, either through envy or a sense of degradation; in short, for the most part it seems not too much to say, that imprisonment for life, to its proper subjects, is almost an improvement of their condition and an increase of their enjoyments. So much truth is there in this, that it is a common remark concerning one of this class of men in the confinement of the strong walls of his prison, "He is better off than were he at liberty." I make these remarks not to undervalue the blessing of civil liberty to those who know how to use and enjoy it, but to show how comparatively inferior, not to say insignificant a thing it is to that class in the community who put it at hazard by the commission of crime; which shows, by the way, how ignorant of the principles of human action are those pretended reformers of social life, who exalt the influence of imprisonment for life to prevent the murderer's work above that of the penalty of death. I charitably hope the former would suffice to deter *them* from the crime of blood, who are so powerfully restrained by a thousand other influences. But how they forget, that if there be any thing that shakes the soul of a confirmed villain, it is the expectation of approaching death; the prospective horrors that give such a wrench to the mental organs, as to crush the rising purpose of blood.

In view then of the comparative insignificance of imprisonment for life in the estimation of those who are likely to incur the penalty, I ask, can it operate or be designed to operate as a legal sanction? Is it, with all the blessings which it leaves unimpaired, a direct and decisive expression of that disapprobation which is demanded for the violation of the supreme law of the State? Can it be supposed to be intended as such an expression? It may indeed serve to show *indirectly*, and when the want of it would show the contrary, that the governor is not indifferent to the welfare of the State. But is it such a direct and decisive expression of abhorrence as is due to rebellion against the State? Plainly, the penalty shows that the government does not so esteem the crime; that the crime is not in the eye of the law a *malum in se*, but a *malum prohibitum*, and that the penalty is designed to influence as so much motive, and not as a legal sanction.

With this view then of the punishments annexed to the particular statutes under consideration, I now recur to the penalty of the supreme law of the State, which is *death*. And here I cannot but remark what I think is strikingly shown in what has been already said, how exceedingly prone men are in forming opinions on the present subject, to overlook the main facts, even every thing which essentially belongs to the subject. What account, in their various theories and speculations concerning civil offenses and their punishments, has been made of the supreme law of the State and of its penal sanction? And yet if there is a moral government over the State, there is such a law involved in the very nature of such a government; and if there is such a law, it has its peculiar penal sanction, and if it has its peculiar legal sanction, that sanction, in view of the preceding discussion, must be the penalty of death. Death must be the penalty of the supreme law of the State, or that law has no penalty. What then is the nature and design of this penalty? I answer generally, that death to man as a being of earth and time, is justly regarded as the supreme evil, and as such is annexed to the supreme law of the State for the purpose of supporting the authority of that law; that is, as a penal sanction, or as the direct and decisive proof or expression of the lawgiver's highest disapprobation of disobedience. The general proof of this is, that if this be not the design of this penalty, then the supreme law of the State has no sanction, and of course has no authority. The penalties annexed to other laws, those particular enactments whose violations are merely *mala prohibita*, are not as we have seen legal sanctions—are in no respect designed to support the authority of government as the direct and decisive proof of it. If therefore this is not the design of the penalty of death, then there is no penalty whatever annexed to law with this design. The law of the State has no sanction. There is, and can be no evidence in the form of penal sanction of the governor's authority. Whatever provision he may have made by other statutes for the welfare of the State, he has furnished no direct and decisive proof of his authority in the form of the requisite penal sanction. On the contrary, by his failure to furnish this proof, he furnishes decisive proof that he has no authority or right to rule, and thus creates on the part of his subjects the right of revolution. There being no penal sanction, there is of course no law and no government. Nor can any penalty of the supreme law adopted by an enlightened civil government, which is less than the penalty of death, be a penal sanction. The reason is, that every other penalty involves, as we have seen, the essential, virtual reward of obedience, viz., the protection of life, and to a greater or less extent other blessings. The lawgiver therefore, by annexing any less penalty than death to the supreme law of the State, becomes the patron of rebellion against the government of the State. Whether therefore the penalty of death be fitted or adapted to the end specified or not, it is either designed to answer this end by the moral governor, or he does nothing to support his authority; but does that which in his own view, and in that of his subjects, unless disqualifying ignorance is his apology, utterly subverts his authority. If either himself or his subjects regard his authority as supported by the requisite penal sanction, they must regard it as supported by the penalty of death, as the direct and decisive expression and proof of that supreme disapprobation of disobedience which is necessary to his authority.

The next question respects the adaptation or fitness of the

end aimed at on the part of the governor. Is it adapted or fitted directly and decisively to express and prove his highest disapprobation of disobedience to the supreme law of his government? And here assuming it to be, as it undeniably is the penalty of this law, there can be no ground of hesitation in regard to its fitness to the end designed but one—viz., that death without torture is not, in strictest accuracy of speech, the highest degree of natural evil which the governor can inflict for disobedience. Hence it may be inferred, that it is not inflicted as the direct and decisive expression and proof of his highest disapprobation of disobedience to his supreme law, but as merely so much direct motive to deter from disobedience. Admitting that in the strictest use of language, death is not the highest degree of evil possible in the case, there are three suppositions to be made and considered. One is, that on this account it is not viewed either by the governor or his subjects, according to the true mode of judging in the case, as any expression and proof of his disapprobation of disobedience whatever, and that it is not designed to be such an expression by the governor, nor to be so regarded by his subjects. On this supposition it follows, that civil government is not in the lowest sense a moral government. There is nothing in it, either in the view of the governor or of his subjects, which answers to the idea of authority. There is no evidence from the penalty, and therefore none from any source, that he has the least degree of disapprobation of disobedience, and therefore none that he has a right to rule; but decisive proof that he has no such right. Another supposition is, that the governor and his subjects, according to the true mode of judging in the case, regard the penalty as expressing some degree of disapprobation of disobedience, but not the *highest*. On this supposition there can be no ground of confidence in his character—no ground for believing that possessing both the judicial and executive power, he will not sacrifice the State, rather than sacrifice the life of the traitor that wars on its welfare and its existence. To test the truth of this, let the fact be supposed, that he refuses to execute the traitor or the murderer, because he is his friend or favorite, or even his son, and would public sentiment reproach him merely for not employing so much motive to deter others from the crime; or would it react on his character, and pronounce him in this respect disqualified for his office, and having no authority? A third supposition is, that according to the true mode of judging in the case, both the governor and his subjects regard the penalty of death as a direct and decisive expression of his highest disapprobation of disobedience to the supreme law of the State, and as such a legal sanction. This plainly is the only supposition consistent with any thing on the part of the governor which can be regarded as authority; or with the doctrine that civil government is a moral government, in that sense in which all men ought, and in which common sense does regard it as a moral government.

But here the question arises, how can the penalty of death without torture, be justly or properly regarded as a direct and decisive expression of the governor's highest disapprobation of disobedience? I answer, that death, in the common conceptions of all men, is the supreme evil to man. It is, as it were constantly, in common speech, and of course in the common conceptions of men, distinguished as the greatest of evils to man considered as a being of earth and time. It is emphatically familiarized as such to all minds. The idea of it is an idea of so great an evil—when it occurs, its object so absorbs thought, by its own magnitude and certainty, that suffering as an attendant circumstance is unthought of as enhancing the evil. The moral governor conforms to this universal and familiar conception of the human mind, and when he would impress every subject with his highest disapprobation of disobedience to his supreme law, he makes that evil which in their common and familiar conceptions is signalized as the greatest, the supreme evil, the expression and the proof of his disapprobation. What so natural, what so fitted to his design? He knows their conception of the evil, and is sure of the judgment which they will form of the degree of his disapprobation of disobedience to his law, when thus measured by death as its penalty. They know how the language ought to be interpreted. He knows how it will be interpreted. By making death, which is universally regarded as the supreme evil to man as a being of earth and time, he shows himself the mortal enemy of rebellion against his throne, and in the most, or rather, in the only natural, obvious, and impressive mode, manifests the highest disapprobation of disobedience to his supreme law, which he can feel toward any object which can come into competition with it as an object of disapprobation. He thus shows the feelings and the character on which his authority depends.

Thus I have attempted to show, that the view which has been before given of the nature of the legal sanctions of a perfect moral government, is substantially that which is entertained by men, of the sanctions of the supreme law of the State. If we find in the wisest admininstration of human government some occasional departures from the rigor of the principles contended for, still the principles themselves are most distinctly recognized. Every such departure is so obviously the result of the necessary imperfection of a human administration, in connection with the comparative inferiority of the interests to be protected, not to say of its corruption, as clearly to show that no such departures can mar the moral administration of an infinitely perfect Being,(whose kingdom is an everlasting kingdom, and of whose dominion there is no end). Here no departure from the exact principles of truth and righteousness can result from weakness or error, or indifference to the end to be accomplished. The magnitude of the interests concerned, the value of the law as the means of securing these interests, the ill desert of transgression, the relation and the authority of the lawgiver, and the sanctions of his authority, are to be estimated not by the standard of earth and time, but by that of eternity. And what can truth, and wisdom, and goodness demand, in the government of a kingdom, where every act of every subject is virtually either the perfect happiness or perfect misery of all; what but a full and unqualified manifestation of the benevolence of Him that sitteth on the throne, in his highest approbation of right, and his highest disapprobation of wrong moral action? How can such a manifestation be made except through natural good and natural evil as the sanctions of his law?

APPENDIX—No. V.

THOUGHTS ON THE EVIDENCE FOR DIVINE REVELATION, AND ESPECIALLY THE ARGUMENT FROM MIRACLES.

1. Miracles defined.—Misconceptions removed.—2. Miracles are credible.—A strong presumption against miracles as contrary to experience.—3. Are capable of proof.—4. Under the circumstances; and, 5. Are therefore credible.—To complete the argument, the historical narrative must be shown to be true and its authors inspired.

It is urged that events like the recorded miracles have been wrought.—Also by Dr. Chalmers, that miracles may be wrought by other beings than God.—This opinion controverted: 1. As inconsistent with the proper meaning of the word; 2. As subverting the object of miracles; 3. As destitute of proof; and, 4. As opposed by reason and the Scriptures.

It is essential to the argument for a divine revelation, that the facts related, the *miracles*, should be shown to be credible, since if miracles, as the opposers of revelation maintain, are incredible, not only no argument from the miracles alleged can be derived, but the whole argument for a revelation is weakened, if not subverted, by the narration of such events.

On the question whether the scriptural miracles are incredible, I propose to show—

1. What a miracle is; and,

2. That a scriptural miracle is no more incredible than a common event.

1. What is a miracle? Different answers have been given to this question. As a general answer, comprising others which have been given, I should say: A miracle is an event which can be accounted for only by ascribing it to a direct divine agency; or which cannot be accounted for by ascribing it to any law of nature, or to the agency or action of any created agent or cause.

By *nature*, in this connection, I mean created beings or things. By *a law* of nature, I mean that established course or order of things or events which depends solely on the constitution, properties, or nature of any created thing, and which admits of no deviation by any created power. By *a deviation* from a law of nature, I mean any departure from or alteration of such a law, whether it includes or involves a suspension, or counteraction, or violation of the law. A miracle then essentially differs from every other event, as it involves *a deviation* from some law of nature as now explained.

How we are to determine whether an event is a miracle or not, or whether it actually involves *a deviation* from a law of nature, we shall inquire elsewhere. What I now affirm is, that no event can be a miracle which does not involve, and that every event is a miracle which does involve, a deviation from any law of nature.

It may be well to remark still further, that by laws of nature I do not mean merely that order of created things by which certain changes are produced in certain circumstances, but also that order or course of things by which certain changes are not produced, or by which they continue as they are, or produce no changes whatever. Thus it is as truly a law of nature that a dead man should remain dead, as that a living man should die when wounded in the heart; that a man born blind, or without eyes, should not be made to see by a word or by the application of clay and spittle, is a law of nature; that five loaves and two small fishes should not be augmented into a quantity of food sufficient to feed five thousand men, is a law of nature; that men cast into a fiery furnace seven times heated should be burned, is a law of nature. Now though each of these laws of nature may in some respect differ from every other, yet all of them are the result of the nature of things, and are established and determined by it; and the opposite event in each instance would involve *a deviation* from the law of nature which pertains to that particular instance.

Some definitions of a miracle given by able writers on the subject demand a brief consideration. Thus we are told by Mr. Horne, in his Introduction to the Study of the Scriptures, "that it is essential to a miracle that it be accompanied with a previous notice or declaration that it is performed according to the purpose and by the power of God, for the proof or evidence of some doctrine, or in attestation of the authority or divine mission of some particular person." The same thing is included in this writer's definition of a miracle. I deem this an error which consists in confounding what is or may be always an attendant of a miracle, or may be requisite to complete the proof of a miracle with an element essential to a miracle. That the accompaniment of the previous notice or declaration specified, is no part or essential element of a miracle, is obvious from the consideration, that the same event without such an accompaniment would be and must be regarded as a miracle. The event actually involving a deviation from a law of nature, would *ipso facto* be a miracle, whether any proof of its being a miracle were furnished or not.

Again: Dr. Brown, in his Essay on Cause and Effect, denies that a miracle involves a violation of the laws of nature. This denial he rests on the strange and mistaken assumption that the word *nature* includes all existence both created and uncreated. From this assumption it follows indeed that there can be no such thing as a miracle considered as involving a violation of, or a deviation from a law of nature; for plainly in this import of the word *nature*, every event must have a cause *in nature*, i. e., a *natural* cause. It is impossible that any event should not have an adequate cause. If God himself be included under the term *nature*, then no event can be above nature, or be supernatural. I need not say that nothing can justify Dr. Brown in giving that comprehensive meaning to the word *nature* which includes all existence, even God himself. He certainly must have known that the word not only in all correct usage, but especially in the common definition of a miracle, is used to exclude the Creator, and to denote simply the range of *created* existence. God and nature are obviously distinguished, because God is supposed to do what *nature* cannot. These remarks expose the futility of what this writer designed to show, that a violation of the laws of nature is a violation of the great principle, that every event must have an adequate cause. For how is this principle violated by maintaining that an event is not produced by any secondary cause, and is therefore produced by God's agency? All Dr. Brown's reasoning to show, that if a miracle be a violation of the laws of nature its reality could never be proved by testimony, because this supposes that the great principle of cause and effect is dispensed with, is owing to a strange mistake respecting the import of the phrase "laws of nature."

But this false reasoning is not the worst consequence of his mistake. According to his definition, the reality of a miracle can never be evinced to the human mind. His definition of a miracle is, that it is an event whose peculiar antecedent is the will of God. How then, if this is its only peculiarity, is an event ever to be shown to be a miracle, i. e., to be an event whose antecedent is the will of God? Why may not the will of God be the antecedent of one event as well as of another? Surely there must be some criterion of distinguishing an event which has this antecedent from one which has it not, or we are not entitled to refer one to the will of God any more than another. What then is this criterion? What, unless the event by some peculiarity authorizes the conclusion that it cannot be produced by any created agent or cause? If we cannot decide this in view of the nature and circumstances of the event, then plainly we cannot decide that it is not brought to pass by some created agent or cause, and of course cannot trace it to the will of God. If we can decide this, then the event, and the only one which can be truly traced to the will of God as its antecedent, is an event which cannot be brought to pass by any created cause, and which is above nature. This is its grand peculiarity; that without which, there can be no warrant for ascribing it to the will and power of God. In other words, a miraculous event is one which is a violation of, or a deviation from the laws of nature. Call it by what name or define it as we will, this peculiarity must be assumed respecting it, or the inference of a divine interposition in the production of the event can never be authorized. I only add, that all correct usage sanctions this application of the phrase *laws of nature*, that the peculiar views started on this point by Dr. Brown resulted from his peculiar notions of a cause, and any controversy on the topic must be a mere logomachy, as the phrase was never before used in the sense which he has given it.

2. Miracles are credible.

There is a strong presumption against a miracle, simply considered. The principle applied to all secondary causes on which this presumption rests is, that *the same causes in the same circumstances produce the same effects.* On this principle Mr. Hume maintains that miracles are incredible and incapable of proof from testimony. Nor can I hesitate to say, that in my opinion his argument on the subject, or the principle on which it rests, has not been successfully refuted, at least not in every instance. On this particular topic his most prominent antagonist, Dr. Campbell, has failed. I do not here speak of the entire treatise of Dr. Campbell, but only of that part of it in which he maintains the abstract principle, that testimony to facts which are *contrary to all experience* is entitled to credit.

Nor when I speak of the presumption against miracles simply considered, do I mean that a case may not be supposed, in which we should reasonably hesitate to say that there is not a miracle, but that no case can be easily supposed in which a violation of the laws of nature is implied, and in which I can be reasonably required to believe in this violation, MERELY on verbal or written assertions. A case in which I might be perplexed can very easily be imagined, but after all it appears to me, that I should either reasonably feel that I did not know all the facts in the case, and on this ground should still withhold my faith, or I should presume that there were *circumstances*, which removed what would otherwise render the narration incredible.

The mental assurance of laws of nature and of their uniformity in the future as well as in the past, is evinced by an experience so uniform and so extensive, as to be scarcely inferior to that given by *our senses* of the reality of external things. And so it must be, or it is absurd to talk of a miracle; for what is a miracle if not an event contrary to all experience except of itself, and incredible therefore just in a degree proportioned to our assurance of the future uniformity of nature's laws?

Miracles ARE *contrary to experience*, and must be thus viewed so long as the question of their reality is agitated. That a dead man should be raised to life *by a word*, or that the fire of a furnace should not consume human flesh, *circumstances being the same*, is contrary to experience. The experiment has been fairly made, and no philosopher could hesitate so to pronounce.

The story of the King of Siam, by Mr. Locke, is a good illustration of the difference between an event *aside* from experience, and one *contrary* to experience. This is *aside* from experience, not contrary to it. But let all the *causes* of freezing exist, and exist in the *same circumstances*, and no freezing ever have occurred since the world began; and then the declaration that freezing would be produced by these causes would be the declaration of a miracle; and if the circumstances were alleged to be the same as in all former cases, the declaration would *not* be entitled to credit. See Campbell, sect. 2; Dwight, vol. ii. p. 460. I cannot subscribe to what these writers say.

3. Miracles in their own nature, equally capable of proof as are common events,—i. e., the testimony of our senses, *other*

things being equal, is to be as much relied on in one case as the other,—the opportunity of judging, the state of the mind, the presumption against their existence, &c., being removed.

4. *The circumstances* of the miracles of Christ remove all presumption against, not to say create a presumption in favor of, their reality. THERE WAS AN OBJECT WORTHY OF GOD'S MIRACULOUS INTERPOSITION. Hence—

5. *The credible nature* of these miracles cannot be doubted; and therefore they may as easily be proved to have taken place by testimony as any ordinary events.

Most if not all the other direct arguments must depend on *the truth of the historical narrative* contained in the Bible. By this I intend the truth or correctness of the account of sensible facts given by the writers of the book, and also of the instructions of Jesus and his apostles. If this be so, then every other argument must conduct us to this conclusion, i. e., the truth of the narrative; for unless we can establish its truth in these matters, how can we come to any conclusion founded upon it? But if on the other hand we can prove the truth of the narrative in these two respects, our conclusion is incontrovertible. If for example I can *in any way* prove that Jesus wrought miracles, in attestation of his mission from God, I prove the validity of his claim, and that what he taught was from God; and if in addition to this, I prove that those who have given us a record of what he taught were inspired, I prove that what they wrote as his instructions was what he taught, and was from him. All this it is obvious depends on the truth of the historical narrative.

To evince the truth of the historical narrative, the arguments which are relied on are various; and though they all bear indirectly on the ultimate conclusion that Christianity is from God, yet it is important if we would estimate their weight, to see the form and bearing of each. Some of these arguments which support the general conclusion that this religion is from God, only as they evince the truth of the historical narration, are the following: The argument founded on the credibility of the writers as witnesses. The argument founded on the reception of the history by Christians at the time it was published. The argument from the coincidence of facts related in other writings—as contained in Paley's Horæ Paulinæ. Now to these and every other argument of the kind, some things are necessary in common, and some things which are necessary to one particular argument are not necessary to all.

On the other hand, some things are necessary to each of these arguments which are not necessary to others. Thus, to make out the argument from *the credibility* of the writers we must prove that it was written by its professed authors; for unless we can identify the authors we can derive no argument *simply* from their credibility. It is true indeed that their credibility may be proved without proving by the second and third arguments before mentioned, that its professed were its real authors; but these arguments prove the truth of the record or the reality of the facts independently of the *testimony* of the authors, and it is quite logical to infer from such a source the *credibility* of the historian. Still the credibility of the historian thus proved, cannot be relied on to prove the reality of the facts or truth of the record. Thus to use it in an argument would be reasoning in a circle: it would be deriving his credibility from the truth of the record. It is true there may be what may be called particular exceptions to these general remarks. For example, we may suppose the credibility of a writer to be proved in the manner now supposed with respect to a very large portion of the facts which he records, and yet not with respect to all of them; and in this case we might reasonably rely on his credibility in regard to those facts which are not proved in any other way.

It ought here to be remarked, that while there are many ways of proving the *truth* of the Gospel history, considered as a narrative of facts, that no one of these arguments terminating at this point proves that the system of religion contained in the Bible is from God; for though we had the very autographs themselves and could ascertain with exactest precision their import; though we were fully convinced of the intelligence, honesty, opportunities for information—in a word, of the credibility of the writers as mere human historians; and though we might from the nature of the facts recorded concerning Jesus, infer that what he taught was from God, still their *record* of what he taught might be very *imperfect;* and though according to the circumstances of the case we should place a greater or less reliance on their account of his instructions, yet we should only have that ground for an unqualified reliance, that the record contains exactly what he taught, and that the

Bible contains a religion from God which the case seems to demand. It is only when we take another step in the argument and show that these historians were the subjects of *a divine inspiration* which led them into all truth, that the mind rests in the unhesitating conclusion that Christianity is from God.

The evangelical history being true, miracles were wrought in attestation of the fact that the system of religion taught by Christ and his apostles is a revelation from God. But God only can work miracles, and he only in attestation of truth. It follows therefore that the system of religion taught by Christ and his apostles is a revelation from God.

This argument, so absolutely conclusive as it would seem to every unperverted mind, is opposed on the ground that events similar to the miracles recorded in the Scriptures have taken place in other instances. To show that this claim is wholly groundless, and that God only can work miracles in the true import of the word as used in this controversy, is the object of my subsequent remarks.

Instead of occupying time with an examination of the accounts of pretended Pagan and Popish miracles, such as those of Pythagoras, of Aristeas, of Vespasian, of the Abbé de Paris, and of others, I refer to Horne's Introduction and other works in which these accounts are examined and sufficiently refuted: Paley's Evidences and Douglas' Criterion.

It is claimed that the magicians of Egypt wrought miracles. If so, the proof must be found in the Mosaic account of their works. But this very explicitly informs us, that what these magicians did under the pretense of working miracles, was done *by their enchantments*, i. e., by jugglery or legerdemain. The facts in the case are obviously these: The magicians of Egypt attempted to resist the authority of Moses' divine mission by performing through the arts of jugglery what would be regarded wonders as great as those performed by Moses. The method adopted by Divine Wisdom to render void these attempts, was not to lay open the real causes of these seeming wonders by unfolding the arts and tricks of the magicians, but in a more direct and impressive manner, to perform works which should be seen at once to be both beyond their power, and beyond all human and created power. While such was the method adopted to convince Pharaoh and the Egyptians of Moses' divine mission, the writer of the narrative appears even solicitous to impress on the reader's mind the fact that the seeming wonders of the magicians were done *by their enchantments.*

There is another claim made by the advocates of Revelation and professedly on its authority, which, as it involves a principle as well as facts, has an important bearing on the argument from miracles, and demands a thorough examination.

The claim is, that created superhuman agents can, and actually have performed miracles. Thus Dr. Chalmers says: "It is presumptuous to affirm that nothing short of Omnipotence can suspend the laws of visible nature,"—"that we cannot tell what be the orders of power and intelligence between us and God; and it is a monstrous presumption to affirm that no archangel, no secondary or intermediate being whatever, can perform a miracle." He asserts on the authority of the Bible, that there are such beings, and that they have performed what are to all intents and purposes, miracles."

To the clearing away of the supposed difficulties of this subject, it is important to remark that the word miracle (*τέρας, σημεῖον, δύναμις*), as used in the Scriptures, is in itself wholly ambiguous. By this however I do not mean that it is so in the least degree in its actual application, in view of all that bears on the question of its meaning in each instance of its use. The fact is far otherwise. Indeed in every case of the actual use of an ambiguous word, there is either an improper and forbidden use of it, or else the connection and manner of use show which of the different possible meanings of the word is the real one. What then is the real meaning of the word miracle, in any instance of its actual use, must be determined by the connection in which it stands.

In the most generic sense of which the word is capable, it denotes a wonder, that is, an event which is unusual and extraordinary in one respect, viz., that it cannot be accounted for by any *known* secondary cause. The word also has two specific meanings in different applications. When applied to the works of creatures it still retains its generic import, and denotes, as the nature of the case and often other considerations decisively show, wonders, i. e., events which cannot be accounted for by any *known* secondary causes, but which nevertheless are of such a nature as not to require, and therefore in any way cannot be ascribed to power above that of creatures. (Vide Matt. xxiv. 24.)

Again: when the word is applied to the works of God, it still as before retains its generic import, and denotes, as the nature of the case and often other considerations decisively show, wonders, i. e., events which cannot be accounted for by any *known* secondary causes, and which require us to ascribe them to power above that of creatures, even to that of God.

With these different meanings of the *miracles* in view, to affirm that *miracles* in the generic sense of the scriptural term τέρατα, or in the former of its two specific meanings, cannot be ascribed to created agents, would indeed be presumptuous. The Scriptures evidently sanction this use of the term. On the other hand, to use the word in the specific meaning which it has, when applied to those works of God which are alleged in attestation of a revelation, and to affirm that created agents can work miracles, is to say the least not less presumptuous. There are in my view, on the part of Dr. Chalmers and others who use similar phraseology on this subject, two errors. The first is, that they do not distinguish between the two meanings of the word *miracle* in its different applications, and treat of the subject as if the word had but one meaning. The second error is, that they use the word in that meaning which it has when applied in the controversy respecting a divine revelation (for it is undeniable that they would be understood to use it in this import), without having accurately ascertained what this meaning is.

The doctrine then—and Dr. Chalmers fully asserts it, and professedly on the authority of the Bible itself—the doctrine that any created agent can perform a miracle, in that sense of the word which is its true sense when applied in the argument for a revelation from God, I deny for the following reasons, viz.:

1. It is inconsistent with the true meaning of the word miracle in its present application.

2. It subverts the peculiar characteristic of a miracle as a proof of divine interposition.

3. It is destitute of all proof.

4. It is opposed by decisive proof from both reason and the Scriptures.

Before I proceed in the discussion, let it be remarked that the inquiry respects miracles only in that specific import of the word which it has, when used to denote a work wrought in attestation of a revelation from God.

1. The doctrine that any created agent can perform a miracle, is inconsistent with the common and only just conception of such a work.

I need hardly say that the ablest advocates of a divine revelation, as well as their opponents, have considered a miracle as an event above the power of any created agent. Is this idea then essential to the true idea of a miracle? If not, then there is no word which usage has sanctioned to denote that class or kind of events which are above the power of created agents. Is this credible after all the discussions which have been had respecting the reality of such events? Will it then be said that there are no works, or that it is presumptuous to affirm that there are any, which some of the creatures of God cannot perform as well as God himself? I think not. But if we are authorized to affirm that there are works which God only, and not creatures can perform, then I ask what are they? The only answer from those who agree with Dr. Chalmers must be, we cannot tell—the works, if such there be, which God only can perform, cannot be distinguished by us from works which some of his creatures can perform. Therefore if water be turned into wine, if mountains be removed, if the dead be raised to life, we cannot decide from the nature of the event whether God or a creature has done it. Is this the common conception or judgment of those who believe in miracles, or even of those who believe in God? Or do they, under the name of miracles, conceive of certain works which God only can perform, and which the human mind can and is bound to distinguish from those which creatures can perform as exclusively the works of God? If the human mind is competent to make no such distinction, then instead of talking of God's works, let us speak of those which may or which may not be the works of God.

Again: I ask in what does a miracle, according to the principle of Dr. Chalmers, differ from an ordinary event, or one brought to pass by the agency of second causes? Not in this, that the former is above the power of any created agent and the latter not; for it may be true according to Dr. Chalmers that a miracle is not above the power of some created agent. Is the difference then, that a miracle is an event which *appears to us* to be above the power of any created agent, while an ordinary event does not? But I ask, how does *this appear to us?* Plainly not from any thing we know or have good reason to believe, either from the nature of the event or the manner of its production; for it is an event which may be brought to pass by a created agent. It does not therefore *appear to us* at all to be above the power of a created agent. We have no means of deciding whether it is so or not. Is it then said that a miracle is an event which lies without the limits and range of what Dr. Chalmers calls "visible nature," or of which we know of *no adequate created cause*, and of which therefore God by direct agency *may be* the cause? But according to the principle of Dr. Chalmers, it is equally true that God *may not* be the cause and that a created agent *may be*. If then it is essential to his definition of a miracle that God *may be* its cause, it is equally essential that God *may not be* its cause, and that a creature *may be*. A miracle therefore would be an event concerning whose author or cause we can decide nothing, except that either God or some creature of God is its cause; i. e., which may be or may not be an ordinary event. What other difference can be supposed on the principle of Dr. Chalmers, I am unable to conceive; and to the question, what is the difference between a miracle and an ordinary event (by which is meant an event brought to pass by the agency of second causes), the only answer is—no difference; at least no one is authorized to conceive or to affirm that there is a difference. Palpably as this conclusion follows from the principle of Dr. Chalmers, it is believed that no one will adopt it.

I recur then to the idea of a miracle as an event which is above the power of any created agent. If this idea be conceded to be involved in the true definition of a miracle, then the very supposition that a created being should perform a miracle, carries in it this palpable inconsistency or absurdity, that a created being can perform what none but the uncreated Being can perform; that a created being has power to do what he has not power to do.

It is plain then that Dr. Chalmers denies in one essential respect the commonly received definition of a miracle. This he must do, or give up his position that some created superhuman agents may have power to perform miracles. With the idea of a miracle as exclusively the work of Omnipotence, if we admit that Gabriel possesses or even may possess the power to remove mountains, then if mountains are removed, we cannot regard the event as a miracle. The very supposition of a miracle performed by a creature is absurd and self-contradictory, unless we abandon the commonly received definition of a miracle.

2. The doctrine that any created agent whatever can perform a miracle, subverts the peculiar characteristic of a miracle as a proof of divine interposition. Dr. Chalmers not only maintains as we have seen, that created agents may for aught we can say, perform miracles, but he asserts on the authority of the Bible, that such agents have performed what are "to all intents and purposes miracles." Having taken this ground, he is fully aware of the peculiar pertinency of the question which he puts—"How comes a miracle, and in what circumstances, to be the token of a revelation from God?" This question he treats under three suppositions; the first is, that the so called miracle, i. e., an event which may be brought to pass either by God or a superhuman creature, is wrought in support of either known falsehood or known immorality. In this case he justly claims that the event must be ascribed to a created superhuman wicked agent. The reasons for this are obvious. It is a work beyond the power of any human agent, and must be ascribed to a *superhuman* agent; it is done for a malignant or selfish purpose, and must therefore be ascribed to *a wicked* superhuman agent. But the problem to be solved is, why not ascribe it to God? I say this is the problem to be solved, and that Dr. Chalmers in his solution of it, has assigned at most only a part of the reason as the whole. The reason which he assigns as the whole reason is, that the work is done for a malignant or selfish purpose. I admit that this is *a* reason and *a decisive* one. God is good and cannot be charged with countenancing falsehood or immorality. But this is not *the whole* reason for not ascribing it to God. There is yet another, viz., the work done is one which according to the supposition may be done by a created being; so that entirely aside from the falsehood or immorality of the affair, there is this decisive reason for not ascribing the work, the so called miracle, to God. There is nothing in its nature to justify us in ascribing it to

tain the claim of the professed revelation on two grounds: first, the absence of every thing which indicates the agency of a wicked spirit; and, secondly, that God would not lend himself, either by permission to others or by direct agency, to the deception of his creatures. So far as the first of these reasons is concerned, if it be admitted to be a sufficient reason for not ascribing the so-called miracles to *a wicked* spirit, it is not a reason in the lowest degree for ascribing them to God, since they may be the works of a good though a created spirit, commissioned by God to bear the message. Again: if the absence of every thing which indicates the agency of a wicked spirit is a reason for ascribing the miracles to God, this reason does not result from *the nature* of the works, but solely from other and distinct considerations, viz., that they are either the works of God or of a wicked spirit, and that they are not the works of the latter, because if they were, there would be indications of his malignant agency. But here the question is, whether the evil spirit might not be sufficiently wise for his own purposes, to avoid furnishing even the least indication of malignity, and whether there is not somewhat of an unreasonable assumption in this argument. But waiving this altogether, and admitting that in the case supposed, there is good reason for believing that the works are God's, still *the reason* is not furnished *by the nature* of the works. Any other evinced to be the results of his direct agency, would be as good evidence of God's interposition as these so-called miracles. Proof furnished of God's direct agency from testimony, or the circumstances of an event, is surely a very different kind of evidence from that furnished by a work which God only can perform. But, says Dr. Chalmers, God would not permit wicked spirits to deceive his creatures, i. e., to furnish legitimate proof that falsehood is truth, by working miracles. Certainly not. But this is not the question nor any part of it; but whether God would not permit them to do those works which they have power to do; and if he would not, why? Dr. Chalmers says this would or might be fitted to deceive his creatures; and this is the reason that God would not permit them to do the works. I answer, that it would not in the least degree be fitted to deceive them; in other words (and this is what is meant), it would furnish no legitimate proof, nor the shadow of it, that falsehood is truth; that works which are not God's works are God's works. Do we not know or believe, according to Dr. Chalmers, that these superhuman beings have power to perform these works? Why then if they actually do them, should we be deceived, and conclude that God has done them? This is the only way in which we can be deceived by them; and why conclude from their nature that God does the works, when for aught we know there are a thousand other beings who might do them? Such deception truly would be wholly gratuitous on our part, for there is absolutely nothing in the nature of the works which can authorize, but that which absolutely forbids such a conclusion.

Take as an illustration, the miracles by Moses on the authority of which he claimed of Pharaoh that he should let the people go. What would Pharaoh have said to this demand, on the principle of Dr. Chalmers? The reply would have been, "Your pretended works of God may have been performed by some other agent. They can therefore neither require nor authorize, but must forbid me to conclude that they are performed by God. Such works can furnish no evidence that God has sent you." Moses, according to Dr. Chalmers, could not deny this. He could only say in reply, that "they are not the works of a created agent, but are God's works." To this Pharaoh might rejoin by asking, "Where is *the proof* that they are the works of God?" Moses answers, "You must take my word for it." "That," says Pharaoh, "I am not bound to do. I might as well take your word that any other work or event is God's, and not only so, I might as well take your word that God has sent you, as take your word that this is God's work. Besides, you appealed *to the works*, as *the proof* of God's agency to establish your claim to a divine mission, and now you ask me to take your simple word for it." "True," says Moses, "but is it not plain that God would not deceive you by permitting a creature to do these works?" "Deceive me!" rejoins Pharaoh; "deceive me in what, or by what means?" "Why," answers Moses, "deceive you in leading you by these very *unusual* works, to conclude that they are God's unless they really are his works?" "I am in no danger of that," says Pharaoh; "so long as I have common sense I shall never be deceived by such works into the belief that they are God's, knowing as I do that they may be done as well by angels or devils as by God himself." And truly, why should he be deceived in a case in which there is nothing to deceive him? Plainly he should not, though all the waters of Egypt were turned into blood.

Dr. Chalmers however, is very explicit on this point. He says: "Though neither a good nor a bad morality stood associated with the message, still on the strength of natural religion would we defer to the authority of *the miracles alone;*" i. e., to the authority of works which, in his view, devils have power to perform, and for the non-performance of which by devils no reason can be given. Is it not plain that Dr. Chalmers in this view of the subject, all the while assumes in his own mind the common definition of a miracle, as that which Omnipotence only can perform, and that in this lies what he calls "its proper force and authority?" and yet in affirming the possibility that miracles should be performed by other beings than God, does he not forbid us to ascribe them to God, and deprive them of every particle of force or authority as evidence of God's interposition?

3. There is no proof that any created being can perform a miracle, or any thing which shall have the semblance of one.

On this point there can be no hesitation, provided we adopt the common definition of a miracle. For then the very supposition that a created agent should perform a miracle involves, as we have seen, a palpable absurdity. But the question now is, whether created beings can perform works which we shall reasonably regard, or which by the laws of evidence we shall be bound to regard as miracles; that is, as works wrought by God in attestation of a revelation. It is obviously assumed by Dr. Chalmers and others, that such works have been and may be done by such beings. This class of works is conceived to be beyond the powers of any created agents, with which we are acquainted, or beyond the powers of "visible nature."

According to the view now under consideration, the true test of a miraculous work is, that it is one which in its own nature is beyond the power of any created agent with which we are acquainted; and which therefore, while it may be for aught we can say to the contrary, the work of a creature, may also be the work of God. Such a work it is claimed, being declared by a witness of a certain character and in certain circumstances to be God's work, ought to be believed by us to be so, and to be regarded as a proof of a divine revelation. According to this view, the real test or proof that an event is a miracle is, that it is in its own nature beyond the power of any created agent with which we are acquainted; for the supposed testimony that it is wrought by God, does not determine it to be a miracle, but only a miracle wrought by God and not by a creature: or if it be said that the fact testified, viz., that it is wrought by God, is essential to its being a miracle, and as such a proof of divine revelation, then the nature of the fact as it falls under the cognizance of our senses, is no more proof of a revelation, than any ordinary event concerning which the same fact should be testified in the same manner. The raising of a dead man to life, viewed as an event within the power of created agents, and yet testified by the supposed witness *to be done by the power of God*, furnishes no more proof of a revelation, than would the death of a living man testified by the witness to have been effected by the power of God; and neither adds a particle of proof to the fact of a revelation, beyond that of the naked testimony of the witness. The witness is no more entitled to credit when he asserts that the supposed work, which according to the supposition may be performed by a created agent, is performed by divine agency, than when he asserts the fact of a revelation. The work itself therefore, in its own nature, adds nothing to the proof of such a fact, and in this respect is wholly useless. This may be illustrated by an example—that of a king, sending his signet by a messenger. If we suppose that there were a hundred or a thousand other such signets, any one of which the messenger might have obtained, it is plain that the showing of the signet with the assertion that it is the king's, would still leave the simple testimony of the witness as our only reliance; and no proof from the signet, or from his possession of it, would be added to his mere testimony to the fact of his mission by the king. One who should believe in his mission would reasonably say—I believe it not because the messenger has the signet, for others have the same, but simply and solely in view of the character of the witness and the circumstances of his mission.

Whether then created agents can perform works which we shall reasonably regard as miracles, or having the semblance of miracles to our mind, that is, works which shall reasonably appear to us, or be regarded by us as proofs of a revelation, is a question which depends entirely on another, viz.: whether we can draw the line of demarkation between those works which God, and which creatures can perform. Just so far as we can draw this line, and no farther, are we competent to decide the question whether an event is a miracle or not. Of every work in respect to which we are authorized, in view of its nature, to say God only can perform it, we can assert that it is a miracle, i. e., a proof of a divine revelation, but of no other. That any created agent has power to perform a work which we are authorized to say God only can perform, cannot be admitted. Of course no created agent, even if we suppose his powers to transcend those of any finite creature with which we are acquainted, or those "of visible nature," can do any work which can be esteemed miraculous. If cases can be supposed in which we cannot decide whether God only can do the works, then of course we cannot decide that they are miracles, and may be in doubt whether they are or not; i. e., we can make no decision, and of course must remain uninfluenced by them. Before then we can decide that any work apparently done by a creature is a miracle, we must decide that it is a work which God only, and not a creature can perform. So that if we decide that a creature has actually done it, then we know that it is nót a work which God only can perform, and therefore that it is *not a miracle*. Or if we decide that it is a work which God only can perform, then we cannot admit that a creature has done it. It is utterly impossible therefore, that any mind should find the least proof that any creature can perform a miracle.

But that created agents can work miracles is claimed on the basis of matter of fact. The cases alleged are such as the following:

The raising of Samuel from the dead by the Witch of Endor, (1 Sam. xxviii.) The design of the narrative seems to be to assert a miracle. Samuel, according to the account, was raised from the dead; while the manner of the event was such as clearly to show that the woman had actually no concern with it. "She cried with a loud voice," that is, she betrayed disappointment and consternation. "She saw gods ascending out of the earth;" that is, in her panic she saw what was wonderful and strange, she knew not what. When inquired of by Saul "what form he was of," her answer was, "An old man cometh up and he is covered with a mantle;" while "Saul perceived that it was Samuel." It is also manifest from the narrative, that the sorceress had not even prepared her enchantments. Thus from the obvious disappointment and consternation of the woman, and from the appearance of Samuel as having no connection with her enchantments, it was apparent to Saul that her pretensions were groundless, and that those who claimed the power over familiar spirits were impostors.

Had it been said in this narrative that the woman did not expect to see Samuel come forth, all the difficulty would vanish. But I ask, had not the writer of this narrative as much reason for supposing that his readers would so understand the matter, as had he expressly asserted the fact? I think so, not only in view of what he has said respecting the manner in which the woman regarded the appearance of Samuel, but for other reasons. That God raised Samuel from the dead we conclusively infer from the nature of the event, and also from the fact that in proof of it, Samuel actually uttered a prophecy and addressed it to Saul. The law against witches was quite sufficient to show that God did not work miracles by their instrumentality, and that he did not authorize them or others to believe that he would; as he must have done had he in this instance, or in any other, have raised a dead man to life in connection with their enchantments. On this supposition, why was not Saul even authorized to make the application to this woman which he did make, and to entertain the expectation from her which he so evidently did entertain? Such must have been the views of every unbiassed Jewish reader of this narrative. Of course it is as certain that the woman did not expect to raise Samuel from the dead, as had the historian asserted the fact. Hence I conclude that the miracle of raising Samuel was wrought for the double purpose of convincing Saul that she was an impostor; by the way in which it was done, and the manner in which the woman regarded it; and also to reprove Saul for his wickedness, and to denounce on him the judgment of death by the mouth of the risen prophet.

Another class of facts claims consideration, viz., demoniacal possessions. These facts as given in the literal interpretation of the scriptural narrative may be admitted. Still there is nothing in them miraculous even in appearance. They must have been regarded by those who witnessed them either in view of their nature, or of their frequent occurrence, or of both, as ordinary events in distinction from miracles. In this manner it is obvious on the face of the narrative they were regarded. Whether we can or cannot assign the reasons why the people of that age regarded them as ordinary events, the natural results of adequate power of created agents, the fact that they were so regarded cannot be denied by any one who admits their reality on the authority of the history. If he admits the reality of the facts, he must admit also that they were not miracles in the view of those who witnessed them. We, indeed, may be obliged to regard them as a peculiarity of another age. But whatever the phenomena were, we cannot avoid the conclusion that their cause was known, and known as an adequate second cause. In these events therefore, there could have been no semblance of a miracle to those who witnessed them. They were Jews who asked, "Can a devil open the eyes of the blind?"

Should it here be said that whatever may be supposed in respect to the people of another age, if the same phenomena were to occur in our time they would be justly regarded as miracles—such as that recorded, Mark, v. 4—I reply, that if the same phenomena were to occur now, either their nature or frequent occurrence, or something else equally decisive, would reveal their nature as the effects of adequate second causes, and of course prevent the possibility of mistaking them for miracles. To suppose that they should occur in such circumstances as to require us according to the laws of faith to believe them to be miracles, is to suppose that God should lay us under obligation to believe that to be true which is actually false. Besides, we never could be required by the laws of faith to believe them to be miracles, so long as we knew or had good reason to believe, that they might be the effects of created power. Such events in such a case could not furnish the least evidence that they are performed by divine power, or that God has any more concern in bringing them to pass, than the commonest events. If we suppose such an event to occur, we might or we might not be able to assign the reason for its occurrence; but surely we could not reasonably suppose, that God designed by it to convince us that he had done what he had not done, and what we should not have the least reason to imagine he had done. If we suppose such a design on his part, it must be our own fault if we are deceived by it. But it may be supposed, that we have no reason to believe that the imaginary extraordinary event can be brought to pass by a created agent, and that all the evidence in the case goes to prove that it is accomplished by the power of God, and that nevertheless God may permit or commission a created agent to perform the work in attestation of a divine mission—and on this supposition it may be asked, whether the event would not be good evidence to our minds of the fact of a divine mission, and in this respect be entitled to the same influence, and answer the same purpose as a divine work? I answer, yes; because all the evidence in the case would be to one point, viz., that it is a divine work. The mere *supposed possibility* that it is a creature's work would be no evidence either way, and the conclusion that it is God's work, would be as truly authorized and required with such a possibility as without it. Why then resort to the present supposition, and especially that of a possible fact, which if real would imply that God should lead us and oblige us to regard that as evidence which is not so in the truth of things, and which to our minds proves that to be true which is not true—viz., that the event is the effect of divine power, when it is not?

I am aware that another than the literal interpretation of the scriptural language on the present subject, has been adopted by some advocates of revelation, of no less reputation than Sykes, Lardner, Farmer, and others. This class of writers admit the incredibility of the narrative when literally interpreted, and attempt to relieve the subject of difficulty by rejecting the literal interpretation. The question here respects the origin of certain phenomena, and not the reality of the miracles wrought by Christ and his apostles, of which these phenomena were the occasion. I cannot however concede to the opinion that the language of the Scriptures on this subject is not to be literally interpreted. I see in the first place no real reason assigned for it, except the supposed incredibility of the facts as given by a literal interpretation. But why are they to be pronounced incredible? Solely on the ground that they are aside from, not contrary to all experience, except that given in the scriptural narrative. Be it so. But this no more establishes their incredibility, than the want of experience by the inhabitants of the torrid zone, establishes the incredibility of the fact that water freezes in a more northern climate; or than the want of experience by the greater part of the human race establishes the incredibility that stones should fall from the atmosphere. Indeed why is it at all incredible, that the facts in question should actually have existed as the scriptural history relates, even from the beginning of the world, considered as the peculiarity of another age, being in their nature well understood by the people who witnessed them, and designed to render the triumph of the Redeemer over the grand adversary of God and man more complete and signal, and to cease, when that object should be accomplished? Besides, no man is authorized to say, *from the nature* of the phenomena, that there were no created agents adequate to their production, known to those who witnessed them. Of course the facts in question in respect to incredibility stand on entirely other grounds than the facts of miracles. In the second place, the language of the scriptural writers cannot in my view, according to any authorized principles of interpretation, be understood in any other than its literal import. On this point I can here only remark, that whether the facts be credible or incredible, the language of the narrative could not be more absolutely unequivocal than it is, that the facts actually occurred. How is it possible that this plain narrative of plain men should tell us of the spirits that held converse with the Saviour; that supplicated his forbearance and a respite from torment; that professed their knowledge of him as the Holy One of God; that were commanded by him to be silent, and that when ejected from those whom they possessed, were permitted by their own request, and in execution of their own will, to enter a herd of swine, and to make new manifestations of their power and malignity? How are these things possible, if the writers of the narrative did not mean to be understood as recording the reality of these spirits, and of the facts connected with their agency? And why should the plain meaning of the language be rejected solely on the ground of the supposed incredibility of facts, which are in no degree incredible? That the writers intended to be understood as giving us a literal account of the facts, cannot, I think, be reasonably doubted. The only alternative therefore, is either to receive it as true, and to admit their authority as historians, or to regard their narrative as proof of their credulity, and of that of the age in which they wrote; which, if this be all that can be said, is nothing less than infidelity. I say *if this be all that can be said*, for there is one thing more at least of what *may be true* on this subject, viz., that while this is literal language, and expressed the actual belief of the age or the people, and also of the writers, *it is still only the language of appearance.* Whether this be so or not, I am not prepared to decide with confidence. I would however admit that in some instances things or events are in words ascribed *to the devil*, as in Matt. xiii. 39, which if ascribed in literal language *to that principle of evil* which is inseparable from a principle of good in the very nature of things, would better harmonize with just and necessary conceptions of God, and of his providential government.

4. There is decisive proof both from the Scriptures and from reason, that no created being can perform a miracle.

This proof from the Scriptures, it is true, can have no influence except with those who attempt to defend the scriptural miracles. With them the question is, what are the events to which the scriptural writers appeal as proofs of a revelation; or rather what is the nature of this proof from miracles? On this point I shall only ask what is it, except that in their view and that of other men, miracles are works which God only can perform? John, iii. 2; Acts, x. 38, 40; John, v. 36, and x. 21, 25; Matt. xii. 24, 28; Ex. iv. 11; Ps. xciv. 9, and cxlvi. 8; John, ix. 32, 33.

The proof from reason that no created agent can perform a miracle, if by a miracle we mean a work or an event which God only can perform, is still more decisive, consisting in the self-evident proposition, that no creature can do that which God only can do. The same thing is true, if we define a miracle to be an event which involves a deviation from, or a violation of, a law of nature; for it is no deviation from a law of nature for a creature to bring to pass an event which he has power to bring to pass.

But it is claimed by some that a miracle, considered as an event brought to pass only by the power of God, cannot be evinced to the human mind by legitimate evidence, not even to that of an eye-witness; and this on the ground that we are ignorant of the powers of nature or of created agents, and that therefore whatever the event may be in its nature and its circumstances, we are not competent to decide that God brings it to pass.

Before replying to this argument directly, I would remark

that I shall assume what it admits, that a miracle as defined, is possible. I shall also assume that whatever presumption there is against a miracle from experience, it is completely removed by the object for which the miracle is wrought. This is fairly assumed, for the question now is, not whether a miracle can be reasonably admitted on the ground of testimony as opposed to experience, but it is simply whether the event, supposing it to be brought to pass by the power of God, can be satisfactorily proved to be, since as it is claimed, for aught that can be shown, it may be accomplished by created power. It is not whether God can work a miracle or bring to pass an event by his own direct and immediate agency, but it is whether he can bring it to pass *in such a way or manner* as to prove to our minds, according to the laws of rational belief, that he has brought it to pass by his direct and exclusive power. It is claimed that he cannot, and this on the ground that the event, be it what it may, and produced in what manner it may, may for any evidence to the contrary, be brought to pass by the power of some created agent.

To this reasoning I propose to reply, by stating and illustrating what I deem sufficient grounds for inferring the reality of a miracle, and by showing that these are sufficient for the inference.

I remark then, in the first place, that the creative power of God may be an incommunicable attribute. By creative power must be understood at least power to create substance—this visible universe from absolute and universal nothing. The true and essential conception of creative power is, that it is necessarily eternal, underived, and self-existent. As such its existence could neither be produced nor be prevented. The mind cannot conceive as it must, power to be eternal, underived, self-existent, without conceiving it to be *necessarily underived*, and in its own nature incapable of being produced or communicated. For whatever is necessarily conceived by the mind as existing by a necessity of its own nature, is necessarily conceived as incapable in its own nature of being produced, created, or communicated. Space, for example, cannot be conceived to be capable of being produced or created.

Creative power is possible or capable of existence, without being created or produced. So is self-existence. Space and duration are possible without being created or produced, and so is the equality of two and two with four. Whatever is capable of existing and actually exists without being created or produced, exists by necessity and cannot be created or produced. It is eternal and self-existent.

Some things however are necessarily conceived by the mind as existing by a necessity of their own nature, *directly*, and others *indirectly*. Thus space and duration are necessarily conceived by the mind as existing by a necessity of nature *directly;* by which I mean, that the mere conception, or as logicians say, the simple apprehension of space by the mind, necessarily involves or gives the conviction of its necessary existence *in re.* In other words, the object of thought has necessarily in the view of the mind a correspondiug reality. The self-existence of God is necessarily conceived by the mind to be necessary in its own nature *indirectly;* by which I mean, that while the bare conception or simple apprehension of a self-existent God, does not necessarily involve or give the conviction of the necessary existence of such a being *in re*—in other words, while the object of thought has not necessarily in the view of the mind a corresponding reality,* yet *when the fact of a self-existent God is given or proved to the mind*, then the mind necessarily conceives it to be necessary in its own nature, and thus incapable in its own nature of being produced or created.

Without claiming then that the mind on the condition of the bare conception of creative power necessarily gives as it does give on the bare conception of space, *directly* the conviction of the necessary existence of the corresponding reality, still it is manifest that it necessarily gives this conviction *indirectly*, that is, when the fact of such power, as in the present case, is admitted by the mind. This necessary existence of actually existing creative power is not the necessity of existence which is given by the mere certainty of existence, that is, the necessity that a thing is while it is; but it is a necessity of existence given in the nature of such power, as that which could neither be caused to be, nor prevented from being, any more than space or duration.

Power could not create in the first instance without being in its own nature *necessarily* uncreated; in other words, creative

* The same thing is true in respect to the bare conception of *an infinite* being, contrary to what the transcendentalists assert.

power which creates in the first instance, is necessarily conceived by the mind to be necessarily incapable in its very nature of being created or produced, just as the actual self-existence of a being is necessarily conceived to be necessarily incapable of being produced or created, and therefore incommunicable. Nor does this necessity that the power which creates in the first instance is itself incapable of being produced or created, result from the mere circumstance that the instance in which the necessity is given to knowledge, is the first of creation; for though given clearly in this instance, it is given as the necessary nature of power which creates from absolute and universal nothing. This conception of creative power thus formed becomes as a necessary conception the true and essential idea of creative power in all cases. It is a conception which involves the knowledge of the nature of creative power as being necessarily incapable of being produced or communicated, and what the mind thus knows in respect to creative power, it cannot cease to know while it knows what it really is. The mind then in its true conception of creative power must conceive it to be necessarily underivable and incommunicable.

I now proceed to say, that no power except that which is adequate to create, or creative power—power which is adequate to give to substances their existence and their nature—can be adequate to destroy, or change, or counteract them. The being who has power adequate to transform the nature of substances, and thus destroy, suspend, or counteract their action as causes, and thus to suspend those laws which result from their nature, has power which is adequate to create substances with their nature. Power that is adequate to raise a dead man to life, is and must be power to give existence to a living man from nothing. Indeed the one power must be identical with the other, since the giving of life to a dead man is as truly and essentially an act of creation as would be the act of giving him life from absolutely nothing. If then creative power is incommunicable, the act of giving life to a dead man must be the act of God, and not the act of any creature of God. This view of the subject I confess myself inclined to adopt.

If it be said that it is too metaphysical to be satisfactory, I ask, why is not also the opposite assumption, viz., that God can *impart creative power?* The proposition that God cannot impart creative power, is plainly no more metaphysical than the proposition that he can. And if my opponent has a right to rest on the assertion that he can, I have as good a right to rest on the assertion that he cannot. But I have not rested the proposition that he cannot impart creative power on mere assertion. Whether the reasons given be sufficient or not, I can only say they seem so to my own mind.

Without however resting the question on the position now taken, let us examine *it on the ground that God can impart creative power to creatures.*

I remark in the second place, it is reasonable to believe that God would not impart creative power to a creature if this be possible. The supposition that he should do this, involves so many things which are inconsistent with a sound theism, that it can hardly require a refutation. If any should insist on the possibility of his giving existence to such a creature, it may be replied that the supposition of such an existence is wholly gratuitous and unauthorized. From the mere light of nature, we have no evidence of the existence of any superhuman beings intermediate between God and man. Should an event be known to occur which is beyond the power of man and of every known created agent, it would be unreasonable to ascribe it to any being but God, since he is known to possess, and is the only being who is known to possess, power adequate to its production. Again: the supposition that a creature possesses creative power, involves the supposition that he possesses infinite attributes. A being who has power and knowledge which qualify to create from nothing, must have power and knowledge which are infinite, that is, attributes limited only by what involves a contradiction. To suppose such a creature is unphilosophical. When the mind is brought to the conclusion of an omniscient and omnipotent Creator, it is brought also to this, either that this Creator is an eternal, self-existent being, or that there is some other. We must conclude that there is an eternal, self-existent being who is the Creator of all created things, or that there is a created creator, or that there are many created creators. If the eternal, self-existent Being is not the Creator of all created things, then there may be as many created creators, with one exception, as there are things created; and to admit this is to violate the axiom of sound philosophy, that we are to admit no more causes than are necessary to account for an effect. Besides, there is a strong presumption against the supposition that an eternal, self-existent Being should give existence to creatures or to a creature, if this be possible, having the same infinite attributes with himself, especially if we reflect that each of these creatures would be able to create other beings *ad libitum* of the same infinite attributes.

Assuming then as proved, the existence of one and only one eternal self-existing Creator, who alone possesses creative power, the existence and the nature of all created things must depend on him to the exclusion of every other being. No created being can either destroy, change, or counteract the nature of created things, which is exclusively the effect of creative power. To suppose the contrary is to deny the exclusive power of God to create, since the being who can destroy, change, or counteract the nature of created things, must have power to create.

Again: from the nature of created things in given circumstances necessarily result what are called *laws of nature*—modes of operating or acting, by which physical agents in certain circumstances necessarily produce certain effects; and while the nature of created things, from which these laws necessarily result in certain circumstances, remains the same, and is neither destroyed, changed, nor counteracted, these laws must remain the same.

As no created being has power to destroy, or to change, or counteract that nature of things from which the laws of nature necessarily result, and since no deviation from these laws can be effected, without destroying or changing or counteracting that nature of things on which these laws necessarily depend, and from which they necessarily result, it follows that no created being has power to cause a deviation from any of the laws of nature.

Further: man is competent to decide to a certain extent what are laws of nature, and what are deviations from these laws. To deny this, is to deny the authority of our senses in matters of universal experience and observation, and on which the senses can solely decide. And here it is obvious at once that if we are not to rely on this authority, then not only the Christian must abandon all his reasoning for miracles, which is founded on the experience of his witnesses, but the infidel must abandon all his reasoning against miracles, which is founded on the experience of the rest of the world. The infidel, when it will subserve his purpose in argument, as strenuously maintains as others,on the authority of experience and observation, that certain causes in certain circumstances must produce certain effects. For example, that a man placed in a furnace seven times heated must be burned: that water cannot be turned into wine, or a dead man be raised to life, by a mere word. These and a thousand similar facts which are laws of nature, are settled by experience and observation, nor can the unperverted mind deny or doubt them. Let it now be supposed that we see a man placed in a furnace seven times heated, and not burned. I say *see* him, I mean that we ascertain (so far as the senses when perfectly employed on the question of fact can ascertain any thing, which is solely a matter for the senses to decide upon), that such are the circumstances of the case. Now the question is, are we to rely on these mental decisions or judgments? What are they, and on what grounds do they rest? The first is, that such is the nature of fire and of human flesh, as God has made them, that in certain circumstances—viz., when brought into contact in a furnace seven times heated, and when there is no cause either natural or supernatural to prevent the effect—the fire *must* burn human flesh. To say that we are not to rely on this judgment or decision respecting the nature of the things under consideration, is either to deny, contrary to all experience and observation, that fire has always produced this effect in the given circumstances; or to deny the self-evident proposition, that the same physical cause in the same circumstances *must* produce the same effect; or to deny both. As no one will deny either, it must be received as a fact unquestionable and incontrovertible, that from the very nature of the things, as God has made them, fire must burn human flesh in the circumstances now supposed.

Another decision or judgment in the case, so far as the senses perfectly employed on the subject can decide, is, that the man is placed in the circumstances supposed. I speak not now of any judgment or influence derived from the fact that the man is not burned. This may or may not modify or change the final conclusion in respect to the facts in the case. How this is, we may see presently. The fact that the man is not burned may be a ground of inferring some other cause or circumstance in the case than any which is cognizable by the senses. The judgment I now speak of concerns the causes and circumstances, as these are cognizable simply by the senses, and aside from the fact that the man is not burned. I suppose the case to be one in which the mind, so far as the senses when perfectly employed on the subject can enable it to judge or decide respecting the case, necessarily judges or decides that the man is placed in the circumstances supposed. I claim that aside from *any inference from the fact that the man is not burned*, the true and only judgment of the mind would and ought to be, that the man is placed in the furnace seven times heated, and that there is no cause either natural or supernatural to prevent the burning of his flesh; and that this decision or judgment, were it not for the single fact *that he is not burned*, would be entitled to unqualified confidence.

But the supposition is, that the man in these circumstances *is not burned*. How then is this fact to affect our conclusion? We are plainly not to conclude that our senses do not give us all the facts and circumstances of the case which are cognizable by the senses. The senses are according to the supposition perfectly employed on the question of fact, and their decision is to be relied on as in other like cases. When thus employed they have never deceived us. In this respect they are to be absolutely relied on. We are therefore bound to believe that the facts and circumstances supposed, are the only facts and circumstances of the case, unless we have reason from some other source for inferring some other cause or circumstance which is not cognizable by the senses. Such reason we have in the fact—a fact given by the senses that the man is not burned. This obliges us to conclude that the effect of burning is prevented by some cause which is not cognizable by the senses when perfectly employed. This must be either some natural cause, that is, some created agent not cognizable by the senses, or it must be God.

Is it then a created agent which is not cognizable by the senses? I answer, first, that we have no evidence from the light of nature, that there is any such created agent intermediate between God and man. As God is the only being who is known to possess power to prevent the effect in the case supposed, the only rational conclusion is, that its prevention is to be ascribed to his power. If on the authority of our senses we could decide that a watch had disappeared from the room in which we are, and that no individual had been in and passed out of it except A. B., we should be bound to believe that A. B. had taken the watch. The reasoning would be this: The watch must have been taken away by some visible agent; A. B. is the only visible agent by whom it could be taken away; he therefore has taken it. So in the case under consideration. The effect must be prevented by some invisible agent, or some one not cognizable by the senses. God is the only known agent who is not cognizable by the senses, and who could prevent the effect; he therefore has prevented it. It is here to be remembered that for reasons already assigned, there is no more presumption against the man's not being burned than against his being burned; in other words, that the prevention of his being burned by divine agency in the case, is as credible as the fact of his being burned in another case by natural causes would be. If we suppose a case in which the presumption from experience against a divine interposition is not removed in the manner already explained, it might be one of difficulty. We might be compelled to oppose what seems to be given by the senses perfectly employed, to the testimony of all past experience, and we might and probably should inquire again, whether what seems to be given by the senses perfectly employed in the case, is really the result of such an employment or use of these means of knowledge; or if it proved to be such, we might begin to distrust the authority of the senses, which is one of the most difficult of all tasks that can be imposed on the mind; or we might suspect that in drawing universal conclusions from universal experience and observation we had gone too far, and begin to think that what has been, at least as determined by experience, is no proof of what will be; in short, we might be in the supposable quandary of being bound to judge on a question, when the evidence on both sides is exactly balanced,—a case which may be imagined, though it can never occur; since if we really suppose such a case, we cannot be bound to form a judgment. The case to be decided on, is one in which it is as credible that the burning of the body is prevented by the agency of God, as that the watch is removed by the agency of A. B. The mere possibility of another invisible agent ought no more to diminish the confidence of our conclusion in the one case than in the other.

Again: the mind cannot reasonably admit the existence of a created agent as the author of the supposed event; but there is good and sufficient reason for disbelieving and denying it. Whenever the senses perfectly employed on the subject have decided on the facts or circumstances in which physical phenomena occur, they have in all cases decided correctly. The mind has often from an imperfect use of the senses, judged rashly and incorrectly. But no erroneous judgment or decision can be traced to a perfect use of the senses. The mind has thus decided, that the facts and circumstances which exist and which are cognizable by the senses, are all the facts and circumstances of the case, to the entire exclusion of any and every cause or agent not cognizable by the senses. This it has done in numberless instances and never found itself mistaken. No cause or agent not cognizable by sense, has ever interposed and by the result evinced the reality of its existence. It is true the mind has other proofs of the existence of God. But it has no proof of the existence of any created agent not cognizable by the senses. And here it naturally inquires, why if there are such created agents have they never evinced their existence until now? Why have they never prevented human flesh when in contact with fire from being burned? Why have they never turned water into wine, or raised the dead to life? Why should they do such things now, when they have never done them before? By this process of thought the mind, in connection with uniform experience and observation, comes to the conclusion, not only that the senses give all the facts and circumstances of the case which are cognizable by the senses, but that these are all, to the entire exclusion of any and every created cause or agent. The senses are in fact, and are obviously designed to be, the medium of deciding on the existence of physical phenomena and their causes. With this authority they do decide in certain cases, that the causes and circumstances which they discover, are all the created causes concerned in those cases. The mind is thus brought to the conclusion before the event and irrespective of it, what the created causes are and what they are not. For example, when it has decided in this way that a man is thrown into a furnace seven times heated, or that a man is dead, it also decides that there is no created agent which can interpose and prevent the burning of the body, or raise the dead to life. Indeed if the mind did not rely on this judgment or decision as one fully warranted when thus based on the authority of the senses, that is, if it admitted the possible existence of created agents not cognizable by the senses, with power thus to interfere with the operation of causes which are cognizable by the senses, and should allow this fact to modify or control its judgment, then it could not decide that any of those things cognizable by the senses are causes of the phenomena connected with them; for all these phenomena might be the effects of the power of agents not cognizable by the senses. A man might be actually burned in a furnace, or killed by being pierced through the heart, or by poison, or sustained in life by food, &c., &c., and yet neither the fire, nor the dagger, nor the poison, nor the food, be the cause of the effect connected with it. These things are sufficient to show, that the mind is under the same necessity of regarding the authority of the senses, when they decide that certain sensible causes and circumstances, which they discover by the senses, are all the created causes or agents concerned, which it is under of regarding these things as causes at all.

Once more: there is another consideration still more decisive on this point. The mind cannot suppose that there are created agents not cognizable by the senses, with power to interfere with the operation of causes which are cognizable by the senses, without supposing created power which is adequate to destroy, or change, or suspend, or counteract the nature of created things, which is exclusively the province of creative power. But to suppose this is to deny the exclusive power of God to create, since it must be admitted that a being who can destroy, or change, or suspend, or counteract the nature of created causes must have power to create. Hence all sound and consistent theism admits, that power thus to interfere with the nature of created things or causes must be creative power, and must belong exclusively to God. Since therefore no created being has power to change, or suspend, or counteract that nature of things from which the laws of nature result, and since there can be no deviation from these laws without either changing, or suspending, or counteracting that nature of things on which these laws depend, it follows that no created being has power to cause a deviation from the laws of nature. Man then being fully competent to decide in certain cases what are laws of nature, and also what are deviations from these laws, and that God only can cause such deviations, is competent to decide that certain supposable events, viz., those which involve a deviation from any law of nature, are and can be brought to pass only by the power of God, and are, according to our definition, miracles.

We have now finished the preliminary discussion respecting miracles, which prepares us briefly to present the argument from this source for a divine revelation. We have shown that—

Miracles wrought for the purposes and ends of the scriptural miracles are credible events; that not only is every aspect of incredibility removed from these events by their object, but a very high degree of presumption—even proof—furnished of their reality.

It follows that: The testimony of the sacred historians to the reality of miracles—thus placed beyond all question—confirms their reality as decisive proofs of a revelation from God.

END OF VOLUME II.

www.ingramcontent.com/pod-product-compliance
Lightning Source LLC
LaVergne TN
LVHW021144110826
845150LV00005B/1117

* 9 7 8 1 4 2 5 5 4 7 7 1 4 *